TO DANCE

TO DANCE

Valery Panov
with George Feifer

ALFRED A. KNOPF　NEW YORK　1978

THIS IS A BORZOI BOOK
PUBLISHED BY ALFRED A. KNOPF, INC.

Copyright © 1978 by Valery Panov

Library of Congress Cataloging in Publication Data
Panov, Valery, [date]   To dance.
Autobiography.   Includes index.
1. Panov, Valery, [date]   2. Dancers—Biography.
I. Feifer, George, joint author.   II. Title.
GV1785.P275A37   1978   792.8'092'4   [B]   77–20362
ISBN 0–394–49882–8

Manufactured in the United States of America

FIRST EDITION

To everyone, everywhere, who helped us

Illustrations

ILLUSTRATIONS

Rehearsing *Hamlet*
(*both photographs: Jennie Walton*)

Rehearsing *Hamlet* with Alla Sizova (Boris Blankov at left)

The same moment in performance
(*Jennie Walton*)

Galina as Aurora in *Sleeping Beauty*
(*Rosemary Winckley*)

Galina in *The Creation of the World* (Baryshnikov at right)

Galina and Valery in *The Bronze Horseman*

Together in *Nutcracker*
(*Jennie Walton*)

AFTER LEAVING RUSSIA

Harlequinade
(*Jennie Walton*)

Valery in *Le Corsaire*
(© *Max Waldman, 1976*)

Together in *Le Corsaire*
(*both photographs: Martha Swope*)

Albinoni's Adagio
(© *Max Waldman, 1976*)

Harlequinade
(© *Max Waldman, 1976*)

Prologue

ONE WINTER EVENING NEAR THE END OF MY YEAR AS AN EXCHANGE
student in Russia, I went to the ballet in the Kremlin's Palace of Congresses. I did not know who was dancing. But even before the male lead
began to move, I knew I was in the presence of a sublime artistic gift.
Some spellbinding quality of his held the huge Moscow audience in his
grip. They responded to him with more fervor than I'd seen them give a
male dancer—or, for that matter, a female one. Leaving the building, I
learned that the magician who had transfixed us was a young man from
Leningrad. This was the only time I saw Valery Panov on a Soviet stage.

He danced *Petrushka* that evening in 1962. A decade later, when I
was writing a novelistic memoir called *Moscow Farewell*, his hour of
wizardry became a fulcrum for all I'd seen during my years in Russia. I
had never experienced a more moving performance—not only in ballet
but in any kind of theater. Panov's fantastic energy and total submersion
in the role spun an enchantment throughout the vast hall; but neither
the intensity of the characterization nor the dazzling dancing itself could
explain his overpowering effect. Panov *was* Petrushka. Russia and the
human condition were his stage. Nothing else could explain his uncanny
ability not merely to delight and entertain but to open the audience to
the ballet's deepest meanings—and to themselves.

Despite treacherous political and personal obstacles, Panov went on
to reach the summit of Soviet ballet. Leningrad's exquisite Kirov Theater
chose him to create almost every leading male role in major new productions during his period as a premier danseur. Because the bureaucrats

who managed Soviet culture clenched their teeth at the mention of his name, the awards and honors eventually heaped on him had a special significance. But the only reward of this kind he wanted was denied him for fifteen onerous years. Aside from a tragically interrupted trip to the United States when he was twenty-one years old—three years before I saw him as Petrushka—Panov was never permitted to travel to the West.

As a result, his reputation did not extend beyond Russia, except among balletomanes. But Western critics who visited Leningrad were stunned by their "find" of the "unknown" star. In 1967, the dance critic Clive Barnes spoke of Panov's Mercutio in *Romeo and Juliet* as "one of the greatest performances I have ever seen in the ballet theater." Praising Panov's dancing as "more brilliant, more electric" than even that of the other Russian masters he had seen in the role, Barnes concluded that "as a pure dancer [Panov] has genius."

The few other Western experts who traveled to Leningrad were also driven to superlatives by the hidden star. Patricia Barnes, a critic in her own right, called Panov "one of the treasures of Soviet ballet." In the early 1970s, Suzanne Massie compared him to the greatest male dancers in history. "*Harlequin* was first danced by Fokine in 1900, then by Nijinsky in 1910," she wrote. "Now there is Valery Panov, who, like the other two ballet immortals, is more than a master of technique, he is a creator. Yet Panov is virtually unknown abroad."

When he did become known to the world public, it was not as this magnificent artist but as a victim. In 1972 he applied to emigrate to Israel and was condemned to two years of vicious persecution. He wanted only to continue dancing and choreographing: to create symbols onstage, in which he was perhaps the world's master among living dancers. Instead, he became a political symbol. In London, Rosemary Winckley, the young Englishwoman in whom Panov rightly saw his angel-savior, would call me with emotional accounts about the KGB's murder of a unique artist. But I happened to be working for the release of other Soviet citizens, including my own mother-in-law, and I took no part in the massive international campaign to save Panov.

Finally, he was freed. A few months later, when he came to London to thank those who had worked for this, I met him almost accidentally, and we talked for several minutes. On the basis of this, he asked me to help him with his autobiography.

My reluctance derived from several assumptions. The hundred articles I'd read about him while he was a political cause célèbre contained nothing to suggest he wanted anything more than a book about his victimization. And now, as we exchanged our few words, he looked to me like the "typical" ballet dancer—that is, a person not best known for mental acuteness. He had an extremely expressive face, and despite his exhaustion, his smile cut through a celebrity-packed roomful of banalities. But he seemed ill at ease off stage. Unable to believe that the star was shy, I concluded he had little to say.

The greatest performer in the world does not necessarily have a story to tell. Panov's ability to captivate audiences, even the genius I had seen in his dancing and in his characterization, were no indication that he had the makings of a genuine book. And I could not join him in a politically oriented documentation of his case. Ghastly as it was, I had read—and written—too much about Soviet persecution to take on another account of it.

Sensing my hesitation, he began describing what he wanted to write about. I could not have imagined his sensitivity, his hidden bent for reflection about himself and his friends. He did not mention anything I'd read in the one-dimensional articles, but portrayed fiery steeds roaming fields of snow and other Chagall-like images of his childhood. He did not talk about his persecution, but about the tragedy of his father—who to that day had remained a dedicated Communist. There was nothing about the "system" in his first memories, but a rush of impressions about *people,* including an odd and luxurious collection of women he had loved. Against the gray Russian mise-en-scène and the ominous political backdrop, his portraits gleamed.

Everything he said disclosed a storyteller's gift. His narrative sweep was equivalent to his ability to move audiences with the fierce emotion of his dancing. And I again felt something uncanny in his presence. His Russia was mine, perceived exactly as I perceived it. But none of my writing about the country revealed what he now wanted to, if only because I had always been on the outside, trying to peer into places where he had been at the center. In three sentences he revealed more about the real workings of Soviet ballet, and of Soviet art in general, than I had learned in scores of visits spread over a dozen years. I knew some prominent Moscow dancers and ballerinas; had even written about them. Not one told me what Panov did: not only about the political pressures but also about the personalities, intrigues, joys, and despairs. Unless someone else of his passion and keen eye defected, no one ever would tell me.

What he said was only slightly more intriguing than how he said it. He talked like a painter, a thinker, a guileless comic. He had a wry wit and a born novelist's powers of observation. His scenes were as vivid as Russian ballet music and folk art. I loved listening to him. The intense sensitivity that gave him his unique voice had pushed him into a bundle of improbable adventures with violently romantic moments. It seemed to me that I was hearing about many aspects of Soviet life—and of life in general—for the first time.

In the context of his panoramic view of Russia, even his account of his persecution, about which I thought I had known everything, was full of revelations. (In fact, I had known only the outline. For personal reasons, the full account was far more gruesome—and inspiring—than I had imagined.) It had almost nothing in common with the cases of Rudolf Nureyev, Natalia Makarova, and Mikhail Baryshnikov. Like Panov, they were principals of Leningrad's Kirov Theater—but they defected when they were abroad. One day they were dancing in a Soviet company, the next day in a Western one. Of all the famous ballet émigrés, he alone did not defect, but stayed—even though not by his own choice—to face the murderous music of Soviet revenge. Only the huge foreign campaign kept him alive during his twenty-seven months as the object of KGB hatred.

Precisely what Soviet rule did to Panov can be imagined only with some specific knowledge of what he had endured during his sometimes nightmarish imprisonment. When I went to New York from London to work with him, I found him in a shabby hotel. Immediately after his victory over the KGB and triumphant arrival in Israel, he suffered an injury caused by the utter exhaustion of his struggle—and he was greeted by bad luck in his new professional arrangements. Without proper guidance to help him overcome his disorientation, the career in the West for which he had sacrificed everything at first eluded him. But if his kind of experiences in Russia shattered "ordinary" people, what could one expect of a highly sensitive artist? He had not lost his genius, but he was badly battered. His natural instinct was to protect his artistic and creative sense, even from television lights, when he at last left Russia.

Notwithstanding his exceptional stamina, his recuperation took time corresponding to the wounds inflicted upon him. In 1977, after three years in the West, his creativity re-emerged. In Leningrad, he had stopped dancing at the height of his powers. If anything, they are now more glorious. Panov has grown in human, and therefore in artistic, stature. Persecution has given him an added wisdom, and his world travels since then have brought new scope and depth to his responses. Today his dancing and choreography have attained new levels, and his effect on audiences is more spellbinding than ever.

But even during the first years in the West, when—with Soviet poison literally and figuratively still in him—he was shaky under new blows, he was not disheartened. He adored his wife, Galya, the young ballerina who had shared his two-year trial. Gratitude for her extraordinary loyalty re-inforced his touching love. Besides, his handicapped start and hard luck fit a pattern: his entire life had been a series of comings-from-behind to surmount seemingly impossible obstacles. On top of everything, he never forgot how close he had come to death in Russia. Although well-wishers wondered if he would ever dance again as he had, he told me he was taken up with other thoughts, prompted by the daily thrill of being alive.

I had never met anyone like him. He was Huckleberry Finn, Peck's Bad Boy, an innate artist—and genuine hero—combined in one. He so loved fairy tales that it seemed natural for him to have become a character in his own fable. Together with grim Soviet circumstances this is what his imagination and passion had made of his life. The steep climbs and dizzying falls of several twentieth-century dancers—Nijinsky, Spessivtseva, Pavlova (and Maya Plisetskaya, were she free to talk)— have been as mesmerizing as their virtuosity on stage. Thirty-six Russian years of haunting coincidences and tempestuous drama put Panov in their company.

As bonuses, I enjoyed the excitement of his charged personality and the roller coaster of his friendship. He cried when remembering his Russian friends; he doubled up with laughter at the craziness of existence there and at life's weird jokes on himself. Although he simply could not talk when he wasn't in the mood (and his notes begging me not to press him contained quite enough spelling mistakes in elementary Russian to confirm his stories of expulsions from a dozen schools), when he did want to talk, he woke me in the middle of the night. I have tried to capture at least a hint of his intensity, the kind often better expressed in motion than in words. In any case, I have invented nothing. I did have to coax him to talk, especially about his bitter years—but the "I" of this book is his voice, telling his story. I was a kind of rapporteur.

In this capacity, I asked questions to sharpen his memory, but I could not change his tendency toward self-deprecation. Without independent knowledge of his achievements, anyone who listened to him as I did could not guess that he is—to quote Clive Barnes again—"one of the most remarkable male dancers of our day." Whatever Panov does onstage is not good enough for him. If he leaps five feet in the air, it should be six; when he stuns veteran critics with the brilliance of his interpretations, he goes on developing them. Controlled by these same obsessive demands on himself, he hardly mentioned his triumphs to me but dwelled on those of others, especially of his Kirov colleagues, in whose virtues he took genuine delight. But nothing on paper could reproduce his effect on audiences. "Panov comes on stage, any stage, and offers an unmistakable image," exulted Barnes. An actor touched by "higher" inspiration, he is one of the few linked to the sublime and the mystical in art—and able to transport his audience there.

This is not part of his book because self-satisfaction is not part of his nature. Nor is routine of any kind, even after midnight. Usually when he shook me out of my sleep, it was to go for a marathon walk in the New York or London that beckoned him—or, when we were in Israel, for a drive in the desert. He could not sit still. He needed movement, *action*. He continued to be the intense, supremely individualistic Candide he was as a struggling "ballet boy," and I loved being with him as much as hearing about his amazing Russian journey. Having felt the fire, I thought I understood the magic of his dancing.

George Feifer
London, January 1978

TO DANCE

CHAPTER

1

I LAY NEAR A LARGE WINDOW OPEN TO THE SMELL OF HAY. A BIG METAL
thing clattered on the dirt street, followed by bare running feet. I tried
to understand the link between my parents' tenseness and the word
"tank." Then village quiet came again, and I was back in the adoring
care of three or four women committed to protecting me from outside
danger.

They were probably my grandmother and aunts in Vitebsk, where
I'd been born in 1938 and where my parents took me during their summer vacation. With the Polish border less than a hundred miles west,
they needed no explanation of why tanks were maneuvering there in
August 1940. The women returned to their gossip, no doubt about Aunt
Riva, the Shulman family's fallen angel. Working as a nurse during the
First World War, she had married a wounded Turk, who bore her off
to often imagined horrors. Aunt Fanny must have been one of those
taking care of me now. Young Marc Chagall, who had lived just down
the street, had courted her briefly. His portrait of her hung in our
wooden "Chagall" house until the German looting a few years later.

Infant blankness took charge again. The only thing I knew was that
I wanted to be moving. Next, I was doing just that—in an incredibly
packed railway car. The three hundred miles from Vitebsk to Moscow
were an immensely long ride with an infinitude of stops. Maybe prewar
train service had as much to do with this as my two-year-old perception.
People seemed worried about food. When my mother or father went out
for anything, I burst into howls. This continued in Moscow, where Papa
left our room early every morning for something called work.

Sometime later we were in another railway station. We stood on the concrete platform a very long time while my father tried to hold our ground against all the pushing and pretend he didn't notice it. This was probably soon after Hitler struck. The new word "war" was full of fear and excitement. "Evacuation" was less interesting.

For some reason my mother wept. My superbly courageous father did not cry but wiped his nose with a handkerchief. The crowds became thicker, but at one point most of the grown-ups disappeared. This left mainly children for my second train journey, an even longer one than the first. Much later, I learned that my group had been sent deep in the Urals, near Perm.

Because of wartime conditions, the thousand miles took many days. Frequent long stops were enlivened by wonderful running for cover, apparently brought on by strange noises in the sky. Everyone shouted "Planes!" and grew terrified. I couldn't understand the other children's tears. Separation from parents was nothing compared to the great gift of the ride. This time I wasn't afraid. The train click-clacked ahead for me. When it picked up speed, life was truly wonderful. I looked around me for the first time and realized I lived in an amazingly large, fascinating world. Field after limitless field called out to me to get off the train and enjoy something beautiful.

Grown-ups stood out like Gullivers in the swarm of children led from the train. We were at a siding next to a glorious winter painting. Pine trees as tall as mountains bordered a huge field heaped with snow. The trees all belonged to the same forest, yet each one stood like a magnificent hero.

Giant men packed a hundred children into brightly decorated peasant sleds. We set off like ten anthills being shifted to new sites. This served as a signal for a fresh chorus of sobs. I held my breath, wondering what would happen to us next. It seemed wonderful that we didn't know. Runners swishing along a path over picturesque hills were enough in themselves.

Soon I was staring at the rear of the horse that was drawing us. Its tail hung down from the towering muscles like an endless stream of water. Suddenly it rose, and magic little pies tumbled out, accompanied by puffs of steam and an intriguing smell. I pleaded for one. It had been many days since we'd had anything warm and delicious to eat. The driver lifted one of his huge hands and shouted to the other grown-ups. They roared with laughter at me. I broke down and joined the weeping.

The mighty steed marched on in a cloud of steam. He pulled us across another white field and into a somber forest. Snow clumps fell on us from the branches we brushed while passing. The driver cried "Whoa!" I couldn't remember Vitebsk, Moscow, or my mother and father.

When snowstorms raged outside the window, a bewitching fear built up inside the house. The matron told stories of people who had gotten lost in the whiteness and frozen to death. When the sky cleared and we were permitted outdoors, the snow was unbelievably deep. I was very frightened of wandering off. But I had to test myself. How could a man go to sleep in the snow? I'd build a castle there with stables for my horses. . . . Something made me push on, despite a desperate yearning to be snug in the house. The matrons ran down the hill and scooped me up. My heart was pounding fiercely.

The evacuation home was apparently very near Molotov, as Perm had been renamed shortly before the war. Our toasty house stood at the edge of a little village. The other landmarks were a well alongside a meandering road and an abandoned church at the top of a little hill. When the snow melted, I longed to run in the fields, hunt through the woods. Why were we indoors so much? From where did all the worries come that restricted our movements? The staff liked children, and we were happy. But it puzzled me that they saw so much danger in everything "outside" and that the other children listened.

In summer the fields came alive with flowers, bees, and insects. Squirrels, birds, and mice got away, but I held my nose to the ground and studied the ants for hours. It was hard to believe that so many things grew and moved. What a playground the world was!

Before we had any notion of what "New Year" was we were a squealing horde in a large barn. We were told that none of the delicious treats could be touched until the tree standing alongside the table was fully decorated. The giant fir, already gay with little candles, made the barn like a sumptuous palace. The heroes of our fairy tales probably lived in such places.

Someone taught me to draw sharp little mountains on scraps of paper, then to cut them out with a pair of scissors. Soon I was told to show the other children how I did it. When the job was finished, teachers solemnly congratulated me for the quality of my product, which they proceeded to attach to the tree. That our little white things were stars, I learned by accident.

The most important parents in our house were Stalin, who loved us with magic, inexhaustible powers, and Lenin, who was also very good, but somehow more removed. Their portraits warmed and blessed the house's main rooms. But the figure of charity and authority we lived in direct awe of was the Director of our own establishment. Even the grown-ups spoke of him in hushed tones. His son had recently arrived to visit him from something involving *the war*. From the way older men cried when younger ones left the village, we suspected that the war was connected with grave hardship. It was somehow the opposite of nature's gifts of color and movement. Yet nostrils flared when people talked about it, so wasn't it also connected with energy and therefore goodness?

We knew for certain only that people who played war were exceedingly important. The Director's son was in a military academy, a real cadet! This was a matter of great pride.

THERE WAS NO EXPLANATION for what fairy tales did to me. I liked where I was, yet needed escape. One matron was younger than the others and very beautiful. Her presence made me happiest, and I squirmed for her to notice me. But what I really loved was my secret picture of her as the Fairy Queen.

The tales made my mouth go dry. The matrons learned to have water handy and to soften the scary and awesome parts. Still, I vanished into infinitely more interesting worlds. Life in them opened my eyes, spun my head, filled me with wonder until I couldn't breathe. Gripped in sharp talons and tugged to the fox's den, the Cock with the Golden Comb cried:

> *The fox is dragging me*
> *Into the dark forest,*
> *Beyond swift rivers*
> *And over giant hills . . .*

Terror almost made me lose consciousness, yet I needed more.

To be certain that everything ended well, I had to hold the illustrations of Ivan Bilibin in my own hands. Bilibin's mastery was a source of astonishment in itself. But it was even better to picture my own endings.

The other children's fantasy went largely to imagining family life.

Not remembering our parents, we saw them as characters from the best tales, representing the highest good. *When our parents came,* everything would be glorious. I couldn't settle for second in this competition. *My Mama and Papa* were the best and most beautiful.

Yet real horses were even better. Winter and summer, second winter and astounding spring, these divine creatures made the deepest impression on me. In daily life, they pulled wagons and plows. Soaring necks were made to droop. But the most magnificent of them all, a huge copper one, was never harnessed, even to a sled. I knew he was made for running free. His owner's understanding of this compensated for much inexplicable injustice to animals.

When this fiery steed galloped in a nearby field, the other children dashed to the house and watched from a window. Their fear re-inforced my own and sharpened my reverence. I tried to understand where such strength and beauty came from. It was unbearable that I would never have them, but at least I could touch the object of my worship. I could fall before him, and he would know. I climbed halfway up the rotting fence that separated us. The stallion trembled and snorted. He had the same impatience to run that I felt when the sun shone. Something secret linked me to my idol.

Then the great animal no longer pawed the field. On the day we were told that he had been taken by the army, war became real.

THE SECOND SUMMER'S NEW PHRASES were "glorious victory" and "pushing the marauder back to his lair." Moscow was free of danger. The appearance of parents to fetch their children spurred talk about these mythical creatures to a feverish new peak. Without knowing what mothers and fathers actually did, we sensed they would have a decisive effect on our lives. The day of their arrival generated unbearable anxiety.

"Whose mother is she?"

"I don't know, I don't know. I don't feel so good."

"Maybe she's not a mother but an aunt."

Everyone knew his fate was being decided.

Early one morning a new matron announced to our sleeping dormitory that one of our fathers had arrived. For some reason she cackled like a sorceress. I jumped up, pretending I badly needed the toilet. Passing the parents' room, I saw a bald man with bulging eyes, sitting there like an evil spirit. He stared at me with a kind of greed, got up from his bench, and started for me. I thought I made out a wooden arm!

Nimble as never before, I dodged his grasp, dashed under my bed, and howled. Peeking from their blankets, the others begged to know what the horror was. When I was certain the creature hadn't followed me, I told them a bad man from one of our tales had arrived.

After breakfast I was summoned to the Director's office. I begged him to take back what he had said. Weeping hopelessly, I ran to tell the others that the man who looked the opposite of all I wanted him to be was *not* my father.

My tantrum affected no one but myself. Someone calling himself "Papa" had come for me, and I could do nothing but accept my tragic fate. Above all, the missing arm haunted me. I decided he had lost it recently, for the wound seemed fresh and the hateful replacement, which he was now carrying under his armpit, was almost new. The appliance seemed to embarrass the man too, as if he wondered why he appeared in such a form.

2

HUMMING A MILITARY SONG, MY FATHER, MATVEI SHULMAN, PLUCKED me out of my childhood and headed, as he studiously explained, toward the railroad station. That we were clearly going to the end of the earth helped me accept him as a traveling companion. Amid fields stretching to the horizon, I pictured a life-ending chasm.

I grew very tired. Wartime shortages affected children least, so I did have boots—two sizes too large and both for the right foot. When my father saw I couldn't go on, he lifted me to his shoulders. I felt far better there. Papa's voice was gravelly, but he carried tunes well, and I sensed a paternal feeling for me. He taught me what was expected of a Soviet lookout, and I was first to spot the railroad tracks yonder in the distance.

We fought our way into a horde of weary men and women at the station, then waited most of the day. When the train finally came, it was already packed, but those who were waiting assaulted it more frenziedly than the proletarian throng storming the Winter Palace. Hauling ourselves into a car against a current of writhing limbs, we established rights to a place on the third berth, just beneath the ceiling. Another family occupied half of it, but a blissful yard of space belonged to us.

The train jerked forward with no confidence in itself. Our car was crammed with soldiers, sailors, and ordinary people trying to settle down on their smelly bundles. When I managed a peek out the window, I saw a fantastic string of cannon and machine guns, which the sailor next to me called an armored train. To my father's vigorous approval, he explained that it could kill "a big bunch of fascists" all in one go.

We screeched to a stop, evidently to make way for the armored train. My father explained—and I instantly forgot—that he needed something and pushed out of the door. The train suddenly lurched forward, while I wailed that Papa was lost, I'd never see him again. Calming voices assured me that he would be back in a moment. Finally, Papa reappeared with hot water for tea. As I sipped mine and he talked about our motherland's tasks after full victory, I felt how dependent I already was on this strangely energetic man.

SOMEONE ANNOUNCED that this was Moscow. We had arrived without warning. I held onto Papa's hand for dear life, while everyone evacuated the train in a greater crush than when we had fought aboard. Soon I was looking up into rich chestnut hair. The lady had her arms around my father. Totally engrossed in their embrace, neither took the slightest notice of me. The other passengers milled about in feverish excitement over their families and their bundles. The entire world had forgotten me.

My secret hopes for recognition shifted from Papa to the woman, for she was the most beautiful I had ever seen. She had a startlingly thin waist and arms. The only time I'd seen a face like hers was when one of the matrons had showed us a photograph of a movie star.

I wanted to be close to her, to absorb her elegance while getting her to admire me. But she laughed, and I overheard "funny-looking little thing" in her whisper to Papa. She seemed distressed by my boots and avoided my dirty-fingered advances while awarding her admirers in the crowd with a dazzling smile of splendid teeth.

THE BRILLIANT WOMAN turned out to be Mamachka. She and Papa led me into an apartment house with an endless staircase. We climbed most of the afternoon. The strange city promised even better dangers than any near the evacuation home. I couldn't have dreamed of a more frightening chasm than the pit of the staircase.

At last we reached a room on the seventh floor. It was enormous, but Mama and Papa wondered how we were going to fit "everyone" in. While they fussed, I sneaked out to my stairway. As if anticipating elevators—a great rarity whose existence I hadn't even imagined—I was tormented by impatience when going down the stairs again. Trains ran on rails, and why shouldn't I? The track was begging to be used. I ran to the top of the house, then zoomed down on the banister. The momentum shot me through the front door and onto the sidewalk.

Performing this little number one day, I soared higher and faster than ever. I glided over the curb and landed in the roadway—directly in front of the wheels of a passing car. I continued my trip by skipping onto the parapet of the quay opposite our building. Good brakes had saved me, but the appalled driver left his car to give chase. Unwilling to risk what I did on the six-inch parapet, he stopped and shouted in rage. I flew home on the wings of fear. The driver followed me and engaged my mother in a marathon discussion. Of course, it ended in the moralizing I'd already learned to detest. At such moments the only sanctuary was the roof. I enjoyed complete freedom there since no adult could negotiate the passage to my little part of it.

My parents had everything wrong. Seeing trouble and evil influence wherever there was pleasure, they sputtered, "Shame!" and "Don't you dare!" *They* associated the roof with distressing reminders of the war, especially air-raid watches. While my mother and I slinked into the basement bomb shelter, my father would clamber up to the accessible part of the roof. His protection was a dishpan with two holes punched out for the eyes.

Night air raids proved my happiest moments. Convincing my mother that I'd only have to get dressed and scramble downstairs when the siren sounded, I went to sleep in my clothes. Sure enough, the sirens did wail, while the Radio Moscow loudspeaker blasted forth. We rushed out, ran a hundred meters, and took cover in the building that served as the shelter. The district defense chief ordered everyone to crawl in on all fours, which none of the local ladies could manage. While ack-ack guns were banging away at thrilling fascist bombers, grannies and aunties were fainting on all sides; this was a regular circus! Down in the basement everyone strained to hear the slightest noise from the street. The world was expected to come crashing down on our heads.

The apartment house was on the Moscow River embankment near where the little Yauza River flowed into it. A few years later it was overshadowed by one of the "Stalin skyscrapers" that would dominate the city's skyline forever after. The huge structure went up almost next door. By that time I knew that our own building was largely a kind of dormitory for my father's institute. Despite the spaciousness I first saw in it, our room measured only ten feet by twelve. Others like it housed up to eight graduate students.

By that time, too, I'd learned that my father's lack of an arm had nothing to do with the war; it had been lost in an industrial accident years before. I wondered why the loss upset him less than it did me.

PAPA'S DEBUT AS A HERO became a grand holiday. He strutted around the room with his dishpan, enlightening callers about the miracle of his head remaining in one piece. Then he displayed the flat hole that flying fragments had ripped in the metal the night before. A sacred war relic, the helmet would long occupy the place of honor among our things.

About this time letters began arriving for me from a strange land called Central Asia. They were pleasantly short on text and illustrated with magnificent drawings of Soviet fighters gunning down smoking Stukas. These works of art were from my brother, who was still in evacuation. I knew about him only that he was fourteen years old, almost three times as old as I was since my sixth birthday was approaching. But because books were much more important for the images their pictures stimulated than for their boring words, I was very happy. What a wonderful brother I had!

Alfred appeared several months later, having traveled all alone on a train. He turned out to be a pudgy boy with big eyes. I called him Alec.

He brought an exotic present he had bought in something called a bazaar just before leaving Central Asia. It was long strips of melon dried in the sun and plaited, like a girl's braids. They were so delicious that I almost swallowed my fingers together with the candy ones.

I would always think of Alec by way of his treat, and other gifts followed immediately. There had been no strong feelings between my parents and me. Nothing in them lived up to my picture of Mama and

Papa when I hadn't known them, and nothing in me made them really like me even when I behaved well. But reassurance of having the same blood linked me with Alec. He gave me the missing closeness within weeks of coming home.

When Alec was in school, life on the seventh floor turned dull. My mother's very splendor seemed to make her remote. Something in me irritated her—my pigeon-toed walk, if there was nothing more handy. "What a sight you are!" she would exclaim. "How can you get across a room on those legs?"

Actually, my walk made things very easy. I simply slipped one foot over the other like a tightrope walker and never stumbled. This is what kept me whole on the roof and on the catwalk of a bridge across the Moscow River, but of course, I couldn't tell that.

Mama's unhappiness with me made it even harder than ever to sit still. One day I saw a group of kids gripping each other's red scarves and making an amusing chain while crossing the street. They entered the courtyard, walked through our entryway, and settled in a second-floor apartment. I ran downstairs and pressed my ear to the door. Happy children's voices came through, and when the door opened, a friendly woman patted my head. Soon I was spending my days there, listening to the fun I was missing. It seemed odd that I was alone so much. I liked being with people, and something drew me to every child I saw. And the kindergarten teacher didn't mind my bowed legs. She even made a pleasant remark to a younger woman about my "excited" eyes. "He's so eager for something," she said approvingly.

One day I returned home from the roof to find her chatting with my mother. Mama's glamour stood out against the background of wartime drabness, attracting everyone. She also loved talking. The teacher smiled and invited me to join the group.

MY DRAWING SKILL earned me pride of place in a May Day showing of kindergarten work. Everyone was amazed at my crashing Stukas, complete with broken swastikas. Taking the credit for my copies of Alec's drawings made me admire him even more, and I even tried some original sketches.

The next event to which my parents were invited was a party for the Anniversary of the Revolution. A little girl asked me to join the dancing—a slight to my masculinity that first drove me deeper into my chair. But some nosy grown-ups saw my response and dragged me to the center of the floor. Surely everyone would know that dancing was a humiliation for a boy, especially when we had just won a war. A crowd gathered to observe and to block my escape. My arms and legs trembled: Mama's strident "Go ahead!" made me wet my pants.

She raised her voice again. It offered only utter lack of understanding. With all my illusions of manliness shattered, sheer shame forced me to move my limbs. Still weeping for this terrible hurt, I began a series of furious movements. When my partner sat down, I felt even more charged with despairing loneliness. It was a confrontation with my insignificance and need to obey others, even with my body. The way out was to spin even faster. This brought delighted praise, mixed with congratulations for my mother. But the hurt of not being understood lingered for weeks. This was deepened by a recognition that my performance had involved me in something supremely mortifying, yet equally triumphant. I realized I was different from the other children, although I couldn't say how or why. In all my best roles as a ballet dancer the inspiration would be just this personal perception of tragedy.

That summer the kindergarten went to a small camp outside Moscow. The gym teacher's quick success at teaching me backbends and cartwheels persuaded me that I was the toughest, bravest boy on two feet. Full of myself again, I acquired the habit of punching fellow campers without warning. No one hit back, and I was convinced I was unconquerable, until I picked a scrappy lad who did a neat job on *my* nose. Through the pain it occurred to me that I might be wise to drop my tough-guy act.

Although this conclusion was entirely self-protective, the bloody nose went on to stimulate my first serious thought. Like all the other children, I had judged everyone by physical prowess. Since I was truly the strongest and most agile in the group, I had been developing a notion of myself as a future superman. The return poke was the first lesson that someone stronger is always waiting to amuse himself with you as you might like to with others.

SUMMER PASSED TOO QUICKLY on the former capitalist's country estate. I was the star performer for every parents' day and even more in demand back in Moscow. "Shulman will do a new number," was the standard suggestion when entertainment was needed. I began to sense that dancing was my personal specialty.

The surge of performance was linked to another set of growing sensations. They came with the perfect little body of one of my fellow campers. One day she lay in the sun alone with me. I caressed her. After this we looked for each other. I yearned to be close to her loveliness, to seize the beauty of the day in my arms. I jumped up to dance for her, too.

3

PAPA CONDUCTED RESEARCH FOR THE MINISTRY OF LIGHT INDUSTRY. BUT offers for jobs promising better living quarters began arriving. A Lithuanian official appeared. His manner was as rare as his foreign car, sent east during the Red Army's march to Berlin. Like a fat capitalist, he plonked luxurious cans and bottles on our table.

Soon preparations began for a move to Vilnius, the capital of the Lithuanian Socialist Republic. We set out early in 1946.

Vilnius was one large country estate compared to Moscow. Independent Lithuania had been as rich and developed as a Scandinavian country until its annexation by the Soviet Union. This had happened a few short months before the German invasion, and it was now only two years since the Wehrmacht had been ousted. The new republic was still far richer than Russia and had greater foreign influences from its colonies of Poles and German prisoners of war.

The phenomenal living standards startled me. Families had apartments all to themselves. Polish milkmaids went door to door each morning, offering real, fresh milk! Some people even gave them their keys, and the girls filled the jars inside while the owners slept. This trust was as amazing as the personal possessions that would have disappeared in a second in Russia. Nobody seemed to steal anything, and there were almost no lines at the shops.

On every corner women sold homemade toffee for a few kopecks. There were a hundred foreign ways of doing things, and meek, hungry German prisoners worked very hard as domestic servants for tens of thousands of Soviet military families. I couldn't link their gentle conscientiousness with the children—for whom they even made toys—to

the grown-ups' tales of their frightening cruelty. For me, the most unpleasant moments were when guards shoved these pitiful people to work
even harder.

Our own living conditions improved dramatically. As manager of
the republic's large Leather and Footwear Trust, my father reported directly to the Lithuanian Minister of Light Industry. The quarters that
came with the new job were the top floor of a solid two-story house built
for prewar bourgeois owners. This palace included our *private* bathroom,
two bedrooms, hot water in the kitchen—and a new roof refuge.

Singing his marching songs, Papa rose early to go to work. Once
a week he got up even earlier for his outing to the peasant market. He
returned with eggs, cottage cheese, fresh vegetables, clean-smelling meat,
and even chicken, which I had seen only a few times in Moscow. But
although Alec and I were the best-fed children in the Soviet Union, we
never received more than the "norm" Papa had calculated in accordance
with his precepts of Soviet upbringing.

I saw him now as a shortish man with strong legs and a powerful
right arm. He had precisely Lenin's degree of baldness to match the
Leader's schoolteacher morality. Thrifty and totally organized, he wagged
his finger to make me the same, basing his instruction on references to
various Soviet texts. No doubt this helped make me the kind of boy who
couldn't remember where he'd thrown his coat, much less remember to
hang it up.

Maybe Alec's war experience accounted for his much better discipline. His age-group had been evacuated to a settlement in Moslem
Central Asia. It was between a vast desert and the desolate Tien Shan
mountains, with China on the other side of the snowy peaks. His board-
ing school in that wilderness had been much poorer than mine—and
sometimes cruel. The local people had no love for Russian adults, and
Alec's classmates, who came from the toughest districts of proletarian
Moscow, inspired no love for Russian children. The gang leaders requi-
sitioned entire meals from gentler children. They also demanded total
obedience. The staff did not either know or care about the certain beatings resistance invited. Even without this terror, Alec longed to return
to our parents. He was old enough—almost twelve when he left in 1941—
to miss them. His two-year yearning for home is what kept him from
eating the delicious melon braids on the long train ride back from exile,
although the aroma tortured his empty stomach.

I was almost his opposite in self-control and in self-esteem. And since he was a physical copy of my father, and I of my mother (although without her beauty), we also looked very different.

My lot in the hereditary draw pleased me enormously. From the first moment in the railroad station, I tried to accompany Mama on her errands. I wanted to bask in her glory, wanted the world to know that the statuesque being was *my* mother. I watched for hours as she prepared herself for an appearance in the street. Few sons even suspected the existence of toilet water. Hers filled the room with an intoxicating magic. Only Papa appearing from work in his old suit jacket snapped me back from the lush world of her narcissism.

Mama adored flowers and pretty things to own and to wear. These were extremely scarce after the German occupation, the postwar hunger, and the sacrifice for socialism. But her occupation was hunting for them in a large flea market. She made her way through the rows of pitiful stalls, which I saw as a marvelously luxurious bazaar, like a queen taking a regimental salute. The bits and pieces of European artifacts implanted my first notions about the outside world's riches, but she impressed me even more. She was surer than ever of her beauty and importance as she examined remnants of jewelry and silverware. My mother was a *personality*.

Alas, her interest did not extend to me. And since my father seemed to understand me even less, it fell to Alec to share my world. My brother's physical and emotional dissimilarity to me made his friendship more treasured. *He* was the one who introduced me to wonderful new discoveries, such as a book with genuine photographs of submarines. Papa seemed intent on suppressing my enthusiasms. Mama's warmest offering was permission to tag along with her.

My parents scoffed at everything that wandered beyond their own conception of "real things." I sensed that the best in me was the "foolish lying" that sometimes lifted me over my own pettiness. Their hostility to this crushed me. Alec used to dismiss my make-believe, too, because it jarred his liking for documentary fact. But soon he began calling me "my own little Baron von Münchhausen," referring to the much-admired fictional traveler who invents as much as he actually sees. He came to admire my fantasy almost as much as my physical dexterity, an additional point of difference between us; he had already developed sinus trouble and a slight weakness of the heart. Only he listened to my stories and hopes, and in this sense he became my parent.

OUR HOUSE WAS IN THE FAMOUS Antokol district, near the city's military garrison in a former monastery. One day my mother, Alec, and I saw an unusual spectacle from the window. The entire regiment was leaving its building and piling into cars and horse-drawn carts. All the soldiers were heavily armed. An even longer string of civilian carts and trucks waited behind the military ones.

A few of the drivers were my neighborhood pals. I dashed downstairs and onto the running board of the one I knew best. Had the war with America begun? We'd all been waiting for it, frightened by fierce press and radio descriptions of Washington's thirst for blood.

"What's going on. Where are you all headed?"

The answer had nothing to do with our forthcoming defeat of Uncle Sam. "We're off to ship the Lithuanian bourgeois exploiters to Siberia," the driver explained.

I waved to the far-flung convoy as it moved off. Yes, the bourgeoisie must be smashed, I reasoned—or shipped if the slogan had changed for some reason. I only wondered why Lithuanians had been chosen when there were so few of them in their own city compared to Russians and Poles.

Years later I realized that this was the start of an appalling tragedy. That day bourgeois Lithuanian "elements" were rounded up for murderous exile. For historical reasons few of them lived inside Vilnius. The great majority of deportees were villagers, but since few exploiters existed anywhere, "bourgeois" was applied to any farmer who had constructed a solid barn with his own relentless work. By the sweat of an extremely independent, hardworking peasantry, Lithuania had once helped feed Germany and Scandinavia. The republic's agriculture was hit as hard that day as when the Soviet occupation began.

The convoy returned toward twilight. It made for the railroad station with a cargo of families crushed into each cart and truck. Guarded by soldiers with tommy guns, the adults already wore a convict look, made even more haggard by their inability to explain their uprooting to their bewildered children.

When the exiles were permitted to return under Khrushchev, their accounts made clear what I had witnessed in 1947. But even at the time I somewhere worried that a terrible mistake was taking place. All evening packed wagons passed by, people moaning inside them. Even children my own age were weeping. Pregnant women had fainted. I ran home, where my father ordered me to be worthy of myself as a Soviet lad, since "those people are the bourgeois enemy." Something was strange. Enemies should have been . . . different. I thought no more about it at the time.

THE FASCISTS WERE MORE SUITABLE ENEMIES. Fresh tracks of the war showed everywhere, but especially in the handsome hills that surrounded Vilnius and the woods that extended into the city. The Germans had used them for storing ammunition, and one of the great adventures of my new friends and me was searching for the dugouts among the bomb craters.

Uncovering an unusually deep hole one day, we crawled into a kind of grotto. It contained a large supply of what we called bombies—mortar shells, as we later learned—lying amazingly neatly in their cases and accompanied by "missilekins," evidently high-explosive bullets. From then on our pockets bulged with bullets whenever we played. Our maneuvers acquired new importance. Jamming nails into the place for the percussion caps, we tossed bullets down from a hill and rapturously watched them explode on the road.

Every free moment of half the city's schoolboys now went to fashioning a range of homemade missiles and incendiary devices. Our supplies formed the arsenal for national justice in the great war between Polish and Russian youth. Enlightened by their parents' whispers, the Poles regarded all Russians as occupiers of their city—with certain historical justification since it had once been a center of the Polish separatist movement. And the Russians labeled other nationalities "fascists," deserving roughly the same lessons recently given to the German variety.

Backed with this sense of mission, the fights drew blood. From every district, hundreds of children advanced into the woods, where the Poles dug in on one hill and the Russians on a nearby one. As in the war films showing everywhere, one side charged the other with a manly "Hurrah!" and the punching went on in the best tradition of asserting national rights. Abandoned German ammunition had already killed two older boys.

As a mature warrior of the second grade I felt obliged to fight furiously. *My* nationality was above suspicion; I was 100 percent Russian, like every real man. Even when waiting teenaged fists made me ill with fright, I forced myself to run toward them. Everything was mixed together: outright fear, love of danger and risk, crowd fever, and Pushkin's "call of clanging swords" that drowns out thought.

My memory of a recent thrilling film made me want even more action. After besieging a Swedish fortress all summer, Peter the Great orders a cannon stuffed with gunpowder. A torch is lit, a fantastic shot goes off—and the great fortress falls to our valiant forebears. My largest cartridge might substitute for the miracle-working cannon. I asked the most reckless of my friends, whom I liked best, to help me empty it through a hole we sawed through the back end. More hands helped stuff the cylinder with gunpowder and buckshot, then carry it to the woods. It was time to annihilate the foreign foe once and for all.

A great battle was about to begin. Our seventh-grade commander's shout of "Now!" heated my joyful fever to new heights. I struck a match, felt the shock wave reach my face, remembered nothing.

Sometime later a terrible scream brought me to. *"Done for!"* One ear heard this while the other still ached with the thunder of the blast. My shirt, hair, and eyebrows were badly singed. Deranged with fear, I stumbled and crawled up the outside access to my roof refuge, where I trembled for hours. I knew that a terrible, irreparable tragedy had taken place.

Evening's darkness helped generate courage. Feeling my way down to the street, I saw a cluster of anxious grown-ups in the twilight. "One boy dead," certified a voice. "And another in hospital badly wounded." When I heard them saying that only a few pieces of my daredevil friend had been found, everything went empty. It seemed absurd that this boy, who had enjoyed exploring the world more than anyone, was gone.

The burial processions passing our house on their way to the cemeteries beyond the Church of St. Peter and St. Paul filled me with dread of death. Weeping relatives followed white faces on casket cushions. For many weeks the terrible mistake that had extinguished my friend dissipated all desire even to see war films with Alec.

4

My escapades filled my mother with increasing horror. Convinced that my passion for "hooliganism" was going to saddle her with a full-fledged thug, she decided to divert me from my path of reckless confrontation with the world. Papa grunted his assent.

Casting about for something to occupy me, she remembered a teacher's prophecy in my Moscow kindergarten. "Your son has the makings of an acrobat or an artist," she had pronounced after one of my dancing performances for guests. My loose limbs, the Polish war, and all the other mischief I kept getting into persuaded my mother that the circus was where I belonged. But Vilnius had no training school for circus arts or for acrobatics. Ballet was her substitute.

The way she introduced me to it showed what she might have attained as a politician. Blending casualness with her usual flourish, she bought tickets for the Lithuanian opera house. Then she suggested that I, rather than my father or brother, might have the honor of escorting her. I already loved whatever we were going to see.

It was Tchaikovsky's *Sleeping Beauty*. The Prince was the most wondrous sight I'd ever seen. The splendor and illusion on the stage were exactly what I had secretly dreamed for myself since I first heard fairy tales. Nothing more glorious could exist on earth.

I left the theater dizzy with love. That night I lay in bed and stared at the ceiling. I knew I had to convince my mother to bring me closer to the magnificent Prince Charming and Princess Aurora dancing there. This proved easier than I imagined. Stirred, too, by the rare appearance of beauty in our lives, Mama was on her way to becoming a balletomane.

She soon found the city's only Palace of Pioneers—a kind of scout center with ideological trappings—offering ballet instruction. I entered this heaven as the second boy among thirty girls. Although I was puzzled by the odd lack of male enthusiasm for ballet, my first class confirmed my discovery: life's meaning could be reached through movement. Wherever I was from then on, this certainty accompanied me.

I also signed up for a dramatic class in the same Pioneer Palace. Alec was in this one, and his ability to memorize whole monologues re-inforced my awe of him. I was assigned to the "popular masses," since my line learning was limited to occasional words and phrases on the order of "Hurrah!" or "Down with" whoever it was. On the other hand, my portrayal of what the stage directions called "agitation among the crowd" was a hit. For "feelings rising among the people," I dashed around to enhance the commotion by shifting chairs and trees. *Action* was what I'd wanted in war games and now wanted on the stage. But I was beginning to love the stage itself and tried to work my way into the Palace's every presentation. My feeble memory ensured that the only impression I produced was of zeal. I could read the puzzlement on supervising faces about whether mine was normal in a boy of eight.

My face was a perpetual smile. I had forgotten what loneliness was like. Whenever someone asked for me, it was: "Where's the kid who's always laughing?" This enthusiasm—along with my strong legs, elastic muscles, and natural flair for movement—also pleased the ballet teacher. I'd been blessed with an early coordination that produced easy bodily harmony. In later years I would make much of my commitment to art and my drive for hard work. But the raw material was physical endowments for which I deserved no credit. Even then I could get some elevation with my leaps, yet control them because of my balance.

This showed most vividly in the light of the other "male" in our class. Godlike Big Benny, five years older than I, was, of course, my new idol. But six months after I arrived, he shifted all his artistic ambition to the piano. My improvement had driven him away, and besides, the girls had begun to favor me. This was not for anything personal. They'd have "liked" a boy with three eyes if he were doing well in class. Dozens of pretty girls dreamed of being a ballerina and of having a partner. Now they had only me!

Eager mothers escorted the girls to the Palace and stayed to watch their progress. Every hour began behind or beneath the piano, changing into the "training costume" of shorts, high socks, and anything resembling a polo shirt. Mama agreed to shield me from the other mothers; women's gazes embarrassed me. Meanwhile, we were struggling to memorize the French names of the basic positions and steps. No one had heard of warming up muscles. But crucial importance was attached to loosening the tongue.

We mumbled the alien syllables, pouting because we'd come to dance, not for more *school*. The mothers nagged. Needless to say, *my* mother was the angriest of all, since I couldn't remember anything. After months of practice every other day the result was perfect pronunciation of the Gallic gobbledygook by my mother's eager lips, while I thrashed about in total inability to memorize even one of the nasal sounds.

The principle escaped me. In order to dance with one's body, why torture one's head with a long list of sadistic terms? But to Mama everything was crystal clear. Her errant son was the worst pupil, as demonstrated by his ineptitude in mastering "the most important part." Years after, I realized that our awesome teacher, an amateur volunteer, understood equally little about ballet priorities.

Each day parents and pupils labored with the language drill while awaiting the teacher's appearance. Our babble would cease instantly when the mother responsible for "pedagogue liaison" burst through the door. We children froze in anticipation at the practice barre. No maternal muscle moved either as a small, slight granny in tutu and point shoes made her entrance into the room. She hobbled on turned-out "ballet" legs as if after a full life on the stage.

She rose up on her toes several times. Later I realized she had acquired this habit after careful observation of real ballerinas warming up. It was also her way of mesmerizing her pupils since the girls were convinced that toe shoes were a marvel only sylphs could own. Perhaps she owed her Palace job to possession of her rare pair, together with the tutu that had mysteriously found its way into her wardrobe. She had once attended a ballet class in another Lithuanian city—but not as one of the trainees. She had been taken in as a token of thanks for her help in compiling program notes. Years later it seemed to me that her fierce love of ballet might have taken her over the split-personality line, especially since she could barely get her feet into position even while gripping the barre. But she inspired us with her reverence for dancing and for art in general. And no one even thought to thank her for that.

Total silence still enveloped the class. The teacher withdrew Vaganova's *Fundamentals of the Classic Dance* from her tattered shopping bag. She opened this bible and pronounced, "Page three!" A rustle of fawning haste sounded as the mothers found their own third pages and mouthed the title of the lesson: demi-plié and grand-plié. Veteran mothers smugly lectured recent joiners, while older pupils wagged their heads knowingly at the young newcomers. "You *still* haven't learned it? That is very, very sad."

The teacher turned toward the whispers. "What are *you* laymen doing here?" her glance demanded. Then she announced, "Pas de bourrée, en dessus et en dessous."

The mothers fell into a cosmic hush and concentrated on their children's torturing according to the system devised by the legendary Vaganova. Someone claimed that this successor to Pavlova was still alive in Leningrad. In any case, Providence had seen to it that our teacher owned Vaganova's treasured book. Without it, we would have been a mass of broken bones.

Yet by the end of the year the classes were my purpose in life. The "source of indisputable authority" I kept hearing in broadcasts about our Party is what the teacher represented to me. I never dreamed of spoiling her sacred lessons with mischief.

Mama stood out like a Polish aristocrat full of pride for her breeding. She was now a bright blonde. In keeping with her status she always sat in the front row. All the other mothers competed to please the owner of the sole male partner for their little princesses.

She never missed a class or a chance to fuss over me. My fellow pupils considered her the ideal mother, while the other mothers, who had no time to think of their own makeup or outfits, saw her as the complete *woman*. But my worship of her diminished as the others' admiration grew. I had begun to feel that something essential was lacking, especially in comparison to our scrawny teacher. Naturally, I felt this chiefly in her attitude toward me. Perhaps she loved me, but if so, it was because I enhanced her own effect rather than for anything I was achieving or failing to. I was wanted because I'd become decorative. I sensed that she'd sought out ballet as much as an outlet for her unused energy as to involve me in something constructive. The good side of this was her drive for my stage success, which was especially important because I had disadvantages neither of us had suspected. It was from her alone that I inherited ambition and a need to draw attention to myself. My father's main aim was to pull my head down to the level of his own.

ONE OF OUR CLASS'S HANDFUL of nerve-racking show projects would long remain the central attraction for gala occasions. It was set to the music of the famous folk song "Kalinka." I rehearsed with a pretty blond girl who led her school class in everything. If I hadn't been the only Prince, she would have intimidated me completely.

She was an exceptionally determined girl for whom ballet was all work and no fun. I was a compact tyke with fluid movements and an ability to soar, but the music often swept me off my feet in the wrong sense. Entranced by it, I'd often rush ahead of the beat or lag behind, confusing and irritating my serious partner with these "improvisations." However, she could not scold me as she wanted to; she was concentrating too hard on her painstakingly memorized movements.

Every future curtain time would bring a horrible dose of stage fright. But this first "Kalinka" seemed fatal. The stage on which I was about to venture floated free from this world. My pulse was a rabbit's at the sight of a wolf. Yet when I was actually *on*, trying with all my might, the dancing calmed me. I enjoyed my own movement.

And of course got carried away. But this time, stage fright had loosened my partner's tongue. "Valerik," she snarled loudly, "you're not in time again." The great laugh that issued from the audience seemed to increase their pleasure. What incredible, thrilling delight when the sketch ended to cheer-laced clapping. We were called to three encores— the same "Kalinka" each time.

The good-natured audience was responding to what would be one of my favorite sights as a mature dancer: children trying with all their hearts on the stage, no matter how awkward they were or how many mistakes they made. It allowed me, at the age of eight, to feel I'd had a triumph. The most amazing thing was winning loud approval for once— and for doing something I *loved*. I took off my costume in rapture.

My growing ardor for ballet bewildered others and mystified even me. My mother's foresight in leading me to it became increasingly clear, for I was a model child only in class. Otherwise, my obsession to prove myself in physical trials continued. If I missed the edge and fell into the ditch I'd ordered myself to hurtle, I might be maimed. If I failed the jump between roofs, little would be left of me. I was terribly frightened; that was why I had to test myself. I would despise myself if I ignored the challenge. I had to win my own approval.

The Neris River was a fine source of danger. Returning from school one winter day, I spied some ice near our house. It was floating just off a point the local fishermen called the "shit shallows" in honor of a large sewage pipe that discharged its contents there. The warmth usually kept ice from forming around it, but this chunk *might* be large enough to support me. I took a run and leaped onto it. The momentum carried me out toward midstream. The little floe went under very slowly, like a submarine with an inexperienced crew. It was not sheer terror that kept me from following under immediately, but my coat, which had miraculously filled up with air. In the few minutes this life jacket would last, I had a chance to pull myself back. I strained with more power than I thought I had, but the closer I came to the shore, the deeper I sank into the freezing water. Choking on the sewage pipe's acrid fumes, I grasped its lip with aching fingers and somehow hauled myself out.

I usually delayed my homecoming from such fiascos as long as I could, but this time violent trembling from cold and fear left me no choice. I grabbed my bag and ran to our apartment, my felt boots squishing loudly and giving off a pernicious smell. Passersby scurried to one side, and my mother's reaction, like the stink confined by our four walls, was correspondingly stronger. I was undressed, washed, beaten, and berated for hours. My determination to learn to swim the following summer began an enduring love affair with unpolluted water.

5

DISMAL FAILURE ELSEWHERE BALANCED MY PROGRESS IN BALLET. IN school I couldn't stomach arithmetic or writing, nasty little inventions for distracting a young man from what was important. My teachers' constant pointing to my betters as models for me was even less successful than their other methods, for I found absolutely nothing to admire in the mama's boys called "achievers." They were bad at games, lacked fantasy, and couldn't put up a decent fight. The study habits that would prevail until my last day in school were well established.

Even in the fourth grade, the scope of my ignorance confounded my teachers. Because I *looked* like a normal product of an intelligent family, they couldn't believe my antipathy to book learning. I managed a few respectable grades in history, literature, geography, and lessons involving nature. But nothing could force me to study when I wasn't interested. I regarded every attempt to push me toward academic dreariness as a sinister attack on my dignity. The approach of spring put even my modest scholastic efforts out of their misery. I was like a captured jackrabbit.

Hitching rides on the coupling links of trolley cars would complete my afternoon of roaming. I crisscrossed the city until dark, eager to keep seeing, exploring, moving. But my travels were also a way of dragging out the return to my parents. My father's commissarlike rebukes of my "abnormal individuality" were always based on my catastrophic school record and accompanied by comparisons to the "good" boys I avoided. Ugh!

BUT MY BALLET IMPROVEMENT won my mother's increasing approval. She decided to grant Lithuania's sole ballet company a look at me. We were received by the balletmaster of the opera house, the same *Sleeping Beauty* Prince who still danced in my memory as a god. A veteran dancer even before the war, Bronius Kelbauskas had grown no more limber since. But because prerevolutionary Lithuania had had almost no ballet, he deserves a place in the country's artistic history, thus illustrating the old Russian saying that a crayfish will pass for a fish when nothing else is available.

Yet then I saw him only as a magnificent embodiment of manly art. Mama was only slightly less dazed by his reputation and had been shivering with pleasure for days before our meeting. It exceeded her hopes: he turned out to be as bewitching in person as on the stage. He elegantly kissed her hand. No doubt remembering our many classes, giddy Mama lowered herself into a wobbly approximation of a curtsy. My jaws went farther unhinged; the Prince's eyes bulged. But the great ladies' man welcomed this striking woman in distress with all the gallantry due both of them. Whenever I chuckled at this incident, my mother swore she had never curtsied to anyone in her life.

The Prince said that the theater's studio was closed for the summer, but its leading dancer—Kelbauskas—would soon be conducting a class in an excellent Palace of Culture. We might apply there, he suggested encouragingly. Mama immediately bought tickets for *Swan Lake*, whose Prince—the stage one—would be danced by my hand-kissing future teacher.

Swan Lake was my second living fairy tale. When Kelbauskas leaped onto the stage for his first appearance, my heart seemed to stop. His dizzying tours brought me close to a swoon. Never mind how awkward or old-fashioned he was or that he operated on his right leg only; I realized this *later*. Never mind that his grands jetés in the second-act coda were flat along the stage like the plonking of a cross-country skier. That evening I saw everything I would ever want for my own life—except that the magnificent Prince was divine and inimitable. I wondered whether children my age could die of happiness.

The next day I tried to copy all I could remember of *Swan Lake*. I had always been one of the most fanatic members of our neighborhood soccer team. Now balls dribbled past me and into the goal as I visualized swans in lacy costumes, who were supporting me in Kelbauskas' role. A kick in the ass from my jeering teammates finally brought me to.

At last the great day dawned of the master's summer class. Most of the pupils were trying to join the corps of the opera house. We waited breathlessly, girls in short skirts, I in my shorts. We peeked through the window, ran into the corridor, and dashed back again for feverish whispering. Finally, the clouds parted, and the classical hero and lover appeared in his irresistible glory. He sported long hair, a wan complexion, and a weightless walk. The noble creature was virtually a girl with the face of a middle-aged man. This was everyone's image—mine included—of what young male dancers should strive for. Providentially, a new generation of Soviet dancers would cut through these affectations. They had powerful bodies instead of the pretty ideal of the time. The images and emotions they conveyed came through dynamic masculine movement. In the 1940s and 1950s their lack of a "proper" Kelbauskas-like bearing would have kept them from leading roles. But the non-standard generation to which I belonged was successful enough to blur a later ballet public's memory of our handicap of looking too athletic.

Kelbauskas looked like a perfect model when he appeared before our blinking eyes. Everyone saw him as a figure on loan from the stage, which was obviously how he saw himself. His principal purpose seemed to be moving through the class and on to grander matters as quickly as possible. It was over before we knew it, and no one had dared interrupt his haste with a question.

We gathered our sweaty things. Suddenly he turned and pointed a finger at me. "That boy there, whom does he belong to?"

My mother's charge forward ended on a turned-out leg placed well forward of her weight. I flinched in anticipation of another curtsy, but she limited herself to the bizarre presentation of her leg to the princely gaze.

"I see," he said as if faintly remembering her from his army of admirers. "Let the little lad try a jeté for me."

My knees buckled. Blackness covered my eyes. Mama had been right after all. My whole attitude to ballet—therefore, to life—was a fraud. Here was the proof that what counted was the French gibberish.

So I was finished before having had a real chance to work at what I loved. If someone were to lead me through the door and straight to a firing squad, I could not save my wretched life by remembering what a jeté was. For some reason, fear always pulled down my eyelids. They squeezed shut now like the shell of a snail. When I risked opening them again, the Prince was a few inches in the air. Instead of booting me out for my miserable memory, he was demonstrating—not without beaming appreciation of his own effort. I dashed after him and tried a leap. It carried me through the door and into the corridor. I shuffled back. The Prince looked me over and smiled. "That's something, eh? The kid's elevation is better than mine!"

Future praise would rarely match those offhand words. Even when someone commended my work in an entire three-act ballet, I would know its shortcomings—and my own. But this approval from my faultless hero left my eleven-year-old heart in bliss.

SEVERAL MONTHS LATER the Prince's recommendation got me into a class at the opera theater. It was an experimental group to test possible accomplishment with pupils well over the usual age for developing dancers. But my classmates counted for nothing since the teacher was everything. Luck had put me under the wing of a remarkable ballet person who wanted to further my "career."

She was Niola Grigorievna Taboraskaite, a graduate of the famous Leningrad Ballet Academy. There she had been a favorite pupil of Vaganova, author of our ballet book. A soloist in the old Maryinsky Imperial Theater, Agrippina Vaganova was one of the few to hang on after the Revolution, when the new Soviet ballet was largely rebuilt around her. At one time, she was simultaneously artistic director of the Maryinsky—renamed the Kirov—Theater and of the Leningrad Ballet Academy, two of the world's greatest institutions of dance.

Vaganova's patronage of Taboraskaite was a hint of my new teacher's gifts. In her I saw both genuine talent and dedicated professionalism for the first time. At twenty-seven, Niola Grigorievna, as we called her, was approaching her prime. Her legs were long, shapely, and strong. She had a wasp's waist and a beautiful face—bred for ballet. Despite her eminence, she spent much time developing even barely trained pupils. She coached me for a year with nearly maternal devotion, insisting I had the physical and emotional potential for further development. Then she advised my mother to take me to the great Leningrad Academy, where she herself had trained.

My mother needed little convincing. She bought a bundle of books and photographs about the Leningrad ballet, the country's finest. Maybe she imagined that after a month or two in the Academy, my portrait would be added to those of the famous stars. With their beaming encouragement we went to the railway station to begin our five-hundred-mile pilgrimage.

IT WAS INDIAN SUMMER. Colored leaves still clung to the birch trees. Lyric poets since Pushkin have been overwhelmed by Leningrad's splendor at this time of year. Each bridge, square, and canal was superb, but the city's glory far exceeded the sum of its parts. It seemed the creation of one inspired moment.

The Academy was on Rossi Street, named after the architect who built many of St. Petersburg's magnificent ensembles. Two identical paragons of Russian classicism faced each other across the roadway. With white columns against yellow façades, they stood like a guard of honor to the Pushkin Theater at the far end. Their harmony and proportion soared beyond anything I had associated with mere buildings.

One of these two structures that seemed reflections of each other housed the Ballet Academy that was founded in 1738, under Nicholas I. Its style, perfectionism, and outpouring of peerless dancers had stunned the world ever since. I already knew of some of the most famous: Pavlova, Nijinsky, Spessivtseva, Karsavina, Fokine, Dudinskaya, Ulanova, and Vaganova.

I was grateful for the opportunity to see this thrilling blend of ballet history and beauty. I expected nothing more of the trip, in fact, and would just as soon not have entered the building. The inevitable disappointment waiting for me inside—where real dancers trained—would slap away Rossi Street's magic.

Mama had no such misgivings. Her enthusiasm for her own plans could shelter her from tiresome facts—in this case, that all classes were full and had begun some weeks ago. She had promised my dubious father that their son would study in the celebrated Academy, and she never doubted the world's eagerness to cooperate. She rushed inside—to cold office voices. "All places are taken. We're overflowing with pupils."

My mother could not accept such a no when her son's career, and, incidentally, the country's artistic future, were at stake. She smiled her way up to the fifth floor. But "Comrade, it's simply too late," stopped her short in the Director's outer office.

Walking back toward the stairs, I saw that a sleek female leg in the corridor had distracted her. Actually, her eyes were riveted not on the leg itself, but on the shoe displayed at its end. The high heel was a hint of Paris in our land of trudging boots. A cry of appreciation escaped my mother's lips.

This flattered the owner. Later we learned that she was Lidia Tuntina, a teacher in the Academy. The two ladies struck up a conversation. The subject switched from fondness for ballet to fondness for clothes, since Mama, as usual, was wearing the handiwork of surviving Vilnius "bourgeois" dressmakers. To continue their chat, the new friends sat down in an outer office.

Later the door opened, and a bent old woman entered very noisily. I noticed that her legs were powerful, yet springy. The office immediately came to life. Striding past, she examined me severely from head to foot. My mother's fancy for "foreign" apparel extended to my wardrobe. That day she had clad me in smart short pants and knee socks, which were no doubt responsible for the granny's attention. All the other children here were dressed very shabbily.

The woman made for the Director's inner office but wheeled back suddenly. The force of her bellow almost blew me down. "Where did you come from, boy?"

"Vilnius," I mumbled.

"Louder!" she shouted.

I opened my mouth to obey the command, but my mother had already hopped to my side like an aroused hen.

"From Lithuania," she crowed. "Li-thu-an-ia."

"You mean out there where Niola is?" The reverberations of the woman's growl filled the room. At length she pivoted toward my mother. "As a matter of interest, who might you be?"

"I'm the mother." It was the rare person who could trim Mama's sails to three short words.

"And what are you doing here?"

My mother began to singsong our story. Halfway through, the woman interrupted with a fresh war cry.

"This boy with the compact build, is he yours?"

My mother nodded.

"Come with me."

She ordered us through the inner door. Inside, a large woman was sitting very straight at the Director's desk. Our battle-ax marched to a chair at her side.

"We're going to sniff at a new boy. I like the look of him." She swung her eyes toward me. *"Get undressed."*

I obeyed. While my shoes and socks were coming off, the Director talked about the school year's having begun, about all vacancies having been filled long ago, about a lengthy waiting list. She went on to general reflections about the need for rules and regulations, "without which this Academy will be chaos." Her monologue reached me, and I delayed removing my shirt. But my dawdling was noticed.

"Take off your clothes."

I was terrified of her, especially since she made even my mother cringe. The shirt was off, and I was down to my short pants. The really terrible moment was coming, for I was wearing not underpants, but an awful pair of long drawers, rolled up above the level of my shorts. They were striped, were far too large, and had a huge opening in the middle. I stole a pleading glance at Mama, but the edge on her voice provided the answer before I could put the question. "Yes, you must!"

I was alone with my drawers, trying to make myself invisible, praying I would never see the strange woman again. She enjoyed a long look and broke into a belly laugh.

"You're some sight, Master Pantalon Pantaloni. . . . Which ballet exercises do you know?"

I looked at Mama again. Her expression told me that an affirmative reply was required.

"All of them," I stuttered.

This nerve shocked even my mother. But a plan of self-defense had come to me. Whatever they asked for, I'd run through everything I knew, not stopping to think, not even listening. Experience had shown that examiners always liked what my body could perform better than what my mind could answer.

"Well then," the woman grunted, "since you know them all, I'll name a movement and you do it."

I resolved to ignore her scoffing smile and stick to my plan. And when she shouted, "Now an échappé," I showed her a changement. Next she asked for a tendu, and I was up in the air with my jeté—adding a few extra steps for good measure. Recognizing the futility, she stopped giving directions. I ran through my entire repertoire with frenzy, trying to make up for doing it all so weirdly.

At last I exhausted my repertoire. A panic-filled silence descended. With a contrapuntal echo from the Director, the old woman broke into delirious laughter.

"Well!" she croaked. "This lad seems bursting with love for our art. . . . You're accepted into the Academy, and I'm going to coach you myself. Comrade Director"—she poked a finger at her—"will take care of the details."

Halfway to the door she spun back to Mama and me.

"Send my regards to Niola," she roared. "She's sent us a good little mite. Pantalon Pantaloni!"

She slammed the door. Her demonlike laughter shook the corridor. When it died away, I learned that she was the mythical Vaganova.

6

THE FIRST MONTHS IN LENINGRAD WERE ALL ABOUT A COUNTRY BOY making good. As a newcomer *and* a latecomer I was the exception to a hundred bureaucratic rules. Agrippina Vaganova bulled her way through them all and even got me into the dormitory. I would learn what this took only when I had to leave.

Vaganova decided I belonged in the 3/5 class: the third year—of nine—in ballet and the fifth—of eleven—in general subjects. My physical development and knowledge of ballet steps, which was better than she had expected from a provincial lad, guided her in this. Sharp as she was, she couldn't have guessed how retarded I was in school subjects.

Two or three times a week she took time off from her other duties
to drill me in fundamentals. My plié wasn't nearly open enough for her
liking. While I assumed second position, she clamped her feet behind
mine to push my hips apart while I bent from the knees. She yanked
with her powerful arms and smiled when she felt no resistance from
my limbs.

She liked to plant a foot on mine and push my other leg skyward
from the ankle. She was amazed that the uplifted leg, which my young
muscles could hardly hold at waist level, could stretch beyond my forehead. Some of my movements—my monkeylike spurts and pigeon-toed
walk—entertained her to the point of outright laughter. But above all,
she liked the easy freedom of my limbs. This allowed them to follow
her example of new steps even when my brain couldn't follow her spoken
orders.

Years later, when I understood exactly who Vaganova was, the
privilege of her individual coaching amazed me. Trained in this same
building under Pavel Gerdt and Nicolai Legat—who also taught
Karsavina, Nijinsky, and Fokine—she was a living link to the nineteenth
century. She became a soloist at the Maryinsky Theater in 1897 and
continued to perform there until 1920, but her most valuable contribution was as a teacher—of Semyonova, Shelest, Dudinskaya, Ulanova,
and most other Soviet primas. Strict, severe, and exacting, she was known
as one of the greatest trainers of all times, even before her *Fundamentals
of the Classic Dance*, the ballet bible, was first published in 1934.

Vaganova established the Soviet system of ballet education. Her
approach was instantly recognizable in other teachers, as well as in her
own pupils. With the strength of the famous "Vaganova back," the
pupils were able to maneuver their bodies even at the top of a leap.
Most of all, she demanded harmony, coordination, and stability of the
entire body, with as much emphasis on arms as on legs. But only a hint
of this superb teaching penetrated my gaping twelve-year-old eyes. Her
voice struck me more. Even when she was in her mildest mood, it
creaked like an ancient cart with wooden wheels.

But most days she was *angry*, and her voice turned genuinely unpleasant. When she was berating a pupil in full view of everyone, her
tongue lashed the mortified sinner. Scorning a sloppy relevé, she became
as crude as a market woman.

I was a frequent target. She taunted me mercilessly for a leg not
properly extended. To soften the attacks, younger teachers whispered

that Dudinskaya, Ulanova, and the other greats had always got the worst of them—and in front of everybody, too. But I hardly needed comforting, even when she let loose her neighing laugh at my failures. For my child's perception recognized that the fonder she was of someone, the more harshly she treated him. Above all, this seemed a kind of masochism: her abuse of her favorites was a mocking of her own affection for them.

Besides, deeds revealed her true attitude better than words. She worked ferociously to develop pupils she believed in and to protect them against bureaucratic interferences. In my case, the private lessons, which cut heavily from the elderly woman's free time, came on top of her personal acceptance of me in the first place and her supervision of my living arrangements. She laughed at me, derided me—and fought for me like a tiger.

But I also sensed that this attraction was not just for a possible outstanding pupil, but for someone bringing an exotic touch to the Academy. Everyone considered Vilnius a foreign city. Almost all my seventy classmates in the various sections were Leningraders who had been together since the age of eight. Maybe because of their success in the fierce fifteen-to-one competition for places, they had already developed a sense of exclusivity.

I was physically different, too. Many saw me as better suited to high jumping or acrobatics than ballet. Vaganova seemed intrigued to see what my nonstandard body and intense energy might lead to.

IN ADDITION to the private sessions with her, I had two forty-five-minute lessons on fundamentals with my classmates. The first weeks were hard. My Vilnius training hadn't prepared me for the Academy's methodical approach to exercises, let alone for the class discipline. But as I caught up, the other boys startled me. Most did the exercises diligently and very precisely—but without a flicker of love or even excitement for what their bodies were executing. Nothing was connected with the exultation of dancing. Even when introduced to the most glorious movements, they remained sullen, while the teacher's comments sounded at regular intervals like some part of the mechanism. "You're not working at all well." Or, "That was a good execution." No wonder so many dancers merely perform movements—that is, merely do their job—on the stage.

I wondered whether I faced six long years without the elation I'd already felt in my amateur performances. We spent a million hours on the five fundamental positions alone. But I longed to get to the scenes the daily exercises would lead to. I wanted to be thrilled even during training. Driving myself to exhaustion promised a hidden, uplifted meaning. I was happy to hear the daily "work harder" sermons and to see mucus flying from gloomy faces—Leningrad's rawness kept everyone in winter-long colds—as my fellow students worked on their pirouettes. Old Vaganova's croaked flogging gave me a secret pleasure.

Sometimes there were moments of performance euphoria. Most came during our "genre" classes of historic manners and morals that offered the minuet, pas de quatre, and pas de grasse, galop, several varieties of waltz, and other traditional dances. The teacher, a tiny woman named Elizaveta Gromova, who knew them all in incredible detail, passionately loved her own instruction. She paired boys off with the little girls in our class. All waited in suppressed excitement to be assigned their partners, and our coaching with its elements of the mysterious game of courting—how to take a woman's arm, when to kneel before her during a mazurka—brought flashes of romantic beauty into our impressionable lives. We left these classes feeling wonderfully grown up and in love with our "ladies" of the hour.

To enhance this pleasure, the practice often took place on a charming little stage in the Academy's own third-floor theater. This miniature playhouse provided a taste of the joyful future of unencumbered dancing. A peek toward the stage as our class passed in the corridor filled me with fierce determination for the next ballet class.

But it was a rough ride in the nondancing subjects. We had five classes a day, teaching the standard curriculum for the entire Russian Republic. Unfortunately the Academy did not take this as a formality. The reading-writing-arithmetic teachers needed only weeks to uncover, then to gape at, my benightedness. Noticing my love for drawing, our art teacher said I'd probably erred in choosing a dance career and suggested a transfer to a special high school for painting. But art was the exception that proved the rule. The general subjects dragged me further and further down, and I was demoted to the 2/4 class in the winter. This hurt doubly because I could still see no purpose whatever in the deskbound courses.

The lower ballet class to which I was transferred was taught by a methodical former Vaganova pupil. She usually pointed to Yuri Soloviev as the class example. The future Kirov star—and my future friendly rival—looked like a runny-nosed boy from one of the poorest collective farms. But his physical equipment was fantastic. A rubber robot couldn't have executed the full range of ballet steps any more easily than he. He was the perfect illustration that elasticity and flexibility count much more than strength in ballet, but he himself was dying to trade with me. Everyone in class—I above all—loved to show off his leaps, while he cried because he couldn't lift himself off the floor.

Soloviev's poses and gestures had a naturally elegant line. By contrast, I was made for movements requiring acrobatic energy and airborne spinning. The daily class consisted of three segments: exercises at the barre, exercises at the floor center, and leaps, ending in all-out efforts, giving everything we had. All through the preliminaries I kept longing for the leaps, and this set the pattern for all my future training. Often my most important work would begin when the other dancers had left the studio. I would carry on alone with the all-out part until my legs stopped working. Now I went quickly to the front in class "feats," but what 1950 observer would have believed that, when his muscles matured, the same Yuri Soloviev who could barely inch himself upward would develop the greatest leap in the world?

THERE WAS NO TIME to answer letters from home. Our first class was at eight-thirty in the morning. After this the day was so packed that even lazy boys finished very tired in the late afternoon.

Russia's circumstances handsomely increased the supply of daily adventures. The Academy had about six hundred pupils. Roughly five hundred were from Leningrad. One or two boys represented the Urals city of Perm, which enjoyed special privileges because the Academy and the Kirov Theater had been evacuated there during the war. Otherwise, almost no one else had come from another Russian city—let alone from the Ukraine, Belorussia, or elsewhere in the huge Soviet Union.

The main reason was severe shortage of dormitory space. I soon realized why Vaganova's steely insistence had been needed to stake out a place for me. Although children were theoretically free to board with local families, spending even ten or fifteen rubles a month was unthinkable except for the richest 1 percent of parents. Russia was just too poor, and Leningrad in particular too shell-shocked after the Nazi siege. Ballet was allocated a relatively huge share of national resources, but neither great institutions nor private individuals could afford to maintain pupils outside their own homes.

The exceptions were youngsters of the "national minorities." Although the Soviet Union had a hundred such ethnic groups, the phrase almost always implied the peoples of Central Asia and beyond. On instructions, the Academy made the "Brotherly Help" propaganda real by enrolling children who otherwise would never have seen a ballet. Thus, the dormitory housed a hundred "nat-mins," another word for "wogs." Thus too, nightly frolics and tortures that were as tiring as the long day.

My room contained two dozen cots. All the others were occupied by boys from Kirghizia, a half-mountainous, half-desolate region bordering China, and from the Bashkir Autonomous Republic, an enclave of the Russian "Wild West" below the Urals. This was the best Vaganova could find for me. I was a "White child"—five years younger than my roommates—among Asian tribesmen.

In accordance with some bureaucratic quota, this particular group of captives-for-rehabilitation had been counted off for "culture." Too far from home to escape to their tents, they messed about with ballet on the rare occasions when nothing more interesting suggested itself to their warrior imaginations. But their principal interests were gang fights, stealing, and shoplifting in town. After classes they sneaked off to a dozen varieties of tasty mischief. I served as the midnight snack.

In the dead of the night I would feel my cot being borne toward the door. My pals would tie my ankles to the knob so that the matron would yank me to the floor when she opened it in the morning. They also kept my night table spanking clean of all treats from Mama. Even before I could rip open a new package, I'd get a breathless summons to report immediately to some administrator. I'd scamper to her office, recognize her puzzled look, and not bother to return to the dormitory. Only the parcel's wrappings would be left.

Masters of the art of surprise, my roommates preferred tricks their audience could "really feel." They would summon me to a room on some urgent business. I would rush there with my usual eagerness, open the door, and catch a slosh of water from the pail planted on the door-jamb. The little barbarians broke up with friendly laughter which I was expected to join. "You're a little Shulman," they snickered. "So you'll just have to take it, won't you?"

Occasionally a gleeful yell would resound in the early hours. "Wake up the Yid. We'll give him a twenty-one-gun salute." An upturned behind, wan in the night, would quickly appear above each cot. The voice of Uran, the leader, cut through the darkness. A toughie with the body of a marvelous cat, he was to become the leading dancer and Artistic Director of the Kirghiz Theater of Opera and Ballet.

"Who's ready out there?" he would shout.

"I am," one of his soldiers answered. "But *hurry*."

During salutes the headman was more like a cheetah than an ordinary cat. In two giant vaults Uran reached the upthrust rear of the lad who had spoken. He struck a match just under it. Then came the bang and shudder of a minor explosion. Uran danced a circle around the cots, ready to light up at the next muzzle to pronounce itself primed and charged.

But this cannonade was performed in a spirit of sincere salutation to me, just as "the Yid" was intended as good-natured banter. Even their birthday present—eating black bread all day to increase their gas production—was meant as a friendly gesture. Later in the year their fondness for me became clearer and clearer. Maybe there were other Jews in the Academy, but I was the only one with whom they had fun.

But what exactly a "Jew" was, I had no idea. One day a pupil read my nationality in the class book and wrote "kike" on the blackboard. Later I understood she meant no spite in this but was simply repeating what she'd heard in her average working family. All eyes in the class turned to my face and stared in frank puzzlement.

Again I understood nothing, but it was impossible not to feel. I remembered that it was not only as an alien *Russian* that Alec had been persecuted during his evacuation in Kazakhstan, but also as a Jew. For some dark reason this was worse than a Russian. I had not wanted to understand Alec's remark that "Yid" occasionally peppered the taunts of the native teachers and his ruffian Moscow classmates.

My parents' attitude confirmed that this was something to keep away from. "Just look at those darling blue eyes, *he doesn't look a bit like a Jew*," my mother often said of Alec. "The nose? Oh, that got smashed up at soccer." When I left for Leningrad, grown-up Alec was admired by his friends for his wit as well as his learning. "Of course, Mama," he would agree. "It's just that all the Jews happen to look like me, your darling Slavic son." My father kept forbidding further mention of the subject "in any form—just don't get involved with those damn Jews."

But much as I respected Alec, I responded very differently to problems. The few times ethnic slurs were tossed in my direction, I refused to accept that they were intended for me. Whatever they meant, I knew that to be less than pure Russian was to carry a shameful, weakening virus in your blood.

I developed a suspicion of those tainted people who might spoil my love of beauty and physical feats. But this was linked to a hidden fear that I bore some defect deriving from my unknown relationship to them. Why did Jews have to burden *me* with their unwholesome existence?

ONE WINTER DAY a teacher read off a list of pupils chosen to participate in a performance of *Fadetta* at the Maly Theater. The children's cast was to include six pairs and one soloist: me! The honor of my first appearance in a genuine ballet was overwhelming, *unbelievable*.

We were rehearsed by the owner of the beautiful instep spied by my mother in the corridor, the gentle, much-respected Lidia Tuntina. She was the chief coach of children's dances in every ballet, but more important to me, she had been my friend from that first day. She taught me much, for the time was coming when I would be borrowed two or three times a week for performances in the Kirov or Maly theaters. Working in actual performances was one of the most beneficial aspects of the Academy's training.

The Maly Opera Theater, Leningrad's second home for ballet after the Kirov, was on Arts Square, just off the famous Nevsky Prospekt. A glorious unity of colonnaded façades, the square was another masterful Rossi ensemble. The building itself, the Tsar's former "French Theater," was remarkable even by St. Petersburg's standards. We were led backstage. Bustling assistant directors had been waiting for our arrival. Wardrobe personnel fussed over our costumes—mine included a blouse with puffed sleeves in the smartest style of the *Fadetta* period—and we were made up as carefully as the grown-ups. My peasant wig and huge hat hid me like some private canopy. I looked like anyone in the world but *me*, which by itself carried me to fairyland. Suddenly I realized that one of the theater's highest achievements is reached when no one can recognize you.

It turned out that we were in the theatrical game not only for spiritual satisfaction, but also for the ultimate in material rewards. The fee for child performers was a "sweet supper" of candy, pastries, and tea. In those half-hungry times, éclairs did more than artistic gratification to sharpen hopes of being selected. My own sweet tooth took second place to none.

But the greatest joy, the moments of total ecstasy, came in the Kirov Theater. Just to hear its full name—the State Academic Theater of Opera and Ballet—touched me with shivers. The sight of the azure and gold palace on Theatrical Square intensified this to delicious anticipation tinged with stage fright. The former Maryinsky Theater awed us all with what had been—and still was—great in art, especially since we already knew that very few of us would attain its stage as adults. Every hall and every corridor were galleries of portraits of legendary and present stars, confirming that nothing had changed in devotion to supreme achievement. The air once breathed by the geniuses of Russian ballet was pure oxygen to my fantasy. Each Kirov appearance strengthened the illusion that I might learn those mystical heroes' secrets.

THE ACADEMY ITSELF was slightly musty and run-down. Layers of powdering paint contrasted oddly with graceful wrought-iron patterns on the balconies overlooking the larger studios. An army of cleaning women smaller only than the Kirov Theater's wiped every nook of the ancient wood every day. Their reverence for the noble building seemed a hangover from its imperial days. Somehow it was hallowed. But the tendency to humble Russian disorder helped make it also homey.

The first door off one of the Academy's endless passageways opened to the studio for our daily classes. The following ones were to the smaller classrooms with their prisonlike rows of desks. General subjects were drilled into us here, and although some of our humanities teachers were capable, they had up to forty pupils in a class, as in ordinary schools. Ballet lessons usually came in the morning, when we were still fresh. Any energy left over from the demanding day went to leapfrog and other afternoon games. By early evening everyone was wilting—and remained so when we were delivered to the Kirov or Maly to perform. In tsarist days, herds of Academy children were taken to their vesper duties in locked carriages to prevent their running away. According to a popular story, the floor of a carriage collapsed under the weight one evening, forcing the still-imprisoned children to run along like coolies, in step with the horses. Our doors weren't locked, but the old carriages couldn't have been more crowded than our cars. And some of us fell asleep during the short drive to the theater.

Thanks to our category of calorie-demanding physical work, our meals were above average and our bread ration was higher than the city norm. But better than average was dismal, especially compared to my family's diet. And extra bread was anything but an honorary award. At every spare moment those who could afford a slice dashed into the cafeteria for one, to be gobbled down with mustard or salt left out on the table.

The lack of a shower was the most rankling shortcoming of the facilities. The Director's efforts to have one installed kept failing, and we continued to use a single cold-water faucet in the lavatory. Everyone who was waiting shouted to the one washer to *hurry*—and to the child sitting on the toilet to stop fouling the air. Kirov dancers who luxuriated in the same facilities put our hero worship to good use. After their final leaps in the large studio reserved for them, they would summon a young boy or two to announce that "Now we'll have a nice crap, get me some paper." The boys would run off obediently and return with the required *Pravda* or *Izvestia*, torn into eighths. "Now how about softening it up a bit?" the soloists would say. "Who's good at crumpling?"

Despite these little trials, the Academy was a happy home. Each Kirov and Maly success was a reward for every one of us. We were all together in something exalted.

WHEN MY SECOND TERM BEGAN IN 1951, I was a cheery boy, somewhat better equipped to feel my way. For years, a fondness for reading had partially compensated for my allergy to school subjects. Alec had re-christened me Manilov after Gogol's *Dead Souls* character who saw the Neva River's ice packs as crystal palaces. My flights of fantasy had grown so powerful that I sometimes had to shout to stop them. In another minute I'd black out and enter my invented world forever.

I had graduated to adult literature as a source of imagery. Personal experience taught that the thicker the book, the better its contents. Kilogram for kilogram, my favorites included *And Quiet Flows the Don, Port Arthur, War and Peace, The Russian Forest,* and *The Three Musketeers.* I plunged so deeply into them that wrenching myself back to reality was painful. Compared to them, everything around me—except ballet—seemed as pallid as Leningrad's raw overcast. I read mostly at night, in the dormitory toilet. During the long, frustrating winter, my free time was spent like a hibernating bear. I lived off the fat of romantic volumes and waited for the first rays of the spring sun, when I'd bring life to the printed page.

D'Artagnan claimed my body first. I solemnly chose three classmates as my Musketeers for dashing through the city's parks and puddles and riding "bareback" on trolleys. Under the impression of Dumas' perfidious women and the amorous problems unraveled by Leo Tolstoy, I developed a secret passion for girls. My Musketeers blinked at the plots I dreamed up for them.

Our favorite girl was actually developing what real women had! She was soon to become and long to remain a corps de ballet plodder. By contrast, Alla Sizova—who ten years hence would be a beautiful woman and leading Kirov soloist—merited only the disdain of our nickname for her: "the ugly duckling." The older girls were always more intriguing, and I tried everything to win their affection. My gallantry included sweeping around a corridor corner to knock one off her feet and pelting another's head with snowballs. Tossing a lump of bread into a fair lady's soup was another winner. I wished I could think of a better approach than these crude futile ones.

The tallest Musketeer, Murat Kumisnikov—we called him Porthos, of course—crawled out of his skin trying to execute even my silliest schemes, but his very conservative parents fretted about my corruption of their impressionable son. My whistle outside his apartment brought him faithfully through a tiny winter-air window, a slice of cake only half squished in his pocket. He didn't care much for pastry, so I gobbled down his half, too. Then we hurried off to the Peter and Paul Fortress to play naval battle on the Neva's ice floes. Like real ships, ours sometimes sank, taking their proud captains with them. Wet to the neck, we'd go back to his place, which was closer than the Academy, to dry out. After his parents came home unexpectedly once, my negative influence worried them even more. I struggled to incorporate their displeasure into my updated Dumas but also took it as further proof that real life was much more niggling than its depiction in art.

· · ·

WELL BEFORE THE DUTY MATRON CAME IN to wake us at eight o'clock, my roommates had done the job by jumping on my bed and playfully removing my blankets. They hated my lingering in bed after they were up.

We hurried to the cafeteria in the main building, then to our ballet instruction. Class brought the pleasure of final leaps, but also certain discomforts. The hardest came to my toes, which stuck out from holes in my canvas ballet shoes. Shoes were given out about every six weeks when supplies were available, and during the last ten days I hotfooted about on bare skin. In the absence of resin the floor was religiously sprinkled with water. The wet wood cut through our flimsy soles like a rasp. Mama was far away; no one volunteered to repair my sweat-soaked rags, so I banged my protruding toes and howled. Kirov dancers who rehearsed upstairs often distributed their used shoes among the older pupils. The young dormitory orphans had to do without.

Our lessons were given in a practice room with a sharply raked floor—a great advantage, since most of the country's stages had the same angle. A slanted stage helps a dancer keep his balance and find his feet for leaps and some of the most tiring turns around the stage circumference. The one drawback is that this series of tours around the outer limits of the stage is usually performed toward the end of a solo number. With his failing strength, it's all a dancer can do to swing his legs up the incline.

Since adapting from a slanted to a flat stage is far easier than the other way around, this was a small example of the professional pains taken for students even of our age. In addition, there were carpenters, costumers, bookkeepers, many varieties of administrators, and the large cleaning staff. The ratio of pupils to teachers and coaches was six or seven to one. The physical layout—the older the pupils, the higher the floor—contributed to our perception of upward progress. The lower corridors with the production charts and portraits of Lenin and Stalin could have belonged to any ordinary school, while each ascending stairway landing was closer to art. The fifth floor was a corner of heaven itself, for here nestled an enchanting little museum with photographs and portraits of graduates who had gone on to become great St. Petersburg and Leningrad dancers.

The large fifth-floor studio, where the Kirov's leading soloists came to practice, was an even greater attraction. *Sleeping Beauty* was created here in 1890. Coaches and balletmasters watched the rehearsals of our day from a high gallery with an iron balustrade. The entire Academy tried to join them or to peek from the studio door. Quivering in anticipation, straining to see through the legs of a hundred pupils crammed in front of us, we goggled at Galina Ulanova, Natalia Dudinskaya, Konstantin Sergeyev, at the fluttering Nicolai Zubkovsky, and at Ina Israileva, Tsarina of ballet beauty. When someone rolled off the huge jumble of young bodies and onto the studio floor, we all were ordered *out*. The pack hunted down the clumsy one responsible for cutting short our glimpse of glory.

But when Boris Bregvadze was rehearsing, no punishment could fit this crime. The dark, manly Bregvadze embodied my vague feelings about what I wanted for myself. Lacking sculptured legs and a noble torso, he violated all rules for a male hero's appearance. Despite his slight unwieldiness, he was extraordinarily exciting. By casting his spell through dynamic *dancing* instead of assuming effective poses, he opened the way for that new generation of male leads who failed to look like man-gods.

Evenings I appeared more and more often at the Kirov, acquiring a small repertoire of child roles. The openhearted old wardrobe women who dressed us would ask for me whenever I failed to appear for a week. At one point they were as worried as Russian mothers about a sick child, for I was excluded for a full month as punishment for a bungle. For the Dance of the Saracens in *Raymonda*, seven other boys and I were fitted with little wrist saucers for beating out the rhythm. Waiting for our cue backstage was like holding in a pee. Naturally one boy always fell victim to the tension and began clacking too soon while the others' eyes popped from their heads in dread. Only a fierce hissing from the wings prevented disaster. The prompting came from Lidia Tuntina, our tireless coach. When I sat in audiences years later, her frantic sputterings to the new crop of children reached me distinctly through the performance. I couldn't understand why no one else seemed to hear them.

In any case, we had completed the dance that tragic evening, and I was scampering toward our exit with my usual zeal. The something soft I bumped my head on threw me back under the feet of the Saracens running behind. In a second we were a squealing tumble on the floor. The soft thing was the stomach of Jean de Brienne. The heroic lead was being danced that evening by a man who thought of himself as a knight even without stage armor. At the moment of our collision he was unsteadily affecting a supposedly exquisite pose on one leg. Spoiling his sacred artistic mood was an even more serious crime; thus my long exclusion from the theater.

Twenty years later I was waiting in the wings of Moscow's Palace of Congresses for my next scene as the Golden Idol in *La Bayadère*. A group of boys were to run toward me from the opposite side as I made my entrance, then form a diagonal line that would serve as a kind of backdrop for my leaps. But no boys appeared, and I was already behind cue. I charged on just as one tyke was streaking with all his might across the great stage to tangle himself in my legs like a soccer tackler. The following moments of a hurdle race over boys cowering in paralyzed confusion added something new to modern choreography.

Still cursing after the final curtain, I remembered my own *Raymonda* mishap. Good old Tuntina appeared with a clutch of boys to apologize. The children couldn't understand why this grown-up idol in the golden body paint laughed them out of their dismay.

MY ROOMMATES AND I settled into peaceful coexistence. One or two even accompanied me to an occasional performance at the Kirov Theater. Familiarity bred affection.

Some evenings I sneaked down to the rooms of Academy graduates living in "bachelor quarters" on the first floor. Some even gave me a pencil and let me draw them. The little group included Anatoli Gridin and Anatoli Sapogov, the spectacular character dancer who would fill the Kirov with pleasure through the coming twenty-five years. There was also a boy named Yuri Maltsev, who was seven years older than I. While waiting in the corridor on one of her visits, my mother had struck up a conversation with him and was taken by his quickness and brightness. *I* liked him because he was tough, was full of fire, and painted well. My mother ended their lively tête-à-tête by asking him to keep an eye on me, a prophetic start to his role in my life.

One first-floor attraction was a Korean named De-Son-Chan. The stories about his fanaticism seemed exaggerated until an older boy urged me to stay downstairs very late. Son-Chan was fast asleep. We switched on the speaker that carried Moscow Radio when the Kremlin bells struck midnight and the booming Soviet national anthem began. Son-Chan leaped out of bed and stood at attention until the last note, then slipped back under the covers, still asleep. Dormitory life got more amusing every day.

THE SECOND TERM ENDED with high marks for me in ballet and the usual flops in general subjects. In June I was back to Niola Taboraskaite's coaching in Vilnius. The Academy remembered her as an exotic foreigner because of her height and non-Russian beauty. After watching top soloists rehearse for a year, I recognized her as a gifted, polished ballerina who surely would have starred in the Kirov had she come from Leningrad. But she had to return to Lithuania because its Ministry of Culture had sent her to the Academy. She immediately became the republic's prima, but there was no hope of joining the Kirov no matter how brilliantly she danced. Too many bureaucratic obstacles blocked transfers between institutions even of the same city.

Niola Grigorievna's devotion to teaching was probably an outlet for creative impulses that the provincial Vilnius Opera House couldn't fully absorb. She was a wonderful, womanly mixture of maternal generosity and skilled instructor. And she knew all the god-like leading dancers I'd watched from afar. Her personal idol was Konstantin Sergeyev, the Kirov's premier danseur and balletmaster. He thrilled me too, although I already knew I could have nothing in common with his superb lyric elegance. Had someone told me we would one day work and even fight together, I would have bitterly resented this as cruel teasing. Meanwhile I greedily absorbed Niola's attention. Sometimes I knew I deserved neither her nor Vaganova's gifts to me, but at other moments I considered it entirely natural that they lavished their time and talents on me. Their extraordinary generosity helped convince me that *I* was exceptional.

7

WHEN LITHUANIA "JOINED" THE SOVIET UNION IN 1940, THE OLD POLISH town of Vilna was renamed Vilnius and declared the capital of the new socialist republic. Feeling superfluous in their own city, many Poles packed their belongings in the early 1950s and left for Poland.

One of my mother's main occupations during my summer vacation was sorting out photographs of herself. Still pampered and striking to look at, she was already developing nostalgia for the period of her greatest glory. "This was my closest rival," she would say, examining a yellowed photograph of a Vitebsk blonde. "She married well. But people placed her second at the time."

Mama also collected more general mementos of the old days. From a former middle-class woman about to join the exodus to Poland, she purchased some furniture that included a treasured stack of Hollywood magazines. I would never have believed such pages could be printed. The rich, shiny paper, the brilliant photographs, the dizzying beauty of the stars of stage and screen! It was like discovering the existence of fruit.

Mama and I thumbed the worn pages for hours while my father and brother puzzled at us. My debt to my mother increased when she also acquired a collection of phonograph records. I stopped listening to them only when my arm was too sore to go on cranking the handle. Caruso, Gigli, Galli-Curci, Titta Ruffo, and Jan Kiepura sounded constantly in my room, and I shouted arias so loudly and badly that Alec nearly went mad. In the middle of a courtyard soccer engagement I would open a window and invite the team to meet Puccini. Although my sporting friends were certain I'd lost my senses, other acquaintances were deeply impressed—by the new marvel of a phonograph. The arias by the world's greatest singers opened me to interpretation as no class had. Without thinking, I absorbed their lessons about phrasing and timing. They would give me the freedom to move even on evenings when my technique was off; the courage to stand still on the stage—to speak in pauses—if that was what the character I was dancing really felt.

Second to the records, I gave my heart to "booty" films. These were immensely popular Western productions the Red Army had seized in Europe at the end of the war, then shown up and down the country without a need to pay hard currency for them. I saved my pocket money religiously to see *Clowns, My Favorite Arias, Tosca, The Great Waltz*, and other inexpressibly noble spectacles. Even when I was old enough to recognize their faults, I remained deeply grateful for their mush and melodrama. Their tenderhearted sentimentality was as essential as fairy tales for emotional development. Soviet films also preached love for "your Friend, Comrade, and Brother." But this was always put into ideological messages: neighborly love through devotion to the motherland or a factory lathe. It was "bourgeois escapism"—human emotions for their own sake—that gave children the longings and the vulnerability to become real people one day.

THE MOST POPULAR BOOTY FILMS dominated my second year in Leningrad. All Russia lay in Tarzan's grip, breathlessly awaiting the next serial. The Academy corridors and the city's canals and tree-filled parks were a jungle setting, crying out for continuation of the last episode's action. The elephant-summoning yodel-yell echoed from tall buildings, and every boy who could cope with his mother went about with hair like fish spines, straining toward the shoulders. Good-looking girls were called Jane, and less lucky ones—including all teachers, of course—were Cheetah. For a full year I swooped out of the last afternoon class with a rhino grunt or a call of a savage tribe. Johnny Weissmuller left his indelible mark on me in swimming, too, which I took even more seriously than before.

My private sessions with Vaganova resumed in September but soon dropped off. Everyone talked of her health and about how she *had* created a galaxy of top stars. Murat Kumisnikov told me that she babbled on one day, confusing him with me.

She took to her bed in October 1951 and died—of old age, I think—a month later. The country's best female teacher was gone. The naming of the Academy after her a few years later only underlined her absence. My personal loss was not only of a great teacher, but of a person willing to go against the grain in everything. No bureaucratic or "cultural" rule interested her, but only how to detect and develop talent. If she had lived even a few more years, my life would probably have been much simpler.

Some changes came immediately. My mother was summoned to Leningrad and told that the Academy had no funds to keep me in the dormitory. But no one in the city had room enough to take me in. After a despairing search she finally found a family. My couch was in the corner of a tiny room. The remaining space was entirely occupied by a bed for the family's two daughters, both younger than I. The mother and father slept in a similar room, and we all ate in a kitchen slightly larger than a closet. The basement apartment was on the gloomily beautiful Kryukov Canal, between the Kirov Theater and St. Nicholas Cathedral. During the autumn rains the younger generation was bedded down on the kitchen table to keep us from drowning in our sleep.

But this was rare luxury. A worker's family living in its *own apartment* instead of being crushed together in one room of a communal one was almost unheard of. Uncle Sasha's work as a construction crew foreman explained it. Everyone in the fantastically overcrowded city curried his favor. And Auntie Tonya carried home a small but regular supply of pinched foodstuffs from her job behind a canteen counter.

I got a share of everything delicious, for Uncle Sasha and Auntie Tonya put me on an equal footing with their daughters. Much nonsense is spoken about the "pure" and "selfless" Russian character, but I would keep meeting their type from time to time, especially in the countryside.

Twice a month Uncle Sasha prepared our birch besoms and took me along to a public bath on Streetlamp Lane, a marbled, heavily colonnaded institution known to many generations of Leningraders. A stuffed bear that had survived all of the city's upheavals greeted us in the vestibule. We sweated together in the huge steam room with the hundreds of slippery bodies, then scrubbed each other. Resting on a worn bench, Uncle Sasha consumed his quarter liter of vodka, helped down with beer chasers. He poured an inch into a mug for me, for what was a *banya* without beer? Finally, we set out along the snowy Moika River, where Pushkin had lived, winding our way in the hushed St. Petersburg darkness to our Kryukov Cathedral.

Meanwhile, classes continued. Studio floors were sprinkled with water, ballet shoes were worn to shreds, and tiny successes in our training were augmented by the great triumphs of the soloists we managed to observe. When Ulanova danced *The Bronze Horseman*, the Academy vibrated with tension and excitement. The Kirov was closed to minors because of the permanent crush for the tickets, but we squeezed in backstage. The chair I crawled under promised the protection of the official seated weightily on it. *His* kind was never asked to move, even to oust a stowaway. I watched a third of a heavenly scene. A fragile Ulanova-Parasha, soon to be drowned in a terrible St. Petersburg flood, was onstage. Suddenly someone dragged me out by my ankles and sent me packing—and to visions of the ethereal Ulanova.

Otherwise, I dreamed about Lelya, who had appeared just as I considered myself old enough for love. Several classes above me in the Academy, she would be turning heads in the street just a few years from now. My incipient taste in women worried me: I liked only those far above my standing. My craving for beauty had nothing to do with the soul or even the body. I simply wanted girls whose glory no one could question—therefore, whom I did not deserve. The prizes lured me into anxiety, as when I had to prove to myself my willingness to risk danger.

When my darling Lelya allowed me to walk her home, the mood was set by statues of brave men taming wild horses on the Anichkov Bridge. It was heaven to be at her side, and when her parents were out, she sometimes invited me into her room. I sat across from her for a half hour, then rose and said good-bye. "My God," I sighed, walking home. "How glorious life can be."

WITHOUT DORMITORY SUPERVISION I was often on my own. I spent more and more afternoons going to plays or simply walking in the city. In the end I stopped even going through the motions of studying. It was indeed "the end," for my miserable scholastic record caught up with me in June. My teachers had given up. My parents were told that they had either to move to Leningrad or to do *something* to discipline me for the general subjects. Their decision was to remove me from the Academy when my second year ended.

On the train to Vilnius I stood shell-shocked at the window. Life seemed finished—until I saw Niola Grigorievna again. After some months of classes with her she advised her own theater to take me into the corps de ballet. At the age of fourteen I was a member of the Lithuanian State Theater of Opera and Ballet.

My thirty-five rubles a month—a charwoman's earnings—seemed extraordinary. People were paying me for doing what I loved. Soon I was puffing in pride and exertion on Vilnius' hills. A sporty bicycle had been bought for me from the earnings that I took directly to my parents.

My fourteen-year-old frame was like comic relief amid the extremely veteran members of the corps. Some had to be set out on the stage before performances like props. But they treated me with paternal warmth, rather than resenting my youth. With no pensions for dancers, the old ones clung to their positions for dear life. The pay was so low and performances were so few that some of the soloists sold apples or flowers from nearby stalls on the evenings they weren't dancing.

Yet my nervous excitement almost burst me before each performance. I was wildly happy, ready to rehearse all day and talk ballet with the janitors if necessary. The only cloud was long winter evenings in an Evening School for Working Youth. "Youth" was a euphemism, since pupils—mostly factory workers tired by their day at the lathes—were accepted to the age of forty-five. Since some older "boys and girls" actually prepared their lessons, the sane thing was obviously to postpone mine by thirty years.

When things became impossible there, my mother took me to a neighboring school. This started a process of petty deceit that would continue as long as I remained in Vilnius. I transferred to a dozen evening high schools, one worse than the next. Whenever I couldn't pass a grade, Mama would talk her way into yet another school, claiming that my records had been lost. She thus "promoted" me to a new class, where I was even further behind. I almost never had two years in a single school. Every "sane" person but me knew the multiplication tables and the rivers of Eastern Europe. The shame of my ignorance naturally drove me deeper into the cycle of defeat. I knew very well that I ought to have learned more. But I'd convinced myself that formal instruction was behind me, and I was locked into my self-fulfilling prophecy.

My parents' cries of "You nitwit, aren't you *ashamed* of yourself?" only increased my inferiority complex and my stubbornness. Totally unable to stimulate a child's natural instinct to learn, they could think only of new insults. My mother filled the apartment with wails about how terrible it was, how tragic her fate, to have a dolt for a son, while my father returned from work with a single question on his lips. When it was answered in the negative, he ordered me to my unfulfilled "task," then patrolled behind my chair.

"You sit there until you've finished the homework. No food until you do. My children are going to be bricks in the building of Communism."

Alec was fed in his room because I *didn't* get food; I could not fulfill my scholarly plan. My love went into him on the tray. The distance between us and my parents grew daily. What did they want of me? Why couldn't they understand my feelings?

Our understanding so little about them, in turn, was more than the ordinary selfishness of children. We knew almost nothing about the truth of our origins. Alec's discovery of the wayward Shulman aunt borne off by the Turkish officer and of the younger one painted by Chagall would come twenty years later, when a final, determined trip to Vitebsk extracted a few facts from elderly uncles and aunts who had survived. Until then we lived in a kind of "historylessness" like Russia's as a whole, where nothing outside Party myth and production statistics was deemed useful to know. Since Mama and Papa didn't fit the "proper" pattern, they pretended they had no past.

Alec's later research suggested that Elizaveta Petrovna Charitonova, as Mama was born, was the product of an unblessed union, her father probably a minor Polish or Belorussian baron. Her mother was an illiterate peasant who hired herself out to farmers near Vitebsk. She brought up her children in great want.

My mother's only item of exchange for escaping poverty was her beauty. It did win her invitations to her rich classmates' parties, but this only aggravated her envy. She yearned for wealth and for respectability. Above all, she was ashamed: of her mother's work-gnarled hands as much as her own illegitimacy. She became the pretty waif who dreams of far better origins and finally comes to believe that she has actually had them. To protect this illusion against her old humiliation, she avoided talk of her family.

In the hope of marrying her daughter well, my maternal grandmother reduced her own diet even further. Her lovely girl needed appropriate clothes. But although her sacrifices may have helped develop my mother's vanity and self-importance, they couldn't bring a good match. In Vitebsk, as elsewhere, the Revolution had finished all men of substance. The problem now was how to feed oneself, not run a handsome house. My mother was still unmarried in her mid-twenties, considered dangerously late in that rural area. Matvei Shulman, who was about to graduate from a local school for electricians, was stunned by her gentile beauty and lofty bearing. After dogged courting she accepted him.

Her exemption from the rule of Soviet women working showed how she dominated at home. This was a wild luxury *and* an otherwise unthinkable deviation from Papa's commandment to *do what others did*. He loved her deeply. He gave her the final word in all domestic matters. And she was happy to follow his political lead, especially since her intelligence, as opposed to her strength of personality, was clearly second to his. Although lacking his fondness for Party slogans, she always parroted *his* parroting.

The happiest aspect of this pattern was its domestic peace, based on harmony of interests. My parents almost never quarreled. The adoration was very one-sided, but respect and affection came from both partners. As a bonus to my mother, Papa often relieved her even of cooking. He also liked chopping wood for the stove, cleaning the family's shoes at dawn, and polishing the furniture.

A trace of Papa's background showed in these oddnesses. The more we learned about his origins, the less related they seemed to his attitudes, which perhaps explained why he proclaimed them so rigidly. Papa was a child of his age. Originally from Poland, the large Shulman family settled in Peskavatik, a section of Vitebsk where our Uncle Arkady studied painting with the same artist who tutored Chagall. It was a district of shopkeepers, traders, handicraftsmen, and wheeler-dealers, with an intellectual and cultural life that almost matched the business and religious sides.

Grandpa Shulman owned a small butcher shop and a log cottage for renting in addition to the homestead. He was apparently an Orthodox Jew. Alec remembered being bundled outdoors with a flock of cousins so as not to disturb his impressive swaying while he mumbled his prayers. But he also fancied himself a local baron and was widely known for his grand manner. Dressed to the nines in a vest and bright tie, he indulged in cardplaying at every opportunity. The ninth child of his second marriage, Matvei was his opposite in every way: no religion, no cards, no jokes, no women, no finery. This was our Papa, to whom I, in turn, was a kind of antithesis.

Grandpa Shulman often talked of Palestine, swearing he would re-settle if he were younger. One aunt actually did go there, a misdeed that would convulse my father every time he completed a questionnaire. But Grandpa went nowhere until the Nazis took him away. Most of his children had left Vitebsk earlier. When my father was off for Moscow in the early 1930s, the old man gave him his valuable silver pocket watch. Already devotedly ascetic, my father refused "such a present" even from his own father, who, of course, was offended.

The trip to Moscow began my father's ascent. He had started as a delivery boy in a Vitebsk textile store that disappeared, like most others, soon after the Revolution. He finally found work in a leather factory, where his arm was caught in a machine and had to be amputated. He went hungry in the mid-1920s, then won his way into the electricians' school where he was studying when he met my mother. He had had only a few previous years of formal schooling but was quick, precise, efficient, and religiously diligent. Using his computerlike ability with figures, following every order with his unswerving self-discipline, he was graduated at the head of his class, but again the ruined economy had no work for him.

On a Leningrad labor exchange he got a job in a lumber mill being constructed by prisoners in the far north. He and my mother spent a honeymoon year in a wrecked railroad car deep in the forest. When they returned to Vitebsk, his old tannery had resumed operations and hired him as an electrician. Soon factories all over the country were being canvassed for able young men to train as supervisors for the first Five-Year Plan. My father was unusually industrious *and* had the diploma from the electricians' school, which put him among the well educated.

The Industrial Academy in Moscow was chiefly for teaching something to provincial Party officials about the enterprises they had taken over and were ruining. My father did homework for some of the near illiterates. Compared to them, he appeared a genius. Again finishing at the top of his class, he was sent on to the Institute of Light Industry's Section of Textiles, Leather, and Footwear. Tutoring others to support us, he managed to earn a degree in "Technical Sciences." He was assigned to defense work during the war. Just after it he returned to teaching, which is what gave us our room in the institute's dormitory near the Moscow River.

My poor father's record did not make him proud but only troubled him gravely. He came not from a Russian working family, as the keepers of the incessant questionnaires surely saw, but from a comfortable Jewish one. His lineage was solidly petty-bourgeois rather than proletarian. This could lead to much worse than failure to advance.

With a hundred daily reminders that all was not well with his "social origins," he learned to hide them. This was the beginning of his sacrifice of personality. Sheer fear did the rest. Naturally timid to begin with, he was petrified by the show trials, purges, and executions during his first Moscow years. He *never* took any initiative, *always* kept himself in the middle of the Party ranks. All his fervor was reserved for slogans already being waved, and he changed instantly with the new ones, even when they made nonsense of what he had been saying yesterday. The great tragedy was that he had begun as a shining idealist, eager to sacrifice for the first truly just society. His original faith in Commu-

nism—the best in him, which fear and enslavement turned to the worst—
derived from a yearning for the highest humanistic goals.

At least my mother loved ballet. My father was suspicious of it because his deviant, dumbbell son was dabbling at the stage to fool people.
"If your mother thinks it's necessary, I'll go along for now," he would
mutter. "But you should do some real work for the motherland. Get behind a lathe, and show us you're *worth* something."

The other vivid difference between my parents was in their dress.
Papa never wore anything actually ragged or holey, for this would have
suggested disrespect for Soviet society. What his wardrobe did consist
of primarily was a suit jacket and a worn coat, both bought secondhand.
He simply wouldn't put on anything that wouldn't blend with the gray-
green masses. When I took out a pair of new shoes, he leaped on this
"foolhardy nonsense." Scuffing the shine off the toes, he lectured on his
central life principle: not to stand out. "Don't you know anything?" he
sputtered. "This is terrible, people will *see*. You're always trying to attract attention to yourself." To be like everyone else was one of his
highest goals. He was deeply opposed to everything necessary for art.

Safe in his secondhand raincoat, he looked like a Soviet version of
Plyushkin, Gogol's Scrooge-like landowner. But a closer look at his
features showed unmistakable signs of a nastier symbol. By now I recognized him as the kind of Jew from whom the caricature is drawn. Yet
he sneered at "the Jews" as frequently as at monopoly capitalists. In fact,
these enemies of socialism were often lumped together, with Judaism
as the yeast. When Alec mentioned that a friend had been rejected by
Moscow's Film Institute, Papa lifted his head from his chicken soup.
"With his nose?" he scoffed. "And he thinks he can apply for the
pinnacle of our Soviet cinematography yet? Typical Jewish insolence."
My father seemed oblivious that his ridicule could easily have been exercised on his own nose and accent. But Jewishness was one of the few
topics that could drive his ordinarily harmless indignation to genuine
anger.

Maybe he felt such a heavy responsibility for our moral upbringing
because he was a dedicated Communist Party member. He scrutinized
several newspapers every day. Later I learned that his type studied every
tedious line because one new word, even a change of word order from a
nearly identical article the previous week, could signal danger to those
trained in the code of newspaper language. But my father's eagerness to

absorb every list of names and production statistics went beyond concern for his own skin. He also wanted to be right about every little detail, and the only fount for all knowledge and wisdom was the various Party and government organs.

Our apartment was full of them. All were more tedious than an algebra textbook, but one day in the winter of 1952–53, an intriguing headline caught my eye: ARREST OF A GROUP OF DOCTOR-SABOTEURS. The article told of nine doctors and medical professors confessing to the murder of two Politburo members by intentionally mishandling their treatment. Five of the traitorous criminals were Jews. I couldn't miss this point because of the further charge that they were connected with a "Zionist espionage organization established by American intelligence." Anything involving American intelligence was as interesting as a movie about counterrevolutionary bandits. I read on. The saboteurs were enmeshed in a center of international evil too vile to contemplate.

The article was the start of a campaign that would become known as the Doctors' Plot. It stopped being a joke when my parents read it. Their fear was instant and obvious. But my father chided, "That's the Jews for you. Thank goodness our Soviet security squashed those schemers before they got to their main mission." The plot to poison the entire Politburo was fully real to him. He was certain the doctors should be shot.

Soon after the *Pravda* exposé, most Vilnius pharmacists—who were Jews—were discharged. People seemed to have an instinctive fear of their assassinating key citizens by tampering with prescriptions. There were daily exposures of more and more "depraved Jewish bourgeois nationalists" pursuing espionage and "wrecking." The newspapers now seethed about enemies of Stalin who were trying to save themselves by sneaking out of Moscow to hole up in provincial cities, such as Vilnius. These articles were more frightening because of the dangers they warned of than because of anything that might affect me. I still felt myself loftily removed from the troublemaking and the problems of Jews. Only some remote compartment of myself accepted that the cartoons of hooknosed murderers in doctors' smocks disturbed me.

My first direct confrontation came when a young soloist at the theater asked to borrow fifty kopecks my mother had given me for a movie. I knew I could get more from home. I gave it to him without a second thought. In the dressing room soon after the performance some dancers were discussing that day's unmasking of Jewish assassins, throwing "Yid" around like a rotten pear. I started changing next to the man who had asked for the loan. He threw the fifty-kopeck note on the floor and kicked it away, snarling "Lousy kikes," to the others' satisfaction. When the talk moved to something else he quietly pocketed the tainted money.

His kick had felled me like a tipped arrow. The hurt was that I couldn't stop others from seeing me as Jewish, even though I knew I was far from being so. I remained on the bench long after the other dancers had gone. Pushing away my unwanted thoughts, I got up and went home.

My father studied the newspapers' increasingly hysterical attacks—and approved. He was pale but stalwart. Then one evening Alec and I returned to an ominous buzzing in our neighborhood. A small crowd was pressed up against a fence on which the local newspaper was displayed. The article that gripped them was about . . . Matvei Shulman. It was written in the style of a Krylov fable about a beast that had been swindling the Leather Trust of millions for years.

My father ran to the newspaper's office to beg them to print the truth. The whole truth was that the under-the-table boosts to his salary were a fraction of the "normal" embezzlement taken by almost everyone of his rank. In fact, he was a righteous impediment to his fellow administrators, who wrote false contracts, sold state merchandise to cash in on the desperate consumer shortages, and stole large sums outright. This helped heat his plea to the editors. When they sent him packing, he dashed to Party headquarters. Finally, he requested permission to resign his post. He said he could not fulfill his socialist duties in a climate of suspicion, but even I felt his hope to leave before his enemies could pounce. He bravely announced he needed more education and registered for economics and management courses.

Warning feverishly about espionage, calling for even greater vigilance, the press ran more and more horror stories. Its language brought down a heavy pall of fear over the country. Stalin's 1930s warnings about enemies who feigned devotion to socialism were repeated to encourage workers to denounce artists and scientists. Only the hope that the collective hysteria was too mad to be real kept it from taking over. But just before the expected bloodletting, medical news about Stalin himself overshadowed the Doctors' Plot. Early in March 1953 the radio announced that he had suffered a stroke. Alarming communiqués about this greater threat to mankind's happiness pushed the Jewish scare to second place. While Alec stood aside, my mother and I joined "the people's" incomprehension. It was inconceivable that our Teacher would leave us.

All the people of Vilnius hung onto their radios for bulletins. Then came the paralyzing announcement that he was gone. "Let there be no panic and no disorder"—but no one could stop the weeping. All Russia was stricken. My mother howled, while father steamed like a samovar. Every few minutes he wiped his eyes.

With no idea how they would get there, many Russians left immediately for Moscow and a last look at the man who had taught them to love humanity. The rest of us sought salvation in crowds. Announcers sobbed into loudspeakers, prompting new wailing in the street. "What will happen to us now?" my mother bleated. An American invasion was her most immediate fear. It was certain to come any moment now that our leader's protection was lost.

The next day I went to a memorial ceremony for the theater's personnel. Stalin stood deep on the otherwise empty stage, bordered in black and illuminated by a single spotlight. Medals painted with infinite pains by worshiping portraitists covered him like a suit of armor. Warlike strength and unchallenged power radiated from the huge painting which would surely come to life during the service. From Director to cleaning woman, we sat in an awed hush in the orchestra. The funeral music was from Wagner's *Götterdämmerung*. I pulled my eyes up to meet Stalin's. He was a python hypnotizing his trembling rabbits.

Dancing Petrushka years later, I carried this image of the supreme dictator with me. The despairing puppet dashes frenziedly about his room, unable to understand why he can't get free to see his beloved Ballerina. Above him hangs a silhouette of his personal tyrant, the St. Petersburg conjuror. To put myself completely into the role, I mentally exchanged the image for the likeness of Stalin that had stupefied us that March afternoon. My puppet's limbs flopped in desolation. By recognizing how monsters use portraits to help crush all individuality, the genius of Fokine and Benois gave me the clue to the interpretation.

8

THE THEATER'S BALLET DEPARTMENT GAVE THREE CLASSES A WEEK, BUT most of my training came in sessions with Niola Grigorievna. After two hours of regular work with several young Vilnius ballerinas she kept me on alone. We covered almost the entire classical repertoire of male variations and codas. "Keep working, keep learning," she repeated. "You break many rules, but there's something in you that can't be stopped. You're going to *dance* one day—maybe very soon." Her words spurred me on. The joy of working with her made it easy to repay her devotion with all the energy I had. It also made the escape from home and school to ballet even sweeter.

MY FIRST WHIFF of serious interest in the outside world began with curiosity at what the outside world thought about *us*. My parents had hardly listened to the shortwave bands on their radio during Stalin's terrifying last winter. But when the nightmare was fully over, the temptation revived. They warned Alec and me about what one word to anyone would mean, then switched on—at the lowest possible volume—to Russian-language broadcasts from the West. My father said his duty as a political fighter required him to hear the enemy's inventions. He listened very intently, then scoffed at the "absurd lies, lies, lies." His answer to every item, even the announcement of a cease-fire in Korea, was couched in newspaper language about the bourgeois press spewing propaganda for monopoly slave drivers sworn to destroy socialism. It was only Papa's amazing rigidity in repeating that day's Soviet editorials that disappointed me. Like everybody but Alec, I assumed that *our* side was right.

The Voice of America went on and on about what it called the Soviet people's endless hardships. This particular nonsense proved to me that our Party represented goodness and truth. I knew as well as anyone that the citizens of our first socialist state in the world, the victorious smashers of fascism and builders of Communism, were richer, happier, and freer than the overwhelming majority of cowering Western workers. Only references to injustices committed by the state could raise a barely perceptible question in me. I sometimes remembered the sobbing convoys that day in 1947 when Lithuania was cleansed of "bourgeois elements."

But this passing image gave me no hesitation about joining the theater's Young Communist organization. A stage career was impossible for nonmembers. Anyway, it never occurred to me to commit the political suicide of the 5 percent who stayed aloof. I believed as much as other teenagers in the Young Communist principles—and the grown-up Communist ones, too. Some of the bowing and scraping to the Party and the motherland was a nuisance, but Marxism-Leninism itself was sacred.

So I marched toward the Young Communist League (Komsomol) with typical outward nonchalance and inner conviction. Although entering was supposedly a great honor, mass processing made the ritual of application, review, and acceptance extremely routine and guaranteed that cynics and hooligans helped fill the ranks of the "ideologically steadfast." My credentials were quickly approved. It seemed no more significant than registering for school.

WHEN A FESTIVAL of Lithuanian arts was scheduled for Moscow, the company was beside itself with nervous excitement. In bureaucratic terms, such cultural festivities were actually "major accountings to the Party and government" of the condition of a given republic's arts. Since the task was to please high officials rather than the public, it was vital that the content have the greatest possible rectitude.

For weeks the theater's lobbies and offices were scenes of a nonstop conference about what to perform, while everyone quivered in dread of making a false ideological step. At last the front office, "guided" by its Party cadres, settled on *Zorenka*. This ballet about a triumphant peasant revolt against domineering Lithuanian landlords was rendered in the straightest socialist-realist style. Asaf Messerer, the Bolshoi dancer, balletmaster, and teacher, was invited to review our production, and everyone was in a frenzy preparing. There were even endless discussions about what props would be most likely to impress the literal-minded Moscow Party overseers. Real rakes and scythes were handed out, and the dancers representing elders were entrusted with genuine pipes, precious rarities in our country of cigarette smokers.

Zorenka was a ballet of old fogeys. When I was picked to be one of a group serving as a backdrop to the bride's parents, I studied the movements of elderly shoppers in the markets. But an unscripted drama the night before the opening queered these preparations. My pipe was swiped from the cloakroom, and when I tried to explain the unthinkable loss, suspicion was shifted onto . . . me.

This double injustice destroyed my concentration. Instead of thinking myself into a doddering mood, I was asserting my youthful innocence of the crime when the famed Messerer entered the dressing room just before the dress rehearsal. Passing me, he turned to his entourage.

"Goodness, what excitable young dancers you have!"

The next morning my name was listed in the new, larger part of the bride's father. I was going to be a soloist at the age of fifteen! Not even the fact that my first role was that of an ungainly old geezer diminished the flow of nectar to my vanity. The change had been ordered on Messerer's recommendation after he had watched me in the group of old-timers. But his approval stopped at that. Niola Grigoricvna could neither impart her enthusiasm for my progress nor win his patronage to get me into the Moscow Academy. Although Messerer thought I had the makings for strong character roles, he saw no potential as a full-fledged dancer. Stabbed by his verdict, I succumbed to my grown-up corps friends' urging to join them that evening.

The banquet celebrating the success of the premiere was held in the theater's buffet. Long white tables were crowded with bottles of vodka and wine. When these were drained, the right approach to the waitresses, which my tablemates exhibited, produced others. I was old enough to know what a Russian does when he is blue. I lost count of the glasses I drank. The next thing I remembered was kneeling over into a toilet bowl while cold streams of water were flushed on my head. Reassured that I was still alive, my drinking companions went back for more.

Sometime later I felt good enough to drag my nausea outside. The first November snows were falling, and all public transportation had vanished for the night. But somehow or other I arrived at our oddly tilting house. Noiselessly I climbed the stairs to our second floor, silently undressed, soundlessly sneaked into bed. And came to in the same hush— a certain sign of something seriously wrong, since my father always woke me with his favorite carol of "Onward, cannoniers, Stalin gave the orders / Forward, lads, the motherland needs the mortars." Apparently my homecoming had devastated my parents. But showing that even they sometimes could solve problems sensibly, they let me sleep until evening. Then they showed me the evidence of my "silent" return. My shirt hung from the sideboard's top shelf, an oak closet lay flat on its back, and the window in the stairway door was broken. Worst of all was the dented fender of my bicycle, from which I had wiped every speck daily. I swore to myself I would never overindulge again. My next lesson was how feeble are pledges that are made on the miserable morning after.

THAT WINTER I DANCED reckless young Vanechka in *Doctor Ohithurts*, a lighthearted ballet based on Kornei Chukovsky's beloved children's tales. Although not a difficult part, it appeared in all four acts and was usually danced by an acknowledged soloist. I made the step forward without faltering and won some praise for expressiveness. The scrimping theater raised me to sixty rubles a month, an eloquent indication of its interest in my future.

During the summer break my sessions with Niola Grigorievna were more frequent. "Messerer's seen too little of you to judge," she soothed. She was more convinced than ever that I had the makings of a leading dancer and must continue my formal training. She applied for support from the Lithuanian Republic's Ministry of Culture to send me to the Moscow Academy for a year's further study. The ministry approved; the Moscow Academy took me after a short appearance before its examining board. In September 1954 I was a student again.

I liked Moscow for its dynamism and pace. It made me feel close to the center of things and stimulated new interests. Amid Leningrad's classical architecture, I had played the noble hero. Here I looked at girls' sweater fronts. The difference was in my age, but also in the atmosphere of the rival cities.

Adolescent preoccupations narrowly focused my observations in the capital. Girls began noticing me, too—that is, began noticing my clothes. My mother outfitted me from a Vilnius secondhand shop to which Poles' visiting relatives sold an item or two to pay for their trips. Moscow's masses were always trudging the streets in grayish Chinese raincoats. A bright shirt was enough to make me appear exotic there.

The girls' vote got me elected Young Communist secretary of our class. A kind of homeroom monitor and distributor of political messages, the secretary helped maintain discipline and encouraged everyone to study. I couldn't refuse the honor; I wasn't "anti-Soviet." But as soon as it became clear who the worst pupil was, another vote was taken.

Moscow's dormitory shortage was as severe as Leningrad's. I was settled in a communal apartment near the Bolshoi Theater. One family of four members was crammed into the largest room, a couple lived in the adjoining one, and my landlady, a typist approaching sixty, had her "living space" to herself, which was why she was permitted to rent out "a corner." But we could hardly move when the door was shut. Every night we unfolded my cot and eased it into the available square inches. I returned as late as I could every evening and got out of the little box early in the morning.

My roommate was proud of her well-preserved body and assumed, with reason, that it interested me. She often undressed for bed in front of me, demonstrating that I was too young to care—or that I wasn't too young. I hated her for mocking me, which is how I interpreted her strip-tease.

The Bolshoi's Leonid Zhukov taught my ballet class—without encouraging results in my case. I sought inspiration; I went to theaters, tried to sneak in to watch the older classes, and kept up my swimming, which had developed every summer in lakes near Vilnius. The Bolshoi Theater had been assigned one lane of Moscow's only full-sized pool during certain hours. After months of petitioning I was given a pass.

The other lanes were thick with Olympic swimmers, whose example spurred me to train seriously—until some pretty girls from the Bolshoi corps appeared one day and admired a diver's gainer-with-full-somersault. "Oh, that's easy," I said on my way to the board. I never doubted that the wish to dive well would give me the necessary strength and skill. My head smacked the water so hard that the entire group in the pool turned to gape even before I howled. And since the pool was packed from morning to night, I never went to the board again.

IT COULD BE EVEN HARDER to attend the Bolshoi's performances than to use the pool. This contributed to the Academy's artistic isolation and to its dreariness of daily routine. As teaching hospitals are allied with medical institutions, the best ballet schools are attached to major theaters. In both cases the emphasis is on the trainee's future perform- ance. Pupils become dancers, then teachers of new pupils—part of a continuous process, when it works as it should, for maintaining the standards and transmitting new techniques. To put it another way, the stage is the laboratory where pupils can observe their progress and draw inspiration for further work. One of the Moscow Academy's major disad- vantages was the absence of this laboratory. The great dancers did not train in the Academy, and we rarely saw them even onstage! Alas, fifteen years later, Leningrad would lose this marvelous opportunity to fuse learning and performing. The Kirov Theater would withdraw from the Academy, ending its rehearsals on Rossi Street's fifth floor. But at least the Vaganova school's students would be regularly sent to the Kirov as part of their education.

The Bolshoi lacked these vital traditions and probably would never acquire them so long as the management had a sold-out house for even mediocre performances. True, every other one of the hundreds of thou- sands of Soviet and foreign tourists visiting the capital daily wants to crown his stay with a Bolshoi evening. But by diminishing performers' ability to distinguish good from bad in their work, these hollow "hits" hurt them as well as the pupils. The Bolshoi *was* moving ahead in some ways, especially that very year, when the company made its first appear- ance in the West. Through a new flamboyance, it was gaining ground on the Kirov's traditional perfection. But the Moscow company's suc- cesses had nothing to do with *us*.

The Academy was on an old street not far from the Bolshoi Theater. In the late 1960s a large replacement on the Moscow River would thin true artistic atmosphere even more. The modern building would com- pletely lack the spirit of prerevolutionary traditions, which is the Soviet ballet's heart and soul.

Living in the routine of practice for its own sake, we had only our teacher's mythical-sounding exclamations for inspiration. "I saw Ulanova last night—fantastic!" Someone else chimed in with a rave for another dancer seen the previous week. Most of all, I missed the Leningrad Academy's miniature theater, where pupils *and* primas performed for a "family" audience. In Moscow the substitute was two studios with a folding wall.

The daily classes went on, with me making slender progress. The ballet staff paid far less attention to my training here than in Leningrad.

A superb balletmaster named Pyotr Gusev, who had once partnered Olga Lepeshinskaya, taught me the rudiments of the lift, but I missed Niola Grigorievna more every week. At least spring came a week earlier in Moscow. When the Vilnius theater summoned me home to join rehearsals for the forthcoming Festival of Lithuanian Arts, I was happy to return. Niola beamed. The next day we were together in our private class.

But something had changed. Lifting her was hard not only because of her size, but also because I couldn't concentrate on the technique that adds strength to the arms. Greater awareness of beauty in general had increased my worship of her, and feelings that had tormented me in Moscow grew stronger and made things worse. The discovery that Niola was a woman kept stunning me. I couldn't take my eyes from her leotards.

She was starring in a new ballet that celebrated Lithuania's socialist rebirth—ideologically pure enough for inclusion in the Moscow festival. I felt that she had been reborn for me, too, as more than just a radiant dancer and coach. Jealousy of her partner on the stage and her husband at the stage door interfered with thoughts about her art. As if to assert his ownership of some luxurious vase on loan, her lumbering husband came to fetch her after every opera house performance. The lackluster gynecologist loved his role as escort to the republic's leading lady. *She* loved his adoration of her: a feeble foundation for marriage. His clumsy body and self-satisfied eyes humiliated me as he waited. She would emerge, bouquets in her arms and triumph in her eyes—the picture of a thirty-year-old prima accepting the city's deserved veneration. I had just turned sixteen.

Perplexed by why I was being deprived of the person who had taught me to strive for beauty, I stared at her and choked. She turned to me with a half-inviting, half-condescending smile. The moment I returned from Moscow she knew everything about my new feelings and ever so slightly toyed with my absurd but flattering adoration. When she turned back to her husband, the smile intended for me lingered on her mouth. A sweet, warm hurt welled up in my throat.

With the soaring new meaning our daily class had acquired, I practiced until utterly spent. My passion for work seemed to arouse Niola, then me, in turn, even more. But the jealousy attached to my first love for a woman would plague me in all my later loves.

One day Niola smiled strangely and said she was "waiting for someone" and therefore would not be performing for several months. The term she used to define her coming leave of absence from the theater was connected to a special dispensation for female personnel. My head started spinning at her excessively casual mention of it. The action decelerated to slow motion. In my sweaty shirt and a ribbon for controlling my hair, which she herself had tied, I slumped against the wall. Reading my guesses about her intimate life, she blushed and fled to her dressing room. I stumbled to a toilet and was sick. A terrible refrain drummed in my head: "My goddess has fallen, my idol has been . . . defiled."

On the hills of our old war games I had sometimes come across busy couples. Soldiers called the girls prostitutes, the meaning of which I only guessed when they laughed about them and their babies. It was inconceivable that Niola had anything in common with this dirty business. Yet her oblique announcement of maternity produced images of her in these terrible poses.

There was more. Becoming the mother to his baby meant that she not only slept with her husband, but loved him. How could this be when she loved only ballet and me? Sobbing and retching, I cursed her for soiling the secret of our life.

9

At last the company went to Moscow for the festival of Lithuanian Arts. The banquets, speeches, and presentations of honors—all designed to demonstrate the republic's affection for the "Soviet family of nationalities"—were more important than anything really connected to art.

The tour provided my introduction to the category of people called admirers. They were more visible and noisy in Moscow than in Vilnius. They flattered me, especially because I seemed to attract more attention than our leading dancers. They even increased my standing in the company itself.

My most persistent followers were four girls who waited with flowers after the performances, switching to candies when they learned of my sweet tooth. After *Doctor Ohithurts* one evening, they presented me with a whole cake. Before my fellow dancers could tear at the cardboard, I hurried to call Niola in her hotel. Just when I was coming to terms with my Vilnius hurt, her belly became noticeable. This was an awful reminder that I would be deprived forever of the person who meant most to me. Yet I had to share my first tremors of fame with her this evening.

The receiver shook in my hand. But she answered casually that it was late and she was sleeping. I said I *had* to come: I had a chocolate layer cake. This "irresistible temptation" forced out her real explanation: she was waiting for a telephone call from Vilnius. But before I could collapse again, she added that I might visit her in the morning.

These holy words again promised the absolute beauty to which only Niola could guide me. I didn't sleep; the layer cake had to be ministered to. In my third-class hotel, a short bus ride from the center, no one would dream of letting me use a refrigerator. For a substitute I went to a little square near the Bolshoi Theater I remembered from my student days. Planting the box in the March snow, I waited.

As I knew from Vilnius fishermen I'd occasionally joined as a boy, morning meant five o'clock. As the Kremlin clock bonged five times across the square from Niola's hotel, I was tiptoeing past the snoring watchwoman on her floor. She had told me her door would be unlocked. I opened it to her blinking amazement.

"My God, you're blue with cold." Then she guessed about my sleepless night. "Take off your shirt and trousers. Do as I say: get into bed."

Shame held me back. She undressed me to my underwear and pointed to the side of the bed next to the wall. It was warm from her body. She kissed me on the cheek and told me to sleep. Her lips had turned me from freezing to burning. I breathed as shallowly as I could, not to break my enchantment. I was lying next to a heavenly woman, the light of my life. And although her back was to me, she arched her neck from time to time to give herself a view of my face.

So she hadn't really fallen. She had lifted *me* up into her bed. Our backs almost touched.

LATE THAT SPRING Bronius Kelbauskas revived what he believed to be the old Fokine production of *Les Sylphides* for the Vilnius theater. He gave me the part of the Youth, which required a full range of technique and strength; the only man onstage, he lifts every woman in sight. Niola had already taught me the role and now helped me rehearse to my physical limits. Deeply melancholy under the influence of the Chopin score, I tried to sustain a mental image of my adored teacher throughout the performance. Vilnius audiences didn't laugh at my comic attempt at tragedy.

Between classes and rehearsals I spent more time than ever in an athletic club on the river almost opposite our apartment. My craze now was for a kind of pentathlon of water sports, including long-distance swimming, rowing, sailing, and lifesaving. I'd been chosen to represent Lithuania in a national competition in Moscow the previous year and again went to practice sessions in picturesque Lake Trakaisky, about twenty miles from Vilnius.

To discourage breaks in training, our camp was on an island a mile from the shore. Separation from the theater—and from Niola—began to gnaw at me there. After an exhausting day with coaches, an August sun would set on the water. It warmed my longing for the most revered of ballerinas and teachers. One day a newspaper announced that a new title, People's Artist of the Lithuanian Republic, had been conferred on her. I had to congratulate her in person. I swam to the nearest shore, where some country houses were surrounded by banks of flowers. Soon I was swimming back to the island. A splendid bouquet was strapped to my forehead with my belt.

It was now dusk. My head piled high with my trousers, shirt, and sandals in addition to the bouquet, I swam three miles to the opposite shore. I had recently bought a motorcycle with a friend. When he was away, he hid the prize in bushes near the water. I jumped into the saddle and streaked to Vilnius. The opera house audience was already dispersing. There had been a special performance of *Swan Lake* to honor Niola for her new title. Soon *my* Odette appeared—accompanied by her husband, the heavyweight without a boxer's grace.

The bitter injustice stunned me. The enchanted creature for whom I had broken discipline, stolen the flowers, and accomplished my land-and-water mission was going off with another man simply because he bore the honorific of her husband. But first I demanded to talk with her alone.

She stroked my forehead. "What is it, Valerik? What's happened to you?" The hurt and shame constricting my throat jumbled my congratulations into an incomprehensible babble. Then the tears gushed out. I ran to the motorcycle and sped to the lake. The final swim to the camp at midnight at last cooled my ache.

MY FIRST PROPER TOUR was a month with the company in Kaunas in the summer of 1955. The hint of something forbidden lingering in its streets and apartments immediately cast a spell. Vilnius had more Russians than Lithuanians. Kaunas, by contrast, was a profoundly Lithuanian city, the former capital of independent Lithuania and the center of cultural life. By determined snubbing of Russians assigned to offices and enterprises, the natives got many transferred to Vilnius, keeping Kaunas for themselves. As a result, national traditions and customs endured there despite Moscow's determination to quench them (the university had just been abolished) in order to found our new socialist order. The country's heritage and spirit of resistance were bound up with the ancient city.

Wistful talk of "the old times" was on everybody's lips. People whispered about Chaliapin's appearances, guiding me through a labyrinth in the old opera house to where a signed portrait of the officially banned "turncoat" hung. The cosmopolitan spirit was strong enough to bring out secrets within my own company. Kelbauskas began holding forth about his "Paris period" with Nijinsky, Diaghilev, and other names I now first heard. He was probably drawing more from his dreams than his memory, but the tales were wonderfully inspiring.

Kaunas' cafés, candy stores, and shops retaining "bourgeois" attitudes to service interested me at least as much as the fourteenth-century architectural monuments. For the first time my pay was mine to spend as I chose. The example of my father, who saved every possible kopeck for a rainy day, wagged its finger at me. But he had never been able to explain anything convincing about this infamous day that supposedly signified a wet end to the world. I, with my pampering, had the opposite urge: to run through my tiny salary as though empty pockets represented purity. Although I rarely swilled my wages in the Russian manner, I developed a compulsion to unload my last ruble on some childish purchase or on treating my friends in cafés. Spending made me feel big.

Alec had begun to joke that I was not his full brother, but the product of some brief encounter Mama must have enjoyed. Papa's stolid seed could not have spawned my "artistocratic bravado," he insisted. My need to splash friends with exaggerated, unnecessary hospitality and my urge to show off with mindless physical feats had to have come from somewhere else.

Alec himself was still racing away from our parents' outlook on everything, but in different directions from me. As soon as the post-Stalin relaxation began, he and his university friends spent feverish days discussing Polish literary journals they had obtained. The Becketts, Ionescos, and Joyces who excited them were nothing to me. But I deeply admired his heroism in getting into serious trouble.

He and some Faculty of Language and Literature classmates decided to revive an old Russian tradition of compiling a student literary journal. Their material was mostly items unsuitable for the faculty's wall newspaper, which carried only the usual announcements and political messages. Alec edited this official "organ" and was also put in charge of the new handwritten venture.

The first number contained witty portraits of teachers, mild parodies of farm and office routine, and sketches of real and fictional life. Then NKVD officers raided the contributors' homes as if seeking out a terrorist organization. They found the manuscripts in Alec's room and led him away to his first interrogation. Party meetings, faculty confrontations, and public condemnations of the "conspirators" followed. Their prospects were worsened by the agents' discovery of a diary containing literary criticism of several Soviet writers in the desk of one of them—together with an old copy of Dostoyevsky's *Notes from the Underground,* a Russian classic that had been suppressed for many years. The NKVD team knew perfectly well what to make of "underground"; the book's owner went to prison. Alec himself was merely expelled from the Young Communist League. But if this hadn't happened just when Khrushchev was preparing to expose Stalin's crimes, Alec would have spent years in a labor colony.

Alec welcomed the incident for its help in opening his eyes to the nature of Soviet rule. After the appearance of the French film, Alec would talk of the "four hundred blows" that taught him that "life in our Soviet Union is not unpleasant but impossible." When he heard soon after this that I'd be touring Kaunas, Alec urged me to observe the city carefully, which is why I became aware of its atmosphere so quickly. He was the teacher I had never found in school.

MORE THAN OLD ARCHITECTURE drew me to Kaunas; more even than the mystery of half sentences and hints of pre-Soviet memories. The most haunting secret belong to *us*. Without her husband and baby, Niola's whole face seemed brighter. Her gray eyes ran up and down me, almost saying something. Men began staring openly at her.

One day a genial dancer invited me to picnic with him. I wondered why he'd picked me when he could have had his choice of almost anyone in our group or stopped any girl on any street. He was the only one in the company with a car.

Leaving the theater after class, I saw Niola Grigorievna waiting outside. She began talking to me in a tone of exaggerated casualness. It still didn't register that she'd been waiting for *me*. "Someone you know has invited me to the country," she said, striking me down with jealousy and hatred of my inferiority. "I said I wouldn't go alone. *He* suggested we take my 'best pupil.' And I agreed, so please be ready in the morning."

Someone else might have seen what Janus, my older colleague, was up to. And how Niola had countered. But that day and night I could not have perceived the plot of a Soviet spy movie. I was dumb with gratitude to Janus for asking me.

The next morning his ancient Moskvich reluctantly climbed the hills outside Kaunas. He and Niola Grigorievna sat in front, conversing in Lithuanian. From time to time she glanced back, her large eyes silently examining me. This time I imagined I read something in them: that her conversation with Janus meant nothing; only *I* was important.

We descended from the hills to a crystal lake framed by tall rushes. We spread a tablecloth and set out the wine. Bathing suits were then unavailable. Niola Grigorievna stripped to a black brassiere and panties, and Janus and I were in our homemade practice shorts. Still trying to engage her in intense private talk, he found ways to rest his hand on one of her ankles, with the sculptured ballet instep. She playfully brushed it away, looking up to make sure that I had seen her gesture.

To deflate my excitement—and call attention to my swimming skills—I uttered Tarzan's idiotic cry and dived into the water. Looking back, I saw Janus increasing his efforts, but Niola's indifference was obvious even from afar. Her eyes devoured my wet chest when I returned, and her patter wasn't even a serious disguise.

"Why were you in the water so long? I was worried about you."

The lie flattered me immeasurably: she knew I was at home enough in the water to have swum Lake Trakaisky with her flowers last year. I burned with her heat.

Evidently she had given a final no to Janus while I was in the water, for suddenly we were packing to return. Niola put on her dress behind an open door of the car. Janus' head, then backside appeared in rapid succession from behind the fender as he cranked the stubborn motor. I carried the remains of our picnic to the back seat, reaching in while Niola did the same from the other side. When her hand brushed my wet one, she took it and pulled me close. "I can't stand this any longer," she whispered. Her breath came as if this were a speech she had both yearned and feared to make. "This can't go on. You must come to my room tonight—eight o'clock."

AT SEVEN O'CLOCK I was looping the block around her hotel. A clock hung from its corner. After each circuit I looked up at its hands. They hadn't moved.

I kept passing a florist's shop on my loops around the block. Each time I was certain I'd bought too few, and I added another bunch. Soon I needed both hands to cope with the bouquet. Eventually my money ran out. But there were still forty minutes to live through.

Her hotel was the city's best. I was certain no one would notice me there. On my second step into the foyer I bumped into . . . our Artistic Director! "Where the hell are you going with all those daisies?" he asked. Mumbling something absurd, I found the staircase, clumped heavily upstairs, and held my breath. Luckily Niola's room was around a corner in the corridor, out of sight from the watchwoman's desk. The door opened almost before I knocked. She was *there*, in a robe with staring buttons down its front. She took my bouquet into the velvet of her hands. Her forefinger beckoned me to her window. I looked out. She pointed to the clock just below us.

"I watched the whole hour," she whispered.

Before I could run, she pressed her hip against me, and I could hear her pulse. Then I felt a soft plateau between her turned-out ballet legs. My mind could not cope with her love tricks. Their images overwhelmed me. She supported me with an embrace. When my head sagged to her chest, she stroked my curly bush of hair.

"Valerik, what is it? Here, come sit down."

She guided me to the bed. "Take off your shirt, you'll feel better. Don't be embarrassed, you must rest." I noticed that she had begun by undressing herself.

Her magnificently sensitive fingers removed my shirt and stroked my neck and chest. When they dropped to my belt, control of my body passed to her. Swiftly she removed everything. Feelings charging out of me like beasts in terror shocked me into a dumb haze. She bit at my skin. Her flowing body pressed upon mine, the convulsions frightening me even more. Rolling me on top of her, she whispered urgently, "Darling, I want you. Please. *Now.*" Her incredibly white thighs opened and closed. I realized this was like going into battle. Something powerful and heroic was expected of me. Something supremely male—but I didn't know what.

Her wild impatience paralyzed me. All I could think to do with my manhood was to push it on her belly so hard that both threatened to burst. The passion in her eyes changed to bewilderment. She could never again regard me as a man, but I still couldn't decipher what to do, where to direct my strength. I slipped from her and to the floor. Sobbing and choking, I pleaded for myself in a fake monologue about her interests.

"But this is shameful, I have no right . . . you have a *husband.*"

She got up and quickly covered her awesome nakedness with a sheet. From the opposite corner of the room I saw tears magnifying in her eyes.

"My little Valerik," she said. "If I'd known the suffering this would cause you, I'd never have dreamed of it."

My lying humiliation of her to save my miserable masculine "honor" was a new jolt of shame. My sinking toward full breakdown dismayed her, and I tried to comprehend how our love could have taken us to this unbearable disaster. But while I wept, she suddenly stopped. A subtle smile formed on her lips: a great woman's gift to her protégé.

Her sheet was like a toga. She stepped to the table, poured from a bottle of wine, and brought the glass to me.

"Drink this, you'll feel much better. Yes, the whole glass."

Chiding that the floor was cold, she helped me back into bed. I drank a second glass and laid my head on the pillow. Slowly and calmly she covered me with the sheet and bent over my face. Her mouth was on mine; her body balanced over me; the sheet fell away. Soon I felt myself plunged into a warm, softly swaying sea, its waters both boundless and ruled by the pull of a strong current. I felt totally tranquil, infinitely happy. Her lips held mine; her tongue explored my mouth. What surged up lifted all of me into cosmic joy.

10

A COMBINED CLASS OF MEN AND WOMEN WAS SCHEDULED FOR ELEVEN o'clock in the Kaunas theater. I could hardly believe I would see my adored one again that same morning. A meeting by the light of ordinary day seemed slightly wrong.

I could barely force my drugged muscles through the motions of our exercises, but Niola seemed aroused rather than exhausted. She was in a state of flashing excitement, pirouetting and laughing so gaily that other soloists wondered aloud. "What's up with Niola Grigorievna today?"

I watched in numb bewilderment. The sickening spectacle of her absorbing others' admiration again reduced me to nothing. I could see only her, think only of our love, while she not only attacked the class with relish, but had the presence of mind for banter. *How could she?*

But she saw me again that evening. Kaunas' intriguingly illicit flavor mingled with our private secret. We usually met in her room, but if I said *"please"* while we were strolling in a park, her eyes darted from passersby to likely thickets. She was recognized everywhere as the city's star by now and couldn't afford the slightest indiscretion.

Toward the end of the month, we went to the far edge of an empty heath bordering the city. A daisy brushed against her mouth during our loving. She devoured it.

Then one evening she told me not to come to her room, offering a feminine reason that flattered me with its intimacy. I popped in at the nearest café. Her husband was there chatting with some soloists! Niola's pretense hit me harder than he could have with his burly hands.

Why hadn't she told me that *he* was the reason we couldn't be together? Was it possible she still could feel something for him after our heavenly passion?

The next day she scolded me for not having greeted him. I tried to convince myself that *I* was wrong. She was so wonderful, and I so lucky to have been with her, that the failure of perspective was mine. But my feeling for her was never quite the same.

Back in Vilnius, the company was happy with its purchases and acclaim, and I was wretched in my loss. Instead of daily hours in her arms, I had brief professional meetings with her that only sharpened the hurt. Desire welled into torment. The image of his hairy hands on her obsessed me. Niola's rejection made it disgraceful to live.

I jumped into the saddle, zoomed through red lights in hope and fear that something might crash into me. Only movement was the answer. Only my motorcycle could share my fate. Calmed by an hour of wind in my face, I would make a last race down Stalin Prospekt, where their apartment was. One day I saw them out strolling. His arm was where mine had been. Wild hatred blacked out any sense of what I was doing. I knew only that I was running toward the self-satisfied giant, at last ready to make him pay. Nothing else mattered except ending his evil.

Tears were wetting my shirt. "I demand that you leave this woman in peace," I ordered. His mouth fell open. Niola rushed between us.

"For goodness sake, Valery, this is ridiculous." She hurried back, and they quickly moved away, leaving me with the shame of my unfinished gesture.

The next day she lectured me. The entire theater knew about us, she complained. She had risked her reputation for me and deserved better than my acting like a spoiled baby.

It was true that everyone knew—even my mother. Although unhappy because only she herself deserved her little darling soloist, she was also secretly glad: Lithuania's prima was almost worthy of Mama Shulman's boy. Niola's interest in me struck her as a compliment to *her* maternal beauty. And in the theater my every new role brought a needling. "Shulman again. Of course, Taboraskaite 'recommended' him, don't you know?"

Still, I couldn't understand Niola's criticism because she said nothing about our love. Could it really be that she cared mostly about maintaining appearances? I stalked away. I would demonstrate my dignity by not seeing her during the next few days.

LITHUANIANS WERE MORE RESENTFUL than ever of outsiders, Jewish *or* Russian, but the Party helped my father look for a new job. Finally, a place was found for him as a kind of efficiency expert attached to the Lithuanian Academy of Sciences. For the next quarter century his work would be comparing production costs and recommending economies in the republic's shoe factories.

During my game of avoiding Niola, I spent more time with Alec. His love of everything mechanical set the pattern for mine. We scrambled for the first of every new "invention" to appear: portable radios, tape recorders, Chinese fountain pens. Meanwhile, he procured the neighborhood's first camera, which originally came from a German prisoner of war. We started our own "photo club," a "serious-minded" pastime of which our parents approved. Pained by the moral wrong, we nevertheless traded an adopted stray dog for a second ancient camera and spent even more time in our improvised darkroom. Alec also adapted his homemade radio receiver there. The radio club he had joined was then very fashionable among the scientifically minded. Constantly warning of insidious bourgeois propaganda, the Young Communist leaders prohibited shortwave attachments, which Alec immediately proceeded to innovate.

AS DAYS STRETCHED TO WEEKS, my "punishment" of Niola pleased me increasingly. Thanks to her position and her reproaching me, she felt she couldn't initiate a reconciliation. Yet our separation was clearly upsetting her. Perhaps for this reason, I noticed with pride and disillusionment that she was no longer my incomparable ideal of feminine beauty. I was developing an eye for younger girls in our company, and just because of Niola a few of these girls, who wouldn't otherwise have looked twice in my direction, began noticing me. Somewhere I felt miserable to be trading on Niola's gift of herself, to say nothing of her huge contribution to my ballet upbringing. But recognizing my cruelty wasn't enough to stifle it. The more I gained control, the more I warmed to our strange new competition.

Professional progress bolstered my outward confidence. After the

Youth of *Les Sylphides*, I was given the Blue Bird in *Sleeping Beauty*, one of the most demanding parts in the male repertoire, which Niola had been teaching me for years. Talk circulated about a real career at the opera house. But although I danced tolerably for an eighteen-year-old, inner doubts about my training gaps and stage rawness began nagging at me more insistently than those about carrying my revenge on Niola too far.

That summer films of *Romeo and Juliet, Laurencia,* and other famous ballets appeared. In dozens of viewings, I studied every movement of Konstantin Sergeyev and Vakhtang Chaboukiani, both Kirov stars. Chaboukiani's sizzling technique and soaring dynamism thrilled me even more—because they were far closer to me—than the lyric perfection of Sergeyev, Niola's favorite. Yet all the varieties of dancing confronted me with my artistic shallowness. And the professionalism of every gesture told me I was a bungling amateur. Lost one day in admiration for the fiery Chaboukiani, I realized that I could never see anything of this level, let alone train for it, in Vilnius. If I wanted to strike out for ballet's best rather than reap provincial glory, I would have to finish my training with what only Leningrad or Moscow could offer.

Niola transmitted her desire to see me in a dozen ways, but the more the balance of impatience shifted in my favor, the longer I wanted to prolong the game. One day I was approaching the theater's studio by a long stairway leading to its door. Something drew my glance upward. She was near the top, descending. Before our meeting, there was a quick revelation of how much had changed. A glint of the same jealousy that had almost made me attack her husband now darkened her eyes.

She reached for my hand. "Valerik, this is no good. I must see you tonight." Although her fragrance no longer paralyzed me, my heart began to race. I remembered everything that had made her my dream.

After the performance we climbed a large deserted hill in a park on the city's outskirts. Our passion, even our old friendship, quickly restored itself. Love was more enchanted than before because we were less unequal.

Afterward we looked down at the city. "I've told my husband everything," she suddenly announced. "That I love you. That he and I can't go on as man and wife."

I prayed that the right words would come to me.

"He said I was wrong to rush into anything silly," she continued. "He was willing for me to move my bed. But he kept saying we should have a trial separation before considering divorce." She added a final plea. "It's you who's making me say these things, take this terrible step, turning me into the butt of everyone's gossip. Forcing me to break up a home, to take a child from its father. But I can't help it, I can't let you go."

Sweating under the heavy burden of this talk of our common future, I again felt I must perform some supremely male act that would make everything right. Niola was asking me to be a man, yet my bones sensed that they were still soft. Suddenly I knew that the only future I could be serious about, the only plans I cared for concerned dancing. And that my dreams could never be realized in Vilnius. A dismaying, yet emancipating discovery struck. I knew I was big enough for only one passion. Now I realized it wasn't Niola I loved, but the ballet I had long perceived as indivisible from her. Despising my own egotism, I chose what I wanted most in life.

But Niola had also to be saved from herself, which would be as close as I could get to giving her the gratitude she deserved. The act required of me was to leave Vilnius and its short-term temptations. I hurried to Leningrad to resume the studies broken off four years before.

11

THE ACADEMY ON ROSSI STREET HAD THE SAME SMELL OF A TSARIST seminar, the same propaganda posters, the same long corridors leading to ballet excellence. The ancient studios were full of wonder.

I arrived in September 1956. My compact, versatile body partly compensated for its departure from the long, graceful standard; my stage experience partly substituted for missing years of academic training. The staff remembered me mostly as a historic oddity: a Baltic "foreigner" in whom the mourned Vaganova had for some reason taken a special interest. My ability as a performer was impressive for my age, but the general puzzlement over how to fit me into the system was greater than before.

Warming up my first day, I sensed the approval of Abdurakhman

Kumisnikov, the father of Murat, my Three Musketeers chum. Kumisnikov taught the class that would graduate in June. When we started the high leaps, he went to fetch the Director. They studied me, pointed to some flaws, and said I could join Kumisnikov's group permanently. I plunged in happily.

The daily ballet class was still the heart of the curriculum. But at this advanced stage it was supplemented by a wide range of specialized courses. Fencing was taught by "Steels" Kokh, a brilliant designer of stage battles for all the dramatic arts. Kokh's obsession for swordplay was feverish; he himself was as thin and sharp as a rapier. His wit was cutting, and he moved with the spare elegance of a thrust to its mark. Cutlasses and sabers flashed through his classes like some massive rehearsal for the Dumas I'd long dreamed of.

Makeup was also loved but for some reason had been assigned a lowly place. The result was that my generation of Leningrad dancers would remain embarrassingly weak in the cosmetic arts, even after years on the stage. Kirov dancers would be saved by the excellent makeup artists there, but we had no feeling for the brush and mirror as helpers in finding what we wanted from our roles and in transforming ourselves.

Acting was far more complicated both in itself and in relation to the demands of the dance. It was taught by Mikhail Mikhailovich Mikhailov, a man of wide experience in the traditions of Russian pantomime and strong devotion to the schools of Stanislavsky and Meyerhold. Mikhailov's classes were like dramatic games without words or dancing. He tried to teach us how to convey thought, emotion, and narrative development merely by walking across the stage or standing motionless on it. But in one way his inspired coaching served as an obstacle to creative acting. Lacking contact with the inner feelings that prompted the master's uncanny gestures, other teachers copied them mechanically. A tendency toward empty, therefore exaggerated, posturing grew in the Academy. Besides, Mikhailov's approach was more suited to drama and opera. Necessary as gestures are to ballet, not poses but dancing must convey most of the thought and action. Unfortunately, Mikhailov's lessons often provided substitutes for acting through ballet movements. No one bothered to say that leaps, turns, pliés, and pirouettes were also supposed to carry forward the story and the development of its characters.

This, in turn, resulted in ballet movements being performed for themselves. Pupils were taught to execute them magnificently but with no sense of their emotional or narrative purpose in given roles. In the stilted tradition of the so-called dramatic ballet, an interval for the significant gesture would follow another for "pure" dancing. There would be much standing around in costumed poses instead of choreographic motion. Even the dancing itself suffered because it was deprived of inner content. People forgot that ballet should not only delight the eyes, but—like primitive dancing—*say* something to the heart and mind.

Igor Belsky, the Kirov's leading character dancer, who would soon be an important choreographer, led our character classes. Yuri Druzhinin, another Kirov character dancer, who would become an outstanding rehearsal coach, was second only to him. Both relied on examples from their huge repertoires, yet worked in totally contrasting ways. The enormously gifted Belsky was the exception to the Academy's rule of endless drill. His somewhat careless attitude to teaching could produce unexpected benefits. Half an hour late one day he flew into class from a rehearsal, still charged with his high-speed stage imagination. To dispel our grumpiness about the waiting, he began dancing a fantastic potpourri of movements from every known ballet. This magnificent treat was a pedagogical tour de force precisely for its avoidance of anything smacking of pedagogy. The spell of his pouring out what possessed him instead of stopping to think of "useful" movements lasted for weeks.

Druzhinin was far less outwardly expressive, but more musically precise, than Belsky. Even among Kirov rehearsal coaches, his choreographic memory was known as phenomenal. He could instantly perform any movement we asked to see from any ballet ever performed in Russia. This was especially important because character dancing was one of the distinguishing elements of Russian ballet instruction as a whole. The West's much weaker attention to it took something vital from the teaching of even lyric and heroic parts, for character work could enliven even dancer-craftsmen low in emotional output. It also stamped everyone with certain aspects of Russian professionalism—proper carriage of the body and head, clear phrasing of movements—which could help sustain the dramatic line, even in cold numbers of pure classicism. Since character dancing is a kind of theatricalized folk dancing—itself a release from hard living conditions—Russia's lead in it was little wonder. I already felt village attitudes and traditions nourishing our work. The enormously varied Russian folk dance was a giant source of inspiration. The Ukraine, Moldavia, and the Cossack steppes were particularly rich in folk forms, but each cultural unit, from the Caucasus Mountains to Siberia, offered something different for ballet movements and patterns.

Every character class was an invitation to bounce my head off the studio ceiling. But the best feasts were the recitals in honor of official holidays. For the one for the Anniversary of the Bolshevik Revolution, I was given Actaeon's variation from *Esmeralda*, a serious piece of work. My athleticism, stage experience, and emotional intensity couldn't keep me from sinking below the Academy's standards for polish and stylistic purity. Still, the staff's attitude toward me perked up a notch after the performance, and I got the Blue Bird variation from *Sleeping Beauty* for the New Year's concert. In general, however, I was still an outsider whom nobody considered for a place in a Leningrad company, therefore not worth much attention.

Meanwhile, the recitals were their own reward. They took place in the Academy's beautiful two-hundred-seat theater, where senior pupils used to turn into gods when they performed. The first row was occupied by Leningrad's most distinguished teachers and by scrutinizing representatives of the ballet companies. The last three rows were taken by younger pupils, packed three to a seat. They roared so after each number that the front of the house had to restrain them before the curtain could rise again. While waiting to go out onto the stage I once had believed I'd never attain, it made me slightly dizzy to remember myself as one of those eleven-year-olds sneaking in to watch the graduating-class giants.

On days preceding a recital the entire Academy was permeated with anxiety, but the greatest tension was felt in the classrooms adjoining the miniature theater. We performers changed and made up on the desks, then dashed down the corridor to warm up in our class studio, where Kokh had established his headquarters. On these occasions, he was armed with a camera instead of his usual assortment of cold steel. As full of himself as a triumphant impresario, he manipulated the instrument to record the great moment of anyone who could stand still long enough for the click. Panting couriers would dart in to announce that the next number was *yours*, and with a thumping heart you would walk out for your inspection. I lived for the fierce excitement.

.   .   .

OF THE GRADUATING CLASS of about fifteen pupils, the Kirov would take the best one or two, and it was for this that the Academy really existed. The ballet world would applaud the new Kirov members, while the rest of us would languish in provincial oblivion.

The truly gifted were even fewer than these successes, for the Academy's procedure of selection and training could not guarantee the presence of talent, as opposed to the grooming of craft and skill. But both the penultimate class, where I studied general subjects, and my graduating one in ballet, had a smattering of future names. In five or six years Alla Sizova would be dazzling Western audiences on the Kirov's foreign tours, although she was now an anemic-looking complainer with red eyes and a voice that nagged whenever she stopped crying. Sizova was a striking example of the caterpillar who becomes a ballerina butterfly.

Yuri Soloviev had retained his superb ballet physique. With his muscles matured, he was nonchalantly perfecting the phenomenal leap that would soon stun audiences. His elevation was like an act of nature that hardly interested him; he simply seemed happier in the air than on the ground. With his farmboy face and attitudes unchanged, he never tried to feign any interest in art. But he needed only to lift his magnificently turned-out leg to the barre to show us what a ballet body was.

Soloviev's opposite in this respect was lumbering Sasha Shavrov. Since his father had been an important Kirov principal for decades, everyone knew Sasha was going there, too. He represented the incompetent children of the great Party kingpins and various celebrities, who were regularly shoved into the Kirov, thanks to its prestige. Position, contacts, and other non- or even anti-artistic influences, including the occasional outright bribe, saddled it with some less talented graduates than provincial theaters got.

But the "misunderstandings" and low-grade scheming were worse. Budding talents were lamed in the constant maneuvering for bureaucratic advantage. And saddest of all was the subordination of natural gifts to the great god of discipline. We all were subliminally taught that great talent counted for nothing in the Academy—therefore, in the nation—unless brought to heel by the established order. The "regimen"—that is, *conformity*—was held up as the highest good of all our work, while artistic brilliance that challenged the "norms" of deportment was positively persecuted. The more gifted a pupil, the quicker the authorities were to expel him if he was rude, childish, or incompetent in general subjects—most of all, if he violated the regulations.

After extraordinary early success, Rudolf Nureyev had come to Leningrad from his native Urals the previous year. He took ballet in the other of our two class sections, and we had only a casual acquaintance. But even the younger children knew his troubles.

An outsider like me, Nureyev was much more the loner. Maybe this was because of his distance from the more cultivated Leningrad boys or because of his arrogance. He was as surly to the Kirov's most illustrious artists as to fellow pupils. He often answered a suggestion for improving his work with a sneer that implied that the critic could not dream of attaining his physical excellence. But Nureyev was also the one genuine prodigy to appear in the Academy for many years. And once dismissed from the Academy, he would have no hope of ever joining a Leningrad or Moscow company. Nobody would ever hear of him again.

He had already been ordered out of several classes, and no one doubted that he was about to join the ranks of the expelled. Only the pleading of his teacher saved him. Alexander Pushkin not only recognized Nureyev's endowments, but was able to see his untamed individuality in terms of future contribution to art. At the last minute he begged the Director for one more chance and averted the expulsion.

DESPITE ALL BUREAUCRATIC INTOLERANCE, I was deeply grateful for the Academy's dedication to professional excellence. Ten years later some of the staff would be those who were unable to dance and therefore tried to teach. But in my day almost every instructor was an experienced soloist or principal who had himself been brought up on Russian ballet's best traditions. They knew their work as only leading professionals could and were living examples even when they couldn't teach.

The instructor I most admired was Alexei Pisarev, whose twisted face masked an extraordinary generosity to everyone. We heard he had had great losses during the war. His grief drove him to alcohol, which is why some Academy administrators mocked the best teacher on the staff, and he remained an unsung cultural hero. Gentle Pisarev waged an increasingly wretched struggle against his drinking. Unable to feel his way home one night in 1960, he would curl up under a fence and freeze to death.

Maria-Marietta Frangopolo was another favorite. She had danced with the Kirov for thirty years and now taught the history of ballet and supervised the Academy's little museum. Graduates and stars joined adolescent pupils in seeking her research help on esoteric ballet subjects. But her discreet counsel was most sought—and she most willingly offered it—by older students with love troubles.

Frangopolo's class in theatrical history was the only sitting subject I loved. Her apartment was a museum of photographs, albums, and ballet magazines, including prerevolutionary Russian editions and even a few Western ones. It was from her we learned our few scraps of information about ballet trends in the West. Otherwise, we knew only the ritual sentences in the school curriculum: "Western ballet is weak. It is characterized by lifeless forms and empty modernistic productions. Its movements are bearers of bourgeois depravity and corruption."

ONCE AGAIN THE PROBLEM of finding quarters put me in touch with ordinary Leningraders. At last a cot was found alongside the fortissimo-snoring father of Andrei Smolentsev, another old Musketeer, now one class below mine. Andrusha's parents were divorced, and he much preferred to live with his mother but now alternated so that we could spend more time together.

We lived across the Neva on the Petrograd side, actually on an island in the river's delta of tributaries and canals. Our district was best known for the famous Giant Cinema, a magnificent structure almost next door that once housed a branch of the Maryinsky Opera. Films for the most discriminating public showed here, and the posters tantalized me on my daily walk past. The likes of us had no hopes for tickets.

Our room in a converted tsarist secretariat of some sort was one of a dozen off a corridor almost as long as the Academy's. Families teemed like mice in the others. An hour of each morning was spent in the line to the washstand, which we joined after waiting in the even more impatient line to the single toilet. But for some reason the residents of this communal apartment got through many days without screaming.

Andrei's mother lived in a suburb called Strelnya, half an hour away by train. Because he liked her much more than he liked his father, Andrusha and I often rode out there. His mother's room was in an old cottage approached through a wonderfully picturesque meadow. But water had to be drawn from a well or lugged home from a hole cut in the ice of a pond. Three other families shared the little house. They took turns splitting the firewood.

A meal of fried, boiled, browned, or baked potatoes always greeted us. Sometimes there was potato soup. The Smolentsev poverty dumbfounded me when I first saw it. Their main food was bread and salt when I wasn't visiting. Without the vegetable garden in which they were permitted to grow produce for their own consumption, they would have starved. To maximize the calories, the little plot was planted almost entirely in potatoes.

The Smolentsevs were average white-collar workers. The mother earned even less as a bookkeeper than the father as a teacher, the equivalent of pennies an hour. Apart from her kindness, the strongest impression she made on me was of the struggle to feed Andrei. She bought no new clothes for herself in all the time I knew her, and so patched the old ones that taking pains not to dirty his shirt became second nature to Andrei, since washing weakened the fabric. He knew what each little item had cost his mother.

Andrei couldn't afford a bowl of soup in the Academy cafeteria. When my monthly allowance from my parents arrived, we splurged on meals, running through most of it in a week. Then I lived his life, stuffing myself with bread flavored by free mustard. But it was only a game for me.

12

WHEN SPRING FINALLY ARRIVED, I FELT MORE AND MORE SUBJUGATED by the Academy's system of bells. Geometry, chemistry, the history of the Soviet Union, and even the Soviet constitution were now tormenting us. Our teacher sometimes failed to poison Russian literature, and my love for motorcycles made the physics section on internal combustion tolerable, but I was still a head-hanging flop in everything else. "What a little dumb ox you are," said the glare of the teachers in general subjects. "Listen, I'm leaving in a minute," I answered to myself. "I don't know how I got here in the first place."

Later that spring a young Kirov ballerina named Alla Osipenko was sent to an international competition in Paris, arranged by Serge Lifar, the famous Russian dancer who had worked with Diaghilev. A few Bolshoi groups had already crossed the curtain through Khrushchev's miraculous openings, but Osipenko's trip held Leningrad in suspense. "Paris" was always half whispered as if the speaker were propelling himself there on a spaceship. As a final hallucinatory touch, the first prize was named for Anna Pavlova, an 1899 graduate of our (then Imperial) Academy.

Just the manner of announcing that Osipenko had won it gave us the shivers. Our training's central tenet had been that no one was inherently more talented than anyone else. If we were able to make something of our lives, our talents and application were incidental to the munificence of the Party, inspired and guided by Stalin himself. He alone deserved singling out for gratitude. The credit never belonged to anyone who made his way into our educational institutions, but to the foresight responsible for creating the institution and the generosity of accepting him there. A lucky graduate was then found work *and* actually paid wages for it, while capitalist workers were starving.

We were unworthy orphans, raised to be grateful for our gifts from the besieged socialist state. After the Teacher died in 1953, it was no longer quite "Thank you, dear Stalin, for our happy childhood," but we were still taught, and somewhere believed, that no skills really existed apart from our leaders' animation of them. Drawing attention to our individual abilities was very wrong. It showed ingratitude—even ill will— toward our loving Kremlin guardians.

But suddenly Alla Osipenko's personal achievement was described almost as if she had something in common with Western stars, as if the state were grateful to *her* for winning the competition! Full-page headlines would not have thrilled artistic circles more than the change of nuance in official mentions of her. I thought our government incredibly generous to have permitted Osipenko to go, then to accept the prize, and finally to praise her for it. And she had left the Academy only six years ago!

Khrushchev's earliest cultural exchanges were with France, and an exhibition of French modern art was showing just then at the Hermitage. It took my breath away. The perceptions of a dozen painters whose names I'd never heard—and was embarrassed to try to pronounce— were like nothing I'd seen. And more exciting than everything I *had* seen in our own museums. They were so close to my unformed feelings about the emotional truths artists should strive for that I pretended these men had captured some of my own fantasies about what I was going to do in ballet.

I plucked up courage to ask some Academy girls to go back with me and began holding forth on Picasso, Braque, and the others I knew absolutely nothing about. Finally, a Hermitage guide asked me to take my nonsense elsewhere, but I felt Paris beckoning even during my shamefaced exit. Daily visits replaced novels for the duration of the exhibition.

THE ENTIRE SECOND SEMESTER had been one long preparation for our final examination. No lecturing was needed to remind us of its importance. The prospect for all but the two or three winners picked to remain in Leningrad pressed on us like a lifetime exile to a November rainstorm.

Graduates of all educational institutions paid a part of their debt to the state during the first three years of working, therefore were not permitted to move from where it assigned them. Later we would be free to transfer from Omsk if we preferred dancing in Tomsk. But none of us would come home to Leningrad until his career had ended. Those born in the city had a right to live there, but only if they worked. Since no Leningrad stage would have any openings, they could return only as plumbers, trolley conductors, or schoolteachers if they found such jobs. Those determined to dance faced twenty-five years in provincial Russia's monumental oblivion.

The exam would take the form of an ordinary class, beginning with the traditional battement tendu at the barre, then the center work, next the more rapid allegro combinations, and finally the various leaps. Based on a system of mastering body mechanics, this lesson is the daily diet for dancers everywhere in the world. Class routine may prepare for art, may even stimulate thoughts about it, when directed by a teacher who brings something creative to basic training. Otherwise, it is an unreliable guide to the real thing since some of the most flawless performers of the daily exercises can't project a thought or a feeling onstage. Yet we were to be judged solely on our ability to perform the drill, like a pianist being measured by his finger exercises. Ballet became scoring points on jury cards instead of moving audiences to think about their lives.

This made us learn each tiny gesture in a kind of mindless rote.

From beginning to end it was two hours of memorization. The very wide range of movements could provide some idea of real potential, but only in a physical sense. Surely a short stage performance would give a better picture of the pupil as a future artist?

Drill is absolutely essential for mastering the movements of classical dance. Nothing can be achieved without bodily struggle. But routine doesn't have to be mindless. Teaching totally repetitive patterns produces a perfectly "schooled" product, which can be as dry as a legal code. Russian schools had become conservative bastions. They plodded on with their unshakable devotion to *the program,* even when some instructors were "plagued" with an unorthodox love of art that came from their inner conviction. Instead of happily receiving unplanned surprises, the Academy felt irritated by their interference with The Plan.

As the year progressed, Nureyev improved before our eyes. With even less formal training than I, and greater resistance to it, his dancing was underdeveloped and unpolished, but *real.* And just this vivid individualism in everything seemed to terrorize the staff. Apart from Pushkin, they went about as if a mustang from the Urals were butting them.

THE STATE GRADUATION EXAMINATION, literally an affair of state, was scheduled for early May. The examining commission would include representatives of all the country's ballet companies and maybe a few from Eastern Europe. Any fate still hanging in the balance would be decided by top directors, producers, choreographers, and balletmasters establishing or ignoring the young name. The main issues were already settled. The selected pupils' triumphant graduation and future stardom had been worked on like long-term projects. The crucial need now—the key moment for every Soviet enterprise—was that all should run smoothly toward the established goal. Parents, artistic directors, even other students had been *prepared* to know the winners.

Although my own future was probably still undecided, it was a side issue. Still the "foreigner" who it served no one's advantage to promote, I interested no one as a possible principal dancer. The exception was Marietta Frangopolo, who let me know—but discreetly, to avoid sparking vain hopes—that she saw promise in me. Otherwise, everything that had always kept me out of the Academy's main plan of preparing its top echelon as the new Kirov generation operated with even greater force as the time shrank. With me, the job had been to shape my animal energy with some last-minute finishing work, then to place me somewhere suitable—and I hoped for nothing more.

On the morning of the exam, anxiety in the graduating classes expanded to the limits of bodily control, and in some cases beyond. One pupil pulled a nerve-pinched muscle while trying to limber up at the barre. Weakened by vomiting, his neighbor fainted. The ordeal had always taken place in the fifth-floor studio where we used to sneak glimpses of Kirov rehearsals. While the class warmed up, spectators streamed toward the chairs planted around its circumference and into the gallery above. The great attractions were Nureyev and Alexander Pavlovsky. The Kirov had taken both when their class graduated the previous spring, but they had remained in the Academy an extra year for more polishing. Pavlovsky had originally been a pupil of the great Chaboukiani and was counted on to follow in his tradition of the heroic lead.

I felt oddly detached. My Vilnius stage experience fended off the fear the others were feeling, and I was further protected by a slightly sour, yet soothing resignation that lay on me like a film. A groan went up as the state commission filed in. Half of its fifty members were teachers, coaches, and directors of theaters, including prominent representatives of the Moscow Academy and the Bolshoi Theater. Balletmasters for whom we dreamed of working took their seats importantly, and everyone froze when a silver-haired gentleman with an elegant carriage appeared. "It's Sergeyev. Oh, my God, *Sergeyev's* here." Niola's old idol was as graceful and refined as the Kirov's Artistic Director should be. Natalia Dudinskaya, his lost-looking wife, rushed in behind him. She taught the Kirov's classe de perfection; together they personified the very essence of our profession.

The other half of the commission consisted of doctors, nurses, Young Communist leaders, Ministry of Culture bureaucrats, and various "cadre" officials who knew more about wrestling than ballet. One or two senior Party men had clearly come just to run their eyes over the young girls—or boys—in the class. Paper for recording our grades was distributed to these and other judges. The best Academy accompanist settled at the piano. Reluctantly completing our warming up, we took our places at the barre.

My last look over my shoulder settled on a radiant face on the edge of the commission. Sitting there so modestly in her Western clothes, the woman could have modeled for an Impressionist. With a skip of the heart I realized she was Alla Osipenko. I knew I must dedicate my performance to the winner of the Paris prize. I had to do so well that she would offer me her lovely hand and ask me to become her partner. *This* was my test.

All audience eyes rested first on the two pupils earmarked for stardom. The decision to keep Nureyev for a second year had paid off splendidly. He had reason to bless Pushkin for the rest of his life, not only for saving him from expulsion, but also for seeing the beauty in the uncut gem and polishing it enough for solo roles. But instead of going forward in *his* extra months, Pavlovsky had retreated to school triumphs of the previous year, as if he had already peaked. Earlier transplant to the Kirov might have caused him to blossom, as he was never going to do now. The two together were proof that a supremely delicate touch was needed to cultivate a dancer's gift. Kirov and Maly soloists saw this immediately. They had joined the crowd pushing in to watch us, but I didn't care. I had never liked a class so much. I knew I would die if I didn't make an impression on my Alla. The same old routine had been transformed into a *performance*.

Not quite able to believe its own verdict, the commission awarded me the highest grade of all. The Academy was amazed, and no one more so than I.

My prospects changed immediately. Sending a boy with the rare A+ to the provinces was unthinkable. But keeping me in Leningrad was going to be a problem. I too might be held over at the Academy an additional year, and some attempt could be made to give me phrasing with which to present my technique. As it was, I simply couldn't perform the full range of steps with the clean lines and polished perfection necessary for a Kirov soloist. Some teachers wanted to give me this extra chance because they felt sorry for not having seen much potential in me before, therefore not "bringing you along as you deserved," as one apologized. But the extra year was only awarded if some Kirov veteran was scheduled to retire soon. The trouble was that a large group of them had left the year before and were already replaced.

Thrown off by my unplanned-for success and worried that they had contributed too little to it, the Academy's staff was in confusion about where to place a soloist—as that one class had made me in everyone's eyes—at the last minute.

Meanwhile, Andrei Smolentsev received my good news as if it were his own. This generosity of spirit would become even more touching after his own graduation the following June. My Kirghizian roommates' games had powerfully re-inforced his normally vigorous Russian dislike for nonwhites. Naturally, he was dispatched three thousand miles from Leningrad—to Frunze, the capital of Kirghizia! After three years in that outpost he managed to transfer to the somewhat less desolate capital of the Moldavian Soviet Socialist Republic. But on his every trip to Leningrad, Andrei would take pleasure in my success.

Now he insisted we celebrate "like grown-ups." Russian life taught that a stroke of luck without alcohol was like an unbaptized baby. My grade would never be "real" unless properly anointed. I remembered the disastrous Vilnius banquet, but not the feeling in my stomach. In a dank, basement café Andrei and I solicited enthusiastic advice about achieving the necessary condition. The most promising recipe was two parts of champagne to one of cognac: three hundred grams, to be swallowed in a gulp and repeated ten minutes later.

We hurried to the street after our second dose. The light of the May afternoon went out before our eyes, and our anguish was more dreadful and lasting than I could have imagined. It satisfied my urge to celebrate success this way for many years to come.

13

THE PROSPECTIVE GRADUATES WERE ALLOWED TO USE THE FIFTH-FLOOR studio to rehearse for the graduation recital. The great test over, it turned out to be a wonderful place to work—full of coziness and emotional uplift because of the Kirov practice sessions there, but also with excellent structural attributes. The most important was the floor raked to exactly the same angle as the Kirov Theater's. When a major overhaul was decided on, it was the Academy's great luck that the workmen were talented enough to leave things as they were. They had discovered that perfectly preserved wooden beams supported the floor. Replacing them by iron or concrete could only spoil the precisely calculated spring.

The proof of this wisdom came when new studios were built in an extension of the Kirov. This modernization, which deprived both Academy pupils and performers of contact with their artistic roots, was a mistake even in principle. The outwardly imposing but inwardly cold studios provided everything but the crucial inspiration through tradition. Besides, they had rigid floors. Stretched tendons, battered calves, and knotted muscles were the dancers' rewards.

This unhappy experience would be repeated during the major, meticulous renovation of the Kirov itself in 1969. Gilt was lavished as in the best tsarist days, and everything backstage was transformed into the most modern automation. But almost every principle of the design of stage floors was violated. The great day for official approval of the restoration was marked by much ceremony. As a Kirov stalwart then, I was asked to test the stage. I danced a pas de deux from *Don Quixote*, but my principal concern was a search for places to plant my feet. Some floorboards had sunk under my first practice jump, but the audience of construction officials, chairmen of state commissions, and proud Party men couldn't make out these defects and were perplexed by what they took to be my bad improvisation. When I lost the music entirely to pick my way across the stage, passionate safeguarders of Kirov traditions began shouting, "Stop the scandalous clowning! Not in *this* theater!"

But more was needed to reverse the bureaucratic process. I took a genuine leap, hung in the air, and landed full on the worst of many bungled trapdoors. The flabby square sank to the level of my knees while I continued spinning. A new floor was ordered. Later, dancing on this excellent one, I sometimes smiled at the memory of my contribution to it.

That was exactly a dozen years in the future. Now, in the weeks between the examination and our graduation recital, I took full advantage of our privilege of using the fifth-floor studio. Spring sunlight played on the old ironwork. I practiced my numbers as if sheer effort could lift me to the level of the great dancers I had seen here.

It was now clear that I was the victim of a fatal flaw in design. My legs were too short, my torso was too developed, and my step too booming to be a handsome-heroic lead. And the same unimposing height and bearing also deprived me of the right to fall in love with beautiful women. But since this was the only kind who unleashed my feelings,

I couldn't even start a proper conversation with anyone I admired from afar. The very glory I wanted would have dismissed me for my lack of dash. Instead, I dreamed. And perhaps because this showed in my eyes, a beautiful woman sometimes took notice of me.

One day I was leaping my head off when I felt a persistent stare. The wife of Fyodor Lopukhov was watching me from the gallery. Professor Lopukhov had been the doyen of Leningrad—and Russian—balletmasters since the beginning of time. He began dancing with the Maryinsky Theater in 1905, toured America in 1910, and, back with the Maryinsky, staged his first ballet there in 1920. Klara Lopukhova, one of the most beautiful women in Leningrad, was a young decoration for her honored, elderly husband. She motioned me closer and complimented my dancing. Her questions about my living arrangements—"I can imagine that Smolentsev's room is no palace"—might have been transparent. But I registered nothing except her mouth. She said something friendly and led me to her apartment. It adjoined the studio, mere steps from the office of Director Shulkov. Her smile soothed my nervousness, and her remark that Professor Lopukhov was on vacation was a hand put out in welcome.

The following weeks I visited every day. The "salon," as Klara called it with reverence, spilled over with artifacts and memorabilia of half a century of work in the best Russian and Western theaters. She took to pouring me an ounce of cognac from *his* decanter.

Klara felt lonely even when her husband was in town. She had probably been prowling the gallery, and since I spent every free hour in the studio—sometimes alone—her choice probably made itself. But she went on to ratify it like a resolution at a Party Congress. When she slipped her arm into mine at a restaurant, conversation stopped at the neighboring tables. Her impulsive honesty of feeling sparked a debate in all theatrical Leningrad about whether Lopukhov should be told. I alone was not consulted.

When the talk reached the Academy's directorate, Party and trade-union supervisors summoned me for a solemn warning. "This amoral adventure is a stain on the Academy's principles and on your character. Young Communists must be crystal pure to work on the stage." This first official interference in my personal life was like having my father's finger pointed in my face. My moral lecturers' curiosity was even more repellent. "How'd you manage to work," someone asked, "on the wife of such a famous man?" I was thinking of my recital debut, like a soldier before an attack. Everyone else was far more interested in what I was doing with Klara.

THE A+ COULD CHANGE NO WRITING on my academic slate. For a proper diploma I would have to return in the autumn to pass tests in chemistry, algebra, and other beloved subjects. Even if I studied all summer, only a second miracle could make up for years of rout. Knowledge that I would leave the Academy as less than a full-fledged graduate dulled my new image, and the Klara mess removed still more shine. When the initial enthusiasm over my examination surprise passed, the staff was as happy as I about our forthcoming separation.

But the problem of what to do with me continued in the Director's office. Even if a Kirov place could be found, sending me there would be an embarrassing admission of errors in my development. This was not quite enough to keep a sexually depraved dummy in the Academy a further year, but depriving Leningrad of his hint of promise was even less desirable.

A vigorous woman named Galina Isaeva thought to turn the debate to her advantage. The Maly Theater's prima ballerina for years, Isaeva now danced as its Artistic Director. She did not need another soloist so much for his dancing, but as a counterweight for one of her two male leads, who "the collective" believed was growing too big for himself. She approached Director Valentin Shulkov, whose dreaminess as a Party official had always been balanced by a real desire to help pupils for whom he saw a future. He took me and two other graduates he was trying to keep in Leningrad to the Maly office, where Isaeva quickly signed me up as a soloist.

I had hoped for nothing better. The Maly was one of the country's best homes for ballet, probably on a par with the Kiev company, and artistically more advanced than the Stanislavsky Musical Theater, Moscow's number two. When I heard that I was the only boy from my class to remain in Leningrad, I was grateful.

ALL TICKETS FOR THE GRADUATION RECITAL were bought out months in advance. This was partly because the recitals were an old tradition in the Leningrad spring and partly because they gave the theatergoing public a chance to measure the graduates' prospects against the luminaries who had previously danced the same pas de deux in the same Kirov Theater. Occasionally arguments led to blows.

The full orchestra under Pavel Feldt provided the accompaniment. Everyone was fully conscious of the honor of dancing to the baton of Leningrad's most famous ballet conductor and composer. I did the pas de deux from *Le Corsaire*, the adagio from *The Pearl*, a ballet derived from Rimsky-Korsakov's opera *Sadko*, and a mishmash from a new work about collectivizing agriculture in the north. When nothing worked as it should have, I recognized that in order to dance well, I had to be doing it *for* something or someone.

The elderly Feldt came to the dressing room afterward. His voice always climbed high so that he could look down it when he addressed himself to pupils. "Dear boy, you have a future ahead of you," he said. "You're going to develop. Yes, slowly . . . but . . . surely."

At least part of the prediction was sound. I did come along very slowly.

The presentation of diplomas came with handshakes, thanks-to-the-Party speeches, and half a glass of wine lest anyone get the wrong idea. Then we left Rossi Street for the traditional promenade down the middle of the Nevsky Prospekt toward the Winter Palace. I wondered whether my liberation could really be true. Could such joy—of not having to sit in class again—be permanent? Now I could plunge straight into the one activity that made complete sense. My nostalgia for the Academy would focus on a few ballet teachers and studios. The bulk of my gratitude would go to Vaganova, for whom the institution had just been named.

Nothing Alec might have told me about how little freedom I really had could cast a shadow over that graduation night. It was late June. Leningrad's brief span of White Nights, when the sun barely sets because of the northern latitude, was at its best. Lilac scented the air, and buildings reflected their royalty into the Neva. I felt in me the elements of life—action, yearning, struggle—out of which something might be made, and I shivered in the presence of my destiny.

14

KARL ROSSI'S ENSEMBLE ON ARTS SQUARE ECLIPSED EVEN THE MASTER-work around the Academy. The Maly Theater, one of *five* great theaters gathered here like a meeting of Greek Gods, was an architectural jewel. Inside, it glittered a gracious welcome. The atmosphere of luxurious intimacy was reflected in the word "Maly," literally "small" in Russian. This was achieved partly by size—it seated only a thousand spectators—and partly by the baroque elegance of the wine-and-silver decor. Although its rake was slightly too sharp, the stage was excellent. The Kirov was Leningrad's gala showplace, the Maly its cozy family house of opera and dance.

The 1957–58 season opened in September, as usual. Perhaps because I'd danced for pleasure in Vilnius, the Maly's strongest first impression came from its strict canons of what constituted theater. The director demanded much more from the dancing than just getting through the movements. The realization that I must rise above mere mechanics to grapple with some of art's fundamental ingredients daunted as much as it delighted me. For although my technique quickly showed itself to be the equal of the other male soloists, I was backward in these general artistic considerations.

The second Maly quality to strike me was the homeliness of its leading ballerinas. Our finest lyrical lead was peculiar from close up, as if Alla Osipenko had removed her head and screwed on an unsightly one in its place. Her two understudies, both excellent Vaganova graduates from ten years before, completed the impression that a search had been made for crooked faces. Never, stagehands sighed, had so many been brought together in one company.

Our dumpy Artistic Director set the pattern. Galina Isaeva had won the Stalin prizes back in the 1940s but was still one of our leading ballerinas—a misleading term, however, since she could barely get up on her toes. Yet she had the power of a natural artist. Transformed the instant she stepped out on the stage, she radiated humor, drama, and excitement. The public most loved the forty-five-year-old mother hen in her roles as an enchanting ingenue. I loved her for her maternal concern for me, which was probably heightened because she felt she'd "snatched" me from other grasping directors. Until her replacement as Artistic Director in 1960, she encouraged me in every way, even telling me that the company's future was linked to mine.

DURING MY SUMMER VACATION in Vilnius, Isaeva had hired Ekaterina Geidenreich, a former Kirov star. Many of my generation knew Geidenreich only by way of the Serebryakova portrait of her youthful glory that hung in Leningrad's Russian museum. A radiant beauty as well as a brilliant ballerina, Geidenreich was also the wife of Leonid Lavrovsky, the Bolshoi and Kirov balletmaster whom everyone associated with the birth of Soviet ballet.

But nothing could save her after a careless moment when the Wehrmacht was approaching Leningrad in 1941. Referring to her German name, Geidenreich whispered that "maybe the Nazis will spare me." A fellow dancer's report of this sent her to a Siberian labor camp. Lavrovsky struggled long and desperately, but the best he could do was win permission for her resettlement in Perm. There she became an outstanding teacher and helped found a ballet academy with the highest standards.

Now that the elderly Geidenreich was rehabilitated, Isaeva invited her for a specific occasion. The Maly was about to go to Helsinki for a Soviet-Finnish friendship festival. It was my first example of our use as an experiment for the Kirov. But all such thoughts were submerged in the company's tidal waves of fear, joy, and disbelief at going . . . *abroad!*

Geidenreich used special exercises to calm the female corps to a rehearsable state. Good to begin with, the corps became truly first-rate under her direction. The women soloists were also highly skilled, especially by comparison to the men. Our leading male dancers were most embarrassing in the standard Tchaikovsky ballets, which Leningrad officials had thrust to the top of the bill because they considered swans and sleeping beauties the pinnacle of our art and an absolute must for a foreign trip. Ordinarily, the Maly had minimal contact with nineteenth-century romanticism.

No one longed to travel more than I. My infant thrill at seeing the world from train windows had been sharpened on the Kaunas tour and every other trip I had ever taken. The need to explore, feed my fantasy, simply to *move* sometimes built up in me and demanded to be released. But there was no time to rehearse me for the long-planned Finnish expedition, let alone complete the procedures for getting a passport. So I could only read dispatches about the Maly's "victories," which were reported largely in the form of quotations from Finnish critics. This was on the principle that if the corrupted bourgeois press said something good about us amid their raving anti-Soviet lies, it must be true.

The corps won more than foreign praise. They returned in Finnish outfits, and all Leningrad dashed to behold the stunning sight in the streets. A few days' shopping in Helsinki had changed even the ugly ducklings as dramatically as any theatrical costumes.

Meanwhile, I was struggling with different material concerns. As a nonresident of Leningrad, I'd been granted permission—required in the country's major cities—to live in a Maly dormitory. But a permanent residence permit was refused on the ground that a youngster striking out on a stage career had no guarantee of making the grade. If I failed, I'd be out of Leningrad.

Because of the Maly's weakness in male soloists, I had been rushed to work on the stage and pressed to master the repertoire quickly. After a full day of rehearsals and an evening performance I fell into my bed's embrace. Its springs had apparently been designed to inform everyone in the building of every shift of a leg. At night the five dormitory floors resounded with the iron orchestra's creaks and squeals, which slowly diminished in volume until a lone bed was squeaking like an amateur's violin solo.

A conscription notice was also disturbing my sleep. My fill of war games had made me not only antimilitary by inclination, but also a stubborn avoider of all collective activity except ballet. I could imagine the Academy's lessons washing away from me and into some ditch I'd dug, while my platoon slogged its boots through the mud under sergeants' curses. Within months of my first real performances, the army's antiballet life would be the ruination of my every trained muscle. Solo roles on a Leningrad stage did not bring automatic exemption; each call-up had to be fought off individually. But if your luck was bad or you'd exchanged harsh words with an influential Party man, good-bye, profession, and farewell, ten years of studio struggle. Most of the good dancers who succumbed to this madness had—*like me!*—no pull.

But the Maly's trade-union and Young Communist committees took up the fight for me. They sent me for "observation and treatment"—not to an ordinary hospital from which my draft board could have extracted me, but to a much less accessible military one that had served the St. Petersburg garrison in tsarist days. The fakery was nothing new either. The doctors would certify a hale young dancer too ill for military service. The Maly would pay off in tickets. The entire medical staff would enrich themselves by watching the art of fit-as-a-fiddle performers—a perfect example of the way jam is cooked for the bread of Soviet life.

The famous old building was near the Smolny Institute. Secure behind its typical green fence, I lay among genuine patients. Since everyone's sole object in this case was to beat the system, I felt happy. And happier still when the secretary of the theater's Young Communist organization visited me and purred that she would save me from training camp. She was a soloist named Liya Panova, a graduate of the Academy five years before. She danced character roles slightly under the first rank, but this wasn't what her body made me think of when she appeared in the ward.

Liya Panova was tall and long-legged, with flowing movements and startlingly feminine arms. Her small nose, fair complexion, and expressive eyes made a face of typical Russian beauty. It was no feat of observation to keep noticing her in the Maly. In our company, she would have got a eunuch moving. And a deaf man would have understood how her suitors were talking about her. A soccer hero and an imitation Frank Sinatra topped the cluster of men waiting for her after performances. Naturally, it never occurred to me to approach this older, higher target of the city's rising young men, but at the Maly's October Revolution party she had pushed toward my corner and betrayed how much she'd been drinking. "Let's have a talk," she breathed. "I've got something to tell you in private." By this time I recognized her tone. We crossed the theater's courtyard and climbed the stairs to my room. "Don't!" she snapped when I switched on the light. I shut it off and waited for the next instruction. It was the "Make yourself comfortable" that I should have said to her. Then: "Come warm me up. I'm freezing here."

Vodka was still flowing, and some celebrants probably heard my springs as holiday bells. For days after that I was dizzy with longing for her incredible skin. Her passion and seductive power excluded all other thoughts.

Klara, too, occasionally charmed her way into the ward. Her husband was home. On the rare evening when I was free and she managed a believable excuse, we met on distant streets and searched for a staircase. But janitors were on guard for precisely such behavior in Leningrad's passion-killing housing shortage.

On one of her visits to the hospital Klara said she'd bought me a motorbike because she knew how much they meant to me. She did not know exactly why I loved them. My Vilnius motorcycle rides had sometimes paralyzed me. Once my terrified foot instinctively stomped on the brake even as I roared ahead, setting the linings ablaze. But I craved the thrill and melodrama of deadly danger. I sensed that the perceptions I needed to make myself a man and an artist lay on the very edge of safety.

But now a suspicion was growing that Klara represented a greater danger than my harebrained riding. Why was she offering such a gift? When I left the hospital with a year's deferment from the army, a second surprise was waiting outside: a self-contained studio in a cooperative apartment building! Klara had used her excellent contacts to jump the enormous line for new accommodations and was selling her diamonds to raise the down payment. My punishment was a gloomy "Yes, I do" in answer to her question asked as rightful payment. It gave me a leaden taste of self-disgust, for when it came to sharing the room with her, I saw how little I did love her.

I told this lie to no other woman. But that was no solution to my present blunder, which my false words immediately made worse. Then I noticed Klara accepting a stranger's appreciation in a café. Their ocular contact lasted just a minute longer, and we were finished.

This excuse contained the usual element of truth. Klara's harmless flirting had actually made me furiously jealous. Some of my adolescent demands on "my" women would disappear in time, but not my need for their utter "purity," even when I was unfaithful.

The unfair double standard derived from some tight interlocking of my childhood experience and my profession. It was incontestable that the man was physically stronger, although not more intelligent. Apart from the "old-fashioned" attitudes of ballet story lines, *his* lifting of *her* prescribed a certain relationship. Women were inspirers and sources of strength. Nothing was more creative than their work of bearing and rearing the family, and my own attempts to create beauty put me in need of just that kind of generous companionship. I needed someone to help channel my turbulence, someone to wash away my flaws so that I might create more than I destroyed. Not surprisingly, it would be many years before such an angel appeared who would put up with me.

Meanwhile, I convinced myself that since my theatrical and daily lives were inextricably linked, my excessive claims had a positive side. I believed that my obsession for work and inspiration on the stage was fed by the same source as my need for female "purity." I could die for the Princess because that was how my own fantasy worked—to the disadvantage and dismay of real women.

BOTH THE MALY'S MALE PRINCIPALS were about five years older than I. Adol Khamzin had been Alexander Pushkin's pupil at the Academy, and Veniamin Zimin graduated a year earlier under the equally famous Boris Shavrov. Khamzin was more important because he partnered well and could at least attempt lyrical roles. Zimin, then thought to be getting conceited, did strong heroic—as opposed to lyric—roles best. Some bordered on character dancing.

I decided that these two had nothing to teach me and set out to do everything my own way. Later I recognized the pattern. Many graduates who bound out of school with strong leaps and nifty pirouettes believe that this young strength qualifies them as accomplished performers— because they hardly realize the need for partnering, acting, and creating characters. Despite their technical skills, they are uninteresting on the stage, except to themselves. Their belief in their own superiority fires the company with determination to take them down a peg.

Sometimes my eagerness to *work* also struck my Maly colleagues as a challenge, even when none was intended. But the administration was happy to use my zealousness. I was the odd exception who actually loved to dance. Roles were piled on me when I returned from the hospital.

The aspiring ballerinas all knew how important it was for them to latch onto a male soloist with promise. The next Maly social occasion was a birthday party for one of the young girls, who jokingly proposed that she and I become partners. Flushed with proprietorial anger, Liya Panova swooped between us and took me to her place. "But your sister, your nephew, your *mother*," I protested on the way, knowing she shared her room in a communal apartment with at least three relatives.

"Forget them, they're dead to the world," she said dashingly.

I liked her style, even the hot jealousy with which she had responded at the party. And when several toughs in her apartment house courtyard threatened me for meddling with "their" girl, she snarled them off. "Lay a finger on him, and you'll have me to deal with." I was never bothered again.

Liya led me upstairs and saw to everything. She was older than I, wiser, surer of herself.

LIYA'S GOOD LOOKS and strong feelings made her an interesting performer onstage. She would have gone further in the Maly if not for two excellent ballerinas ahead of her in the roles she did best—and if she had worked harder. As it was, she took the attention to her attractiveness as a compliment to her talent.

When she wasn't performing, she watched from the audience. Her congratulations and encouragement were a boost to me. She genuinely liked ballet and feared a younger ballerina might capture me to advance her career. We saw more and more of each other. Her mother closed her eyes to all-night visits. After a few weeks, Liya said it "wasn't nice" to go on as we were because everyone in the theater knew. Her solution was marriage.

Our romance became a melodrama. The first act was played in the Maly, where one and all dished up juicy gossip about Liya's previous affairs. The snide remarks only excited me more by demonstrating the power she exercised over many men. And I was young enough to know more than anyone who tried to get me to think seriously about what we meant to each other. Besides, there was no time; everything happened too quickly.

Then Klara's motorbike went. It had been standing in the Maly's courtyard—still store-fresh, for I'd never touched it. While a handyman wheeled it away, my colleagues jabbed me in the ribs and praised its qualities. Anonymous letters to the Maly management began to arrive. They exposed my sins and—for disguise—those of some minor administrators. I saw Klara and tried to explain. The second act closed with my believing that she understood and she convinced that I was a noodlehead. But at least I persuaded her to stop the letters. No one stayed anonymous for long when the police got interested in "slander of Soviet officials."

In the third act my parents pressured the Maly to prevent their juvenile son from marrying. Over the telephone from Vilnius my mother wept and my father ordered me to stop my "foolishness with that dancing girl." What they probably wanted to say was that I was emotionally shaky, even for a nineteen-year-old, and that Liya might retard my development. But I winced at my mother's supposed joke—"Now *that* was the match for you"—about People's Artist Niola Taboraskaite. And I deeply resented their treating economically independent me like a child, even if I behaved like one.

I wanted to hit back at their high-handed *demands*, and lust-and-love confusion helped me choose the wrong weapon. Films and plays taught that sleeping with someone was to commit yourself forever. I sensed the hypocrisy here, but my mistake with Klara lured me toward just this notion. I didn't want to be treacherous again or to lose what I had.

Meanwhile, Liya drew my attention to other men's glances at her, and I reared up like a rooster. My adolescent pride raged and fumed. I had to defeat all rivals—especially those older and stronger ones—and prove she was mine.

Before I knew it, act four was taking place in a shabby registration office in December 1958; as a divorcée, Liya was not entitled to a civil ceremony. And as the final curtain rang down, I changed my name to Panov for good measure. Since my parents had "officially" disowned me for disobedience, I could do the same to them.

But this name change was more than a spiteful gesture. The Doctors' Plot and related episodes had suggested my own solution to the Jewish problem, better than my father's fatuous ridiculing. When Alec had turned sixteen, he had himself listed as Russian on his identification papers. Every policeman and personnel director who checked them after that would also examine his face. It and the name that went with it always earned the same taunt. "Comrade *Alfred Shulman* is honoring us with a visit. He's . . . ah, *Russian*, of course."

But I looked like Mama. When my turn came, I easily persuaded myself that Alec's humiliating encounters had nothing to do with me. I went to the Vilnius registration office happy with my parents' instruction to take my mother's nationality. Although Russian as far as we ever knew, she had been registered as Belorussian for some obscure bureaucratic reason. So it wasn't only profound official racism but also our own pathetic complicity that led to this categorization of people in the same family. The way that many of the ruled tried to cope with the rulers' dark bigotry was to submit with frantic enthusiasm. This was the fatal combination that brought my father joy when he saw something other than "Jewish" in his sons' papers and pride each time we undressed.

Since my first Maly successes, I'd been given to know—by the Personnel Department as well as by Liya—that "Shulman" had the wrong ring for an important theater. "Believe me, it can only complicate your career." So I took the opportunity of marriage to join my father's cowardice. I still did not know the full futility of this kind of dodge in the face of sick Party, secret police, and personnel officers who relentlessly search out nationalities. A trace of Jewishness is the last thing that can be hidden from people who regard anyone not "our kind" as a potential enemy.

That mistake became apparent very slowly, but Liya's and mine nagged me from our wedding day. I couldn't admit that my overbearing parents might be right. The same obstinacy made me ignore my own fears and see the decision through. My bride would give me many delicious hours. But I always felt stupid and hopeless with her.

15

A MARRIED BOY, I LEFT THE DORMITORY TO JOIN LIYA'S FAMILY ON Rubinstein Street, just off the Nevsky Prospekt. Three other families shared the tiny communal apartment: thirteen people, including us five and a daft hag who kept mailing denunciations of all her co-residents. There was one faucet—without a bathtub—for washing. The lone toilet transformed a stomachache for one into a tragedy for all.

Our twelve-by-eighteen-foot room contained a wardrobe, a bed, four chairs, and three persons: Liya, her mother, and me. Liya's sister squeezed into the adjoining pantry together with her five-year-old son. This menace awoke at the crack of dawn. Since he preferred banging his toy hammer on live objects, I awoke at the same time with a new black and blue mark on my forehead.

When Liya's sister was assigned a room in another building three years later, the minuscule pantry was freed for us. But the thin plasterboard that separated us from the main room did not quite reach the floor. Our every sound in bed went right through, and all toilet noises sounded just as clearly from our other side. The pantry seemed designed to prevent rest and present maximum interference with any mental preparation for noble ballet roles. Bone-weary of these conditions, I would appeal through my diary: "Oh, Most High One, give us a real apartment. Save our work and our marriage. And please don't ruin everything by giving us a child."

THE MALY OPERA THEATER was home for some of the country's best voices, but the dancing standard was lower. After the Maly had functioned as an opera house for a century, its ballet company was founded by Klara's indefatigable husband, Fyodor Lopukhov, only in 1931. The early Soviet period was as exciting and tempestuous as any in the history of art. This was the time of Meyerhold, Mayakovsky, and modern music. In every cultural field, brilliant talents were feverishly experimenting to make art a beacon for the new social era. Since St. Petersburg remained the center of Russian culture long after the Revolution, the Maly was a natural choice as a kind of laboratory for developing a revolutionary approach to musical theater.

Radically ambitious projects were launched, attracting men of enormous vision and energy. Experiments in putting Mayakovsky to music were tried, and Meyerhold himself came from Moscow to stage new operatic productions. The goal of the huge creative search was fresh forms to reflect and inspire the country's new socialist progress. The artistic tendency, therefore, was to infuse everything with deep social content. "Naked" singing and dancing were mere screwdrivers and wrenches for theatrical construction of political ideas and visions. Like writers, directors were to be engineers of the human soul. Mime was at least as important as singing and dancing because it could drive home points with great force and clarity.

The new approach centered on the "dram-ballet," presumably from "dramatic." Mime, motionless poses by impressively costumed actors, and startling stage effects were used more than actual dancing to convey the message of these new morality plays. The art form grew in proportion to the place of ideology in theatrical work and the demand that mass audiences understand it. Choreography became secondary, and the Dancing Director—for two directors were often employed—was subordinate to the Director in charge of dramatic-ideological development. Even ballets based on Pushkin were imbued with revolutionary purpose.

When the new productions worked, it was chiefly because they radiated great sincerity and energy. Idealism heated to enormous pressure broke through into the theater. Russia was blessed with an incredible collection of freethinking talents, but their deep belief in the universal importance of today's rehearsal and tomorrow's curtain was just as crucial. Even the dram-ballet adapted from the supremely propagandist novel *How Steel Was Tempered* made good theater. Something audiences sensed as important to themselves was clearly expressed and movingly conveyed. Whatever the politics and the amount of real dancing, art was *alive*.

All this took place under Sergei Kirov, Leningrad's Party chief, for whom the Kirov Theater was named. When Stalin had him murdered and the purges began, all artistic innovation ceased. The country's creative spirits were either physically liquidated or destroyed as artists.

Fear and fierce orthodoxy finished more than the Maly's brave new ventures. Far more than the old tsars, Stalin made his power felt in everything. His very absence from the Maly drastically lowered its significance. For when in Leningrad, he visited no lesser place than the Kirov.

More than ever, the Kirov became the concern of the powerful and privileged. And as it flourished with lavish appropriation, all other artistic establishments declined; the Maly became truly *maly*. Grim hacks and terrified yes-men replaced the great directorial, choreographic, and musical talents. The theater was left with a huge weight of murdered hopes and a short tradition of dram-ballet, now emptied of all artistic— as opposed to political—meaning.

After Stalin's death, fumbling attempts were made to return to the prepurge spirit. The theater again became relatively more daring than the Kirov, but the political atmosphere still discouraged genuine creativity. Without clear rules about where the new efforts might or might *not* go, nothing came from the heart. Fine coaches were hired to try to improve the dancing. But the leading ballerinas increasingly switched to Party duties because they did more to advance careers. Few cared deeply about ballet. And the repertoire was an aimless collection of inferior classics, old dram-ballets reduced to little more than a series of decorative tableaux, and new productions that were even worse. The Maly lacked a personality.

Reverence for the Kirov also helped glue a "second best" label on everything we did. The Maly had seemed wonderful when I was faced with some distant assignment, and it *was* far better than any provincial theater. Yet we gaped at the Kirov aristocrats, with double our salaries and ten times more in privileges. Since we lacked the right blood for transfer there, no one strived for it. The Academy's selection and stamping had been once and forever.

Purely practical obstacles to improvement were even more demoralizing. Later I would wonder how I could have danced leading roles on my salary. Toward the end of each month too little was left for food to fuel my furious work output. But at the time I seemed to be earning a small fortune. And it *was* unusual for the Maly—even the Kirov—to pay a hundred and twenty rubles to a nineteen-year-old. What was not unusual was sixty rubles for our grown corps de ballet dancers with children to support. Few even tried it without moonlighting for workers' clubs or in odd jobs unconnected with dancing. It was hard for such dancers to consider art as being above money or believe anyone who expressed such a sentiment.

The bright side was the relative freedom from what came with the big money and big prestige of national importance, where everything had to be irreproachably Soviet. The Maly's easier atmosphere immediately proved a great advantage for me. My first parts were in *Schéhérazade* and *Ivushka*, a ballet based on Russian folk tales. During the first winter, rehearsals began for *The Seven Beauties*, a production previously abandoned several times because of its demands on the male lead's stamina. A combination of lucky circumstances gave me work well above my age and ability: these central roles immediately and forty new ones in the coming six years, including some of the world's most technically arduous. The Kirov's new recruits, including Yuri Soloviev and Rudolf Nureyev, had joined almost as one group. Eager and highly competitive among themselves, they also had to share stage honors with a dozen aging greats, including Konstantin Sergeyev and Semyon Kaplan, both my future teachers. Not even the Kirov repertoire could satisfy the aspirations of these extremely promising talents. They had two or three major performances a month. I was onstage more often than this every week, stretching myself to my physical and artistic limits.

The very handicaps that had kept me off the top-billing conveyor and shunted me to the Maly gave me precisely what I needed now. My body still produced no song without tedious slogging. Only my enormous load of this most practical labor led to a degree of ease on the stage. Some of my work was hack stuff, done under great pressure, but the harder

I pushed, the more I *had* to develop, at least in some ways. Only I knew the cost in terms of body punishment and that no brilliant plan of mine, but rather the luck that had placed me where my compulsion could lead to something, would account for any progress.

The Maly's very shortcomings provided extra opportunity. Its dram-ballet tradition forced performers to create their stage characters from within themselves. In the antidance productions you had to dance your own way through the undanceable moments. I could not have asked for a better education.

The final bonus was that my theater was free of the big-time stresses and rewards that would have finished me—if the competition of the polished Kirov group hadn't. As it was, I could watch their star-bound performances on my free evenings, then experiment in the far more easygoing Maly, trying to reach their level in a wide variety of roles.

AFTER REHEARSALS I sometimes crossed Arts Square to visit a wreck of a man named Valery Dorrer. Dorrer was still sober enough at that hour of the day to be one of the country's best theatrical designers, and he used to give me ideas about playing off a character's mood against the background of a set. He also coached me in how to look at paintings, including works by Malevich, Burliuk, and Chagall hanging in a little museum he had access to. A lifelong pattern of friendships with people outside ballet was beginning.

That winter I was taken to a party of Leningrad's top young "swingers." Someone introduced me to a handsome lad whose French sports jacket could have been an exhibit in a museum of modern art. He spiked his invitation to visit him at home with an offer to hear genuine Western jazz. My mild interest in jazz from the Voice of America was nothing compared to Volodya Sverdlin's knowledge. Since a single American record could make a social lion of the shyest wall-flower, his collection represented a playboy's fortune. We quickly became friends. I said hello to a few foreign tourists in his room. They were even more amazing than the records.

Volodya enlightened me about aspects of life abroad, which he picked up from avid listening to Western shortwave broadcasts. He also revealed a new side of Leningrad itself, in that his tight circle of friends was growing more and more dissatisfied with the Soviet system. He described how foreigners were followed and police methods used to persecute and blackmail dealers in black-market clothes.

His own records obviously came from trade with foreign tourists. I would sprawl on his shabby couch, lost in admiration for Benny Goodman, Dave Brubeck, Errol Garner, and Oscar Peterson. But on my walk home, the attacks on jazz as a decadent medium designed to subvert the Soviet system interfered with the "high" of these artists' revelations. I had already imagined a ballet to the music of "Take Five," Brubeck's most danceable number. I couldn't accept that the excitement these rhythms and subtle dissonances created was only an ideological trick. It was even harder to understand how my vision of a modern ballet made me a potential wrecker serving our enemies' interests. I was still a political ignoramus, but the incessant linking of the music I adored to heinous evil prompted conscious annoyance with Soviet rule. What were people afraid of? Why did fear express itself so often against other peoples' inventiveness?

LIYA WAS VERY MUSICAL but didn't like jazz. Her taste ran to Soviet ballads and to the folk song broadcasts constantly presented to stiffen native patriotism. So Alec was right in some ways. His opposition to her had nothing to do with her age, professional prospects, or the other considerations that troubled my parents. He simply saw her as an unchangeable product of her background. Despite spurts of generosity and artless charm, the narrow-mindedness of the Russian lower class extended to a suspicion of everything Alec regarded as civilizing and important. Their Marxist-Leninist slogans, which he considered just peasant chauvinism in a more dangerous form, depressed him particularly. He put Liya in this category after their first conversation, purposely using the cliché "gray" to stress what he took as her instinctive antagonism for everything interesting.

Her distaste for him exceeded his for her. She knew what was good for me, and it did not include that "library mole's stupid smart talk." This steady disparaging had no effect. It was our own physical and emotional differences that were prying Alec and me apart as we settled into our adult lives. He had embarked on a life of inner purpose. When he was a teenager, others' hopes for his career were as high as his own. But the unauthorized university journal made him unemployable as a teacher. It also taught him that all his important perceptions and thoughts were unwanted.

He wrote what he could without lying: chiefly theatrical reviews and humorous sketches for Lithuanian magazines. But most of his intellectual energy went to re-investment. Convinced that he could change nothing in his world, he dedicated his scholarship to himself. He spent days in libraries and in procuring East European journals. He developed his camera skill and his knowledge of cinema history. The more he learned, the greater his contempt for Soviet rule and resistance to taking any staff job. Knowledge of his gifts would bring offers of many comfortable jobs in the coming years. But they all required too much compromise from him. He also abandoned his ambition of serious writing, sacrificing his career to his principles. Some of what outsiders saw him as—a flop—slowly rubbed off on his own conception of himself, and he became increasingly humble.

He still cared for me deeply, but he had hoped I would be a companion in his exile from what newspapers called "our motherland's uniquely rich, energetic, and joyous life." His small circle of like-minded friends meant much to him. In their highly intelligent company he could not take pride in his frivolous kid brother.

My letters to him no doubt increased his disappointment. He assumed my barely literate scrawl was more adolescent clowning. His own experience told him that worthwhile men did not take learning lightly. Besides, I didn't share his opinion of our inimitable papa. I had broken with our father because I was tired of having my personal freedom laced up with rigid restrictions. Apart from this and his addiction to slogans, I had no broader quarrel with him than with the Soviet system he continued to extol like a rooster. But it was these very political beliefs for which Alec, who was still living in the same house with our parents, had developed a scorn. Alec was convinced that dictatorship was the only real law of government behind Marxist-Leninist camouflage. And he sadly accepted that I was too shallow to see what he did.

My profession was further proof of this. Alec knew ballet only by way of the Vilnius company, therefore had no cause to be impressed by it—especially since he saw dancing as essentially trivial to begin with. For all his opposition to our parents and to Communist sermons, both had formed in him a liking for the standard, solid, and correct. This was so strong that well after some talented Leningrad artists had commended a few of my drawings, he tried to teach me to re-do them—in his old realistic way.

He just couldn't understand my love of silly ballet, and that was our greatest barrier now. Still keen on mechanical devices, he admired me as a well-made windup toy. This had once been amusing to him, but now it was clear that I would never grow up. I still loved and respected him. He was wiser than ever in many ways, but his advice no longer seemed infallible. I felt he was joining that large category of people who did not understand what I was striving for.

At least Liya appreciated my work. From the first she accepted that I would go further in dancing than she, and she did what she could to encourage me. I was a child in need of discipline—*hers,* she assured me. And I agreed. At my request she made notes from the audience on my performances. To keep clear of my spelling and grammar mistakes, I also asked her to take down my own professional thoughts. For all the differences in our views of what dancing was for, she did this conscientiously. Most of all, she wanted to weed out juvenile notions that would keep me from being a star like other stars.

At home she tried to see to my stomach and to clean linen, for this was in her peasant tradition. But cooking was no fun in our miserable communal kitchen, and the fat-soaked meals she and her mother turned out there represented the best they had known in their stark poverty. This poverty was what they were always striving to escape from—and into "middle-class" respectability. And Liya's attention to her man's physical needs only emphasized how little we gave each other in other ways. Everything "funny" or "foreign" in me provoked embarrassment and resentment in her and her mother. They were resigned to, indeed expected, occasional binges from a man. But Liya felt that even my fondness for all-day rehearsing made me slightly peculiar. And the higher my professional standing rose, the more hurt she was by my failure to live up to it in terms of respectability. She couldn't understand why I didn't cultivate Party functionaries for friends.

Her steady stream of "that's not normal" and "people will talk" demoralized me even more because love prompted it. She loved happy evenings—provided they were in the good old vodka-and-herring tradition. Anyone like Valery Dorrer and Volodya Sverdlin who enticed me away from making a success through the proper channels was bad. And success was mainly for improving our nest. Nothing was more important than upgrading our furnishings and winning the competition with other wives. That was why a child was needed. We simply had to have one because—well, all upright families did. It was second only to having a refrigerator. Besides, being a father might straighten me out.

A baby now—and under our conditions? Liya registered the force of my protest and relented. She also gave me generously what I could never stop being grateful for. Her body was indescribable. I would wake up hoping things had changed. Surely our nocturnal honesty and understanding would soon carry over into the day? But breakfast always brought the same recognition of how far apart our interests were, and I walked to the theater convinced that my satisfaction lay only in dancing.

16

IN THE FALL OF 1958 THE ADMINISTRATIVE DIRECTOR SUMMONED ME to his office for some astonishing news. "Leningrad," he pronounced solemnly, "has recommended you for a visit to Poland. We think you will agree to go."

Not quite the entire populace had picked me to represent them, as the man's officialese implied. Party officers responsible for army recreation were forming a troupe of opera singers and vaudeville acts to help Soviet troops stationed in Poland celebrate the Anniversary of the Bolshevik Revolution. But whatever the trip was for, I needed no administrator's help to know how grateful I should be for the honor. Foreign tours had already shown themselves sources of huge advantage in prestige, adventure, and worldly goods. Everyone applied any influence he had to pry himself aboard them, causing a great top-heaviness in coaches, administrators, and Party supervisors. In this case, a former Artistic Director of the Maly had arranged for his wife to go. She was an aging Maly ballerina whose dancing was almost a parody of the old academic style. My name was added as the company's specialist in classical pas de deux, which were considered essential for our homesick soldiers.

Poland began for us in cold, uncozy Libnitsa, home of Soviet headquarters. The packed audience gave ballet the lustiest cheers of all our acts. Since Soviet troops were powerfully discouraged from mixing with the "fraternal" natives, a bare-legged blonde created a stunning impression on soldierly hordes yearning for the female form. Pandemonium followed us everywhere. I needn't have appeared at all.

We danced and drank every day. At first I doubted that anyone could perform on the half pint of vodka obligatory at every banquet. But some days we coped with two or three thrown by Russian and Polish units in turn. Toasts, overindulgence, and mellow group sentiment were the accepted forms of contact between "our two great peoples."

Poland seemed fabulously rich compared to us, and its people less downtrodden. The little town of Shetin had more night life than all Moscow. New Polish friends took me to a restaurant that was packed at midnight. Compared to the bright lights and towering ceilings of Soviet restaurants—easily mistakable for metro stations—the darkness of this place was wonderfully tempting. Sure enough, the pretty young girls the atmosphere cried for soon appeared. A few sat right down on our laps and asked, "How many zlotys have you got?"

I had precious few but would gladly have spent the last one. Our armylike medical warnings about the dangers did nothing to stifle my curiosity about the Polish beauty. But our tour leader's constant eye kept me in my seat.

In addition to our tour leader—the official eye always trained on us—we traveled with an unofficial boss. This was the man with the real power and the sharper vigilance, to whom the group leader subordinated himself. Midway through the trip, this policeman turned excited impresario. He dashed to every nearby town, arranging additional concerts for five hundred extra zlotys a time.

In some ways the six weeks were a grand waste of time. The performances were thrown together with furious haste, and most stages were terrible for ballet. But moonlighting gave us an even greater chance to see and explore than on an ordinary tour. I was abroad!

Our last stop was Warsaw. It exuded economic disorganization, heavy bureaucratization, and some sort of national anxiety, as if trying to personify Poland's moodiness. Everyone understood Russian, though few cared to hear it spoken. But hearts melted when ballet was mentioned, and embarrassing generosity followed.

Our last evening in the capital began in the Palace of Culture, an exact copy of the Stalinesque skyscrapers that ruled Moscow's skyline. We kept hearing jokes about the architectural absurdity, and symbol of Russian domination, that overwhelmed the painstakingly restored ancient city center. "Where's the only place for a good view of Warsaw?" "The Palace of Culture, of course." "But why?" "That's the only place you don't see the Palace of Culture."

Foreigners were always treated to a show in the giant's basement nightclub, a bizarre attempt to marry the ponderous to the tantalizing. The hall had all the intimacy of an exhibition of economic achievements pavilion. A large fountain squatted in the center. When it was still a lump of wet clay, all possible extremes of decor had been stuck on it. Yet the dim red lighting would have triggered off a police raid in a Soviet city. The Poles at neighboring tables seemed to be waiting for something. The object of their impatience soon appeared in the spotlight. She was a tall woman in a white sweater that clung to her torso. I was impatient, too, for I'd heard that Wanda Z., the best-known Polish vocalist, was on the program. Her voice on recordings could not have told me about her eyes. They were penetrating and indifferent at the same time.

She sang as if entertaining two or three friends in her living room. Her melancholy tangos expressed the country's spirit. Nothing could have been more different from our popular singers, who were always summoning their weary listeners to march somewhere or accomplish something. All Poland seemed sad to me, and I felt partially responsible since Russia's power made itself felt more here than at home. But Wanda managed to make this our common problem.

Our unofficial eye thought he'd better put himself on record. "That's not singing; it's pure decadence. The only way to put up with it," he added more cautiously, "is to get loaded." While her songs grew more romantic, he proceeded to set the example.

I stood up. The white sweater, beautifully sad face, and melancholy melodies about Polish tragedies drew me to the performers' bar. I guessed she would appear there after her last number. I was right. She entered. And sat down with two men who offered her a drink. But she spun around and stared at me, then excused herself to her friends. She could not ignore the high voltage of my gaze. Her speaking voice and her mouth had the substance of her songs.

By this time our "eye" had accomplished his mission to oblivion. He was so happy that he announced we would all get favorable behavior reports. The troupe had shared the moonlight money fair and square with him: enough for five extra synthetic rugs, which were rumored to have huge re-sale value at home. Now it was his duty to souse the successfully concluded tour in alcohol. In the morning he would remember nothing—certainly not my absence.

Wanda and I went up to the street like old friends going to a reunion. A comfortable taxi appeared. Soon it was cruising nocturnal Warsaw.

"Where to?" the driver asked from time to time.

I vaguely remembered a line from a booty film. "Anywhere," I answered.

Wanda apologized sadly for being unable to take me home. It was far too cold to leave the taxi. I buried my face in her fur collar. We kissed until blood boiled.

At dawn I gave my last zloty to the meter and returned to our seedy hotel. Numb with exhaustion and happiness, I saw nothing until my colleagues started shouting at me. They had informed the police of my disappearance and were waiting in panic for the consequences. But since the tour had officially and successfully ended, our behavior was slightly less important. I got a hot scolding instead of the drastic punishment everyone expected.

The troupe set out for a farewell concert at the Soviet Embassy. I was excused for lack of a suitable stage for ballet but prohibited to leave my room except for the embassy. Wanda knew my address. I lay down to dream she would come. When she did, her beauty in the light of day brought back my uneasiness for a minute. Then she removed her silky blouse and as part of the same frank preparation disconnected the bell to the room.

A violent pounding on the door broke through gradually. I came to just as two Kirov coaches burst into the room. Wanda looked for a place to hide, but they saw her celebrated face and started apologizing. "We were only worried about . . . the gas heater, we thought it . . ." Words even less plausible emerged from my open mouth. Four supposed artists cringed in dismay.

THE WINTER MOON reflected off the snow crust of vast empty spaces. The railway tracks cut through like ink lines on a blank page. We crossed the border. In Russia the snow became deeper, the fields more monotonous, the moon more tragic. The memory of Wanda's good-bye was doubly crushing because of its uncertainty: "I want to come to you— over there."

She had an idea that a Polish citizen could settle in Russia with no problem. This was salt on nerve endings ripped apart when the train pulled out. And on top of it came my dread at what my raging admiration made explicit about my marriage. If I loved her, what I felt for Liya was something different. If those nine hours were what a man and a woman could talk about and feel in common, Liya and I were doomed to live like a pair of animals.

Work gradually broke the spell. A former Kirov coach fired for his drinking came to our theater more and more tipsy. In this state, he coached me for hours in what we called ballons en l'air, of which he had been Leningrad's master. But most of my concentration went to *Solveig*, a new production.

The part of Olaf, the hero, was full of unusually difficult lifts and stunts such as tilting backward on one leg, in defiance of gravity. Finally, the Ice Maiden kisses Olaf, whose legs are flat on the ground but whose trunk is upright, one arm stretched to embrace her, with head raised like a stargazer's in loving awe. Since her touch freezes ordinary mortals, the trick was to hold this devilish position for almost fifteen minutes.

The Grieg score sounded; the curtain opened; I came to the test. Halfway through it, my neck felt stretched by a medieval rack and my Adam's apple was about to rip out of it.

"What willpower!" came a cry from the wings.

"What stupidity, the stubborn nut!"

My outstretched arm had turned to stone. I tried to think of something distracting, but one thought canceled out all the others: I'll die before giving up. During the final minute everything went black.

Applause sounded from the wings, but the audience was indifferent, and the audience was right. The terrible pain produced nothing either beautiful in itself or helpful in getting to *Solveig's* inner meaning. It was an empty demonstration of my physical advantages. Yet the same childish perversity also drove me to the development my work needed. The roles were there in rare abundance. I wanted to excel partly because I genuinely believed I could give more in them than my uninspired rivals.

Solveig produced a grudging acceptance that I was the company's leading male. The first violinist predicted more. "The Maly's never had dancers like you and never will. You'll go on to something higher in coming years." But in the coming weeks all I knew was that my Adam's apple was a ball of lead and my neck full of torn ligaments.

THE KIROV'S INTERPRETATION of *Swan Lake* was acknowledged the best in the world. When Fyodor Lopukhov decided to stage the same ballet for the Maly, his problem was obvious. He solved it by returning to Petipa's original version, as first presented in St. Petersburg in 1895. Even under the pressure of the Kirov, it was a success. A small public was now coming to see me. One evening, Marietta Frangopolo gave me a portrait of Sergeyev, whom she considered the best Soviet Siegfried. "You can be second," she said, and I knew that at least some of the Academy's lessons were beginning to fall into place.

17

BY THE END OF MY SECOND YEAR IN THE MALY I WAS A CROSS BETWEEN a leading dancer and a jack-of-all-trades. When I wasn't Siegfried in Lopukhov's new *Swan Lake*, I danced everyone but a swan. Spanish tango, pas de trois, and Hungarian czardas were all in a day's work. Appreciation of my versatility flattered my ego. A sixty-ruble boost to my pay pleased my stomach, too.

Then came a staggering bonus. Shortly after Moscow officials observed my Siegfried early in 1959, I was recommended for a trip to the United States. The big, bad land of suffering and injustice was the place everyone wanted to see most. We had been reared on daily horror stories of plane crashes, strikes, and seething resentment of monopolistic exploitation. This strange superpower of riches sucked from social evil held an obvious fascination for even the people who hated it so. America was surely hell to live in but promised the ultimate in excitement for a visit. My stock in the neighborhood zoomed when people heard I *might* go.

The government also considered the American tour by far the most important ever mounted. The competitive examination for selection included a pas de deux, an adagio, and a third number of one's own choice. Mine was a Maly piece about a slave who struggles through torture to his arms and legs and finally breaks his chains. It had provided the first inklings of the emotional roles my temperament best suited me for.

The examination was conducted by a small commission from

Moscow. Zaren Vartanyan, chief of the country's musical-operatic ballet theaters, was the chairman. A Party boss to his fingertips, Vartanyan had no room left for art. I danced my *Slave*, the pas de deux from *Le Corsaire*, and a third selection. Although the commission seemed pleased at first, their agitated discussion at the end was a certain sign of failure. Cultural bureaucrats resented anything that provoked intensive debate. The art production line should run *smoothly*.

At last Vartanyan turned to me. *Slave* was unacceptable, he said gravely. American audiences might imagine that the dancer was hinting that he himself dreamed of liberation. Or—he did not explain the contradiction—Americans might suspect I was summoning *them* to break their bondage. "The objective truth is that only a Negro can sever America's chains of slavery and exploitation," he declared. "But you're white; therefore, this item misrepresents the historical struggle." Of course, I *could* perform in black face, but American audiences might consider this untactful. . . .

The reprieve came while I was cursing the bad luck that had snatched away my chance. The commission suggested I substitute a bravura pas de deux from *The Flames of Paris* about the valor of the Paris Communards.

We rehearsed a full month that spring. I'd never seen such intensity and attention to details. The tour would be linked to the opening of the first Soviet exhibition that summer in New York and thus had the highest possible priority. After Richard Nixon's visit to the Soviet Union, America was preparing to make the acquaintance of Nikita Khrushchev. In keeping with established tactics for readying an important political maneuver, advance cultural groups were being sent out to win American hearts. The Moiseyev and Beriozka folk troupes had already made a deep impression on American audiences, and the Bolshoi Ballet got tumultuous receptions.

Two hundred singers and dancers from all over Russia would take part in a Russian Festival of Music and Dance preceding Khrushchev's visit. For good measure the full ensemble of the celebrated Pyatnitsky Choir was included, together with a ballet group from Kiev, Bolshoi Opera principals, and my partner and me. When I thought about it, we two seemed to have been appended at the last minute to carry the standard for otherwise-unrepresented Leningrad. This was an indication of the advantages of performing in Moscow, in constant view of ministers. But why had they chosen us rather than a celebrated Kirov pair? Whatever the reason, I was ecstatic.

My partner was Tatyana Borovikova, a Maly leading lady who learned to cope with the *Flames of Paris* pas de deux only after much tearful struggle. The other dancers were all very friendly to me, probably because I was the festival's youngest participant. Everyone whispered hope that I would bear up under our heavy responsibility.

The "sensitive mission" talk sounded exaggerated until the dress rehearsal in Moscow. Rehearsals were interspersed with *three* talks in a Central Committee building. The country's most experienced lecturers put us on to a dozen different forms of treacherous temptation that might confront us on America's street corners. "The main thing is vigilance. They'll all be trying to disgrace you." Sad incidents of previous Soviet performers and athletes were cited. A speed skater had entered something called a self-service store, which no doubt reminded him of the well-known Russian saying that "swiping a little from a rich man is only sharing." He mastered his bedazzlement at the counter displays enough to pocket a few pairs of gloves for himself and his deserving wife. Our lecturers exposed the store's stacks of unguarded gloves as an intentional provocation to unsuspecting Soviet visitors, since Americans themselves "obviously" couldn't afford them. "This is the kind of devilishness the enemy uses. You must be triply careful."

The warnings about the American tactics of shamming generosity were more specific. Any so-called gift offered us would, of course, be a provocation from a Washington agency. If not categorically refused, it would naturally be seen as payment for espionage. And if an American were to invite us home, we must not forget that this trick was calculated to exploit Russian openness, friendliness, and naïveté. The host of the specially prepared apartment would be operating under orders to give a fake impression of American living standards. Or he would ask us to take letters—all containing spy materials—to so-called relatives in Russia. To help us avoid such traps, we were to go outdoors only in happy foursomes in charge of a senior person. Wandering alone in a foreign country was "exceedingly frivolous" anyway, and anyone witnessing such a lapse was to notify his leader immediately.

Some emerged from these consultations with chattering teeth. Whatever the possibilities for shopping, it might be better not to venture into the capitalist inferno. Meanwhile, mysterious and dreaded exclusions had begun. Suddenly a member of the group, then a second, next a third were dropped. Because they never knew the cause of their downfall, they had to assume that the KGB suspected the most terrible things about them. Maybe the purged had merely incurred the displeasure of a Party boss during rehearsals by wearing too "freethinking" a tie or seeming too cosmopolitan to come from solid Soviet stock. But we also knew that security checks continued to the last minute, and we racked our brains to remember whether anyone had seen us talking to a foreigner. Anxiety about the blackballs swelled in geometric proportion to the approach of our departure date. Talk had it that receipt of one's passport was almost a guarantee of making the trip, but maybe this too was wishful thinking.

But whatever the chances, no one could afford not to stock up on grub. A million items from nylon tights to diaphragms, woolen sweaters to ball-point pens would have to be bought on our foreign currency pay. With this chance of a lifetime, no one was fool enough to waste a penny on food. Besides, every uncle, aunt, cousin, and sister-in-law would be crushed if you returned without a shirt or an oilcloth to decorate their lives and tantalize their neighbors. All thoughts about pirouettes and grands jetés were buried under stockpiles of sugar, sausage, canned fish, condensed milk, tea, and immersion heaters.

We were also busy in a hidden department of GUM with Polish suits, Czech sandals, and other imported items unavailable elsewhere in the country. We were issued ration cards and told to raise our appearance to European levels. The tour's astute planners did not want Khrushchev-type shoulder pads to make us America's newest comedy act. The main consideration in everything was to avoid humiliation to the motherland. Some dancers dashed home to make their own sleek trousers on patterns they drew in the rationed clothing shop. This left more money for salami and salted cucumbers.

The task of gathering enough food to exist on during our two months away helped relieve the strain of waiting. Still, we trembled like children when our passports were distributed one by one in the Stanislavsky Theater. But the treasured red folder in our hands did not exclude the possibility of being snatched back from the airport.

Two days later we were there. Four more hours for re-counting, re-checking, and agitated last-minute conferences . . . and we saw the plane! Inch by inch, we lugged our suitcases toward it. The last question was whether the TU-104 could possibly cope with sixty days' rations for each and every one of us. The sigh of relief as it headed sky-ward overcame the jet's ear-piercing thunder.

THE FLIGHT TO COPENHAGEN was my introduction to flying, and the plane did what it could to re-inforce our recent earthly anxieties. Bouncing down the runway and shooting up at an absurd angle wasn't enough; it also had to teach us about air pockets. At last we leveled off for an hour or so. Then I looked through the tiny porthole and saw . . . *the sea*. And a ship underway on the wide-open waters. I could feel its mast ripping through our banking fuselage.

Somehow we avoided the obstruction. The wheels touched down. The plane stopped alongside a handsome terminal. It was hard to believe the quality of everything. Wherever my eye expected a tumbledown fence or peeling paint, it saw sleekness and high style. It was as though we had been shot forward to some more advanced society, where every little detail was smooth, well designed, and beautifully cared for.

Then I noticed the smiles. People moved with carefree ease. The physical surroundings were far less ponderous than in Russia. Everything was lighter, neater, more colorful, but could life itself really be so free of our burdens? The general easygoingness infected us even as we disembarked, especially since someone else was going to transfer our provision-packed suitcases to another plane. Unchained of them, we tripped happily into the dazzlingly modern terminal. The interior was even more luxurious, and without a single line at a single counter. Immigration officials "processed" us with eye-stopping speed, precision, and courtesy. In moments, we were zooming along a highway grander than any modern construction I'd ever seen.

Next we were in fairyland Copenhagen itself, on a smaller road leading to the entrance of our hotel. Stunning girls in amazingly chic clothes met us in the sumptuous lobby. We tried to look as if we were accustomed to all this service. After a rest and an elegant supper there was just time for a bus tour. The bustle and lights of the city center silenced everyone, but best of all I loved the cozy town houses where Hans Christian Andersen's characters might be living. I wondered whether I'd ever have a chance to look inside them.

In the morning an SAS plane felt the weight of Russian luggage. It too won the struggle, and we were off to the New World.

. . .

THE PLUSHNESS OF THE PLANE was incredible, the engines so quiet that you could hear the music from the speakers. What a passenger cabin! But foreign dangers started immediately. "If an unscheduled landing must be made, please put on a life preserver, which you will find under your seat." Seeing the announcement freeze us rigid, the steward started serving cocktails. The delight of gulping one in an *airplane* almost got several singers over their apprehension of breaking some rule if they asked for more. A minute later Vartanyan's glass went out for a quick refill, then was rushed up to his chest to hide the maneuver from general view. A steward's reply that more was indeed available sent tremors of gratitude through the plane; yes, alcohol would restore our lost Russian bearings. Pockets were reached into, in vivid memory of our lectures *to pay*. But the stewardess made clear that all expenses were included on this chartered flight.

When the unheard-of concept of unlimited drinks for everyone penetrated, a great surge of joy wiped out all fears. Through our happy haze, an excellent lunch was served—and with smiles. Even the most ideologically keyed-up activists were enjoying the holiday of their lives.

We approached New York slightly sobered. Everyone pushed toward the windows. To the surprise of those who'd flown on Soviet planes, no one stopped me from taking photographs of the airport. The landing was smooth. Like geese in a file, we followed Vartanyan into the arrival hall. A corps of conspicuously Soviet men joined us there. They introduced themselves as "spare artists," who had come along to help out in difficult moments. They were an arrogant type, but on balance, we were relieved to have them on our side. Who knew what provocations American agents had cooked up for us in gangsterland?

We headed for a massive glass structure glittering in the sun. Inside, customs officers opened our suitcases and gaped. Evidently there was a strict regulation about importing meat. Our resolution not to spend a penny on food went down a chute, together with a thousand cans of hash.

Everything was obviously true about America's being a land of fearful extremes. The airport was from the twenty-first century, yet young men wore gym shoes because they couldn't afford real ones. And the June heat almost fried us during the short walk to the futuristic bus waiting at the curb. But either American efficiency had been overplayed or the Washington agency planned to suffocate us. Every last window was stuck shut. The big boys from our opera chorus went to work trying to pry them open. A taxi driver, frightened by the rocking of the bus, ran for the police. Total lack of comprehension on both sides festered toward the dreaded clash between two cultures and superpowers. Only Russian endurance averted it, for our "spare artists" finally got us to sit down and bear the lack of air.

Then the bus drove off toward the city, and an inexplicable, delicious coolness appeared. Our translators added "air conditioning" to a list of terms none of us had ever heard. A great happy laugh went up—until Vartanyan turned around and told us we had the same equipment in our southern cities. "And stop acting like children; stop being so impressed with their stupid tricks."

THE BEDS WERE PERFECT FOR MY BACK, but I couldn't sleep. The city down there was too immensely different from anything my nervous system could relate to. We all used the toilet frequently. The shock would have been milder if it were only the riches we had to take in. But the variety and dimensions of everything—the *scale* of what man had built—were bigger miracles. One highway exchange of this mighty, magical country had more concrete than all of Russia's roads. The Manhattan skyline was unbelievable, even from our hotel room on the twenty-second floor. Our instructions about what to expect were like lectures on Richard Strauss to tribesmen who had never heard orchestral strings.

Like an adolescent in love, I saw nothing negative. Even after our orientation week the pace was astounding, the traffic stunned. It was as if I had climbed over a huge fence separating the Russian steppe from the center of exciting *movement*.

Our managers astonished us too by advancing us a week's wages. And in this roaring inferno of capitalism, almost everything could be bought on credit! The shops in their incredible numbers, each beckoning us with a fantastic abundance and assortment of wares, were difficult to focus on. To escape the maddening conflicts and temptations, I quickly plonked down all my dollars on the first payment for a sixteen-millimeter Bolex camera. As their suitcases emptied of soup and sprats, my colleagues were filling them with fifty brassieres or five hundred ball-point pens, which they would re-peddle for a zillion rubles back in Russia. But I was enthralled with my magnificent mechanical device, especially since photography was an art form Alec took seriously.

We were scheduled to open in early July in Madison Square Garden, a slightly shabby sporting arena that seated a huge audience by ballet standards. Nevertheless, we learned that our shows had long been sold out. Some Bolshoi principals had remained in New York after the company's long tour of America and were added to the program. It was evidently going to be a major event in the city's cultural life.

On opening night I gave my performance everything I had. At the age of twenty-one I still lacked the style of a full professional. I'd had to supervise my own rehearsals, and anyone who knew what the coaching of the Russian masters could accomplish could see my roughness. But this was the first time Americans had seen the *Le Corsaire* pas de deux, and the soaring lifts and other feats overwhelmed them. The applause was ecstatic, and I pleased our own directorate by pleasing the audience. Deeply grateful to my country for this dazzling opportunity, I grinned in permanent delight.

So it went, up toward absolute happiness—until a stab in my groin almost felled me during a performance. The pain was drastic, but I knew I must not reveal it. I forced myself through the performance and dragged my leg to the dressing room. The cover-up continued until one day Vartanyan himself asked me why I was limping around the stage. I broke down. Vartanyan's answer to my appeal for help was a stern recommendation that I continue with my "task." "Otherwise, you should go back to Moscow," he added. "People with bum legs don't go on trips."

The pain grew worse with every performance. Noticing me on all fours one day, Sol Hurok, the famous American impresario handling our tour, issued an order to summon help. The doctor's diagnosis—stretched groin ligaments with a threat of hernia—threw our bosses into panic. The doctor assured them that a truss he prescribed would allow me to dance without danger. But who would take the risk of authorizing the necessary expenditure of our nation's hard currency for a second-rate attraction? Finally, Vartanyan made the hateful decision to use state dollars without calling Moscow. Wrapped up in the truss, I swallowed the pills the doctors had also prescribed. To Vartanyan's joy, Hurok paid for everything. The whole miserable nuisance and worry were forgotten.

Dancing again with much less pain, my good cheer returned, and maybe my vigilance slipped a little after the crisis. I went everywhere with my treasure of a movie camera, controlling my excitement enough to record all the marvels I was seeing. I was resolved to get at least Broadway on film for Alec.

Slava Vlasov, a fine young Bolshoi dancer, shared my passion for film. I was slightly worried about exploring with only him and his ballerina wife. But he had arrived months earlier with the Bolshoi. As a fully "trusted" veteran of this duration he assured me that slight lapses such as not taking a fourth person along were overlooked so long as we behaved with full decorum.

I went for a great shot of street bustle one day when one of the "spare artists" slightly darkened the lens of the Bolex. He had the flat face of the Cossack hinterland, and his black eyes glimmered with suspicion. Among the crowds of busy New Yorkers, he stood out like an amateur actor playing a detective.

He approached me and asked how I managed to buy such an expensive camera. "How'd you like to tell me how *you* got that kind of money?" he asked in a tone of vigilance barely disguised with fake chumminess. State security was obviously necessary, but I wondered why the people responsible for it had to leer all the time. Since my wages could never have covered the luxurious camera, he had proved to himself that the money had to have come from an anti-Soviet organization.

Alas, I had re-inforced his suspicions by going around wide-eyed and gawking since we arrived. Our lectures had made it clear that we were supposed to disapprove of everything American. The favored posture was head down and eyes dulled with lack of interest to indicate that all we saw was fake, boring, and in any case not comparable with what the world's first socialist state had. Any "heightened" interest in things American was therefore a warning signal to the tour leaders—and I had given many such signals. Head straining to take in skyscrapers, peering through crowds not to miss a new-model car, I took myself for a modern Columbus, with every fantastic discovery registering on my half-baked face.

The final proof of my treacherous intent was the zoom lens I was thinking of buying for the Bolex. It wasn't quite clear why my American intelligence contacts needed me to photograph Broadway with this piece of obvious spy apparatus, but the "spare artist" could work out the details later. Zoom lenses were unknown in Russia. His eyes narrowed.

"I didn't buy it," I answered matter-of-factly. "They gave it to me to try out."

This bum "excuse" proved to him he was on to something big. For what legitimate American shopkeeper would lend a Soviet dancer, of all silly people, such expensive equipment? It was too wildly remote from everything he knew.

To ease my unhappiness, I bought a sport shirt, the likes of which all Russia had never seen. Cheered up by its orange stripes, I continued filming with friends, then went directly to the Garden. Vartanyan and his assistants were dashing around in jitters backstage. Comrade Frol Kozlov, who was Khrushchev's number two, had just arrived from Moscow and was going to be watching the performance that evening. Hurok had invited the entire troupe to a celebration after the show. We had been directed to appear in white shirts and jackets. The orders were to go directly—all two hundred together—to the party. *Now* I remembered! Somehow I had to change my orange stripes.

I rushed around and begged. Someone lent me a jacket, but no one had a spare white shirt. I might have stepped outside, dashed fifty yards to the nearest shop, and returned with one in two minutes flat. But not unaccompanied.

Everyone else was intensely busy making up and warming up. I appealed to one dancer after another—even to my sleuth friend, whom I happened to see as I peeped out of the stage door toward the forbidden shop, which was in the Garden's arcade. Finally, I raced out to buy the necessary shirt, together with a bow tie—both about to join the Bolex in my collection of ill-starred purchases. The Cossack blocked my way back. Outrage and triumph twisted his face.

His declaration was in a steely voice appropriate to catching a spy in the act. "You have committed a grave violation, and on a very special evening. This will be reported to the proper authorities."

My detective went on to elaborate about the "enemies of our country" who "dream of staging an incident" to embarrass Comrade Deputy Chairman. "But, for goodness sake," I started, "I even asked you to go with me. . . ." The cold eyes of a viper stopped me. The vigilant operative marched me backstage, seated me in my usual place, and ordered me to make up.

I spent most of the banquet with a youngish Soviet diplomat from our Washington embassy who was helping take care of us. He drank so much that my eyes squeezed shut when he drove us back to our hotel. I lugged him to his room. "I know about your case," he mumbled as he plopped into his bed. "But we'll figure out a way to get you out of it somehow."

IN CHICAGO WE PERFORMED in the smallish Opera House. I already missed the giant theater named New York. The least the Chicagoans could have done was to blaze away at each other with tommy guns. We waited impatiently for this, but it was our luck to see nothing resembling a gangster film during our entire two weeks there. We did witness a day the American government had dedicated to sympathy with enslaved peoples—which included us! Leaflets tossed into the theater declared that Soviet citizens were wretchedly downtrodden: you could never see one in a restaurant because they were saving every penny by not eating or drinking. The public took the appeal to heart and thrust dollar bills into our hands as we pushed through the stage-door crowds. I wondered what we'd have gotten if they had known that two ballerinas had fainted from undernourishment after three weeks of eating out of cans.

In the "Windy City" Vartanyan began pouring out vodka backstage for a group of middle-aged Americans. Soon we learned they were Communists, lovers of the Soviet Union who threatened to atomize in ecstasy at every sight of us, the motherland's artistic representatives. We wondered how *we*, a collection of camouflaging have-nots who all lived in communal apartments, could be so sacred to *them?* They arrived at our hotel in gigantic cars, drove us to their country houses, and enlightened us about the cruel realities of American life. Then their children arrived in *their* cars and drove us back to town for a tour of hotel bars. All coped admirably with their hardships.

The next stop was Los Angeles. Hollywood was crammed with tingling associations of the movies that had brightened my childhood. We were shown the sumptuous houses of the stars and the sidewalk outside Grauman's Chinese Theater, hallowed with the footprints of great performers, including Rachmaninov and Chaliapin. These dents in the cement moved me more than I would have thought possible. The local press was with us and got around to asking us our favorite Hollywood performers. I leaped in first with Mary Pickford, Douglas Fairbanks, and Johnny Weissmuller. The booty films I'd devoured in Vilnius were the latest ones to show in our land, and I was delighted to show off my knowledge of the American cinema. The young reporter nearest me winced as I named every hero and heroine I remembered. Finally, he asked me to give someone else a chance. "Please name a *current* star I can write about." His dismissal of *my* America hurt me.

CALIFORNIA WAS SPECIAL, even in the New World. After our month in the States, this brand-new place retained the power to amaze. I tried to keep from gaping, but *everything* here was a reminder of Soviet backwardness. On the other hand, Americans' notions about Russia could be even more prehistoric. Some sincerely believed that bears prowled our streets.

Our encounters with Russian immigrants troubled me more. Groups of them pressed around us as we left our bus for performances. Out gushed the love for Russia that had lain in their memories like a dream of a beautiful childhood. They saw us as particles of their native earth, for which they both grieved and yearned. They brought along their children to talk Russian to us, although they themselves often spoke it more grammatically than we. There seemed so much both right and wrong in their conception of Russia that I wished I could talk to them. But of course, I pushed past them rudely. For these passionate people scared us silly. Our lecturers had told us that while *some* "real" Americans might not be spies, *all* White Russians were. And their children, too.

No one loved Hollywood more than I. I spent hours swimming back and forth in our huge hotel swimming pool as if I owned it. When I remembered my origins and my evacuation home, I almost burst with a sense of luxurious well-being. I should have known that any expression of joy was as suspect in American water as on American soil.

The next stop was San Francisco. Vartanyan began glancing at me, then knocked on my door just as we were about to leave for an evening performance. His heavy arms embraced me. "Steady, lad," he said hoarsely. "There's bad news from home. You must return immediately." Catastrophic alarm drowned out everything, yet it was only what I had expected. Underneath the surprise and the shock, the fear and the incomprehension, I knew, knew, knew. When I found my voice, I asked what had happened. "A very sad event, I'm afraid." "Sad event" was a standard way of informing about a death in the family. For a second, I sensed it was Liya. But this was a dodge. The marriage conflict with my parents had never really been resolved. But to avoid my guilt, I couldn't force out the question about whether it was my mother or my father who was dead. It was easier to sink into Vartanyan's reassurance. His face was full of grief, and his voice hoarse with compassion. I had acquired a lifelong friend, he consoled. The chief of Soviet musical theaters would take me into the Bolshoi, manage my wonderful professional future, try to replace my father.

Curtain time was approaching. He gave me his handkerchief.

"You're a Young Communist. You must get a grip on yourself—and go on with the show."

An hour later I did go on. No one saw my sobs.

But the news shot through the troupe like shock waves. "What happened?" people whispered to me. Whiskey gave me the strength to find out for myself. Hurok's American translator pushed forward with an offer to telephone Leningrad. But Vartanyan vetoed all calls to anywhere and showed her the door. As he turned to me, his voice regained its tenderness. The first report might have been inaccurate, he said. It wasn't clear yet whether the bad news was for me or for my partner. "Personally, I believe it's her," he comforted. But like the knight I was, I'd have to accompany her home—and, of course, not let on what I knew.

While the others slept, Tatyana Borovikova and I left San Francisco the following morning in the company of a Soviet diplomat. Colleagues from the Washington embassy joined him in New York. Despite their efforts to rush us home, we were delayed a day, maybe because of some visa requirement or difficulty with tickets in the summer travel peak. Our officials practically held our hands throughout the twenty-four hours. For some reason, they seemed as nervous about us as about American intelligence. Cars they identified as "FBI jobs" ringed them as they themselves ringed Borovikova and me.

We were still wobbly when we boarded our plane. While it waited for takeoff, Borovikova and I tried to comfort each other, as we'd been doing since we heard the news. She stopped a few minutes later, looked into my eyes, and lowered her voice. It was full of suspicion, disgust, and weariness. "What did you really do to ruin us?" The sudden abandonment of her sympathy laid bare Vartanyan's ruse in one awful instant. Her one important question, which she had been afraid even to ask while we were in America, seared me. Yes, I had caused it all. Whatever it was, I was responsible for everything, including the damage to her.

We had a brief stopover in Brussels to wait for the connecting Soviet flight. I sat in the transit lounge, my head in my hands, my knuckles rubbing at my temples. Whatever was awaiting me three hours from now would cripple my career. But my own weakness was harder to take. I couldn't move or think. How could I live the West's wonderful life when my childishness and illiteracy kept me backward? How could I survive if even now, when it was vital, I had neither the intelligence nor the courage to analyze my situation and reach a decision?

Our flight was announced. I hunched in my chair, trying to delay, to understand what I had to do to save myself. Borovikova pulled at me. . . .

A SURLY DRIVER from the Ministry of Culture was waiting at the Moscow airport. But first I called my parents in Vilnius and a friend of Liya's in Leningrad. Liya was touring Volga towns with a Maly brigade. The friend assured me she was fine. The only thing wrong with my parents was their shock that I was home.

An official at the ministry relieved us of our passports and held out tickets for an evening train to Leningrad. With nothing more to lose, I refused to take them without an explanation. I was told to leave the office. I said I was going nowhere until I got an answer. He disappeared for half an hour. A more senior bureaucrat emerged and put his arm around my shoulder. "We're very grateful for your triumphs in America. We only recalled you because we had to cut down on costs. The other soloists will also be back very soon. Now off you go for a good rest. We need you in the best possible shape for the next trip."

I convinced myself to believe him. I put a smile on my face and rushed to join Liya and her Maly brigade. It was my first trip to the Volga region. Its poverty and dirt bowled me over. To the Maly dancers' astonishment at my early return, I calmly repeated the "because of necessary economies" phrase. But Liya looked hard at me.

The second-string Maly group was working its way down a series of small Volga towns. Lacking enough money for hotels in all their stops, I bought a ticket for a trip directly downriver, where I would rejoin them. As I was about to board my boat, Liya casually mentioned that she was going to have a baby. I had to reach for the railing. The victory in Liya's eyes was for overcoming my opposition by making the decision without me. Cockroaches and crying in a communal apartment were drowning out my memories of the Hollywood Bowl. I didn't want a baby. I wanted someone to be a father to *me*. And for life to stop smashing me with blows I couldn't stand up to. The river cruiser's whistle blew a second time. Naturally, Liya had waited until this moment to tell me. I went aboard and stood at the deck while we headed into open water. Apart from great hydroelectric stations spewing smoke, the Volga was mile after mile—hundreds of miles in a single stretch— of solitude and eroded banks. All earthly cares seemed insignificant in the spell of timelessness and haunting melancholy.

Days later and six hundred miles downriver, the boat docked below the cliffs of Stalingrad. I begged myself a hotel room and settled in to await the arrival of the tour brigade. Backwoods Stalingrad had a winter gloom even in the heat of summer. I drifted in unhappy thoughts about my damaged career and family trouble, tinged ·by premonitions of difficulties ahead. Much as I wanted to believe the ministry's explanation, I now saw it as a quick invention to get rid of a simpleton. A great conflict lay ahead. Walking the dismal streets, I welled up with a longing to dance again.

When the brigade arrived, I requested permission to join it. Since summer tours to such hick places were for coasting and pocketing extra rubles, my fellow dancers were amused. But I worked harder than ever before, more purposefully even than in America. I had asked to do the demanding Diana and Actaeon adagio from *Esmeralda*. I rehearsed with a savage fury and performed as if I were on trial for my life.

The administrator asked me to stay on until the end of the tour. The more I danced, the less opportunity depressing thoughts had to sneak through. While the other troupe was the toast of Washington, Philadelphia, Montreal, and Mexico City, I was giving everything I had on an assortment of splintering Volga stages.

18

THE MALY'S INVITATION TO GULBAT DAVITOSHVILI AS A GUEST CHOREOGrapher for the new season eased my nervousness about returning to Leningrad. Davitoshvili, a Georgian dancer come home after decades in European emigration, was our closest link to Western ballet. He was preparing Ravel's *Waltz, Bolero,* and *Daphnis and Chloe.* The company's dancers charged toward these new one-act works like horses from exhausted pastures.

I was chosen to try out for *Daphnis,* but *Bolero* so excited me that I became the leading contender for it, too. This stormy ballet was one of the first attempts to combine "ethnic" dancing with classical leaps and other feats, such as double spins in the air with one raised leg. Bestowing two new works on one dancer was considered a violation of the collective spirit, but this was Davitoshvili's big chance outside Georgia. He resisted pressure to "share the honors more evenly."

It was finally agreed to give me both premieres, provided I was willing to dance them on the same evening. This was a welcome way to lose myself in raw exertion. I was even more grateful for an emerging conception of how to deal with my huge work load. My first independent thoughts about an artistic style were beginning to surface. I called my approach "conscious interpretation," in which every choreographic movement must reflect the character and his mood. More than my obsession with work or my physical equipment it was this concept that won me roles. In many cases, my competitors could have beaten me easily if they had *thought* about what they were dancing.

DURING THE RAVEL REHEARSALS the Maly took a large step toward upgrading its ballet by hiring Semyon Kaplan to teach and coach. When I had watched Kaplan performing during my Academy years, he represented to me the highest Kirov professionalism without the flare of genius. He danced a wide range of lyric, heroic, and character roles in everything from *Giselle* to *The Red Beacon.* Always a half step behind Sergeyev and Chaboukiani, he nevertheless won titles and Stalin prizes before retiring from the stage in 1958, at the age of forty-eight. His excellence in everything standard gave him the promise of becoming a fine instructor.

He entered his first class at the Maly with a big smile on his broad face. By the time it was over his attention was directed almost entirely to me. By the end of the week he seemed to live for my development. No matter what rehearsals were on, I never missed my daily class with him. After it we often worked together on the empty stage. I bounded around its perimeter, practicing the cabriole, jeté en tournant, and other steps in which I could exhaust myself. The trick was to convert my energy to expressive power through better technique and body control. My style was becoming one of uninhibited movement, with little patience for standing-still scenes. I asked for more and more of Kaplan's hardest tasks as if I could breathe only in an atmosphere of arduousness.

My life was little but this. No male teacher had ever shown any real interest in me. But jovial, unstinting Kaplan was here now, and he sweated with me to discover what I really could do. In comparison to the graduates who had leaped to glory directly from the Academy, I was very late for such probing and training. But the lapse of three or four years gave me a certain reverse advantage. By now I had some conception of dramatic line and the beginnings of a conscious approach to art.

Of those who had won quick acclaim, Rudolf Nureyev was my favorite. His technique was still uneven, but he was as full as ever of his supercharged individuality. Even his clichés were bearable because they came from *him*, while his best roles were revelations of vividness and emotional brilliance. Kaplan wanted me to better his effortless effects: the splendid soaring and haughty pulled-in hips for which other dancers loved him. We reconciled ourselves to accomplishment only with buckets of studio sweat.

BACKSTAGE RESENTMENT OF ME grew in proportion to the applause for my *Bolero*, but I was too wrapped up in myself to see this as anything but a compliment. I was also dancing in *The Forty-first*, as a captured White Russian officer being guarded by a young Bolshevik girl whose pistol has already dispatched forty counterrevolutionary officers. She falls in love with her prisoner, but when he tries to escape, duty triumphs, and she pulls the trigger again.

Although a choreographic clinker, *The Forty-first* took me further toward my new artistic approach. My wide range of roles—from classical-lyric to comic-grotesque—sharpened my hunger for a philosophy to deal with them: some unifying sense of what ballet itself was all about. This strengthened my impression that some deeper understanding of his part must guide a dancer in fashioning all its movements and gestures. I began to see that ballet was not really for visual pleasure, but something far more important. It was all the more expressive and universal for its lack of written language. It had the power to reach *all* people directly by speaking to their most basic emotions.

But rather than diminishing my interest in airborne feats, this wobbly philosophical base gave me more strength for them. With its larger purpose than merely the dazzling of audiences, mastery of technique beckoned me even more strongly. *Flowers* was another new Maly ballet, this one to the music of Shostakovich. My role included twelve solid minutes—three times the length of the average variation—in a series of emotional episodes involving the first cosmonauts. I charged up the ramp of the forestage, which was dressed like a greenhouse, in a whirl-wind of chaînés, broke into huge soaring jetés, and flew down through the glass. Back into the air again with more jetés, I crossed the curtain, while it opened to the main stage behind. Flowers were tossed from the wings. The blossoms turned into maidens. The maidens, soon the entire female corps, surrounded me. I flew over them—lengthwise and across, changing my leg position at the top of my leaps—in a waltz of wild joy. The audience rubbed their eyes.

Kaplan and I spent hours of every day in "impossible" experiments: horizontal turns in the air like upside-down double assemblés, shifting to one leg for a kind of sissonne and ending in an arabesque. The steps were dubbed "pas-nov." Several were actually accepted into the general repertoire, although few of my immediate successors cared to try them, on the sensible principle that if they fell flat, no cheers would lessen the shame. Sometimes I could hardly believe what my body had performed. When applause for my best performances built up my vanity, I sometimes gave in to a slight relaxation in training. I immediately began stumbling instead of soaring "effortlessly" through the air. This taught me yet again that I was nothing without my huge doses of work.

KAPLAN'S DRAWBACK AS A TEACHER was that his enormous ballet knowledge came with no sensitivity to his pupils' feelings. As with many veteran soloists who turned to coaching, he had no training for his new job; it was simply assumed that he'd pick up enough along the way. He could indeed teach technique to the most advanced class, but he was no psychologist. It was a mistake to use only me to demonstrate the exercises. My worse mistake was to suppose he was serving art through me. Slighted egos wanted revenge.

Immersed in my development, Kaplan noticed nothing. When others demonstratively marched out of class, he was dumbfounded. We were summoned to the office of the Artistic Director, Isaeva's replacement. Angry male soloists demanded that Kaplan leave the theater, and if he found it hard to leave alone, he could take me with him. But the Maly could not afford to lose anyone who helped sell tickets. The crisis ended in an official censure of Kaplan and my transfer to the corps de ballet class.

With this setback to draw us closer together, Kaplan and I simply waited a decent interval, then moved to an empty studio. My old need to overcome self-imposed physical challenges heated our sessions. My weaknesses were driven home in Kirov performances by Nureyev or my former classmate Yuri Soloviev. I had to match them.

Kaplan showed me a hundred technical pointers, including "innovations" that were actually forgotten steps he had learned from Vladimir Ponomaryov, who was considered the Academy's best male teacher when he trained Kaplan. He remembered everything danced by everyone—even abandoned experimental steps—during his forty years in the Academy and at the Kirov. And his joy in my work came from a sense that he had been given a second career. After our sessions he massaged my legs, then sometimes invited me to the cafeteria to make sure I had proper food. He took me for fresh country air some weekends or to his apartment for the comfort of an "artistic" Leningrad home. His wife, who sang in the Kirov Opera, gave him little affection or admiration. His daughter blinked whenever she saw "that terribly selfish man," as she called him, being so generous to me. "He never loved me or even my mother," she said. "It's as if he always wanted a son."

Yet Kaplan walked away whenever I tried to talk about what was really troubling me. He knew that I was trying to exhaust myself partly out of despair at being made a minor public enemy, but he wouldn't say a word about this. I had already been excluded from a few small foreign tours. That might have been accidental—until I heard that an Australian impresario was specifically interested in me as someone who might go down well with his public. I featured in three one-act ballets for the audition. He thanked me and sang, "See you soon!" When the group left for Australia, I remained in Leningrad.

My first instinct was to find out. But all my queries produced the same brief answer. "*You* know what you were involved with in America." The touring troupe returned from Australia with brochures unused there because my photograph was inside. If only someone would say what was wrong with me!

Since I couldn't escape the talk of my American adventures, I treated it with scorn, which only fed the rumors. "Panov was operating with the Zionists!" "Panov was peddling Soviet goods!" Some stories cited the makes of the watches I had dealt in, though without explaining why Americans would want to exchange their own elegant timepieces for our Soviet time bombs.

I sprinted from one office to another, asking every official who opened the door what I must do to clear myself. With one voice, the secretary of the theater's Party organization, the secretariat of our city district's Party organization, the secretariat of the Leningrad Party itself assured me that my suspicions were imaginary. Everything would soon be best for me—no, was already best—in this best of all possible worlds. And if it was foreign travel I was concerned about, in addition to local recognition and my handsome salary, that too would be mine the next time.

But the next time the departing group was warned to "learn from Panov's example; never behave as he did." Exactly how Panov had behaved was never spelled out. But my fellow performers began to shy clear of me, especially when a lengthy voyage was in the offing.

I asked my old teacher Abdurakhman Kumisnikov why his son Murat had stopped seeing me. Although I had guessed, his wife's reply cut. "We're afraid association with you might affect our boy's career," she said. "The Kirov is making its selections for a new foreign trip." The Kumisnikovs' rejection pushed me further into my own loneliness. I had hoped being the outsider would be a temporary role. It was becoming the central fact of my life.

To ease the hurt, I returned to the search for Mother Truth. At last I went to Smolny, the Bolshevik nerve center during the Revolution. It was still a Party headquarters, now of the city of Leningrad. Something intimidating lingered in its well-kept walls. I started by telling the official who had received me that I was at my wit's end. The last news to reach me was of a Party lecturer expounding on my links to an important espionage ring. "Who told you that?" the man snapped. Since political instructions for artists going abroad were supposedly secret, anyone I named would be bumped from his trip. I left Smolny slightly farther down my dead end.

At last it dawned on me that no one *wanted* to investigate the stories. I was needed as a warning to others, to beef up fear of the "enemy." And my colleagues were indeed frightened that *something* was wrong with me, just as I would have thought the worst if someone else had been the victim. If you wanted no trouble yourself, you believed what the leaders told you.

Then it occurred to me to write to the one person who might certify my innocence. The only thing I knew about Nikita Khrushchev was that he was taking us in the right direction. He had removed the mask from Stalin, liberated most prisoners who were still alive, permitted "thaw" literature. His peasant manners offended sometimes, but everything felt easier and healthier under his leadership, and he was known to be open to personal appeals.

Two young writers who liked my dancing helped draft my appeal. I told Khrushchev everything I knew about the American trip and implored his help in at least finding out why I'd been made an enemy. Instead of producing facts, people called me terrible names. I hinted that my faith in Soviet goodness and justice would shatter unless he got me out of my impasse. And how could I dance with a witch-hunt destroying my peace of mind?

While I waited for an answer, a Young Communist meeting was convened to call the spy to account. We awaited it in mutual anticipation, I convinced that the "collective's" secret would at last be revealed to me, they eager to hear a confession for my still-unspecified crimes. But the meeting was suddenly canceled—on orders from above, as Liya informed me. "This is a matter of state," the KGB informed our Young Communist officials. "The meeting is not authorized." Without an open discussion at which the truth might have emerged, I remained intact as a scapegoat. And a dozen tales—"either he stole something or something was stolen from him; I'm not quite certain except that it's bad"—continued to stick to me like birch leaves in a steam bath.

Months after my plea to Khrushchev, loyal friends told me that lecturers had stopped referring to my espionage. My letter wasn't answered, but I never gave up hope of hearing from the First Secretary.

No ONE BELIEVED THE ACCUSATIONS more staunchly than Liya. She was still a Young Communist secretary, as convinced as ever that her organization was always right.

"You did something wrong in America. Something serious."

What did she think this might be, I asked for the *nth* time.

"You said something there. Maybe even met somebody you shouldn't. Anyway, you weren't careful enough."

This was the domestic hollowness into which our son was born. We named him Andrei after Andrei Smolentsev of my Academy years. He was incredibly pretty, but Liya and her mother kept him from my "rough" voice and arms. Instead of bringing his parents closer together, the innocent infant helped propel them farther apart. Now that the miracle of creation was cooing in his crib, my resentment of Liya for having had him against my wishes was despicable. But it didn't disappear. And Liya matched me for petty spite. I was bringing home far less than she thought I should for her angel's layette. Ballet's big money was in hard-currency earnings, from which my stupidity or treachery had excluded me.

Liya's determination to give her child "the best" included protecting him from my screwball ideas. After rehearsing my legs off all day, I ran to a friend's studio to paint instead of standing in line for bananas or coming home to knock in some nails around our miserably overcrowded room. I deserved nothing so precious as Andrei, and the real hurt was that she was right. I wanted him to have what my parents had never given me. But I was still an emotional baby myself and could hardly give a real one what it deserved.

In the summer of 1960 I saw a movie about our American trip. It had been taken by Slava Vlasov, my camera-bug companion in New York. The Kodak colors made a great impact. There was talk of showing it in ordinary cinemas, until Party supervisors saw that Vlasov's lens made America look too rich and happy. Footage of myself in the pool of the Hollywood hotel deepened my depression. I remembered how well Vartanyan had acted his role. I guessed that a *real* death in his family would be kept from a touring soloist, on the principle that state interest—the foreign-currency earnings—always takes precedence over the individual. Exactly this would happen soon to a ballerina who was told that she had lost her father only after she had completed her engagements.

The FBI agents who had so panicked my Soviet guardians on my final New York day also came back to mind. "Surely they're not interested in *me?*" I had asked. "Of course, they're interested in you," was the answer. Now that my armor of political innocence had been stripped, the reason penetrated. The Americans had suspected that my recall to Russia foreshadowed trouble for me and wanted to give me a chance to defect. At the airport they had allowed me through the passport checkpoint, then cleverly detained my escorts by scrutinizing their documents. I had only inched away from the FBI men in pathetic fear.

I wondered what I would have done had I known about the persecution awaiting me. And that once I understood the terrible trick about a death in my family, the authorities would assume I *would* defect if they ever gave me another chance. . . . But what hurt most of all was the probable cause of my troubles in the first place. I had been on a list of tour members requiring special observation. The secret police knew New York was a "Jewish" city. It made no difference that I considered myself Russian to the last drop of my blood. The KGB officers saw me first of all as a potential traitor waiting for his chance to sell out Russia to his Semitic brothers. I could do nothing about this. I had been doomed from the beginning. The Maly talk about my involvement with "the Zionists" was more of the same. It made a mockery of my father's frenzied efforts to prove he wasn't a Jew, and my denial that I'd ever been one.

Brooding about this one day, I noticed a newspaper announcement of a vacancy in the Bolshoi Theater. I rushed to Moscow like a scout escaping from an ambush. The admissions commission included Galina Ulanova; the great character dancer Sergei Koren, now a Bolshoi ballet-master; and Professor Leonid Lavrovsky, the celebrated Artistic Director. I danced the pas de deux from *Le Corsaire*, a variation from *Bolero*, and a third number. They applauded my range.

"That's it, you're accepted as a soloist," said Lavrovsky. He was eager for me to start on new productions of *Don Quixote* and *Laurencia* for the coming season. I rehearsed for a few days, then raced joyfully back to Leningrad for the papers that would formalize the end of my run of niggling luck. The Bolshoi was a marvelous rescue from the spy stigma *and* a wonderful promotion. But when I pushed into his office, the Maly's Personnel Officer was waiting with a sarcastic grin.

I would not believe what he said. Heart pounding, I ran to the Director's office. A telegram on his desk expressed regret that the Bolshoi Theater could not take me that season. Once again the explanation was in terms of "economic considerations."

"But there was an official panel," I cried. "A secret vote. I know they liked me."

The Director produced a smile. "Dear Valerik, if you can't figure out how things stand, I'll try to explain. You'll dance for me as long as I give you the job. Otherwise, you won't be our neighbor any longer, so drop your foolish notions about moving."

The threat was that if he decided to fire me, I would lose my right to live in Leningrad. I was a handy outcast for the Maly; disgraceful enough to make a lurid example of, yet still acceptable for use in helping fill the house.

Again, the truth came later. I had begun working on the leading role in *Don Quixote* and listening to talk of a future full of Bolshoi roles. But the real test had come the day before I left Moscow, when I had filled in my questionnaire. It was administered by the Personnel Department, which effectively controlled everyone's employment and punishments. This was the local KGB checkpoint in the nation's every institution. You answered the questions—the standard ones, required for every little change in your life—and waited for consultation of some central file that would determine your fate.

My situation was clearer than ever. So was the nature of my country, which needed scarecrows to keep its citizens frightened stiff. For the first time I was fully aware that my owners could do what they wanted with me. But instead of acting on what I knew or even thinking about its full implications, I repressed it. The largest truth was that I wanted to continue living, which meant not accepting what I really was.

I could not hit and could not run. I could not answer the ceaseless shout that I was living in the best society in the world, enjoying civilization's highest achievements. What I could do was keep working on my échappé to shut out the intolerable suspicion that everything around me was wrong. And keep pretending that my problem was only temporary.

19

THE APPARENT ANSWER TO MY PRAYERS CAME FROM THE BIG HOUSE itself, Leningrad's KGB headquarters. Here was proof that our security police eventually sorted things out—and tactfully, too, for this was their way of telling me, without admitting that a "case" had ever existed, that mine had been properly resolved. I was invited to entertain border garrisons for the holidays honoring the Anniversary of the Revolution. The KGB were directly involved because all border troops served under them. Naturally, their invitations were never refused—this one less than any because of its clear promise that my troubles had ended.

When the major with the invitation squeezed into our room, I hardly knew whether to ask why they had picked me or how they had known I was at home at that hour.

"Don't ask unnecessary questions," he pronounced paternally. "We know everything." My heart soared higher. They even knew how much I loved foreign travel. This trip was obviously a preliminary test. Anyone admitted to a border zone had already earned one of the highest rankings of trust.

Our military bus set out for the Finnish frontier. A hundred miles above Leningrad, it passed Vyborg, which had been acquired from Finland during the war. The once-gay resort town had the pitifully neglected look of Poland's former German cities. War rubble lay everywhere, as if we were expecting to exchange it next week for some greater concession from Finland.

The men of the villages to the north wore ordinary peasant clothes, but they were unmistakably KGB officers. Apparently no one else was permitted in the broad band of forest below the border. No one at all lived in the ten miles of the "neutral zone." The immense prohibited area was dead.

We performed in the headquarters of garrison posts, spaced about fifteen miles apart, up and down the border. Few stages were large enough for dancing, but this made no difference to the soldiers. I'd never seen their type before, even on the poorest collective farms. It was as if an army of village idiots with good eyesight had been recruited: physically developed, mentally retarded boys so devoid of thoughts that none could possibly interfere with their shooting anything that moved in their sectors. They stared blankly at the performers.

But maybe the border had anesthetized them. A fifteen-foot wire fence running along its thousand-mile length was scrutinized by soldiers with tommy guns, posted on giant watchtowers. Twice a day teams raked and rolled the thirty-foot band between the fence and towers so that the footprints of squirrels showed up perfectly.

An amazingly complex barbed-wire system bordered this manicured strip. It would take hours to cut through the intertwining strands, all yards deep and rooted to a nightmarish pattern of stakes. These were followed by a forty-foot canal filled with jagged barriers that could be crossed only with climbing equipment. Finally, an electrified fence brought squads charging at every touch by a deer on the Finnish side. When the soldiers talked at all, it was in memorized phrases about rabid Finnish aggressors who dreamed of seizing the motherland's territory. The eeriest factor of all was their failure to see that everything was for keeping us *in*.

I returned to Leningrad more confident than ever that I'd passed my test. It took exclusion from the next few foreign trips to prove that it had all been a bureaucratic mistake: the Big House's entertainment section hadn't been informed about me.

MY FIRST APPEARANCE at a gala concert for a revolutionary holiday came in 1961. A deeply admiring public attended these events to cheer the Kirov stars. It didn't matter a bit that some of the male idols were thirty-year veterans with behinds like cement bags. They appeared onstage; their cascade of flowers was released; everyone was happy. The little trifle I danced brought feet stamping just because it was that kind of evening.

Audience reaction affected me tremendously even though it said nothing about artistic accomplishment. When the house was indifferent to me, my energy spilled out into a spooky vacuum, leaving me lifeless. When it was hostile, I could be hopeless. Masses of stylistic defects marred my pyrotechnics. A kind of telepathy with the audience told me whether these faults were being noticed. Four pairs of disapproving eyes deep in the balcony could freeze my limbs.

But approval was the most potent possible stimulant for muscles. Love for the ballet music surged through me like lightning. I wanted to sing at the top of my lungs with my body, and I could do this; I could dance for joy forever. Many traditional ballets were designed from beginning to end to win ovations for the leading dancers. Not to receive them deflated me too much to allow me to claim the Princess' heart. When they came, they brought me the self-satisfied bravura that changed me into a Prince Charming.

But audiences gave me even more. Something so wondrous began happening in my third Maly year that I could only tell it to old confidants like Madame Frangopolo. At times I passed into a magic unity with my role. I was not moving according to the choreography; the character itself was dancing. Inspiration from a truth higher than ballet lifted me out of myself.

I did steps in this state that I'd never tried before and would never knowingly try again. Some brought me down on the floor so hard that people insisted I should have been a corpse. "How the hell did you do two turns after landing on your stomach like that?" Wondering how myself, I tried to repeat what they described the next morning. Without

Valery's father, Matvei Shulman,
in 1925

His mother, Elizaveta Petrovna,
in 1926

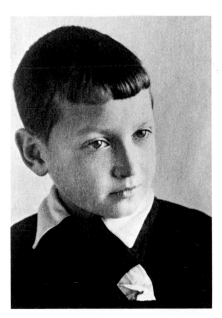

Valery, seven years old

Valery in class at the Palace of Pioneers in Vilnius

The only boy

At fifteen

With his first wife, Liya Panova

Liya

Valery and his son, Andrei, in Leningrad, 1961

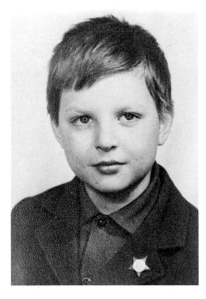

Andrei in 1969

With Semyon Kaplan

Valery's parents in 1970

Valery and Galina's marriage, 1970

Galina with Nadezhda Pavlova and Ludmilla Sakharova

Galina's mother in 1950

Galina and Valery

Natalia Dudinskaya

Konstantin Sergeyev

Dudinskaya and Sergeyev in Raymonda,
late 1940s

Yuri Soloviev and Natalia Makarova in Le Corsaire

Kaleria Fedicheva in Swan Lake

In Pushkin, 1968: Kyoko Ishimatsu, John Cranko, Marika Bezobrazova, Marcia Haydée, Valery, Galina, Marcia Haydée's mother, and Richard Cragun

Valery by the Neva River in Leningrad

With his brother, Alec, after Valery's release from prison, 1972

With Galina in Leningrad

A demonstration in London, 1974: Laurence Olivier, Joan Plowright, Paul Scofield, and Donald Sinden

A New York demonstration with (center) Betty Comden, Lotte Lenya, and Hal Prince

Galina and Valery in their Leningrad apartment

Before leaving Russia

Arrival at Lod Airport, Israel, June 1974

the strength the higher calling had given me, I couldn't even begin. *I hadn't done the movement; it had been that outside force acting through my body.*

The Great Inspiration struck every other month or so. I could not bring it on or even know when it was coming. But some preconditions were essential. Life with Liya had to be smooth enough so that nothing disturbed my concentration. I needed to feel extremely confident in the part; with all the inspiration in the world, ballet is nothing without discipline in its uniquely specialized demands. The last rehearsal in particular had to have gone very well. Above all, I had to know that the public was with me—that is, expecting something from me. I could give more than I thought I had not to disappoint them, but indifference was still fatal.

I did what I could to ward off evil eyes. To counter the effect of faultfinders in the audience, I concentrated on people who liked me, catching the signals they sent in my direction. I would do this for hours before a performance, especially in the roles requiring strong transference. Or I would ask "my own" people—Liya, Kaplan, Frangopolo—to attend. Sometimes I invented a great love in the audience or went further than imagining. Walking to the theater, I would pick out a pretty girl as the one I had to dance for.

My most faithful fans were certain to be there. In my first Maly season I had become the favorite of a circle of elderly ladies. They all had matronly buns and one "theater" dress. They were former teachers of European languages and proofreaders for scholarly journals—survivors of the "old" intelligentsia who had become the picture of spinsterish virtue. Most were on tiny pensions and sacrificed sugar in their tea for the uplifting experience—ballet!—that made their lives worthwhile. After "discovering" me, they took turns standing in line for days for tickets to my performances. They made a collection, each according to her tiny ability, and plied the director of a flower shop to make up a bouquet of peonies or narcissus, all in one color, as they knew I liked.

The most faithful of the elderly ladies was named Serafima Alexandrovna. Although over seventy, she constantly wrote to newspapers, the Supreme Soviet, and the Council of Ministers about issues that disturbed her sense of right. When not writing, she worried about my health. I fell during a difficult variation one evening. The theater gasped, and Serafima Alexandrovna had a heart attack.

When she recovered, her doctor warned against further excitement, but she limped to the ticket line as soon as she could, saying she wanted to die watching me dance. She had a second attack in her seat, was returned to the hospital, and did die soon afterward. The other women kept her death from me during a week of almost nightly performances, and I regretted this. I was always conscious of giving very little in return for the support of these adopted grannies and aunts: a bouquet on their birthdays and attendance at an occasional "reception" devoted to talk of the wonderful old days. It was wrong to miss the funeral of the one who had most devoted herself to me.

MY INTRODUCTION TO *Petrushka* overwhelmed me as completely as my first view of ballet itself in Vilnius. The art I had always loved revealed much more of its divine appeal. Here was the proof that ballet could reach life's most important emotions and truths.

Work on the Maly's revival began early in 1961. Our balletmaster, Konstantin Boyarsky, enlisted the help of elderly pensioners who had performed in the last production of *Petrushka*—in 1921. That one featured Benois decor, the "magnificent" Nicolai Orlov as the Blackamoor and Leonid Leontiev, whom Sarah Bernhardt called a theatrical genius, as Petrushka. As the first Stravinsky ballet of any kind sanctioned since then, our experiment marked the beginning of Soviet reconciliation with at least some of his masterpieces.

After our forty-year deprivation, the score was as moving a revelation as can occur in art. Even my fiftieth hearing gave me insights about Russia that I had "always known" but couldn't articulate to myself without the vividness of this musical observation. Its tragic elements said something indescribably beautiful—because true—about my surroundings. It was hard to believe that such keenness to the spirit of contemporary Russia could have been expressed half a century ago.

Boyarsky wanted more actual dancing than in most Western productions, which leave Fokine's original 1911 choreography almost intact. This change helped make the part of Petrushka more important to me than all my previous ones, despite attempts to disenchant me with it. "You're a full-fledged principal now," counseled many acquaintances. "What on earth do you need with that clowning stuff? Screwed-up limbs and simpering grimaces—that's not going to further your reputation."

Fokine was almost as great a revelation as Stravinsky. Best of all was the organic communion of music and choreography. After this, I would encounter only one other such collaboration—of Balanchine and Stravinsky—in ballet. But even after I knew the New York City Ballet well, *Petrushka* seemed stronger to me than anything in the New York repertoire, perhaps because it was pervaded by genuine drama and conflict, the discoveries of the early twentieth century's creative geniuses.

The uncanny parallels I saw between my situation and Petrushka's made the role a personal statement for me. We both were victims of taunting, inscrutable forces. I believed I had a mission to portray the "little man," whose feelings no one understood. Why were bosses always beating him? What did they gain from thwarting his happiness? The puppet's innocent yearning to be with the Ballerina opened my eyes to the fate of all dreamers. Everywhere I looked, they were being punched and pummeled.

The same fervor that produced Petrushka's love for the Ballerina also made him defenseless against the tyranny of those who controlled him. And the festival crowd to whom he pleads for help against the Blackamoor's pursuing saber treats him like a joke—just as my troubles prompted quips from my Maly colleagues. The rehearsals built up my love for the role and for the poetry of Petrushka's soul. The helpless puppet was a martyr to human feelings.

Late one afternoon I rushed from the Maly stage to an artist's studio to paint a portrait of Petrushka. It was finished in one burst, like a passionate passage onstage. I had never used oils before and could hardly hold a brush. Over the years I slowly learned to work with them, but nothing I would do was nearly as good as this portrait. Without professional training to lean on, my painting showed even more than my dancing how bad an artist I was when I forced myself. Only sheer desire to express my suffering through Petrushka's made him come alive. Eventually I learned to paint only when driven.

When *Petrushka* became what it did in Leningrad, the little Academy museum hung the portrait prominently—until it was ripped down one day in 1972. In the following years, when it seemed I'd never again dance *Petrushka*—or anything else—the painting became very important to me. But Madame Frangopolo refused my pleas for it, assuring me it would hang openly again one day. And even the Academy Director—a stiff Party member who had ordered, "Take that thing down!"—muttered, "And save it" under his breath. It was still my best painting. The role had remained my most beloved. One came from the other.

THE PREMIERE OF *Petrushka* was in May 1961. Each subsequent performance was a feast for my masochism. I would sit in the pantry called home, reconstructing every bit of bad luck I could dredge up. I worked myself into the Petrushka mood with diligent concentration, fusing my own mistreatment with its artistic exaggeration so that I actually believed my insults were as painful and potentially tragic—as the puppet's. I found grievous inspiration even in my domestic situation. I would convince myself that I was wholly alone in the world, and my self-pity sometimes grew so mighty that praise for my performances upset me. It proved that not even my followers understood my inner hurt but thought I was merely *acting*.

Petrushka's final curtain often fell on a tense silence. When I realized that the emotion of the final scene made applause difficult, this hushed interval was greater reward than the ensuing ovation. But I was totally oblivious to the audience on truly good evenings. I went straight to a large empty dressing room where I loved to rest and brood. The Maly had relatively few flowers and backstage visitors and little post-performance fuss. Only Liya was likely to appear with some juice, for in such things she was a constant support. Besides, the better I danced, the fonder she was of appearing alongside me in her best clothes.

Thoughts of my lucky breaks sometimes elbowed in among the reversals. But analysis of my just-completed performance pulled me back to the mood of the Wounded One. Newspapers were commending me. "Petrushka is pitiful, funny, but most of all, terrifying for his infinite despair," wrote one. And: "Although grotesque in form, Valery Panov's Petrushka is almost heroic. . . . It is less a puppet's wooden angularity and nervous jerkings that he displays than the excruciating pain and fury of a human being. I believe his is a new interpretation, at least in Russia, for he stresses not tragic predestination, but a burning protest *against* it." But the stronger the critical praise, the larger the lump in my throat.

Reliving the performance one evening, I realized how much I had improvised. But since I hadn't consciously worked them out, the snatches of choreography evaporated from my memory as fast as they came to me.

Soon I was taking time every evening to try to remember the best of them. The idea of a professional diary came from these attempts at reconstruction.

Everyone—even Alec and Liya, who agreed about nothing else—had been telling me for years that I must learn to control my feelings, not express them. Alec's worry was that outsiders would interpret my exaggerated gushings as simplemindedness. Liya's instinct was that my feelings themselves were shameful, and I would be destroyed if people knew about them. But when I did try to be more "grown-up" and discreet, my dancing immediately became constricted. This convinced me that a diary deserved to be kept despite the reasons against it—including my writing problem. With no hiding place from Liya at home or in the theater, I couldn't put down everything I thought. But I did grope toward the something I felt was trying to coach me to dance better.

November 22, night*

Rehearsed *The Lady and the Hooligan* with my heart in the work, which is tremendously important for me. In this mood I can review and revise meanings, as well as technical points, from the very beginning. Ideas for new movements—even whole new concepts—overwhelm me.

But I desperately need a true teacher to help me direct them. Someone to help me choose and shape what tumbles out of me. I dream of maturing enough to exercise this control myself one day, to lead myself toward *meaningful creativity*. . . . Meanwhile, I'm without the deeply cultured, truly wise choreographer I need to guide me.

November 23, night

Legs ached from the moment I got up. Yesterday's overload almost finished me. Still, forced myself to rehearse *Flowers* and *The Meeting*. The sweat paid off. At last I found the right movements for the end of the variation.

I like to recall every detail I can of the Balanchine tour. I loved the refined precision and the perfection of completed designs

---

* Night was after a performance. The year was 1962.

and then the meticulous finish that coated the creativity with a wonderful gloss. After his refreshing, dynamic outlook, everything strikes me completely differently.

I went to some Balanchine in New York but didn't really *see* anything. I kick myself for missing that great chance to learn. My seeing more now than three years ago means I'm growing—but how slowly! How badly I need *study!* Too little stimulation from people more sensitive than I keeps holding me back. Whenever I do meet someone like this, he immediately sharpens my eye for the insincerity and artificiality of my interpretations, especially in classical roles.

The hardest of all is doing classical variations with my "consciously interpretative" approach. Because I keep trying to go for the *meaning* of the whole rather than just stringing together a series of beautiful steps. But what's the meaning? That's where I need an artist's voice.

November 25, night

Very enthusiastic reception for *Flowers* performance: audience cheers from first appearance to final curtain. But it was all mediocre; I felt heavy. Fuzzy pirouettes at the end, inexcusable for me. The lesson is how dangerous losing control of your development is. How easily sham success can lead you away from control.

December 4

Paquita yesterday. Very severe classical conceptions, and my goal was to dance them with great purity, à la Balanchine. But am also trying to put in the life and interpretative content that the Americans lacked. Without this, their strict classical forms seemed methodical and dry, even pedantic.

Maybe I'm getting there. But the new trouble is failing technique. I just don't have enough strength after shaping *Hooligan* and *The Meeting* all day. I'm working all out on these new things even when I do *Paquita* the same evening. Very harmful, since *Paquita*'s classical movements mustn't be muddied with contrasting styles, especially *Hooligan*'s turbulence.

This is exactly what Kaplan shouted to Belsky [the Maly's Artistic Director] after the curtain: "That's not how the boy can dance when he's in full strength. He needs *rest*. He needs a reasonable performing schedule. It's your duty to supply one."

December 10

Danced the Pilot in *Flowers*. Was counting on my passable performance four days ago to carry me through, but this time I was disgraceful. First of all, I went on without rehearsing in the morning or properly warming up. Before my last Pilot, I worked myself into the mood, but yesterday's *Paquita* spoiled my concentration. I must stop trying to perform on consecutive days.

Even class is sad. My head leans to one side in pirouettes; my legs don't extend properly. I have no feeling of doing things *properly* or of the smoothness I yearn for. Kaplan's no help in establishing some kind of work priority. He can't remember himself as a performer, doesn't know when I should stop. His drive for me makes it even harder to get out of this overloading.

First of all, I must get up earlier to give my senses time really to wake up. Get everything mentally and physically prepared—like a tuned motor—for the day's work. Get myself in the *frame of mind* for making the right adjustments to gestures and movements.

It's essential to get the fundamentals right. To be scrupulously clean getting into "fifth" and starting battements tendus. This sets the pattern for everything all day. Above all, concentration must be absolute. Part of me still hates the dreary drills. But I'm absolutely nothing without them. Even the slightest cheating on the exercises breaks my concentration. This can lead to loss of control, the most damaging thing of all. If you don't overcome your tiredness, your end is in sight. Hollow success among your admirers may keep you on the stage a few years longer, but you'll be a dead man in terms of real ballet.

You'll tell yourself that "just a few things" aren't working for you and postpone your promise to pull yourself together "just until tomorrow." Tomorrow you'll pull a muscle, and you'll conveniently forget that without the basic steps you're pooh-poohing to yourself a dancer is gone. Even if he has the best imagination and highest artistic intentions in the world. To be a real dancer, the first criterion is what it always was: the fundamentals. Everything else follows from this. But in our fuzzy-wuzzy Maly, we concentrate on everything *except* the fundamentals. We're always rushing around, hunting for "effective" substitutes. No wonder our company sags. But what's my own answer? How can I pull myself up to the level I admire?

SEVERAL DAYS after the *Petrushka* premiere Rudolf Nureyev visited the Maly. He saw me rehearsing, waited until I was finished, and asked what had really happened to me in America and after. He listened very intently to my story, then went off on an important Kirov tour. Shortly after this, Soviet ballet suffered a humiliating defeat. Nureyev was gone for good. Still the brilliant individualist with the sometimes stunning bad manners, he acted on an impulse for self-protection. Soviet diplomats had taken him to the Paris airport. He was told that he too was to be sent home from a foreign tour, and my example of what that would mean to his career stared him in the face.

The first reaction of the Leningrad Party chiefs was to fire half the KGB watchdogs and their superiors. The witch-hunt was frenzied; *someone* had to pay for this unimaginable blow to Soviet prestige. It was only a pity that the Kirov Director had to pay with them. The Party's knee-jerk answer was to replace this tolerable man with a hard-line hack, certain to "intensify vigilance" and to crack down on the theater's "impermissible liberalism."

A surprise attack on a border garrison could not have caused more chaos and fright. One man's departure had shaken the whole hierarchy to its roots. When the KGB recovered from the shock, they organized a "trial" of Nureyev. Never mind that he was safe and happy in France. Measures had to be taken, lessons drilled home, and the collective intimidated. Everyone who had had anything to do with the missing man was grilled. Although he was full of years and honors, Nureyev's former Academy tutor, Alexander Pushkin, who had continued to develop him in the Kirov class for leading male dancers, bore the brunt of the fury. This saintly man suffered for all he had done for his star pupil and for ballet. The massive trauma taught the police only the wrong lessons. By bringing the worst of the system to the fore, they guaranteed repetitions of what they feared most.

Nureyev's behavior in Paris had been judged suspect. The more I found out about the special attention to him—from tour administrators and leering agents who had felt he was fraternizing too freely with Frenchmen—the more painfully my 1959 tour returned to me. His escape was a normal reaction to insupportable demands, but my suggestion of this in the Maly's dressing room produced only quizzical looks. All the others condemned him unequivocally.

Uncoached indignation sounded everywhere. Nureyev was a "turncoat," a "toady for dollars," and a "traitor to the motherland that had fed and created him." But what really frightened me was that only my own experience of why a man becomes suspect made the others' reaction appalling. Without this, I might have been mouthing something similar about Nureyev myself.

As it was, he did me a personal favor. By providing a more dramatic catchword for the perpetual campaign to keep everyone in line, he much reduced the "Remember what happened to Panov" whispers. The epithet *"Nureyev!"* now stood for everything potentially dangerous, from failure to meet a production plan to a wrong answer in a political exam. Only "fascist" was worse.

IN NOVEMBER 1962 a wall newspaper went up in the theater with a drawing of a huge pair of scales. The entire company was squeezed together in one pan. A caricature of me was in the other, which the weight of my bloated smile was breaking to pieces. The caption read:

> What matter what all the others feel,
> When Panov knows *he's* the big deal?

The widening gap between me and the other men was embarrassing. Much as the administration wanted to share out the premieres, it feared the risk and banked on me. But maybe because my illusions retarded me emotionally or because something in my nature required I be an underdog, I didn't *feel* like a genuine star. Besides, I knew my professional shortcomings better than anyone. But to "cope" with my social problems, I pretended they didn't exist. I posed as a self-contained young man who knew it all and was destined for the top. This adolescent affectation intensified the resentment of my success and pushed me further into my lonely predicament.

My rivals were more and more eager to put me in my place.

Pretexts for doing so were easy to find, especially since I so rarely ventured into the Maly's fields of extracurricular activities. Almost every day a meeting of one kind or another was held by a new or old "social" agency trying to make things run on the textbook diagram of "socialist communal life." I never attended nor volunteered for any of the civic-minded enterprises. Even if their purpose would not have been to invade privacy, undermine individuality, shape us all to a standard pattern, I had too little time.

I even asked to be relieved of certain ritual rigmarole because of my work load. I did not write a "little something" for the wall newspaper, did not tag after everyone on payday for Young Communist dues, did not serve time as a representative of the theater's Young Communist organization to its trade-union branch, which seemed a double waste of time since both organizations were slogan-pumping fronts. These lapses made me vulnerable. Political misbehavers were almost always sentenced, not for reading prohibited books or uttering impermissible comments, but for "stealing" or "dealing in foreign trinkets." Similarly, someone marked to be taken down a peg for reasons better left unmentioned was disciplined by jumping on his failures as a "member of the collective." There were so many theoretical obligations that *everyone* could be faulted; in my case, with satisfying ease.

As a measure of social correction, I was appointed a trade-union organizer. The collective's money got all mixed up with my own, and I blew the lot at the first opportunity. The real punishment was making up the deficit from my salary, which never lasted more than two weeks in the best of months.

EARLIER IN 1962 the Maly had had a brief Moscow tour to open the Kremlin's new Palace of Congresses for ballet. That trip had been for ironing out backstage bugs, and late in the same year we went back to the Palace as guinea pigs for Stravinsky's re-introduction to the capital. Our second tour coincided with the composer's first visit to Russia in fifty years.

I first saw him through a peephole in the curtain before it went up on *Petrushka*. Having heard he might be there, I looked toward a loge reserved for high cultural officials and state guests. To the left of this was an even more special one for government leaders. Like the Tsar's box in the Kirov, it remained empty if none came. But that evening everyone knew it was going to be occupied by Somebody. Plainclothesmen had surrounded the Palace, checking every handbag even at the stage door. As I peeped, a bent, little man with a nose as large as the rest of him entered the box on the right. The huge audience rose and cheered him for many minutes. The much less enthusiastic reaction to Nikita Khrushchev's entrance caused an awkward moment, until Khrushchev turned toward Stravinsky and clapped, hands raised high in his inimitable manner. Neatly slipping out of the embarrassing situation, he even won affection. Once again I felt he might unscramble my case if it ever got to him. Then I pulled back into the Petrushka mood.

At the final curtain the audience stamped their feet. The newspapers cheered. PANOV IS A BALLET EVENT ran one headline. I was described as a dancer of wide range, from *Bolero*'s strong character part to the pure classicism of *Paquita* and *Swan Lake*'s Prince Siegfried to the big bravado of the Pilot in *Flowers*. Most of all, the press wrote about my Petrushka, calling me the puppet-symbol's apotheosis.

The Maly's relatively meager promise was largely responsible. Expecting little, the critics were surprised by the strong dancer they saw. Besides, my style had greater appeal in Moscow, with its traditional love of the dramatic and flamboyant, than in more courtly Leningrad. This trip set a pattern of my being "recognized" far more in the capital than at home.

Stravinsky's reaction gave me more encouragement than anything. The master's first viewing of a Soviet production of a Stravinsky ballet put him in no mood to see a second one, but I escaped the sour verdict. "You have made two productions of *Petrushka*," he told his Ministry of Culture hosts. "One is Panov's powerful feeling for the part. The rest is simply mediocre." Serge Lifar, who was accompanying Stravinsky, said Nijinsky's Petrushka had used more mime, but mine worked because of the emotional impact. "Panov's technique is equal to his ability to move the audience," he said. "Compared to this, the rest is sugared water."

Khrushchev, too, passed a booming "I like it" on the performance. Later I heard that his wife went to most of my remaining performances on her own and spoke very warmly about them. This prompted congratulations from all kinds of formerly distant people. "It's all fixed, old boy. The Bolshoi will send for you; you'll soon be raking in foreign fame and fortune. . . ." But the supposedly monolithic bureaucracy was actually a tangle of agencies pursuing unrelated or contradictory policies, as when one organization striving to win friends for the country or develop scientific knowledge invited a foreign expert to lecture in Moscow and another stripped and searched him at the border, turning him into a determined *enemy* of the motherland. Without a specific order from Nikita Sergeyevich to strike me from the blacklist, Madame Khrushchev's appreciation led nowhere.

High on Stravinsky's comments, I resolved to throw all caution to the winds and somehow arrange to meet him. This was partly Alec's work. Still condescending about ballet—and therefore my future—he encouraged me to "spit on the degrading rules for getting ahead" and meet foreigners whenever I had a chance. This terrified Liya, who not only understood the rules, but cheered them. She sneered that *Alec* had no career to lose and was trying to drag me down to his senseless devotion to failure.

Liya was hardly alone in her caution. More than one Bolshoi leading lady, even of the world-famous variety, lived in constant fear of a chance encounter with a Westerner. If you suggested one, she would turn white and call you crazy. A telephone call from a well-intentioned New Yorker was a potential catastrophe. Some prayed theirs wouldn't ring. In any case, with Alec in Vilnius and Liya at my side, she prevailed. I went through the proper channels—starting with the Personnel Department—to request permission to call on Stravinsky. It was refused. I told our Party secretary that both Stravinsky and Lifar had said they'd like to meet me and pleaded that I would talk *only* about ballet. The answer held. While I was pondering how to proceed, a meeting happened by itself outside the old National Hotel, where the party from France was staying. Liya and I were hurrying past it one morning to a rehearsal in the nearby Palace. Suddenly Stravinsky's cane gingerly emerged from the triple doors. My heart beat furiously as we moved toward each other, his face chalky and his steps tentative. I was about to speak to the creator of "my" Petrushka, the man who best understood my Russia and my heart! Something wonderful had to come of it.

Liya's vigilance shot up like a gas flame. "What do you want now, to ruin *both* our lives?" she hissed. While she pulled me back a moment, Stravinsky was bundled into a limousine. I saw a piece of his hat brim as the big car sped off.

This took a little luster off the Moscow trip, but the few weeks there raised me a large notch in the opinion of the Leningrad establishment. I was advanced to the Maly's highest salary for a dancer and allowed the top fee for outside concerts. The opinion of one illustrious foreigner reversed the attitude of cultural officials who had seen nothing in me for years.

The company's hopes for good things after Stravinsky's and Khrushchev's approval were well grounded. By the end of the year we would be re-christened the Academic Maly Theater of Opera *and Ballet*, with an Order of Lenin for good measure. My personal award was Alec's head lifted in my direction. Much as he despised the Soviet press, the printed word always influenced him. And there it was in black and white: articles about his frivolous brother somehow involved with giant world figures such as Stravinsky, Lifar, and Fokine. *Petrushka* sparked his first intellectual curiosity about ballet.

20

OUR COUNTRY WAS STILL JERKING ITSELF OUT OF STALIN'S CULTURAL paralysis. Hard put to sustain themselves in the easier atmosphere, dram-ballets were expiring like dinosaurs. Together with the worst films about factories and collective farms, they had reached the end of their tolerability to enormously weary audiences. Young choreographers were warily trying new trends as replacements. These included Yuri Grigorovich, who had recently become a Kirov balletmaster and would later win international recognition with the Bolshoi, and Igor Belsky, my former teacher of character dancing, who had become the Maly's chief balletmaster. The failure fully to wash away the old rigidity and to allow these gifted men to realize their full potential is the story of all Soviet ballet after Stalin. The sponge bath swabbed off only the crudest ideological restrictions. But at the time progress seemed like a tidal wave.

The visit of the New York City Ballet in the autumn of 1962 came at just the right moment. The dazzling company propelled our young choreographers, therefore the whole of Soviet ballet, forward. The liberating effect of their two months in Russia could be appreciated only by those who knew the Soviet's resistance to change.

Balanchine's revelations were amazing. The paradox of a Russian émigré—for Balanchine was as culturally Russian as anyone in Leningrad, despite his Georgian birth—letting loose a revolution on his "revolutionary" homeland struck hard. We were the last supposedly developed country to recognize his genius, even though it was *our own* cultural heritage, as Russian as Stravinsky's music, that he brought home to us!

The company's impact began at the Leningrad airport, where the Kirov's Artistic Director was waiting. "Welcome to the homeland of the classical ballet," said Konstantin Sergeyev.

"No, the homeland of the classical ballet is New York," Balanchine answered. "Russia is the homeland of the romantic variety." This story flew around the city. We had believed with all our hearts what had always been at the core of our education: that the Soviet ballet was the only "true" one. Months before Balanchine arrived, the credo "Nothing is greater, nothing will ever be greater than the Russian classics" was chanted daily, as if in fear that the orphaned Russian company, now the handmaiden of New York money and bourgeois ideology, might subvert our faith.

This fear seemed wholly unnecessary since no one imagined that a foreign company could compete in beauty or significance to ours. We were the descendants of Marius Petipa and Alexander Gorsky, whose traditions we were faithfully carrying on in the masters' own city, ballet's world capital. For all its intriguing dash, New York, of course, produced something vulgar and inferior. Now Balanchine dared to claim that Soviet ballet represented only one part of the Russian tradition. Almost all our dancers had been brought up in the 1930s and 1940s, therefore knew nothing of the Russian trends murdered at home but still developing abroad.

The New Yorkers were given a secondary theater, making the crush for tickets even fiercer. For ten days they transported Leningrad into the 1960s. They performed Stravinsky's *Apollo* and *Agon*, Benjamin Britten's *Fanfare*, and *Prodigal Son* to Prokofiev's score. Ballets to Bach, Mozart, Weber, and Morton Gould were new enchantments.

Not everyone was thrilled. The conservatives who feared threats to established canons rejected the "empty stuff." But I was in the vanguard of Balanchine's worshipers. Despite Soviet ballet's splendrous staging and execution, I recognized it as heavy, solemn, and provincial. Stravinsky's importance also became clearer. He had written the most evocative ballet music of our time, an inspiration to contemporary choreography comparable to that of Adam, Delibes, and Tchaikovsky. This is what we were still deprived of, except for *Petrushka*. The claim that we were the only real ballet was Soviet romanticism's Maginot Line.

The tour was an enormous stimulus to everyone who wanted to explore. I myself could not borrow anything until I improved more. But the New York style would come to my mind every time I tried to work out a choreographic pattern to suit my temperament.

THE BALANCHINE "INNOVATION" that the Maly most quickly adopted was his extensive use of the one-act ballet. Soon we were rehearsing *The Firebird* and *Orpheus* to add to our Stravinsky repertoire. No one in Leningrad remembered any of the old productions of *Firebird*. In the end Slava Vlasov, the Bolshoi soloist and amateur photographer, rescued us from the puzzles of re-creating it from thin air. Our pattern was the *Firebird* of Britain's Royal Ballet, which he had filmed on a recent London trip. The problems of *Orpheus* were greater. Our veteran balletmasters tried to master the necessary approach by studying visiting Western troupes but were much too weighed down by rigid tradition. Every time I danced the leading role I felt how far we lagged behind in everything the twentieth century had brought to ballet.

I squeezed a session with Semyon Kaplan into every break in rehearsing our new and old productions. Although it floundered in interpreting *Orpheus*, his Academy-Kirov approach was magnificent for assigning the right duties to every bone and tendon. Perfect placement in every detail was the goal of the Russian school, and when my feet at last fell into place in some movements, Kaplan found grave fault with my arms. He showed how a tiny gesture of the wrist could convey a large emotion.

The most expressive wrists happened to be in Moscow then. First on my list whenever I went to watch the Bolshoi's performances was Maya Plisetskaya, whose arm movements came from some inherent genius, independent of any school. Her body was far from ideal, but she seemed to make it so in the studio. Her enthusiasms flashed out with her smile. She wanted to be an uninhibited child of nature, and this excitement radiated from her on and off the stage.

It was no task to watch Plisetskaya, but I learned to study everyone

I could in Moscow and Leningrad. I had the same instinct as anyone to criticize my rivals, but the very force of my competitive urge helped me control it. Realizing that only analysis of their strengths could help me acquire those I needed, I put my full endowment of jealousy to constructive use.

EARLY IN 1962 I sent new petitions to the Central Committee, to Nikita Khrushchev, to anyone who might end my ostracism. I could not continue working, I implored, unless my burden of unnamed guilt was lifted. *What had I done? Whose enemy was I?* A certain wistfulness tinged my appeals. They were like paper boats carried away by a forest stream.

"The Party doesn't make mistakes" was my comfort whenever *I* made the mistake of seeking it at home. Girls might have provided more consolation. I admired men who started down the Nevsky Prospekt with an announcement that a fine young thing would be on their arm by the end of the stroll. The miracle almost always happened, and the happy couple were on their way. But I simply didn't have the dash to carry this off. I was still attracted only to Princesses who made me sweat if I even thought of approaching their splendor. My Bolshoi friend Vladimir Vasiliev bemoaned the same problem every time we shared a bottle. "Valera, it's all for nothing. We just don't have those long 'ballet' legs, so that the ladies will never believe us when I tell them who we are."

My ache built up for the times when I danced myself as Petrushka. It gushed out—raw, yet puzzlingly joyful; a blessed opportunity for release through art—when the Ballerina, the symbol of the beauty that flashes into the little man's life, betrays him to the highest bidder.

One April evening I danced that very excerpt at a concert. To avoid the undercurrent of suspicion even at such "outside" performances, I warmed up alone in a dressing room. To enhance my own bewilderment, I thought about what such hostility might do to me. Then I went on.

A visiting Italian dramatic troupe had been invited to the performance. But I hadn't danced well partly because of the cramped stage. Alone again, I stared at Petrushka in the mirror, wondering how we had managed to find each other. I did not remove my makeup. The approaching babble of voices seemed to come from a warmer planet. Suddenly my door was flung open, and a cluster of chic, laughing people burst into my room. These were the Italian actors, a Florence company that had brought *The Diary of Anne Frank* to Russia.

The actress who stood out was a tall girl of about twenty-five with a Roman profile. Her black eyes blazed. She came forward, took my hand, and sang, "Bravo!" "Fantastico!" so many times that the others took up the chant. Her gaze told me that she had come to share my troubles. I looked around for someone to interpret. But we did not need help. Elvira refused to leave with the others. She was still staring into my eyes when we left the theater together.

Our knowledge of each other's language was perfectly matched—neither knew a word of it. But with each step we understood more about one another. Actually, it was she who was doing the understanding and I who was being understood. She knew all about the pain I'd been unable to express to anyone else. For good reasons, many Russians feel able to unburden themselves only to a passing foreigner. But her comprehension went beyond this. She seemed to say it was her duty to draw the hurt from me. While I released all I'd suppressed for years, she strained for every syllable, telling me with the squeeze of her fingers that it wasn't a fantasy: she *did* understand.

We followed a bank of the Neva to the Fortress of Peter and Paul. As the river lapped against the stone, Elvira's silent offer to bear everything with me brightened even the Neva's blackness. We didn't kiss but only kept walking. And shivered at our morning parting because the use of so much energy left none to resist the cold.

I called Elvira a few hours later. I said I must see her. I couldn't go to *her* room; our involvement was risky enough without that. I named the Hotel Astoria—a room belonging to a Pole named Voitek who was in Leningrad for advanced ballet training. Foreigners puzzled by Soviet life often chose me for a friend.

Handing me the key, Voitek repeated his grave doubt that Elvira could possibly have deciphered my directions. Fifteen minutes later there was a tremulous knock on the door. First there were tears: hers falling hot on my chest, mine on her hair. A single word—"Petrushka"— explained the boundless sympathy in her eyes. I offered her the champagne I'd bought on the way. But her brows asked why I didn't understand that alcohol could only sober us.

The day passed pronouncing *dolce, mia amore*, and *caro* in ever new intonations—a full language for us. I danced to show my gratitude to her. As the spring sun waned, she urged me to go to my evening performance. I asked her for a photograph. She opened her handbag, found her passport, and ripped out the first page.

Voitek told me that inquiries had already begun in his hotel. He begged me not to see her again; the KGB seemed very angry. In the morning he went to the railway station where Elvira's train was waiting to leave. She had stood on the platform, shouting that she must remain in Leningrad. Her troupe literally lifted her aboard when the last whistle sounded. I stared at her passport photograph. Her Latin eyes still penetrated mine, urging me to *talk*.

AN EXCITING NEW BALLET CALLED *The Lady and the Hooligan* was the Maly's treat that spring. It was based on the 1920s film written by Vladimir Mayakovsky, in which the rampaging poet himself appeared as the Hooligan. Shostakovich had provided an appropriate score.

My early work on the Hooligan was far weaker than that of two other contenders. Coaches tried to take the sting out of my failure, assuring me that "a boy" of my gentle upbringing couldn't be expected to make something real of the role of a semi-thug. They advised me to give up and concentrate on what suited me. Impressed by the others' progress and by the universal opinion that I was inherently wrong for the part, I did give it up.

But here was a chance to apply my homilies about studying rivals— in this case, Veniamin Zimin. My Hooligan gradually emerged from his strengths. After weeks submerged in his increasingly powerful interpretation, I knew what to try for. To everyone's skepticism, I plunged in again, first working with Kaplan on the dance movements themselves. As usual in the Maly, these were weak compared to the dramatic element. At the final audition, the selection panel gave me the premiere, and Hooligan became "my" second role after Petrushka.

Until recently most of the Maly's dramatic moments had grown out of revolutionary exploits. The "degenerate's" tale was a stunning success. At first appearance, my Hooligan was an utter ruffian, a product of his hangout of bandits, gamblers, and prostitutes in the time of postrevolutionary violence. I wanted to provoke not only laughter at his blustery bravado, but also frightened revulsion for his "incorrigible" criminal tendencies. When love at first sight for the Lady pierces this gangsterish shell, a great longing for gentleness emerges, transforming him into the innocent child he never was. Although the audience unconsciously knew what the only resolution to the conflict between the two incompatible selves had to be, the tragedy of the spiritually reborn man going straight to his death brought gasps. Briefly torn by competing emotions, the tough guy has become a love-struck puppy yearning only to be at his mistress' side. Mortally wounded, he inches up to take his leave of her. He is deeply distressed that she has to watch his unpretty end. All he hopes to do is to die with the sight of her in his eyes.

When the Hooligan apologizes, the spectators were transfixed. When the Lady bends to kiss him, most sobbed aloud. The kiss momentarily revives the dying man. He dances his grateful swan song with his last breath, then crawls to the forestage to transmit his joy to the world: the sublime happiness of a person who dies knowing his idol loves him. His smile as he expires put the audience in a kind of trance.

Mayakovsky's understanding of the easily wounded, deeply emotional being beneath the Hooligan's blustering aggressiveness moved me as much as anyone else. I had long been drawn to this intensely individualistic poet who stumbled to despair of the Revolution he had fought for and from there to suicide. And there was no need to draw diagrams for me about how young men strut around inside shells. Mayakovsky's most telling insight was that these were built to protect not only vulnerable feelings and an unused capacity for love, but also a supposedly cocky youth's secret dismay at his defects for coping with civilized society.

These associations did not by themselves take me closer to genuine art, but they again convinced me that only emotional involvement could. A group of genuine hooligans, attracted to the foreign territory of a theater by the title, approached me after one of the early performances. How did a square like me, they asked, manage to reproduce *their* gestures? I felt I'd made an enormous achievement with this thirtieth role in five years.

SHORTLY AFTER THE PREMIERE Konstantin Sergeyev and Natalia Dudinskaya visited the Maly to see my Hooligan and Petrushka for themselves. I had already danced them at command performances for leading members of the Party and their state guests, but this was my most distinguished audience.

Dudinskaya was a Kirov balletmistress and Vaganova's successor teaching the classe de perfection there. Stages and studios had permanently calloused her feet and her bleached blond hair had roots of gray. Altogether, she looked more like a harried housewife than a prima ballerina. But Sergeyev was immensely devoted to her as his constant helper and partner.

Sergeyev himself was a masterpiece of masculine grace. I remembered Niola's awe of him as her male idol and the Academy shivering when the paragon arrived to watch my graduation examination. His perfection began with his long, supple ballet proportions and flawless executions. Now, as the Kirov's Artistic Director, he was the living image of the lyrical roles he had graced for thirty years. His voice matched his silver locks. Backstage after the performance he said my dancing was impressive, but that I had better stop exhausting myself in marathons every third evening because "your resources might be needed in the Kirov Theater." This was pronounced with such perfect modulation that the implications remained hazy. He offered me his hand and fluently withdrew.

21

I CONGRATULATED MYSELF FOR NOT GIVING IN TO FALSE HOPE. THE categorical "no" that Sergeyev received from various cultural offices indicated that transfer from a lesser theater to the Kirov was disliked as much as ever. He had little influence with the bureaucrats who could order an audition for me. Even if I was granted one, political blackball would keep me from getting any further than I had when the Bolshoi accepted me.

Meanwhile, I rehearsed furiously with Alla Shelest, who had asked me to partner her in two Moscow concerts she had been granted permission to give. Shelest was of Dudinskaya's generation, with an equally dizzying reputation as one of the great Soviet primas. Her help in developing Nureyev's gifts in the Kirov gave an extra boost to the honor of her unexpected invitation.

It was only a pity that I was rehearsing not with the brilliantly inventive ballerina herself, but with the remnants of her glory. Her pelvis bones had pushed up toward her armpits with the years, and her energy had waned along with her flexibility. I wondered how she would be able to cope with our extended recitals.

Ignoring everyone, she would seek flattering positions for her failing limbs, then press up against a studio mirror to whistle coded words of confidence to herself. Long soliloquies with her insteps and wrists preceded every new combination. She would travel to some distant place this way, then spin back to me with an authoritative "Fine! Let's continue." I saw her mental wavering as the privilege, or even the product, of great talent, but later realized that years of terrible pressures had caused it. A strong individualist in her art and personal life, she would not take her "proper" place in the Kirov's magnificent scheme of things.

Despite her age and mannerisms, Shelest immediately showed her powerful, intensely personal vision, that rarest ballet gift. If the circumstances had been right for her, she would have been even more important, to the degree that she was more profound in her every role, than Ulanova. She was the model for younger ballerinas of great dramatic force, including Maya Plisetskaya. This made the atmosphere surrounding our rehearsals even more puzzling.

Natalia Dudinskaya began by peeking into our studio to see what Shelest was up to. She found me alone one day and gravely implied that the recitals could do me no good, especially since I actually did have a chance at the Kirov. "Believe me, you're foolish even to be seen on the stage with her." When I hinted about this to Shelest, she sent a frightening laugh into the mirror. "Of course," she said. "They'll stop at nothing to ruin my concert. The whole company, they *must* destroy me."

The "whole company" didn't seem to *me* to be trying to deprive Shelest of the honor of a personal appearance in the capital. Certainly Sergeyev himself was too immersed in the Kirov's artistic concerns to pay real attention to anything outside his theater. But somebody was doing something to interfere, and surely this must have been Dudinskaya. Her rivalry with Shelest went beyond what might be expected for performers so close in age and parallel in achievements. And her gusto for demolishing real or imagined challenges to her position probably caused her to exaggerate the importance of Shelest's "independent" venture. Partner after potential partner was assigned to Kirov performances on the Moscow dates, making them unavailable to Shelest—

and leaving only non-Kirov me for her. As we approached the dress rehearsal, these obstacles turned her from a nervous woman to a nervous wreck.

This was my introduction to the intrigues that flourished on the scale of the Kirov itself, partly just because of its grandeur. But I understood nothing. I couldn't imagine what to make of the buzzing in my ear from artists I had worshiped for years. And Liya's repeated "You *must not* spoil this chance to move ahead" came with no specific advice about how to avoid some great mistake.

My wife had come to take command of me again. I'd continued living apart from her for a week after Elvira left. When Liya found me, she started by reminding me how inadequate I was for coping with real life. In fact, it was easier to believe I couldn't do without her than to go pay the electric bill myself, or remember what political lectures I mustn't miss. Besides, she had all the money—which she always managed, together with our domestic affairs. I said that we'd better think things over. She casually mentioned the pack of men who were lusting after her. Liya knew that my youth compared to the age of my potential rivals made me want to butt against them like an unproven stag; that the one humiliation I couldn't stand was someone else touching her. Sexually, she was more desirable than ever. I followed her home.

My thinking about my professional choices was just as feeble. I could only see that the "impossible" and "crazy" labels stuck onto Shelest were unfairly exaggerated—but not even she, with her greatness, could remove them. In the end, I stayed with her out of simple embarrassment, or stubbornness. And even despite Shelest's occasional lapses on stage, her recitals were a triumph. Moscow seemed eager to give her the recognition that hometown intrigues had long deprived her of in Leningrad. Each number earned her half a dozen bouquets. By the last one, the stage was dappled with petals, one of which I slipped on the first evening, landing flat on my back.

Afterward, Ulanova came backstage to congratulate Shelest. Although she seemed much like her extremely modest stage heroines, I wondered whether this might be a pose that had become second nature. Something told me that she was someone to be careful with—even feared if she considered you an interference. "See?" she said. "You fell and your public loved you even more for it. You've had another Moscow triumph." But I detected that she was being patronizing in her outwardly friendly remarks. Plisetskaya was also there to rejoice with Shelest, her stage prototype. She showed Shelest genuine respect and affection, and although some of her questions made me squirm, I felt more comfortable with her brazenness than with Ulanova's famed gentility.

ONLY THE KIROV'S UNUSUAL NEED explained Sergeyev's success with the cultural administrators. Ordinarily, nothing I did or did not achieve in the Maly would have meant more to them than, say, Martha Graham's plans. With rare exceptions, the Kirov's soloists were still picked years before as Academy youngsters, then finished on the conveyor belt between the two institutions according to the requirements of The Plan. But the infamous Nureyev had sabotaged the gears. The Kirov had revived several major ballets largely as vehicles for him. No dancer had enough strength to fill the gap he left in heroic roles. Then a series of accidents plagued the knees and ankles of my former classmates who came closest. Some of the most popular productions—*Don Quixote, Laurencia, La Bayadère*—were without a male lead.

This combination of circumstances overcame the theater's reluctance to look "outside" for a replacement. Even so, no one would have glanced at the Maly had it not been for the happy accidents of Stravinsky's visit following on my success in *Petrushka*. The composer's offhand remarks had turned some Kirov eyes toward me, and the Maly's Moscow tours also brought me more attention than anything I was doing half a mile away from the Kirov. All in all, I was pronounced worthy of a tryout.

It was to be as Basilio in a Kirov performance of *Don Quixote*. The Maly's summer vacation began in late May 1963. I had a month to prepare, and the fervor of Kaplan—who had danced Basilio a hundred times in the same Kirov—to help me.

My partner was Gabriella Komleva, Dudinskaya's favorite in her class of leading female soloists. Komleva was my age—and a stage opposite. Emotion seemed to frighten her, but her academic excellence showed me up as a bowlegged amateur. Sloppiness that went almost unnoticed at the Maly stuck out badly next to her perfection. My legs were insufficiently extended, insteps tended to be pigeon-toed, arms slanted off in irrelevant directions. The raw strength and energy were there for the most demanding solo roles. But my strong leap and sturdy technique in pirouettes and air turns counted for little without the famed Kirov refinement. How far I was from the great theater's tradition and from my own wish to express deep emotion, which could never be achieved without Komleva's control!

Although Kaplan knew every movement by heart and demonstrated a thousand times what the Kirov expected, I couldn't get an insight into the role as a whole from him. On the contrary, the enormous attention to polishing individual steps *prevented* me from getting into the character. The Kirov's one truly inspired Basilio had been Vakhtang Chaboukiani, whom I'd tried to copy when I was an Academy pupil. But Chaboukiani—who was to heroic and demi-character roles what Sergeyev was to lyric—had left Leningrad long ago to direct his own Tbilisi theater.

The day of the performance passed in a protective haze. But just before my first entry, everything felt totally new. It struck me that I was about to dance a leading role in *the Kirov Theater*, for the first and surely the last time. The stage suddenly seemed different: spacious as ever compared to the Maly's, but now also cozy. The lavish costuming of the extras in all their numbers was the final opulent touch. In addition to the huge orchestra in its pit, a chamber ensemble was playing in the wings. And these were all accessories for me! The extravagance made me too drunk for stage fright.

As the old Maryinsky Theater had been the favorite of the Romanovs, the renamed Kirov was the darling of the Party elite. That evening the foreign statesmen who were there to crown their visits were hosted by power-loving Vasily Tolstikov himself, the First Secretary of the Leningrad Communist Party. People called him "the Tsar"—in whispers. He ruled Leningrad as if it were his personal fief. Although his suspicion of "culture" was renowned even among Party authoritarians, the splashy *Don Quixote* got through to him. Sitting in the former imperial box, he allowed himself an expression of pleasure at the rich spectacle before him. "You've got some okay boys working here," he breathed during the curtain calls. He pointed a stubby finger toward me. "Who's that one over there?"

No one in his entourage dared suggest that the dancer he had singled out was not a member of "his" theater but was only there for a quick examination, before being dispatched forever. The reaction of the directorate was now only a formality. As the Tsar was being helped on with his coat, I was a Kirov soloist.

Liya rushed back to see me, already cooing with the prestige of a Kirov husband. She was now prepared to tell the entire city that I was its most promising dancer. Sergeyev entered next with Pyotr Rachinsky, the Kirov's Director—and Tolstikov's underling. Rachinsky's grunt that I'd pleased "certain high guests" of the theater confirmed that everything had been decided.

I was told that Rachinsky wore a condescending smile when the Kirov's supposedly sovereign Artistic Council, the body empowered to appoint new members of the company, met the next day. In the Party's own theater, the "decision of the collective"—even of the directors—meant even less than in the Maly. Questions here about why something was being done one way rather than another were often answered with a finger pointed "above."

Tolstikov's comment also put a quick end to the Maly's efforts to keep me. The official who seemed most upset at my leaving was the First Secretary of the city district that encompassed the Maly, a woman who had been truly dismayed by the official failure to answer what my "crime" was. She backed the Maly's request that I leave gradually during the next year. This would give other dancers time to work on the ballets that sold the most tickets.

The last Kirov performances that season seemed glorious in ways I'd never noticed before. Every scene was polished to a perfection undreamed of elsewhere. But more than in exquisiteness of style, the Kirov differed from the Maly because of its unwritten law that every performance was a holiday. I saw soloists putting on their costumes and walking toward the stage in a mood that matched the grandeur of the setting. Despite my backdoor entry, despite my misgivings about what I lacked to be a principal there, I set out for my summer vacation bursting with gratitude for being taken into this home of all that was best in ballet.

22

THE BLACK SEA TOWN WHERE LIYA AND I VACATIONED WAS A WELL-known stamping ground for members of Moscow and Leningrad artistic circles. We soon ran into a leading Kirov ballerina who had been touring Afghanistan with a small brigade while I was rehearsing for my tryout.

Kaleria Fedicheva was a taller, darker, more vulgar version of Liya. Her blazing temperament made her best in highly dramatic roles. Party officials loved her for them and for her sultry good looks and her friendly sauciness. She loved parties, was a big spender, and wasted no time on books. Her sauntering around the little resort town reminded me that she had left the Academy for a time when she was a young girl because she felt she wasn't getting the attention she deserved. Her eyes flashed, and her large-boned body strained at her halter and shorts.

Her openhearted smile welcomed me to the beach. She mentioned that her father was an old Party friend of Director Rachinsky's, but Kirov gossip had centered on a different connection between herself and Rachinsky. Everyone talked about her steep rise immediately after his appointment. She had been twenty-six then, past the age when great things were expected of her. But she suddenly emerged as a new star, leaving behind younger girls such as Natalia Makarova and Alla Sizova who had been ahead of her in every way. In two seasons she had overtaken every other ballerina in performances and awards.

"How awful that I wasn't in Leningrad for your tryout and you had to do it with that frog Komleva," she said in the same breath as congratulating me. "Never mind, everything's going to be wonderful. The Director will do whatever I want . . . so it's all decided: we'll be partners—an unbeatable team!"

I took a long swim and tried to figure out what was on her mind. The ballets for which the Kirov wanted me were the ones containing her best roles. It would be a blow for her if I were paired with Komleva or another of the younger ballerinas. But I sensed something more than just a proposal to work together. Her verve excited me.

She went out of her way to be friendly to Liya and to demonstrate that her interest in me was strictly professional. But Liya couldn't control her jealousy any more than Fedicheva could suppress her appetite for mischief. If she liked someone—usually a man—it had to be fully. She could switch to equally strong dislike in a minute. Forceful feelings and uninhibited reactions were too rare among us. It was more than just working with a ballerina of great temperament and physical strength I was looking forward to.

AFTER THE SUMMER OF SUN AND SEA I entered the Kirov as if it were a cathedral of art. The near-holy faithfulness to the imperial era, when it had been the center of world ballet, was striking. Tiny alterations had been made during restoration after the Second World War's bomb damage, but in the fall of 1963 the building looked almost exactly as it had a century before. It still conveyed a sense of royal grandeur and space despite its relatively small seating capacity of two thousand. The color scheme was the same noble azure and gold. Chaliapin said he never saw a more beautiful theater in all his world travels.

In the best imperial days the ballet company consisted of two hundred dancers. Apart from the thirty or so extras and the fifty Academy pupils who could be supplied when necessary, two hundred was the present complement. The season used to open with Glinka's opera *A Life for the Tsar*. This year the offering was *Ivan Susanin*—the same opera renamed. The nineteenth-century tsars had treated their beloved Maryinsky Theater as an adjunct of their court, lavishing on it a million gold rubles from their private purses. The Party leaders lovingly preserved this arch symbol of class privilege, largely for themselves.

The changes that had been made, such as the addition of two dozen bookkeepers, were in keeping with Soviet bureaucratic procedures. While the size of the company itself remained constant, the supporting and administrative staffs multiplied into a giant enterprise of fifteen hundred people, only slightly smaller than the Bolshoi. Metal fabrication, carpentry, and special effects were designed and produced in superbly equipped workshops. Fifteen men served in the props department alone, and more put together the sets and decor. An army of assistant directors worked in the wings at each performance, including one nervous man whose sole task was to dash around, urging everyone not to be late.

Since the catering department was subordinate to the one that served the Party elite, the "crumbs from the barons' table" in our cafeteria were delicious and cheap. Each soloist had his own dressing room, which came with semiprivate makeup man, costumers, and wardrobe mistresses. A brigade of dentists, doctors, surgeons, osteopaths, physiotherapists, and venereologists looked after us, and a detachment of gynecologists attended to the ballerinas as if each monthly period were an affair of state.

All this pampering constantly reminded us that we were the elite's special pets, just as dancers in tsarist days had been. Access to rest homes and other vacation places was easy, and a Kirov artist was one of the few who could obtain materials to build his own country place. Everything confirmed us as the descendants of St. Petersburg dancers and choreographers who were still classical ballet's greatest inspiration throughout the world. Even the sometimes rigid reverence for the past was uplifting; Karsavina, Pavlova, Nijinsky, Fokine, Spessivtseva, Ulanova, Semyonova, and others seemed to drift in and out of the studios and corridors. Ballet here simply had to be performed and loved as nowhere else.

But the cynicism seeping into the theater from under the Director's door was poison. Personal rivalries and plotting for advantage were far more important than in the Maly because of the "imperial" theater's relationship to the givers of privilege at the political top. There were constant whispers about catching the eye of those who could influence selection for roles and for trips abroad. I couldn't avoid them because I was indeed put to partnership with Kaleria Fedicheva, as she'd planned. The whispers swelled every time she passed.

I could hardly believe her influence. It was all so depressing and repugnant, especially when I sensed that I was supposed to participate in courting her. The fault wasn't really Fedicheva's. She wanted no more than many other women with her ambitious energy. She could have been a splendid member of the company, her generous Russian nature providing much cheer. She knew how to be a ballerina, but Rachinsky of the piglet eyes had no idea of how to be a Director.

Although "happily" married as a good Party boss must be, he brandished his favoritism, partly by ignoring all other ballerinas. She was the example of artistic excellence cited to everyone, and often to her own disadvantage, for he kept pushing her into roles she wasn't suited for. Her long arms, large step, and powerful jump made her a striking heroine in flashy roles—especially as *Don Quixote*'s Kitri— but Makarova and Komleva were much better in everything requiring delicacy.

When important guests were present, Rachinsky played the happy host from his box. Otherwise, his blank face cast gloom all around him. After the curtain he would go backstage to congratulate his pet—and demonstratively to ignore all others. A dancer passed without a glance after some stage lapse was made to feel that the best he could hope for was a dismissal notice rather than a firing squad.

A film of dirt everywhere coated the greatness and glory. Yet I had less right to feel disappointed than others—not only as the newcomer, but also as a beneficiary of Fedicheva's influence. She speeded and smoothed the transfer of Semyon Kaplan back to the Kirov so that there was hardly a break in our work together. Kaplan was like a coach who had been developing an athlete for many years. On the afternoon before a performance—which was as crucial to the Kirov as a big game to a football team—he could measure the effect of personal problems and of the weather on my muscles and therefore prepare me with suitable exercises. He started each day's private session with work to match my mood. I needed his coaching—and his photographic ballet memory of the best Kirov stars in my roles—more than ever.

As my partner, Fedicheva had a vested interest in recruiting Kaplan from the Maly. But purely personal kindness entered when she visited me at home. The toilet noises, communal kitchen's curses, and lack of space for Andrei distressed her, and she informed Rachinsky that I needed to live where rest and concentration were possible. For six years I'd been applying for refuge from the joys of communal living. Now I was quickly assigned a self-contained apartment, and a supply of ballet shoes came with the three whole rooms because Fedicheva had seen me mending mine. Soon Liya, her mother, Andrei, and I were settled in a recently completed apartment building on Cosmonaut Street. The majestic new quarters gave us space enough for several full steps without bumping into something, and I could close the door on my mother-in-law!

Fedicheva was more than friendly in the theater, too. Her Black Sea talk hadn't been idle. She worked to establish what she considered my rightful place in the company, opposite her. I continued as Basilio in *Don Quixote*, but with her as Kitri. Her emotional interpretation helped me with mine, and her whispers to Rachinsky helped ensure my immediate appointment to Frondoso in *Laurencia*, the Blue Bird in *The Sleeping Beauty*, and the Water God in *The Little Humpbacked Horse*. In the spring Solor in *La Bayadère*, Mercutio in *Romeo and Juliet*, and the Man in *The Distant Planet* were added. Fedicheva even guaranteed me that my foreign travel ban would be lifted just as soon as she had time to brief Rachinsky properly. "The main thing is that we're partners," she assured me. "The rest will fall into place. Believe me, it won't cost anything to get your whole mess straightened out."

In a way, it already was. The Director considered me the most promising male dancer. When he put stacks of postcard-type photographs of me on sale, I had a moment of disbelief, remembering my mother buying similar ones of Sergeyev, Chaboukiani, and Kaplan all those years ago.

What was wrong? Fedicheva championed me in the same way she

pushed herself forward everywhere. She tried to cement our partnership by comparing me too favorably to other male dancers. And her travel promises—"You name the country, anywhere you want to go"—could sound like someone indulging someone else's weak points. Unwilling to admit how much my shining fortune depended on the light in the Director's eyes, I shifted my irritation to *her*.

Besides, I sensed she wouldn't stop at making me her permanent partner and her personal admirer. This would not be enough for her. It seemed that Rachinsky made her feel she *had* to take whatever she wanted since everything was there for the asking. Once in possession of the something new she'd always needed, she moved to the next item, with no time to enjoy either.

This drive thrust me far over my head into dangerous situations. Before I knew it, I was being recruited into longstanding Kirov feuds. Dudinskaya felt I owed everything to Sergeyev, not to Fedicheva—and with good reason. After bringing me to the Kirov, he was extremely gracious to me and thoughtfully supervised my approach to new roles. Sergeyev and Dudinskaya wanted me paired with the meticulous young Komleva, who danced the same roles as Fedicheva.

Traditionally, the Director took no part in such matters, which were the Artistic Director's province. But Rachinsky used all his powers against Komleva. As Fedicheva's rival, he hated her. He opposed almost everything else supported by Sergeyev, his antithesis in all matters. As the friction between the Director and Artistic Director intensified, Fedicheva urged me to speak up. "This is your chance," she lectured. "And for my part, I'll see to it that Sergeyev's dropped. He spoils everything anyway."

If it was true, as Fedicheva insisted, that Sergeyev was helping mummify Soviet ballet, I had to fight against him and toward the freedom of nontraditional roles. But for once in my life, I did not jump in feet first. Thank God, some intuition told me not to conspire against the old-fashioned master.

Nothing deeper than Sergeyev's personal bearing held me back. The electrician's son still had the blunt features of the Russian peasantry, but exquisite gestures and manner gave him a princely refinement, as if his intense work to acquire breeding for his roles had taken complete control of his life. In street clothes he was still the "Greatest Tenor of Soviet Ballet." Although he was my stage opposite, the crude talk of eliminating this paragon of lyrical excellence unnerved me.

It was enough to see how the two sides fought to know which possessed the elevated behavior associated with our art. While the anti-Sergeyev faction schemed, he so remained his genteel self that they couldn't believe this was sincere and labeled it tricky tactics, just as they called him a homosexual because of his "excess" refinement. Apart from an occasional polite suggestion to Rachinsky about artistic points, Sergeyev seemed oblivious to the plotting and lies about him.

Fedicheva's remarks about Sergeyev were among many that stung me—a certain sign that I was frightened. Like Liya, she was a stronger person than I. Her powerful influence combined with her greater maturity as a dancer could dominate me. A grown man would have found an inoffensive way out. Somewhere I decided I must also proclaim my independence while doing it, like the self-indulgent, grievance-nursing child I was. When the time came, I'd show her what I thought of her, no matter how I might bruise *her* feelings in turn. Because I knew she attracted me as a woman, I'd make sure to offend any sexual interest she might feel for me. And because she was almost the Directress, I'd add a gratuitous insult or two, just to demonstrate that I was above such considerations. It was as if I sensed I could develop only through hardship and struggle, and set about producing the necessary atmosphere for myself.

THE COMPANY'S SEVENTY MEN needed little encouragement to provide the hostility so necessary to me. Some coldness toward the first soloist taken from another theater in so many years was inevitable. Like certain exclusive schools of the old regime, the closed Kirov was permeated with archsnobbery and smug conservatism. Since the age of eight, the dancers had been reared with faith in the Academy's Plan and in their own superiority. It was just too much that the Maly upstart had been whisked from under his black cloud to leading roles they had been eyeing for years.

Disparaging the odd newcomer seemed to boost their self-esteem, and the Kirov's ancient customs permitted them to feel righteous doing so. I made everything easy for them. Somewhere I knew I was as rough compared to the Kirov soloists as when we had all left the Academy, but guilt-spurred vanity had forbidden me to acknowledge myself as their inferior while I starred in the Maly. I was a principal, too, and pretended we were equal.

Now I produced the same saunter that had served me so badly then. To protect myself from their haughtiness, I assumed the pose of a cocky young man whose body was invincible; everything else was a mere trifle. The more Kirov classes and rehearsals I saw, the thicker my camouflage became, for the clearer my defects were. None of this increased my popularity very much.

One October day I was rehearsing *Laurencia*'s most difficult variation. Kaplan and I had restored some Chaboukiani steps—double cabrioles forward and back along a diagonal—that had been dropped when he stopped dancing. Since visitors and corps dancers in the studio had applauded everyone else in the cast, I anticipated an ovation for my feat. Instead, Sergeyev's polite clapping and Kaplan's triumphant chortle echoed in a dismaying silence.

The others had resolved to shoot down my smirk. I was determined to win their admiration. I would do it with the most difficult, expressive movements Kaplan and I had devised when we were largely on our own in previous years. During the following weeks I tried them in the studios and even onstage. This drove me into my first head-on collision with the Kirov's rigidity. I was forbidden to change a thing—not the placement of the fingers, not the angle of my head—from "the way we do it here."

Trying to regain my slipping position, I could only think to move farther in the wrong direction. I fired shot after daring shot from my arsenal of bravura steps. My body was inexhaustible; my naked technique, almost astounding. I was more impressive than ever in leaps and twists in the air that produced audience gasps—and weaker than ever in presenting them properly. Every device I tried to conceal this only drove me away from the Kirov finish and closer to panic. Rachinsky still loved me because Fedicheva still needed me, but in the shaping, fitting, polishing, and use of bodily positions—that is, in everything that made up the essence of the Kirov—I deserved the company's disdain. I couldn't convince even myself that it all derived from jealousy of an outsider.

Instead of delivering me from my troubles, my transfer to the Kirov threatened to break me. The company began calling me a "trickster" and a "stunt man." If only the whisperers had known how I despised my showy striving for effects! If only they had understood how unhappy I was!

23

Toward the end of 1963 Sergeyev had revived a century-old
ballet called *The Little Humpbacked Horse*. Everyone knew it for the
Water God variation, one of the most difficult in the male repertoire.
Near the end of this grueling test of technique and strength, the
Water God advances from the rear to the front of the stage in a devilish
combination of movements based on a double turn in the air, performed
three times. The near-impossible design is repeated thrice, making
eighteen turns in all.

When I was assigned the role, Yuri Soloviev was performing it as
well as anyone could. This was the same straw-haired Soloviev who
could have danced with a head of papier-mâché because his body was
perfect. Just my age, he had Nijinsky's legs and a farmhand's smile. His
face was as flat as a pancake awaiting its sour cream and completed the
picture of a typical Russian peasant lad, although he was the nearest
thing to the Kirov's leading male. He was one of the few who welcomed me.

Soloviev was tentative in everything requiring interpretation, but
he then had the greatest elevation in the world and a fantastic plié. He
took off like a jet and stayed aloft like a dirigible, sucking the audience's
breath away. And since the Water God's crucial requirement was not
collapsing during the variation's fiendish last moments, his mastery of
the jumps made competition seem useless.

Kaplan practiced with me until I couldn't move. I was relieved that
I could exploit my resources to their limit and also refine my technique.
The satisfaction of accomplishment had been very rare since the summer.
Now my body promised that it had potential for further development.

But despite some progress in doing the hardest passages *cleanly*,
the variation in six-eighths time continued to lick me. In my second
performance I wobbled with exhaustion after landing—supposedly hero-
ically—with a wilted back to the audience. During my solemn reprimand
for this I secretly rejoiced that I hadn't done worse.

Soloviev and I divided the ten performances of *The Little Humpbacked Horse* that season. Two of mine were disasters that had me

praying I wouldn't collapse. Both had been preceded by a Maly performance the previous evening (I was still phasing out of their repertoire) and followed by something the next day at the Kirov. The Kirov's maximum of six or seven major roles a month began to make sense. A soloist might have the physical energy to appear more often, but not the total concentration needed to marshal all his strength.

Oddly, good feeling for me in the Maly had shot up from the day the Kirov took me. The sharp contrast with the Kirov's attitude to me made a welcome refuge, but my new work simply couldn't support the interference. Regretfully, I withdrew entirely from the Maly. As it was, my rawness kept me in classes and practice longer than anyone. Besides, I'd learned that my mistakes on the stage, down to the smallest lapses, were being added up as with no one else in the company.

FEDICHEVA'S REPERTOIRE made unusual demands on her partner, and her great fear, which probably accounted for her original interest in me, was that her big-boned weight would lose her performances. The strain on a permanent partner was particularly severe, and she was relatively indifferent to her cavaliers' difficulties and anxieties. Maybe she hid her worry about her weight under studied nonchalance. In any case, the final delight was her occasional insistence on three or four more tours of the stage over her humbled suitor's head before he could rest. The hernia I was developing was serious enough to merit discussion about an operation later in the spring.

Early in 1964 we rehearsed *La Bayadère*. Weary of Fedicheva's demands that I oppose Sergeyev, I complained to someone backstage about "her goddamn clumsy bulk." My life in the Kirov turned miserable from the next day. In two seconds Rachinsky went from my protector to the marshal of the attack on me.

Fedicheva continued working with me through gritted teeth until she could find a replacement. For May Day we danced a pas de deux for high officials and their guests. All went well until she made a last spin on her toes and went into an arabesque. In this position, I was to lift her from my own plié and bear her to our exit, a difficult maneuver even with a lighter partner. But one of us misjudged a step, and Fedicheva left the stage not triumphantly airborne, but trying to pull up from what looked like a flypaper on my chest.

Even that evening's audience couldn't miss the disaster. And it was the Party royalty, above all, the givers of the subsidies and titles, whom Fedicheva wanted to impress. In the wings she shouted a furious accusation that I had purposely missed the lift in order to disgrace her. I fought back by putting everything I had into my solo variation, which served as her and Rachinsky's final proof of my treachery. The next day my photographs were removed from the kiosks, no doubt for burning.

"What a fool I was to have done so much for you," Fedicheva seethed. Her anger drove her to one excess. In implying to her friends that I was a homosexual, she failed to reckon with Comrade Panova. As an old Young Communist hand Liya knew how to counterattack through Soviet organizations. The whispers reached her with the speed of light. My loyal wife charged to the Party office and demanded that the spreader of stories account for herself. Recognizing a potentially damaging case of slander, Fedicheva's agent produced a letter of apology, while Rachinsky took measures to stop the talk.

Fedicheva's scythe had struck Panova's stone, but nothing stopped it in the Kirov itself. Two weeks after my "clumsy bulk" comment Rachinsky informed the Artistic Council that something had to be done about me. "We made a grave mistake accepting Panov. Let's get him back to where he belongs before he lowers the tone of our work." His patronage had pulled me up too high, too fast. Now I fell correspondingly.

The worst was that Fedicheva had been right to take offense at my remark, which I must have known would be passed on to her. I *was* a little boy, just as she now called me. An adult man would never have abused a woman who had befriended him. Knowing what would pain her most, I pressed on her sore point about weight. Knowing my attraction for her, I played the adolescent pretense that I was above such things—and insulted her to a stagehand.

Soon after the event I saw her glaring at me between rehearsals. Shame for the way I had "liberated" myself from her had continually been close to the surface. The impetuous woman had always been generous to me. The least I could do was apologize.

"I'm sorry," I said, approaching her. "I hope you can forget that stupidity one day."

Her black eyes widened with anger. "So at last you've got the picture about how things work around here," she stormed.

Perhaps she assumed that only fear for my career could have made me swallow my pride. This would only (slightly) increase her contempt for me. Rachinsky warmed to the task of getting rid of me. "Panov just hasn't got the stuff," he pronounced everywhere. "Panov lacks a Kirov repertoire. Panov is a mistake."

Pyotr Rachinsky was a typical manager of Soviet culture. His model was probably Zaren Vartanyan who, as chief of all Soviet musical theaters, was his boss. The principal qualification of these bureaucrats was being one of the boys, and shared hostility to everything "un-Russian" is what really made them at home with one another. They were all *anti*-intellectual, *anti*-Semitic, *anti*-Western—and *anti*-art, since they saw art as a Party instrument for moving the nation toward its goals. And because the Party was actually the Party *members*, they personally chose the goals and used all art as they pleased.

Rachinsky's type staffed all the Party's upper-middle levels. They could be in charge of a mine one day and of an orchestra the next. They kept their status, no matter what. One of them could be found mis-managing—or stealing from—his factory. A fuss might be made, but six months later he would be the Party boss of an agronomy institute or a publishing house. His enterprise could come crashing down around his head, but while others were exiled, he would be tapped for the next promotion. Protected by cronies and by a reluctance to admit that the Party's trust had been awarded to someone unworthy of it, he steadily advanced. Loyalty to the gang was the chief criterion.

Rachinsky's career had begun as a member of the Leningrad Conservatory's fire brigade. He still blustered indignantly when a cigarette was dropped into a pail not specified for such purpose by fire regulations. He and his Party friends came from just that stock favored by Soviet rule. Deciding to advance himself in the field he knew best from his watchman's work, he enrolled for a course on cultural subjects. From there he was sent on to a Higher Party School, essential training for the Party's general staff. After a spell in the bureau that supervised Leningrad's cultural activities, he was made overseer of the city's publishing houses. A scandal over massive stealing of books ended in criminal convictions of many managers and workers under him. He was made Director of Leningrad's Literary Fund. After fourteen people around and under him there landed in disgrace or in jail, Rachinsky was promoted to head Leningrad television, where another great crash failed to reverse his career. One of the first measures taken after Nureyev's defection was to get a solid man in at the top of the Kirov. Rachinsky was appointed.

He was not an entirely revolutionary phenomenon in Russian ballet. He could cite Alexander II's attacks on *Sleeping Beauty*, one of the greatest scores written for classical dance, as a precedent. Diaghilev was in constant conflict with the tsarist cultural bureaucracy, which consisted largely of retired army officers. And Nijinsky's dismissal during the last Romanov's reign had much to do with a stultified artistic policy that produced superb performers but a deadened repertoire.

But even in comparison with the sorriest functionaries of the most reactionary tsarist periods, Rachinsky's ignorance was special. Before my folly with Fedicheva, he tried to pay me a compliment after a performance. "Well, lad, in general . . . I mean—not too bad. But when you moved over there, to the right, you really got yourself into something, *I'll* say." After three years as Director of one of the world's great companies he knew no movements, but only that, for some reason, I had "moved over there, to the right."

Rachinsky had been installed in the Kirov to put things in good Party order. He was always lecturing about the irreproachability of Soviet morals, and the need to make them "even more irreproachable. . . . A Soviet artist is pure in mind and spirit. He is ideologically armed with unqualified trust in our Party. In turn, the Party trusts him with the grave responsibility of bringing culture to the masses, even of representing Soviet culture abroad."

Shortly after I arrived, he prohibited the company members from participating in outside concerts, whatever our free time. Since no dancer would dream of accepting any engagement that interfered with his Kirov performances, Rachinsky's only motive was to assert his authority.

Although no more than sixty of our two hundred dancers were ever engaged in a single ballet, he closed the stage door to everyone not performing that evening. A Minister of Anticulture could have invented nothing crazier. Dancers, whose first spare-time duty was to study their colleagues' work, were to be kept away!

His attention turned next to the theater's little buffet, with its elegant sky-blue decor and unusually pleasant service. It was an old custom for all personnel, from elderly violinists and bookkeepers to young dancers proud to open a bottle of wine for their girls, to have a drink in this approximation of a genuine European café. Resolving to extinguish this traditional amenity in the life of the Maryinsky-Kirov, Rachinsky forbade any form of alcohol to be served to dancers. However, the most savage rulers had learned the danger of interfering with Russians' drinking habits. The fireman's new blunder sparked a fierce rebellion, and he cast about for something safer to be put in order.

WHEN THE DIRECTOR did not interfere, the Kirov's best qualities remained so good that only comparison with the Bolshoi made sense. Nothing was spared; nothing was haphazard. Principals in particular were treated with extraordinary respect. We were allowed to fit rehearsal times to our moods and muscle condition. Even last-minute cancellations were considered our prerogative. We could also choose our own class. Most principals trained with Alexander Pushkin, but I alternated between him and Kaplan, who had the soloists' class. Nicolai Zubkovsky, who occasionally substituted for one or the other, was often better than either. Crudeness and stupidity hampered him in everything, but his extraordinary natural flair for teaching produced inspired combinations of exercises.

Pushkin, a soloist but never a principal, sometimes seemed to me to lack the necessary stage experience for certain facets of teaching. His defects as a demonstrator were most obvious in the arms. But as a person he deserved all of his legendary reputation. He loved his charges like children, opening his home and emptying his pockets for even the mildly gifted. Understandably, the awe of his extraordinary purity sometimes carried over to praise for his teaching skill, all the more because he conducted his classes with the same modesty and tenderness.

It was only later that I fully appreciated our phenomenal abundance of excellent coaches. It was hard to believe that our kind of schooling existed almost nowhere in the West. As I understood it, their dancers trained here and there, under one system and then another. They sought out their own teachers, dashing from one to another because someone had said A was best or B could improve their hands. Did young pupils really have to cut through a jungle of competing styles themselves, and did their parents have to *pay*?

Balanchine had clearly managed to forge a genuine unit, with its own school and style. But when we heard how members of other touring groups had been trained and selected, the reason for their lack of coherence seemed clear. They were not companies as we understood them, but collections of independent entities. Their various styles clashed—sometimes effectively, but often jarringly. Besides, each individual was an assortment of fashions. Having taken bits and pieces from a haphazard series of teachers, he either chose a "school" himself at a certain age or continued searching throughout his dancing life. This had the advantage of keeping him a perpetual seeker, but after a certain age, no effort can give a dancer's muscles the bodily harmony needed for unity of style.

By contrast, all participants—except me!—of the Kirov classes were total products of the Academy, as tight and coherent a school, in both senses, as anyone could imagine. It was generally accepted that what hadn't been learned about technique itself in fifteen years could not be acquired now. Therefore, teachers rarely summoned someone to extend his leg fully, turn out more in fourth position, place his arms *there* during a plié. Their task was helping find the most effective display of what we had, coaching us to dance as artists, not students. Not responsible for the steps themselves, which the Academy had seen to, they worked only on fitting them into patterns and presenting them in the best possible way. And always in the course of shaping actual roles they knew by heart.

My first winter in the theater ended with the acquisition of three major roles and one inescapable conclusion: I would not soon become a part of the magnificent machinery for producing performances with the Kirov hallmark. The exactitude and care for every detail were just where I was weakest. I was twenty-six years old. Maybe it was too late.

24

THE WEST APPARENTLY BLURRED THE DISTINCTION BETWEEN HEROIC and lyric male dancers, maybe because most men were dainty and the very conception of heroic roles was weak. It was these the Kirov had hired me for, and measured by my assignments and number of performances, I was among the top four or five principals. My technique in individual steps matched anyone's, yet nothing hung together. It took a winter amid vivid examples such as Yuri Soloviev, the perfect stylist, to show me the full extent of my defects. I was overwhelmed with problems I hadn't even seen before, thanks to my stunted ballet education.

The central weakness was the absence of a consistent style and the necessary approach to achieve it. I had no polish because there was no overall concept of form. My movements and ideas, collected from scattered dancers I liked, lacked the unity essential to a genuine work of art—especially in the Kirov, whose first commitment was to noble contours.

And to labels. I was hardly the only one to suffer from this. Whenever I had a moment to look up from my own problems, I kept seeing victims of deadly typecasting. Half a dozen corps de ballet dancers would never become soloists only because they had developed after all places had been assigned. Failure to blossom on the system's schedule wasted enough talent and suffocated enough hope for two or three more companies. Our Kirov attributed such significance to its own labels that almost nothing could rip off "corps material" once it went on.

In some ways, five Maly years had taken me further from what I'd needed at graduation. Performing every other evening taught me much about theatrical expression, but the Maly's emphasis on this, rather than on perfected movement, accentuated my native tendencies, all at odds with the Kirov's primacy of style. I not only lacked a Kirov physique and polish, but in some ways represented their opposite. I was emotional; the Kirov, coolly controlled. I believed art came from an inner vision; the Kirov sought it in the achievements of past generations' masters. The theater's byword was the *norm*, which I fitted nowhere.

The Kirov's rule of rules for young dancers was that they must strive to resemble a given role's paragons: Pavlova or Nijinsky, Semyonova or Koren, Chaboukiani or Sergeyev. A role was to be learned, not developed. To improve it was to chisel closer to the accepted pattern, not deeper toward a personal understanding. Polishing a part meant helping evoke the prototype's interpretation, rather than anything the dancer's own body and disposition might discover.

My new colleagues took the model-copying goal for granted. They concentrated on landing perfectly in fifth position, turning out their hips as in the textbook illustrations, looking like a "Kirov" product. But the Maly had encouraged personal little "finds" in shaping new roles. Its emphasis on expressive acting had prepared me only *not* to follow in anyone else's footsteps, which was the last place I wanted to go anyway.

The coaches' idea of practicing everything to a superbly honed, interchangeable perfection seemed to me as close to ballet's purpose as watchmaking in Zurich. They were wedded to what they themselves had mastered in the great days of their youth or, worse, what the rivals who had bested them had mastered. In bearing and muscle control, they were supreme, but it was not necessarily supreme *art*. For no one had encouraged them to express their inner feelings. The individual creativity that feeds true art was beaten out of them in the strict process of training them for their triumphs. Now they were doing to others what had been done to them.

The cultural managers encouraged the coaches to keep their productions "pure" of personal emotion. In the name of preserving it, our classical inheritance was being deprived of the very creativity that originally made it great. For how could even works of the highest classical content, such as *Giselle* and *Swan Lake*, have been born without an outpouring of feeling? The absurd notion was accepted that a prince or a knight must not "tarnish" the part with his own personality, whereas the opposite was true: *only* strong personal expression could bring these venerable roles alive. Heads spun around when I tried a new angle during an arabesque or a tense position while watching the heroine. "For God's sake, Panov, who are you anyway? And what's all the searching for? The whole role's been beautifully worked out."

I appealed to the gods. "Yes, worked out for Sergeyev. The whole manner and style are perfect for him. But look at me, I'm a bullfrog by comparison. I need something different, or people won't believe in *the part*."

"I don't understand your craving to deviate every minute. Anyway, they'll never let you do it."

My critics were right: all my "mutations" were eliminated, and my stubbornness dug itself in. I would show what I could do, silence the ill-wishers, establish my right to be different—all by making my creativity *live*. But except in the moments of exalted inspiration, a performer's innovations are chancy without shaping and polishing through repetition. A dancer's muscles must adjust to the new movements, smoothing them into the role as a whole.

Since the coaches gave me no chance for this during rehearsals, I resolved to experiment during performances—the ultimate arrogance. Onstage the "right" and raw "wrong" renditions jitterbugged in my head. Neither had seeped into my reflexes or was even clear in my memory.

I demonstrated impulsiveness, not creativity. Undeveloped under the keen eye of a coach trained in the Kirov tradition, most of my "gifts" to the choreography only harmed it. In my nervous inability to concentrate, even the few apt changes emerged uncleanly—as more "tricks." Rachinsky's campaign gained support. I had the bitter realization that my dismissal would be caused less by fighting for my individuality than by stupidity while doing so.

At last I realized that I could struggle for my artistic personality only if I achieved perfection in the Kirov sense. Before taking anyone else on, I would have to drag, force, twist my body into the refinement it had never had. I worked harder than I'd ever imagined I could.

THE KIROV'S MAGNIFICENT *La Bayadère*—which the West knew only through "The Kingdom of the Shades," its final act—had long gone unperformed because a suitable male lead was missing. The role of Solor had enchanted dancing passages, some of which had been added in the 1940s by my model, Vakhtang Chaboukiani, the extremely vivid masculine dancer who leaned to character parts. Since the pattern I had to follow was perfect for me, my strengths could show themselves while I tried to shape them. Solor's overriding task was to maintain at all times the presence essential for the traditional Kirov male lead. It was in just these "details" of body configuration and stage positioning, the sum of which identified the true professional, that I fell behind. Scrutinizing every movement from several angles, the coaches worked on my dead arms, empty gestures, and indifference to nondancing posture. Gradually, I got some idea that meaningful positioning of the parts of the body—and the whole of it in relationship to the setting—was the narrative language of traditional works in between leaps and pirouettes.

But by the time I'd made a start speaking it, Soloviev was dancing Solor far more naturally. Besides, Rachinsky sometimes had me temporarily dropped from the part as punishment for some infraction. Or I would be scheduled to perform with Komleva, my usual partner now, when news came that high state guests were expected. The Director would quickly substitute Fedicheva.

KIROV GROUPS TRAVELED to several countries in the spring of 1964, and I was quietly slipped into the breach. My first "substitute" role was in Sergeyev's fantasy about the cosmos entitled *The Distant Planet*.

Only Yuri Soloviev had been dancing the Man, probably because everyone else would have seemed a spaceship grounded by a technical fault. I was gradually allowed to throttle down Soloviev's timing, which helped my more dynamic turns and stronger characterization. After a few months of frantic work on myself Sergeyev smiled. Finally, he put his arm around me and said, "What a pity you weren't with us in America!" He meant that the Kirov would have demonstrated greater range if I'd been on the trip.

Sergeyev gave no more personal attention to me than to the other leading soloists. But in my ostracism, his fairness meant much more to me than to the others. I also needed his professional help far more than anyone else. He had the pleasure of my drinking in his comments, then seeing his advice work before his eyes. Still, his kindness to me did not lead to the slightest contact outside the theater. In almost ten years of allied work and growing mutual respect I never visited his apartment. We did not share a single drink or meal together or have one real conversation about personal matters. He was utterly correct in all his relationships, but also distant. His life was his Romeos, Siegfrieds, Albrechts —which made his attitude to me all the more puzzling.

I attributed his encouragement of my striving and his defense of me against Rachinsky to his devotion to the Kirov. I had something his beloved theater needed. Gradually it occurred to me that my very artistic and temperamental contrasts wth him might have been the attraction. Maybe he'd reached an age when affection developed for the emotional intensity he had never had—and in someone young and beholden enough to be his son.

Only a person with the purest love of art can encourage a younger dancer with leanings seemingly antagonistic to his own. I mouthed all the proper phrases about Sergeyev's masterful control and technical perfection. But it took more years of watching ballet, including contemporary Western works I was then infatuated with, for a similar appreciation of his work to enrich me. When I at last began to *feel* them, I realized how close his lyric heroics came to ultimate art. And that there was no need to consider his approach an obstacle to mine. Unlike artistic techniques, artistic temperaments are unique. A dancer giving of himself has no reason to feel threatened by any other.

. . .

THE COMPANY LIVED COMFORTABLY and in relative peace. Kirov salaries brought few luxuries unless hard currency was earned abroad, but the financial security Russians dearly love came with ample time for fishing, drinking, and other relaxing pastimes. In addition to their average four or five performances a month, the principals were supposed to attend classes and rehearsals with some regularity. But when dancing well, they enjoyed princely working hours and conditions. As mature professionals they were allowed to drop out of class at any time or not go at all if they felt "off."

Dancers traveled far more than singers or actors and had more contact with foreign visitors. A trace of worldliness rubbed off, but the same foreign travel turned the company into a nest of vipers. Cutthroat competition for places on forthcoming trips was enough to do this, and KGB rewards for informing caused even worse damage. The Kirov motto might have been: "Denounce your rival, the payoff will be big." With rare exceptions, the price of getting on the travel list was the same for everyone: sell out a colleague—that is, yourself. Even innately decent, upstanding dancers succumbed because there was no other route to the airport.

My lone Kirov companion was the older boy my mother had asked to watch over me in the Academy. At that time Yuri Maltsev let me paint with him in his room instead of nagging me to study. I liked him immediately for this. He had grown up, a tough, self-made specimen, in the city of Perm, which also kept cropping up in my life. Maltsev was now a broad-shouldered, bull-necked man who looked more like a boxer than a dancer. The muscles produced by years of weight lifting and a head that looked swollen by punches completed the bruiser's image. Scars under his chin were reminders of his miraculous power of survival.

He had gone directly from the Academy to the Kirov, where he danced character and minor heroic roles vividly enough to be selected for a group sent abroad in 1954. Impulsive Maltsev struck up a conversation with the driver of a car that the Soviet garrison commander of East Berlin had made available to Ulanova, the troupe's star. The soldier hailed from the Urals, too, and they hurried to celebrate the reunion of "compatriots" in the usual way. To crown the drinking bout, they went for a joyride. Maltsev's lucky star guided him to a crash in *West* Berlin, whose morgues wired possible corpses to new electronic equipment. The driver was finished, but Maltsev made a needle twitch. When doctors had patched him together, they marveled that his constitution had saved him. Still more dead than alive, he came out of the anesthesia. "This place is boring," he breathed. "Get me out of here, Nurse. Or fetch your younger sister."

His recuperation lasted a year and a half. Although the scars were the only permanent disfigurement, the long layoff on top of the deep shock to his system had ruined his dancing form, which had depended largely on his explosive energy. *No* amount of willpower or desperate determination could haul him back into shape. But just before the Kirov was about to dismiss him, the Personnel Department made representations. From 1956 he did minor solo roles requiring more acting than dancing.

His acting talent and strong muscularity surely helped him stay. He was naturally theatrical on and off stage, and somehow an academic thirst for everything connected to footlights coexisted with his urges to belch, break wind, and entertain passing girls with suggestive endearments. But there was no doubt that the agency behind all personnel departments had arranged his re-instatement. Even before we became close, a dozen people had hinted that his KGB connection was much stronger than the usual occasional informing. This seemed a slur—the usual vinegary gossip—on my friend's free-wheeling spirit. But when I asked him, he immediately admitted the truth, only objecting that the others understood nothing about him. "The whole theater *doesn't* know who I am or what I do. But I'm not ashamed to tell you."

He *wasn't* ashamed or motivated by fear—at least not any ordinary kind. We once came on a thug beating his girlfriend while a partner brandished a knife to warn off passersby. Everyone else scurried away, and Maltsev dived straight in. Two brutal minutes later he was dragging the pair to a police station. Bruised and bloody, he prowled for his own girls as usual that evening. He lived opposite a dormitory on Decembrists' Street and called the damsels he got from there "my little Decembrists." Somehow he found time to recruit and seduce one every other day.

Yet this energy, and his great courage and strength in some things, went together with voluntary subordination to police types with whom he had little in common. He was one of those who felt that the only way to express himself was through the state power that dominated the country. The rationale was that in order to have something, you must surrender something.

But maybe this is too pat. He was so full of contradictions that I never knew what he would come up with next. Artless and totally open in everything personal, he worked for the *secret* police. As crudely nationalistic, sometimes, as a soldier from his Urals, he educated himself in all aspects of world culture with one crash course after another. He could be as rude as a village lout, yet truly loved every manifestation of art. He wrote with natural flair, and one of his hobbies was designing books.

We poured over artbooks together in my few free hours or visited museums. He took me to exhibitions where artists discussed their work. When we sketched each other, Kirov jokes about the oddball duo appeared; he was considered slightly "touched" since his accident.

His KGB connections didn't disturb me in themselves. A few of the most interesting, cultivated people, as well as many of the most repulsive, maintained them. In one way, Maltsev's were an added attraction; he hinted that his "friends" would break me out of my official isolation. But his affection for me meant more. I knew how strong this was, and not only because of my interest in painting and willingness to go somewhere with him in the middle of the night.

He was the same age as Alec. His smile put huge cracks in his punched-up face. He was *himself* as almost no one else I knew.

25

I BEGAN THE 1964–65 SEASON STILL GROPING FOR THE KIROV STYLE— and under constant threat of being told to go elsewhere. Rachinsky took the opportunity every time I inquired about a foreign trip to remind me of my shaky status. "Wake up, Panov. You should be on your knees with gratitude just for staying in the Kirov. If you go anywhere, it won't be abroad." I was not the only victim. Rachinsky's effect on the entire theater grew steadily worse. But his Party friendships made him invulnerable so long as no serious political scandal stained the Kirov. This made us realize that no one at the top really cared about ballet.

Now that I knew the anti-artistic spirit in which he worked, Sergeyev seemed a saint. Lifted to our highest selves in his presence, we all behaved the way I used to assume dancers behaved in the world's most refined company. He had to endure the bossing from hacks who contributed less to art in their entire lives than he during one demonstration of a difficult variation. I learned of scheme after scheme to remove him as Artistic Director. The men who had power in the theater—and in the various ministries and Party offices that controlled it—were deeply suspicious of him.

It wasn't only that he was not a Party man. Most genuine talents had no time for the endless meetings, political briefings, and conferences about comrades' private lives that Communists had to attend. Sergeyev's deeper drawback was that he also wasn't "one of us," and could not be recruited into plots about repertoire, programs, and casting to satisfy the Party lords' tastes and whims. When Marietta Frangopolo saw my respect for him, she told me that he was the main link to her photographs of the Maryinsky's well-bred stars and that his devotion to work and his dignified personal bearing were what set "certain people's" teeth on edge. Intriguers and mediocrities, joined by unthinking dancers under KGB influence, continued to claw, scratch, and gnaw at his position. His survival was as rare as his excellence. As long as he stayed politically "clean," which explained his dutiful pronouncements of loyalty to the Soviet system when absolutely necessary, he was simply too good to fire.

EVEN MORE THAN THE MALY, the Kirov was a warren of committees, councils, and "volunteer" bureaus supposedly discharging the collective's will. Hundreds of hours went weekly to stupendously repetitive discussions by the Party organization, the Young Communist organization, the trade-union organization, and something called the All-Theater Assembly, which served the superfluous function of pulling in any employee not already dragooned into a sitting of one of the smaller agencies. Many of these meetings were for regurgitating production statistics and the standard newspaper messages about the Party and the motherland. Cheers to socialism as the world's best system and to us as the world's best people alternated with sermons to control our drinking, cease our disorderliness, and become even better—that is, to pull ourselves up to "world standards." At our political lectures, attendance was taken, and absent members were later spoken to. But few needed reminding whenever a foreign trip was in the offing.

With no hope of getting on the list to begin with, I took scant advantage of the political enlightenment. I almost never attended the gatherings of the various organizations either, but bad news from them reached me quickly enough.

"Comrades! I hardly need remind you that foreign travel is a magnificent honor and privilege conferred by our own true Party and by our Soviet government. I am sure you are as inspired and grateful as I am. I am sure you will all demonstrate that this highest trust in you is completely justified. We are going to the class enemy's very lair. Vigilance is as important as unity of purpose and political preparedness. Many of you will have heard how a certain wayward dancer was affected.

"In connection with the difficult problem of Panov, I must tell you again that accepting him into our great theater was a damaging mistake. He is unable to master our wonderful traditions. We have just observed him in *Don Quixote*, doing it all wrong again. You saw it, comrades. How should he dance the role? You know how he should dance the role. Not as he *does*."

Sergeyev alone argued that the charges were untrue, provoking Rachinsky's even greater resentment of him. By himself, the Director was not authorized to fire any more than to hire. The trade-union committee and full Artistic Council had to vote on this. Some members hesitated because I was still the only hero for *Don Quixote* and *Laurencia*, the most popular ballets, and also because the casting committee saw in me a fanatic who would take on any part, any number of times, when leading lights were abroad or indisposed. Other members wanted to stop Rachinsky's meddling in artistic matters. An extremely powerful inertia also resisted him: every employee's virtual immunity to dismissal unless he was wildly incompetent or had committed some shocking transgression. Peace above initiative was the central fact of Soviet economic life. Combined with an ancient Russian dread of starvation, this made *security* the highest good a job could bestow. The comfort of knowing they were on a state-backed payroll for their working lifetime softened most people's dissatisfaction with their work. This went together with an instinctive reluctance to banish even a disliked colleague into the cold steppe of unemployment.

While Rachinsky campaigned like a true politician to overcome this, my battle with my stubborn defects continued. My legs refused to stay extended at all times, à la Kirov; my hips were not truly turned out.

When my muscles acquired a trace of Academy habits, my rough gestures tormented me. On the rare day when the body positioning went tolerably, a bureaucrat materialized to say I would not get a part, not go abroad, not be able to use my training as others did. I had to jump as high as Nijinsky and have a step as elegant as Sergeyev's; otherwise, "Panov, why on earth did you take on the role?"

My work load approached what it had been in the Maly. Leading soloists who performed five or six times a month were considered overburdened. Preparing for debuts in new roles almost burned out my nerves, and in addition, I danced up to fifteen three-act ballets a month in the next four years. Since any relaxation would have been leaped on, I could not pace myself for the "big" performances. Yet my schedule was the only solution. If I'd done what Fedicheva wanted, I'd have remained as muddy as Rachinsky's fan photographs of me. Her "star" label for an easy route to the top would have been worse than the "outsider" one stuck to me again. I had to jump over the challenge of disaster to show I could be a real Kirov principal.

THE KIROV CUSTOM of assigning Mercutio to veterans began when experienced masters, especially Sergei Koren, made him *Romeo and Juliet's* most complex character. But aging performers eliminated the difficult dancing moments, some of which were the most interesting. When my turn came, I started restoring the cuts. As the creator of Prokofiev's Romeo in 1940, Sergeyev had a special fondness for the work and for the full Mercutio he used to vanquish.

Mercutio's variation at the family's famous ball contained the most exciting of the pared-away sections. But first came the problem of the costume, which deserved a prize for ballet's heaviest, most inappropriate design. I was decked out in a lined cape, a tunic guaranteed to last to the hundredth anniversary of Soviet rule, and a winter coat of mail with rows of real medals, ballast to keep ten of me anchored to the floor. This was obviously the point, since Mercutio's mask covered my face like a diver's helmet. "No, no, no," came the answer to my plea to lighten it. "It's so beautifully painted. And everybody's always used it." The Kirov law that a dancer may change nothing unless he's at the top strewed his long, hard way with a thousand extra obstacles.

In ballet, as in track and field, each generation improves on the technique of the last. Legs are stretched higher; leaps get more amazing; elevation and speed increase. But try to keep up with this progress by changing a Kirov cape from one generation to the next! No one listened when I said I was trying to enliven Mercutio's role with some very strenuous passages. But when I explained that I was adding nothing of mine but returning to the *original* conception, my pleading to directors finally won a slight reduction in the costume's gross weight. The tunic's hem was raised almost high enough to let me really move my legs, and I could suck just enough oxygen through the lightened mask to sustain myself in the hard dancing moments. The first act went reasonably well.

The second act was one of the tragic ones that fitted me like leotards and had taken relatively little work, except for the scenes of Mercutio's celebrated swordfight. My coach for this was Mikhail Mikhailov, my teacher of acting in the Academy, who had seemed ancient even then. We now saw him as an old-fashioned ham, but his quivering love of the stage and scrupulously professional attitude stimulated receptive dancers to use their own imaginations, even when rejecting his melodramatic gestures. Mikhailov fumed at bravura technique that courted applause without carrying forward the story. Working with him again convinced me that dancers must conduct the same search for clues to roles as actors.

The Kirov's fabulous lavishness was almost enough to move audiences all by itself. Love of show was as strong as in the imperial past, and everything was done with the flourish that only Russia could mount. The cost of this escape from climate and daily drudgery hardly mattered. Squads of assistant directors worked every performance and reported along the chain of command. From the size of dressing rooms to the deference shown stagehands according to their seniority, everything was strictly hierarchical.

Riches from the massive props department—silver trays, jeweled crowns, golden goblets—were also distributed to dancers according to their rank. Eventually my Mercutio won enough acclaim to merit a very valuable rapier. After Tybalt stabbed him during their furious fight, he would fall to his knees, his head braced against the sword's beautifully embellished crosspiece. One evening the fine steel bent like a drawn bow under the burden of the dying man carried away by the story. The blade snapped with a bell-like twang, then fell at Mercutio's side as he expired—a perfect effect. But the props chief nearly broke in half together with the sword. He was one of my most steadfast fans among the

Kirov's auxiliary personnel—who, like audiences, were far warmer to me than the dancers were—and had risked giving me even better arms than authorized. The curtain came down. He rushed to retrieve the useless halves of the treasure he had guarded and polished for thirty years.

Mercutio's end was positively joyful compared to the sight of this elderly man. I pushed a few rubles into his hand after the curtain calls, and he hurried toward a side door without a word. A food shop with a well-stocked spirits department was located a hundred yards from the Kirov and the Conservatory. All its sister establishments closed much earlier, but if this vital service station for fueling Russian art had not stayed open until midnight, most performances would have finished with the second act.

I was no exception to the need in my tense and unhappy moments, and it was also my duty to help others wash away their sorrows. My shaken friend returned in two minutes with our bottle and led me to his little medieval armory behind the stage. I tried to console him while he discharged his grief. In the early hours we stood up and made for the door, steadying ourselves on chairs and tables. Outside, a light snow lay on St. Petersburg's façades. We clasped each other to say good-bye, knowing that the right amount of vodka in the right company had released all the disappointments of our lives.

For all my self-pity, I would not have changed places with anyone in the world. Some of my colleagues were already tiring of ballet, but with each year I found it more wonderful in general and more suited to me in particular. Words had always seemed to me very limiting. They encouraged speaker and listener to think in categories rather than images, to make contact through logic rather than feelings. They often acted as camouflage. The Incas tested the truth of a man's statement by making him dance. I loved dancing because it couldn't be manipulated to fool oneself or others.

Whenever I tried to describe something that had excited me, I heard long speeches coming out that never got to what I'd seen and felt. What I really wanted to do was stand up and move. Human beings spoke a dizzying number of languages, all but one of which, your native one, were incomprehensible without painstaking study. But even the Kirov's ultrarefined *Swan Lake* moved people throughout the world, because it was close to every human heart. Its beauty, its struggle of good against evil were a universal language.

TWO MONTHS BACK IN THE MALY were a relief. My old company was full of welcome. With no personal intrigues or jockeying for prestige running through rehearsals, the summer there was as good as a Black Sea vacation. I had been invited to dance the leading role of D'Artagnan in a new production of *The Three Musketeers* for the fall season. After rehearsals I sometimes visited the places where my classmates and I had staged our Musketeers "adventures." Here was the old upward cycle of my life again, trying to tell me that my fantasies were real.

The ballet role of D'Artagnan was even more enjoyable because of the Maly's attitude to my suggestions. After the Kirov, it was surprising enough that the choreographer listened. Without argument, resentment, or explanation about why one or another change *could not* be considered, he actually accepted whatever seemed worthwhile to him.

A brief movement by the girls in the corps heightened the interest in the new work. They went from first to second position and down again, in a stroking rhythm, their front parts "exposed"—some charged "thrust" —to the audience. Cultural overseers unleashed a stream of reprimands about "this intolerable vulgarization of the Soviet stage." It was said that Vasily Tolstikov himself, still Leningrad's feared Party boss, raged ominously. The production was dropped. The public buzzed. A few "erotic" moments were cut, and officials forgot about the incident or closed their eyes, their righteous protest having been recorded. The dangerous work was back again, to be enjoyed by a full house, including the same officials.

But the godlike thunder at the Maly's *Antony and Cleopatra* might have convinced the public that an evening of depraved sexual displays was being rehearsed. Weakly trying to defend himself, the choreographer said he was attempting no more than a pale copy—ten times more modest —of a few movements of Maurice Béjart's Ballet of the Twentieth Century. When Béjart's compositions were shown at Moscow's first international ballet competition a few years later, the cheering Soviet audience expressed its long ache for choreography that searched for new forms. Béjart's superiority in originality was so obvious that the award for the best choreography was dropped. Everyone "knew," after all, that his work was a "decadent bourgeois distortion of true art." The *Antony and Cleopatra* choreographer blundered in referring to Béjart's company by its full name. He should have known perfectly well that a reference to some foreign ballet bearing the name of the century in which the Revolution was made could only offend the cultural bureaucrats.

I thought it a great pity that the ballet was going to expire before reaching a live audience. "Finally, someone's trying to do something new," I found myself saying at a gloomy conference with Party and city officials following the censorship showing. "And the only reaction is to stop him." This drew astonished glances even from the embattled choreographer. "Imagine that," he gasped afterward. "Panov getting up there and putting two sentences together—a whole speech!"

It was my last one for many years. I shut up and watched a few others trying to pull the "intolerably depraved Western filth" labels from *Antony and Cleopatra*.

LIYA LIKED THE FUSS OVER MY DEBUTS. Attending the Kirov's gala evenings suited her; she dressed strikingly for them and built up attention for herself as a personality. She encouraged my work and complained less, but my outside interests still bothered her.

I was assigned a little cubicle for my hobbies and for "listening to all that music all the time." Actually, I had too little money for the records I wanted. But I could afford indelible paints and established my independence in a floor-to-ceiling mural on Indian themes—white horses, driving snow on the plains—inspired by *Amerika* magazine. Then I tried sculpture. In my likenesses of Liya I sought what was missing in our life. An old superstition taught that a bust brings unhappiness to its subject. When Liya took slightly ill, her mother threw my "junk" into a garbage can.

At such times I would leave to visit my neighbors, a middle-aged artistic couple who represented everything my family wasn't. She was the daughter of a famous explorer for whom Siberian mountains were named; he, the son of a prominent mathematician liquidated in the purges. Their own lives had been spent in one of Leningrad's finest dramatic theaters, to which they often took me. We'd then go home to talk over what we'd seen. We also discussed books they lent me from their huge collection. I always had three or four volumes "out"—the kind they hoped would broaden me without strain.

Another friend lived directly across the street. A brilliantly intelligent physicist, he had been graduated with the highest distinction from a special English-language school that then trained mostly diplomats and spies, even perfecting regional American accents. My friend's superb scientific mind saved him from that work, but during a year in America as an academic fellow and another one in France as a scientific adviser, he helped with industrial espionage.

His spells abroad helped open his eyes "to everything," as he would say. As our mutual trust grew, he gently tutored me in his view of "reality." He knew every nuance of Marxism-Leninism and liked to summarize their "imprecisions," as he called the failures and camouflages. But after exposing and analyzing, he smiled ruefully at the Don Quixotes who dared to protest. "I know our iron state's magnetic fields," he said. "Only a Peter Pan or a suicidal type would try to oppose it with his own force." Maybe this was his justification. Despite his hatred of the lies and his necessary accommodations to them, he loved Russia fiercely. But he wanted me to see and think—even about literature, for he was reared in a family of poets.

The first thing I did see was my good luck in having learned nothing in school, which would have had to be unlearned if I were ever to be educated. The whole of Russia's real intelligentsia was self-educated for this reason. Soviet schools sent *everyone* marching off together in the wrong direction. Only the exceptionally curious or bright could push back against this indoctrination. I had nothing to forget. My mind was unstamped because it was empty. The ideas and passions of people I admired were the only teaching it had ever been open to. Everything that had penetrated this way now turned me away from all that the state felt I should have learned.

Alec had traveled through much of the Soviet Union and written a travelogue, illustrated by his own photographs. It was published in Eastern Europe, but no Soviet editor would risk it. A few of his television programs were produced, but his other books were "unsuitable," and ideological demands had ruined so many of his screenplays that he kept turning down offers to collaborate with well-known writers skilled in adapting to censorship demands. He earned most of his living as the director of a jazz club. When the KGB disbanded it, he became the supervisor of a photography hobby group for youth. Then he got an obsession to "go to the people" and operated a lathe in a metalworking factory for two years. But he retained his passion for the theory of art, especially the relationship of personality to creativity.

Gradually, I noticed him studying *me*. His questions about my fantasies showed that ballet had become real to him, even given him a goal to live for. I, at least, could strive for a goal, and he could cheer me on. I could do nothing to stop the wastage of his life.

I visited Vilnius at least twice a year. The heartache for what he was doing to himself eased when we were together. His friends among the Lithuanian intellectual elite all led double lives. The lover of Tolstoy's philosophy taught Marxism-Leninism for a living; after their hour a day of eyes-shut journalism, the poets rushed back to the theological and humanistic questions that dominated their "closed-door" reality. No one fought openly for anything since the only truths that mattered concerned their private interests.

Alec now took me to this circle's evenings of mind-spinning conversation. He also made certain that books by Bulgakov, Solzhenitsyn, and other favorites unfit for Soviet libraries were on the sofa where I slept. Each return to Liya from his horizons was more like a forced retreat than a homecoming. But I allowed the half-truth of my concern for Andrei to serve as the whole one.

Then Alec married someone with whom he shared even fewer interests than I shared with Liya, such a repetition of what he'd always warned me against that we laughed about it. My new sister-in-law was a Lithuanian peasant girl educated in a catering school. Her thrift and love of hard work quickly advanced her to chief cook for the Lithuanian Central Committee, the republic's highest Party organ. Despite the famous "He who does not work, neither shall he eat" commandment, everyone knew that the Party bosses did least and ate best. It was impossible not to take home smoked fish, good salami, and fresh cheese— all unavailable elsewhere—from the pantries of the better public kitchens. But it was also impossible not to show them off to a neighbor. Impossible for her not to bid for them. Impossible for a second neighbor not to sniff out the delicacies and denounce the dealers. In our homeland of shortage and disorder, access to a rich larder was a shortcut to the good life or to jail.

Donutya was the exception who never engaged in trade. She took only enough for her own daily use: caviar for the appetizer, then a fillet steak carved from a Party side of beef. Alec hardly noticed what he ate, but he had a passion for coffee, a "deficit" item, and liked treating his friends to liquors he could never afford. Donutya served them in her own room, with delicious pastries she herself had baked. Then she sat

in a corner, waiting to wash up. Alec would not endure a marriage ceremony by a Soviet official, but after six years of friendship with Donutya,
he moved in with her and signed the necessary papers.

When Alec came to Leningrad, I introduced him to *my* friends.
Some of the sculptors and artists were Jewish, some so determinedly
Russian that they recited poets like Nekrasov all day and bristled at the
growing cult for everything Western. As members of the Union of
Artists they had well-equipped studios. I gave them tickets to my per-
formances; they gave me a place to paint—and to get away.

I first met Sandrik M. this way. He was a painter and an architect,
but he loved ballet best and became a devoted fan. His friends were art
critics and historians who would have walked across Europe for one
look at the masterpieces they'd been studying all their lives. Art was their
religion. They suffered for it; so much of what they wanted would
never be available. Yet they loved their own country more than all the
Party people together.

Candlelight set the mood of their meetings. When I joined the
circle, it was in the forefront of a Sergei Esenin cult. "Esenin" evenings
consisted of vodka, readings from the poet's lyrical verses, more vodka,
discussion of artistic trends, and songs to a guitar, including the first
Jewish songs I ever heard. Sandrik M. and his roommates worked in the
Hermitage and talked for hours about its treasures, including those kept
hidden from the public. Later Blok became the central poet and the
tone of the evenings became more "anti-Soviet."

Volodya Sverdlin represented the opposite extreme among my
friends. He was even more interesting now than when he had introduced me to jazz and foreigners. I was in his room one day when six
KGB men barged in. Supposedly searching for secret messages, they
smashed his entire record collection. Each record had cost an average of a hundred rubles, and the policemen's sneers revealed their real
purpose was to destroy this wealth. But Volodya watched bravely.

When he was released from arrest, his first thought was of how to
put together the king's ransom to buy new records. His scheme began
with a recently dead doctor who had been doing abortions for twenty
years. If he had put his fortune in a bank, an investigation would have
been ordered the same day. He bought diamonds instead and kept everything stashed in his bedroom.

His widow was too frightened even to open the safe when he died.

Her nephew told the story to Volodya, who considered how to "relieve the poor soul of her burden of stolen money." Sooner or later a neighbor would denounce her. Better he got the loot than see it confiscated by the state. He recruited friends, faked documents, assembled blue uniforms. The terrified woman was enormously relieved to hand over the illegal treasure to Volodya's "policemen." The perfect crime left everyone happy—until the nephew drank and bragged. For good measure, charges of "links to a fascist organization" and "slander of Soviet rule" were added to Volodya's indictment. This time he went to prison for six years.

26

MY 1959 NEW YORK APPEARANCE HAD RECEIVED A MIXED CRITICAL reaction. "They danced it with everything they had," wrote Walter Terry of my pas de deux with Borovikova. "Their flamboyant style may be rather hard to take—Mr. Panov is particularly guilty of hamming— but the dance tricks they accomplish skillfully."

Now—six years later—roughly the same criticisms applied. Feya Balabina occupied Vaganova's old position as the Academy's Artistic Director. She had never taught me but always stayed a friendly observer. I asked her for a full critique of my performance as Vatslav in *The Fountain of Bakhchisarai*. She said that something was missing beneath the booming technique. "You're expressive, but all on one level. You haven't learned much about subtlety." I was beginning to drag myself out of the whirlpool of my disastrous start: some ragged edges had been smoothed, but I still did everything "big," bounding around the stage with all my strength instead of shaping and suggesting in halftones.

CHOREOGRAPHED FOR DUDINSKAYA and Sergeyev in 1949, *The Bronze Horseman* had never left the Leningrad stage. The famous Pushkin poem on which the ballet was based showed how action on a grand "Russian" scale—in this case, the agonizing building of St. Petersburg from a swamp—can lead to unpredictable, often tragic consequences. In 1965 I began working on the central role of Yevgeny, a humble young St. Petersburg functionary. Timid, frightened, and alone, Yevgeny is submerged in the tsarist bureaucracy's ranks and regulations. He wanders incon-spicuously in Senate Square, dreaming of meeting someone to share his life. But he manages only to brush against a general and almost faints when he snaps out of his reverie and recognizes the epaulets. Joy over-whelms Yevgeny when he falls in love. The first act ends with a long adagio that extols the glory of Peter the Great to a gentle girl named Parasha. It was Peter who overcame many terrible obstacles, who called for colossal sacrifices from peasant workers, to construct the glorious city in which they met.

The Kirov had long done *The Bronze Horseman* as a kind of dram-ballet, with impressive staging but relatively little dancing. The man-agement's reluctance to push anyone from our huge company onto his pension always guaranteed a surplus of aging dancers for the stately, slow-moving parts. But Sergeyev decided to pare the pageantry and re-store more movement. He demonstrated the role of Yevgeny as he himself had created it, and "tradition" again allowed me to put back the sections dropped after he had ceased playing the part himself.

Sergeyev's studio work showed why the few foreigners studying in the Academy and the Kirov never acquired full polish. They attended regular classes and rehearsals but otherwise were kept at arm's length from the crucial "inside" finishing skill of personal coaching by the great masters. Some visiting students never even knew what Sergeyev inspired as a demonstrator. One reason for his preeminence was that he ran through everything, including the hardest lifts. Rehearsal was a sacred ceremony. His exquisitely controlled body told us that ballet was above all a system of scrupulously devised muscle movements, which time and tradition had made inviolable. And he was alone in the art of leading a ballerina by a single finger. He had partnered Ulanova in the Kirov's first *Nutcracker* and liked to illustrate from its intricate configurations. Winding the Sugar Plum Fairy around him and seemingly through his arms, he provided as much pleasure as some full ballets.

"Natalia Mikhailovna, might you please help me for a minute here?" he would say when we had fudged a difficult passage. For some reason, he and Dudinskaya were not officially married and maintained separate apartments, but they had been man and wife for more than twenty-five years. Second to art, he loved himself as its servant, and she loved herself as his. She would rush up, assume a pose, and gaze at him "with a million eyes." In an instant he would have her winding, twisting, and pirouetting around him. Her waist was an old tire tube, but under his direction she became a beautiful woman. They danced as if they had invented the duet. Melted in love for their creation, they would take a moment to pull apart. They kissed and returned to their seats. All their old duets were running in the film covering their eyes.

"Well now, my unfortunate ones," Sergeyev would say. "Let's see what *you* can do." "Unfortunate" was only half in jest. He and Dudinskaya waited with full awareness that their professional beauty could not be equaled. All they could do was nudge us a bit toward the best *we* could manage.

Sergeyev made an exception in my case by not wincing at my "big" ballet effects. He seemed resigned to them if they didn't come at any old time the mood struck me and if the spontaneity revealed nothing amateurish. He worked long and hard with me to make sure my emotional outbursts would come out with polish.

Yevgeny was an easier role than some for me since it was one of those with which I immediately felt at home. With a range of vivid steps to express his violently shifting moods, he was another little man oppressed by giant, incomprehensible forces. Without one direct word about the cruelty of Russia or of Peter, Pushkin's "simple" tale of an "insignificant" man portrayed everything there was to know, and to grieve about, in both.

Soon after the appearance of love transforms this timorous "nonentity" into a handsome young man with a spine and a bundle of dreams, the Neva's waters overflow their banks, totally flooding the former swamp. Desperately striving to reach Parasha's cottage, Yevgeny finds refuge atop a granite lion. The terror-breathing figure of Peter—in the form of St. Petersburg's famous statue of the Bronze Horseman—appears from beneath the waves. The former Tsar and his present subject stare at each other in this awful confrontation, and the audience realizes both are madmen. The one whose statue symbolizes the city's dominating spirit destroyed everything for the sake of a great goal. The other is now demented by the might and mania of the city's founder.

My standing had developed enough to give me slight leeway in restoring the full role, even in adding a few steps of my own to increase the dynamism. This tolerance was accorded to the actual movements, but not to my reaction to the story. Talk about *my* derangement began during rehearsals of Yevgeny's madness scene. His movements are retarded in a kind of slow motion—a circle of jetés that becomes ever narrower, squeezing into each other as he is sucked into the obsessive image of Parasha that has appeared in his eyes. To show his loss of control, I avoided every movement of classical ballet. The frenzied hero views his delusions through a dangerous backbend, eyes sagging to the floor to stress his illness. Dropped into the abyss of insanity, he moves in fitful jerks and violent falls. Yevgeny completes a final rotating trek around the entire stage—an extremely difficult maneuver against the Kirov's rake— ending flat on the floor and cherishing the wreckage of Parasha's cottage. The stage darkens, leaving a single spotlight on a wormlike body fried in its own madness.

The extraordinary effect on the audience intensified the disapproval of Kirov watchdogs. Even Academy pupils wondered how "pathological Panov" could execute such double cabrioles. But technique was secondary for me. My main duty was to the personal and social tragedy. Backstage dismissal of this mission strengthened my association with Yevgeny as a man destroyed by a hostile environment. Depicting madness was one of the hardest tests I'd faced. Professional training told me not to become *too* involved with the role, but I often felt myself merging with it. Yet the unorthodox movements required more body control than most standard, highly practiced steps.

Critics had argued about my interpretations for years. Now the "antis" shouted even louder that my "trash" sullied everything the Kirov represented, while others insisted that I was just what the company needed. In retrospect, both opinions proved to be exaggerated, as most are when something new is attempted. But I felt more strongly than ever about the need for individual contributions by dancers. Dancers had to listen to their own emotions. Maybe I indulged myself by improvising too much in dramatic ballets, but at least for me, it was clearer than ever that imitation was wrong, damaging, and even impossible.

My moments of "heavenly" inspiration began to return in *The Bronze Horseman*, especially when my concentration was intense. I knew I wasn't keeping perfect time with the orchestra, but some alternate sensory capacity was responding to a "higher" rhythm. Chaliapin said that when the bell of higher inspiration pealed, the actor himself did not know what was happening to him. I fell once, dancing mad Yevgeny. I wasn't aware of this or of anything after the second act. When I came to in the dressing room, I noticed blood on my collar. It was collecting in a pool under my wig. The duty doctor said my concussion must have come from a severe crack on my head during the fall.

After certain performances I withdrew into myself for days in order to live the thoughts of my victimized hero. I would walk around in a daze, then come home to re-read Pushkin's poem, the edition illustrated by Alexander Benois. This was so moving to me that I had to return to Yevgeny's streets. Life and art could never be fully separated in Leningrad. Russia's inner spirit as captured by Pushkin and Benois hadn't changed at all. I looked up at Peter the Great, who was as dominating as ever on his bronze prancer in Senate—now Decembrists'—Square. Yevgeny had shaken his fist at the blind ambition that crushed him, then fallen to his knees in fear and contrition. How dare he assert himself against his ruler?

A RECONCILIATION WITH MY PARENTS had taken place after they accepted the fact that they could not prevent my marriage, and I learned not to bear them a grudge for their foresight about it. But despite our friendly surface relationship on my Vilnius visits, we didn't even try to bridge the chasms underneath.

Although still better-looking than far younger women, my mother bore the inner tragedies of beauties who once believed they would never age. Her interest in Alec and me—slightly greater as she looked for something to occupy her middle age—seemed to tire her because she was so unfamiliar with it.

My father had become fully and irrevocably a slave. Far from recovering—even when the country did slightly after Stalin's death—he grew worse. Malenkov was "our genius" because the still-revered Stalin had picked him. When he went into disgrace, Bulganin and Khrushchev were the new "leaders of all progressive mankind." He had developed into a genuine anti-Semite who hated all Jews, including himself. I noticed that many Party workers of his generation had become almost incapable of sane conversation. They had no opinion on any question whatever that could not be expressed in a slogan. Alec and I could no longer laugh at him to ourselves. We only regretted what political forces had done to normal human feelings.

At first my father had refused to believe that his dunce of a son was good enough to perform in the motherland's State Academic Theater of Opera and Ballet. When a second season passed without an announcement of my discharge, he wrenched himself away from his hearth to make his own inspection tour. He arrived in his best secondhand suit and full of the skepticism of a man who knows his Marxism-Leninism—and therefore everything subordinate to it, such as cultural policy. Folk ensembles and Russian choirs were the only worthwhile forms of "highbrow" art.

Confrontation with the Kirov's magnificence weakened him slightly. The next blows were the curtain-call ovation for his son in a leading role and the backstage fuss, largely by fans who had carried over from the Maly. The last of his resistance collapsed at a supper in his honor arranged by the same fans. The rich table brought tears to his eyes, and he mumbled about his "incorrect" treatment of me. Someone put his glass in his hand. Two swallows of vodka hit him as it would my Andrei. He gazed at me from his train window as if I were an Important Person and wrote me from Vilnius more often than before.

SOMETIMES THE WHOLE HURT of not going abroad was reduced to petty envy of the company's car owners. Even a few minor soloists had them now, and while I stood aside like a mechanical know-nothing, they discussed carburetors and winter lubrication with more fervor than anybody showed for ballet. To me even the perpetual spare-part crises seemed like sweet agony. But no matter how hard I worked and how many performances I gave, it was unreal to think of buying as little as a set of valves for a car. The only way to amass the necessary fortune was to drop everything and become a speculator in underpants or Tashkent rugs. Or to earn foreign currency, which quintupled your salary. A tape recorder bought for a hundred dollars in a duty-free shop fetched a *thousand* rubles in Leningrad. Six such deals provided enough rubles for a Volga.

Not everyone would kill his mother for this, but almost everything else fell within acceptable limits. "Business" experts knew which hardware brought the highest profit and took orders in advance for special items down to brassieres in the right style and color. Each troupe left the airport like traveling salesmen representing an entire nation of thirsting cousins and aunts. No matter how many times he'd been picked before, a person grew giddy when picked again. But material gain was only one reason for this. The exhilaration of tasting something forbidden to everyone else was another. The greatest lure was that foreign travel was the surest mark of approval and status. Even before his departure the lucky man's friends talked about him respectfully, while he basked in the recognition and the *reassurance* of having been examined and passed. Nothing could equal this. No one from a country where travel was your own affair could understand it.

The reverse was equally true. The threat of losing the privilege was a terrible intimidation. Some dancers passed over for a few trips were so stricken that their muscles stiffened. *Not trusted*, they could not concentrate on work or pleasures. "It's like being in prison," whispered a soloist who had fallen out of favor after becoming addicted to tours. "How can you stand it year after year?"

The practice of purging people already on the list was especially unnerving. Several dancers had actually been removed from their planes. This did not necessarily indicate that anything incriminating had been found in their records. Intriguing for places went on until the very last minute, when the KGB at times succeeded in substituting their own man. But the rejects knew only that someone in a position to do damage might suspect them of something. The flimsy official explanations increased their dread.

I had always loved traveling. I learned only by seeing and experiencing for myself. I yearned to spread outward. I knew I could never develop close to my limits without contact with the world. Besides, only the opinion of the West really counted in Russian arts. Western critical judgment was the highest standard back in tsarist days, when claims were being made about Russia's special mission in the world. And the louder the Soviet derision of "bourgeois idealists" and "handmaidens of capitalism," the clearer it was that their opinions were more important now. Our very isolation made their verdict godlike. In the Kirov in particular, everyone knew that a triumph *there* solved all problems *here*. Earning hard currency for the state partly explained this, but it also came from a deep veneration of the "enemies" our propagandists most attacked. "Well . . . I mean, *over there*, you really pulled it off."

My understudies had been winning foreign applause for six years. I, too, wanted this recognition. I longed to show myself to the judges. What could I hope for without the stimulation and criticism I needed? Every year that passed without travel was part of a punishment. I also wanted justice. Why did I have to see soloists who'd been crash-trained as substitutes in *my* roles go time after time? I worked as nobody else in the company did, was rewarded with slaps in the face, and *no one would tell me why*.

"Why am I not going this time when I'm the only Basilio?" I kept pleading.

"Nothing's wrong, it's just a technical decision," said the officials who tried to humor me.

Others resented questions. "If I were you, I wouldn't stress your strange foreign interests so much. You're not dancing enough? You lack something?"

A dancer left behind was a pariah. No matter how he improved or how well he performed, he was not really to be reckoned with because the authorities had put an X next to his name. If it was possible not to give him a new part, it went to someone else. If a privilege could be withheld without affecting the others, it was. Four years is a large chunk in a dancer's stage life. Compared to others at my level in the company, I was that far behind in acquiring an honorary artistic title. These things weren't as silly as they sounded since the extra money brought a corresponding increase in respect and that margin of advantage in winning parts and leeway with them.

Sometimes the dread broke through and so devastated me that I could hardly get out of bed, could think of nothing but my persecution. Even my old opera records were alien because they were full of life and I was doomed. I felt that if I didn't go abroad the next time, it would be too late ever to apply what I might someday learn there. If I were permanently incapacitated and could never dance again, then they'd feel sorry. . . .

27

ANOTHER LARGE GROUP FLEW OFF TO THE WEST IN THE FALL OF 1965. My one compensation was that "good-bye" sometimes brought with it a Kirov tidbit.

Before Sergeyev left, I asked him to give me *Giselle*. Physically,

I was anything but the handsome Count, but his dramatic side tempted me, and it was a part to stretch my range. With sixty dancers globe-trotting and only one Albrecht left in Leningrad, I'd never have a better crack at it. Sergeyev consented. He made specific suggestions for my rehearsals, then, looking deep into my eyes, pronounced, "And please change nothing in the choreography."

Of all Sergeyev's triumphs, this had been the greatest. Throughout the 1940s he had been the very incarnation of the role. He carried the weight of his fifty years when I first saw him in 1961, but I thought that if the Western companies so fond of *Giselle* had seen him even then, none would have dared bring that ballet to Russia.

For once I wasn't sorry to see this perfection depart. Nothing could have been more cramping than his eye when feeling myself into a strange role. I was more convinced than ever that ballet could not be made by following in another's footsteps. No matter how great the original and how skilled the copy, dancing that lacked an emotional source seemed lifeless to me. I took chances in *Giselle* not to test this theory but simply because my body could not sustain the standard approach to Albrecht. I *had* to do it differently, and that could come only from within.

The early weeks were full of the pleasure of independent search. Then it came to me that my Albrecht should not be a haughty, calculating seducer, but a youth intoxicated on his bubbling fancies and unaware of what he is doing to Giselle. Albrecht deceives no one intentionally. He merely forgets his responsibilities during the delicious game of being enraptured. Conscience and the tragedy of lost love torture a completely changed man in the second act. I saw Albrecht yearning to join Giselle forever in death but kept from her by her unwillingness to grant him this rest. Preservation of his life is the ultimate punishment.

Maybe this wasn't a new interpretation, but the Western Albrechts I'd seen seemed too preoccupied with getting gracefully through the second-act variation and coda to give much idea about his inner thoughts. The dancing itself was taken for granted in the Kirov. At the end of Act Two the sun's first rays magically restored the Count. All ended happily, *and* he had learned his lesson. Without tragedy there was no connection to real life, no significance to his suffering, no dramatic jolt of vengeance from his own conscience.

My debut took place in December 1965. At Kaplan's insistence, the Count tramped about in jackboots during his first appearance on stage—proof to the audience that he *was*, as the plot said, returning from a noble hunt. Sure enough, I stumbled in them, and the weight of the obligatory tunic almost toppled me. But I felt my Albrecht "worked" as a character, and when he returned, Sergeyev said that he could not condemn my attempt. "There have been many Albrechts over the years, and all went astray somewhere. Your feeling something and trying to shape it comes through. But"—deep sigh—"it would have been better to leave him as he was."

I was the first to acknowledge that one Albrecht of his was worth a hundred of mine. But the *Masters of Soviet Ballet* film that had overwhelmed me as a boy also proved part of my case. The style with which he had thrilled the public then already looked stilted. Yet his dancing was so full of real images that it gripped audiences as strongly as ever.

Ballet technique was now advancing not only with each generation, but even with each decade. And while audiences loved the pyrotechnics, their appreciation was purely sensory, as for football or acrobatics. After a few days they forgot the leaps and pirouettes that had made them gasp. But ballet *characters* stuck to the emotional ribs. They expressed something essential about human striving. As the high-water mark of her time's technical development, Dudinskaya represented mostly a historical interest now. But Ulanova endured in people's memories because her interpretations transmitted her generation's feelings about its heroines. Even the most brilliant virtuosity was only an instrument for relating what the heart had perceived.

THE ONLY ADVANTAGE I could think of to not going abroad was avoiding certain traumas. In Vienna a few years before, the constant scrutiny of one "representative of culture" so disturbed a trombone player of the Alexandrov Ensemble that he believed he was going to be eliminated. He ran headlong; the KGB cornered him, pointing his trombone case at them like a gun, in a cemetery. He was rushed home to many long years of peace.

Later a minor Kirov soloist remembered the pretrip lectures and started fearing for his life the moment he crossed the Soviet border. He tried to leap off his train, shouting that the choreographer Igor Belsky was an imperialist spy sent to kill him. The theater took him back after a year of treatment, but he had to return to his hospital several weeks each spring.

The next victim returned with the 1965 Kirov group. She was our best piano accompanist, a woman of great gusto and intelligence. Everyone was still affected by cultural shock while abroad, especially in America. The first few days were spent in an odd exhaustion, often accompanied by slight nausea. Even when people had seen the unimaginable affluence before, their nervous systems needed time to adjust. Before the accompanist's did, she received half her hard-currency payment. Thanks to an improved technology of packing suitcases. with dehydrated soups and canned sardines, none had to go for food. In shop after shop, she saw more mind-boggling items to buy with her five hundred dollars and hurried on. Her mind raced, but fingers couldn't count out the bills. The second five hundred dollars finished her. She stood at appliance-store windows, mumbling to herself, the untouched fortune in her clutched handbag. She was met at the Leningrad airport, and we never saw her again.

Yuri Maltsev hadn't gone abroad for seven years after his Berlin crash. But now he was traveling again and came directly to me after each trip. During his free time abroad he had separated from the bargain-hunting flock to tour museums and architectural landmarks. For days he could talk about only this. He put his boxer's energy into analyzing every statue. He seemed to despise everything that kept Russia from having the same wealth of art and excitement in its daily life.

His passion for European enlightenment would last about a week. Then he was back to his other self, insisting that life "there" was impossible except for imperialists and militarists. The pendulum had swung back to his early Urals attitudes, or the KGB had switched him around while he was making his reports to them. But he reconciled this to himself by insisting that he *wanted* to serve. "I'm not one of those punk informers like every second dancer in the company. I help out because I believe." Then he would explain why having personal ideas was a kind of treachery, even though he himself was full of powerful individuality.

In settled periods between his trips Maltsev argued that as a whole, the Soviet system was truly best. Anyway, it was wiser to believe this than to trouble myself with useless doubts. But he also worried with me about my "case." He volunteered to draft new petitions for me, assuring me that he knew the right people in the right office to approach. No one else told me anything, but on the eve of his trips he would take my head in his hands and moan. "I couldn't help you, Valera. Maybe nothing can."

THE FOLLOWING SUMMER Rachinsky dropped me at the last minute from a season in the Kremlin's Palace of Congresses. Now I was to stay at home from Moscow trips, too. The company departed, but Sergeyev pressed Rachinsky with unusual persistence. "We must show our full range in the capital," he said. "Panov is essential for us all." I was sent for two weeks later and had forty-eight hours to learn a new combination of scenes from *The Distant Planet*. The rehearsals were like impromptu exercises, but the opening-night reviews used superlatives. Two days later the critics singled out my "unsurpassed" Yevgeny. A delighted Sergeyev showed Rachinsky the paragraphs about me, and he absorbed their implication—from the highest Party and government newspapers of our Soviet capital! The easing of his frown was a Roman candle indicating that the siege against me was lifted.

This first full triumph with the Kirov was followed by a huge outdoor concert. Komleva and I were treated as the program's stars. My hard years seemed to be quickly drawing to their end. Natalia Makarova was backstage for congratulations, and we left the pavilion together. She'd been a chubby girl in the Academy who, as she well knew, tantalized the boys of my older class. I'd worked with her only once or twice since and hardly knew her personally. That evening she was as happy as I, having just returned from winning the gold medal at the international competition in Varna, Bulgaria. As if in reward for our triumphs, we somehow found two free seats in a restaurant.

Natasha pooh-poohed my stopping at one glass because I had another performance the following day. Nothing restrained her when she was in the mood for a good time. "I drink as much as I want, whenever I want," she said, shaming me into a proper celebration. When the restaurant closed, we walked down a wide avenue. The summer air fanned in our faces by the cars of Western diplomats seemed a breeze of freedom. Natasha's figure was like the stem of a champagne glass. Her giggles resembled the drink itself.

I studied her dancing more closely from then on and realized that her shimmering talent came from the same source as her occasional frivolity. Natasha identified totally with her roles. She did with utter ease everything I worked at so laboriously. This made her mediocre sometimes, but breathtaking at others. She had a special radiance and a unique enchantment onstage, for she was the personification of her romantic heroines. A perfect sense of balance and timing allowed her to do wonders with her fragile body. She burned with feelings, from the sensual to the ethereal, and conveyed them with every line of her face and arms. She was Giselle herself, more innocent, pathetic, gullible, and tragic than I'd realized even when immersed in dancing Albrecht opposite others. My progress with the meticulous Gabriella Komleva hadn't fulfilled the hopes of Sergeyev and Dudinskaya. I saw one tilt of Makarova's head bringing her heroine home to the audience with stunning dramatic force. What set her apart from ballerinas with equally impeccable musicality and training was the inner passion that lighted her work. My wish came true that fall. Makarova and I were paired for a recital together.

I had never worked with anyone like her. Her feeling for her partner was so enveloping that I sensed her every gesture, even when we were at opposite corners of the stage. I could not think of *my* movements. Her totally feminine responses made us a unit.

Since the recital was in Dudinskaya's honor, Sergeyev supervised our rehearsals with extra concern. Makarova fitted his partnering technique perfectly. A motion of my wrist controlled her turns, making me appear wholly unconcerned about guiding, supporting, and lifting her—and therefore in nonchalant command. The audience would believe this gift from her was the power of my "will."

At the recital itself her beauty and skill won us the kind of acclaim she had had too little of in the Kirov, thanks to Fedicheva's jealousy. But she turned down my every proposal for more work together. I never asked her why. None of the possible answers would have elated me. Maybe she thought less of my partnering than I of hers. But the most probable explanation was my "situation." For a ballerina with her dream of tasting the world's delights and of expanding into the roles she deserved, I was a dead end. For years I thought of the professional couple we might have been. Instead of the song of exhilaration with her, partnership with others often produced grunts, groans, and barks.

I sometimes wondered how couples went onstage with their love scenes after rehearsals had prepared them for war.

From the male standpoint, the females had unfair advantages. Many ballerinas seemed neat and dainty—until you tried to lift them. Some of the airiest-looking things laid their stage longshoremen low with torn ligaments in knees, heels, and backs. Of course, it wasn't a woman's fault if she had this kind of constitution. She too suffered when partners avoided her, and dieting weakened her muscles—the same ones that achieved miracles onstage. But the weighty egos that often came with the leadlike compactness were a suitor's worst woe.

After my enlightenment from Makarova, I conducted a little survey of professional couples. Many combatants were husbands and wives who had acquired proficiency with each other's bodies through long experience. But try to find the affection and deep respect needed for a genuine duet, which, above all, is an exchange of feelings! Younger partners tended to wrangle even more loudly than their elders.

Most of the noise usually came from a ballerina lecturing her gasping man about how to lift her. Despite some recent progress in the campaign for men's liberation in dancing, most ballerinas continued to believe, as they'd long been encouraged to, that the male was essentially a prop for female works of art. Yet nagging from a lady was in itself a major obstacle to a real partnership. My little survey confirmed what Makarova had demonstrated: that a good woman makes even a sluggish mate appear effective. This was because she did most of the actual dancing when they were together. He seemed to control her, but only if she was willing. She also knew that *he* must decide what was most comfortable in the one movement that most depended on him. Otherwise, he'd drop her from a lift one day, no triumph for either side.

Nothing in ballet was more beautiful than a duet that grew out of mutual fondness. The harmony of a perfect two awakened thoughts about pairs in nature and the purpose of life. The tenderness of couples who loved each other (at least professionally) released the most soaring feelings, and you didn't have to hold your breath watching in case she was taking too much out of him. Since everything was in balance, their joint adagio left enough energy for the individual variations that followed. Alas, few ballerinas understood the toll that lifts exacted or were willing to adjust to their partner's strength. Most men managed to struggle through the adagio itself, but the subsequent variations—the vehicle for expressing the bounding emotions the duet was supposed to have aroused—were often undermined.

My own first precept for duets was that a woman must trust her man's powers. Her hardest job was ridding herself of fear in lifts, which was essential for developing the very solidity she most needed from him. The second was that it was time to reconstruct the traditional pas de deux; modern audiences expected more and more actual dancing from the man. The best women partners understood this. But no such "teaching" was worth much if the couple could not draw on some form of good feeling for each other. Nothing real could be achieved on a shaky emotional foundation.

These thoughts pleased me until I realized how much was missing in my own development—and as a person, as well as a dancer. I was still without "my" partner.

PARTNERSHIP HAD TO BE SEEN in the context of the rapid growth of the male role in ballet as a whole. Apart from exceptions such as Nijinsky, women predominated in the early part of this century. Until the birth of the Soviet school in the 1930s, men hardly danced at all; they did a few lifts, took a few steps, and retired into Apollonian poses. Then a new tribe of magnificent dancers—Messerer, Sergeyev, Chaboukiani, Koren, Kaplan, Bregvadze, Yermolaev, Zubkovsky— inserted variations everywhere which began switching interest to them. When Nureyev took this idea to the West he stimulated a great growth of interest in male dancing.

Someone told me that Balanchine called ballet "a woman's world in which man is the honored guest." If the report was true, I felt the belief couldn't be more wrong. Many Western men of less schooled companies than Balanchine's *were* disappointing, but this was because they did not use what nature had given them. They were sweet instead of strong, cute where they should be elegant—in other words, effeminate.

No sexual problems as such existed in ballet. If freedom was important anywhere, it was in love. But *on the stage*, artistic rules applied. A dainty-looking hero evoked anything but belief. The contrast between his and his sweetheart's body, which underlay the dramatic development of many ballets, turned into a confusing, unhealthy sameness when both moved their muscles like girls.

Much more than dance language suffered. A ballet's narrative core was cut out from the start if the male principal did not look like a Prince while struggling to win the Princess. His dancing might be graceful, even brilliant. But if the audience could not believe his love for her, the real meaning of the story, the deepest dimension, was gone. At best it would be a delight for the eye—but no gift to the soul. Yet the rare virile man in visiting Western groups seemed apologetic, as if his manliness somehow violated the spirit of ballet instead of being essential to it.

Maybe because of foreign trips and a desire to impress foreign critics, a tendency toward feminine gestures was beginning to grow in Russia, too. But ballet's status as a full-fledged profession protected us from mass disaster. Boys began their apprenticeship before the "artistic" world had influenced them, then grew up in a relatively normal atmosphere, with real men as their teachers and models and real manliness as part of their work.

But in the West training often apparently began in adolescence, when many already had homosexual stirrings, and some saw ballet's appeal precisely in this. Sometimes they were taught by women—a grave error. Sometimes men teachers fond of the male form chose compatible company for the little nests they'd built in their schools. Boys were encouraged to develop a female coquettishness instead of expressing male feelings in ballet's powerful vocabulary. Parents were frightened of what would happen to normal sons there, and the most potentially gifted boys were kept away.

On top of everything, critics came to take the unnatural mannerisms as the standard. They propagated delicacy as the highest criterion of male dancing and dismissed truly masculine movement as "gladiatorial." Of course, ballet needed beauty in its men—but a beauty based on, and expressing, their own nature. Tenderness and grace did not add up to delicacy.

With ballet's penetration to the deepest, most instinctive emotions, it was natural that so many works until recently were based on what was considered the essence of romantic love. But the days of strict, old-fashioned division between the sexes—the woman as Fair Maiden, the man as Brave Warrior—were ending. There was no reason not to choreograph new works for a different kind of man, even an effeminate one, so long as it reflected a truth about him. There was no reason either why men with the strongest homosexual drive could not continue to dance the most traditionally romantic parts, so long as they stayed true to art's demands in their professional work.

It was common knowledge that some of the world's most perceptive critics, many creative composers, and most exciting dancers were homosexual and that this preference in general seemed linked to a heightened sensitivity to the arts. Certainly this was true among my painter friends and personal fans. But whatever the celebrated dancers were in their private lives, their performances conveyed the height of masculine charm, power, and attraction. This proved that sexual questions were totally irrelevant so long as dancers did not violate the artistic spirit of their roles.

THE PREVIOUS FALL THE BOLSHOI had invited me to be a guest soloist, and I was invited back regularly after that. Each visit taught me more about Moscow.

The old Maryinsky's precise and perfect style mirrored the tastes of the St. Petersburg court and aristocracy whom it was intended to entertain. But in the sprawling village of Moscow, the Bolshoi had catered to expansive merchants who liked Gypsy girls in their taverns and spectacle in the theater. Although not nearly so polished as the Maryinsky's, the Bolshoi dancers were more encouraged to project emotional excitement and artistic vision.

As the birthplace of classical ballet and protector of its highest standards the present Kirov was still considered the final arbiter of taste. But when the capital was shifted after the Revolution, Moscow got the ministries, the foreign visitors, and the need for display for both. Since ballet was still the showpiece of Russia's rulers, the Kirov could no longer compete in prestige, whatever its excellence. The Bolshoi was where Stalin—and therefore the money—went.

From subsidies to actual life and death, bureaucrats decided everything. Personal contact was crucial in winning tiny mercies, and there was a hope if they had just seen you in a performance. Starting with Ulanova, some of the finest Kirov performers and balletmasters transferred to Moscow in the 1930s and 1940s. When the Bolshoi began to travel in the Khrushchev era, they accommodated themselves slightly to the international "market," while the Kirov upheld its strict standards.

Some Bolshoi productions mounted chiefly for "abroad" were empty failures, but the general effect was beneficial. Life there became more interesting as the productions came closer to the limits of the permissible on a Soviet stage. The cycle speeded up as the company went abroad more and more often. Opening up to foreign tastes brought incentives to develop individual styles and personalities. Departures from traditional models were much more likely to be tolerated when they made an impression on audiences. But this dash of the American entrepreneurial spirit was also in keeping with the heritage of Moscow, where the public wanted colorful pageantry.

The difference almost bowled me over when I began rehearsing *Don Quixote* on my first Bolshoi invitation. Everyone was keener about color and effects. Even my suggestions as a guest prompted serious interest rather than winces. But although I felt far more at home in Moscow, Leningrad was still the right place for me. The Kirov's hard schooling was what I needed more of, rather than easier, quicker success in the capital. What the Bolshoi's open welcome did give me was a chance to learn from its more varied dancers, who also brought back more and more ideas from abroad.

The man I liked most in friendly Moscow had been one class below me in the Moscow Academy. For years after he was graduated, Vladimir Vasiliev was dismissed as a trickster because of his "stunted" shape and "twisted" style. He was the one who complained that the ladies didn't look at him when he left the stage door. But the Bolshoi learned to live with his athleticism, and he bounded to the top when he was allowed to feel his own way. Although an unusually late developer as a principal, he would soon be one of the world's best male dancers, my personal inspiration in almost everything. He had Nureyev's animal magnetism, but with more polish. Great native intelligence hid behind his unassuming appearance. He worked hard for exactly the touches he wanted but was delightfully easygoing as a person.

"Let's do some drinking," he'd sing when I arrived in Moscow. "We haven't talked for months."

"You're crazy. You're on tomorrow—and a matinee. Twenty-four hours is the minimum for sobering up."

But he pulled me toward a liquor counter. His tremendously powerful performances could shake off almost any handicap. Besides, he knew how to listen to his moods. He danced for love, and all his strength came from being natural.

Year after year he grew steadily better. At thirty-five he was twice as good as he had been at thirty—so exciting that I floated after seeing him in a new role. When I climbed as far as I could in the Kirov, he was setting a higher standard in the Bolshoi.

THE BOLSHOI CELEBRITY SCENE was either vulgar or appealing, depending on your taste. Foreign trips were more frequent and the Central Committee much nearer than in Leningrad; therefore, the rivalrous intrigues were even more murderous. But they seemed confined to middle-level soloists, while the leading dancers were more worldly and interesting than in Leningrad. And in general, the company lived as though just a hint of the American style—big cars and shiny kitchens—had penetrated here as well. More travel and less straitjacketing of stage personalities made the Bolshoi relatively happy. Ten years later seven leading Kirov dancers would be permanently abroad, but no Bolshoi star would have defected.

The top stars rewarded their most ardent supporters with expensive gifts. After a successful performance the fans gathered to eat and drink at the stars' apartments, as they felt entitled to do, since "we worked hard and helped her have a big night." The big night ended in a happy party, often transferring for a nightcap to one of a few famous "salons."

Among Moscow ballet lovers *the* Party was represented by the daughter of one of its heads. The dark young woman with heavy eyebrows bore an unfortunate resemblance to her powerful father. She was known as "spicy" and was in love with a handsome young Latvian named Maris Liepa, whom the Bolshoi accepted in 1960 after withdrawing its offer to me.

Onstage Liepa lacked much that muscles can do, but he was unusually graceful and full of sensitive gestures, which he unselfishly tried to teach me. His refinement and wide cultural interests kept him an outsider for years, especially since the "boys" of the Personnel Department hated his breeding. But his elegant good looks made him a matinee idol of the wives and daughters of high officials. His lovely wife and two children were no obstacle. The entire Bolshoi knew who sent him bouquets of red carnations. The color had no political significance.

The prospects for rehabilitating myself seemed brighter in Moscow than in Leningrad, and Liepa's contacts in particular were a convict's dream. Only some freak personal intervention could get me a visa now. The higher the rank, the greater my hope. It surged yet again when a young ballet lover invited me to spend an evening at the apartment of his father. He was a son of Anastas Mikoyan.

The taxi driver spun around and looked at me when I named the address. He drove to a central but secluded quarter behind old Arbat Street. It was full of consulates and ministerial residences, and although not a soul was in sight, I wanted to ask someone for permission to breathe. The man for this, an unmistakably sullen type, materialized the moment I left the car. I had hardly begun to answer his questions when he interrupted. "That's right, I know. Follow me."

The yellowish building looked typical from the outside, but the elevator was Finnish, and the interior decor came from Hollywood. Inside the Mikoyan apartment, the kitchen was American, the furniture Scandinavian, and the lighting Italian. Not even any of the custom items the best Soviet craftsmen made on special Party order violated the unity. From floor to ceiling it was a gleaming outpost of the West.

Young Mikoyan was entertaining several young engineers obviously headed for the top. They talked of the economic waste and outright chaos they observed in their jobs and of an old émigré priest who had recently returned to Russia—with much publicity—out of love for the country, but who was already disgusted with the moral corruption. Mikoyan junior listened carefully but hardly joined in. I resolved to make a direct bid for help as soon as I could get him alone.

"Look, there's no point in fooling you," he said. "I think your whole situation's a shame, but I simply won't get involved. What I will do is tell you how to write your petitions and whom to send them to."

His advice sent me off on one more detour, looking for the right string to pull.

AFTER THE MOSCOW SUMMER Rachinsky gave up campaigning for my dismissal. His new respect for me was the kind shown an enemy who has staved off defeat. Even Fedicheva smiled at me occasionally. She was happy on her own account because she'd just given a personal concert. The great prestige was another stepping-stone to People's Artist of the Russian Republic, which she would win the following year. Meanwhile, my invitation to her celebration party after the concert was a clear declaration of a truce.

Her parents' apartment was large enough to squeeze everyone in since her father was a trusted Party worker. Cultural officials intermingled with the police and Party bosses whom Fedicheva loved to impress. Rachinsky raised his glass and bumbled an accolade. It was clear why he liked to stray away from his shrill little wife, who was looking daggers at him and who froze everyone by rising to speak when he finally finished. "Yes, we congratulate Kaleria Ivanovna Fedicheva for her . . . er, interesting evening," she whined. "But I beg you all not to forget that we have other ballerinas worthy of this honor. We have Natalia Romanovna Makarova, for example."

Rachinsky might have taken the hint to honor Makarova, if only to make life less unpleasant for himself. But she would never get her own evening, or her rightful place in Leningrad.

FEDICHEVA STILL HAD ONLY ME to partner her in certain numbers, and we had been mismatched from time to time ever since our break. Now we returned to an almost normal working relationship. Most of all, we were paired for special performances of the big "heroic" ballets for honoring the high revolutionary holidays and foreign dignitaries. The Kirov was taken over for this five to ten times in the average year, and I found myself entertaining heads of state whose names no one bothered to tell me.

In the summer of 1966 we were assigned to do our old party piece *Laurencia* for Charles de Gaulle. His host was to be Alexei Kosygin, the head of the government. As with all such command performances, preparations for this one advanced under "strict regimen" procedure. The audience was composed entirely of stalwart officials and their guests, including a large sprinkling of security men. Our every move was watched. It was taboo to call the plainclothesmen anything but "representatives of the general public." In dark serge suits, white shirts, and funereal ties—Rachinsky's daily uniform—they kept grimacing and glancing over their shoulders. They milled about backstage, causing incidents and misunderstandings by their very profusion.

In the first act I prepared to enter the stage as Frondoso and declare my undying love for Laurencia. Ever since our failed lift, I was very eager to avoid mistakes when partnering Fedicheva. I tried to work up some ardor for her while following the action carefully from the wings. Hands seized me seconds before my cue. I spun around to the leer of two "representatives." Apparently I'd been looking in the direction of Kosygin and de Gaulle. Having detected this unsanctioned interest, the agents swung valiantly into action and began tugging me away. Fedicheva would have killed me if an apoplectic assistant director hadn't rushed up. "*Panov*, for the love of God. You missed your cue!"

I recovered. That scene—and all of Act Two—went well. During the last intermission a legion of officials sporting medals on their suits entered my dressing room. The objects they were carrying were made of genuine leather, a great rarity in our land. They were dyed the color of our national flag and embossed with national emblems the size of a bear's jaws. Pages of gold-printed messages about Franco-Soviet friendship nestled between these covers. The commander of the task force, no doubt at least a vice-minister of something, carefully opened both official souvenirs for the heads of government. "So you will sign here, as this occasion's male lead. But first, wash your hands."

As the final curtain fell, plainclothesmen surrounded the stage. Dripping sweat, Rachinsky told us our honored visitors were coming to see us. State guests came backstage through a bulletproof door of lead and iron. For lesser officials a carpet was dispensed with. For superior ones, a striped material was used. For the present personages, a spread of thick red pile was unfurled, just as a band of hectic reporters and photographers appeared. Then frail Kosygin came into view, looking more ordinary than ever alongside Charles de Gaulle. Before my second blink at his imperial grandeur, a "representative" had shoved one of the souvenir books into my unwashed hands. "Don't forget, young man. You present this one here to Comrade Kosygin. And address him as 'Alexei Nicolaevich.' " He thoughtfully supplied the tone with which I was to suggest a cozy respect.

Fedicheva was instructed with the proper words for de Gaulle and successfully bestowed on him his souvenir book. But he struck up a conversation with us, blocking me from Kosygin, who stood a courteous step behind. De Gaulle kept shaking my hand as if I were a tank officer, then startled me with an invitation to "come to Paris forthwith. I assure you that the French people will welcome your talent." This was pronounced with great elegance, but also with the force of a command. The majestic one was apparently going to settle the details of my visit there and then.

The KGB chaperon behind me had other ideas. Observing the

crimson leather still unpresented and convinced that my kind of theatrical simpleton could be relied on for nothing, he grabbed my elbow and half lifted me, no doubt with the skill of many arrests, in Kosygin's direction. What he couldn't see from behind my shoulder was that de Gaulle's handshake was still pumping away.

The general retreated a full step. His aplomb disintegrated. My guide completed my hand's strange shift by pushing it directly into Kosygin's limp one. The whisper came hoarsely into my ear. "Remember! Call him Alexei Nicolaevich."

Alexei Nicolaevich accepted his souvenir and shrugged to suggest that Russians will be Russians. The "representative" who had successfully completed his assignment evaporated, together with my short-lived dream of a trip to France on a summons from its personification.

28

PARTS CAME THICK AND FAST IN 1966—IN SCHUMANN's *Le Carnaval*, Gounod's *Walpurgis Night*, Khachaturian's *Gayané*, and four other ballets. Dudinskaya asked me to partner her in *The Path of Thunder*, Sergeyev's work about the brutality of apartheid as symbolized in the murder of a white woman and colored man who loved each other. Rehearsals left little time for brooding.

I still kept popping up like a loose screw in the immaculate Kirov machine, but this no longer tormented me. I had the body control and stage bearing to put in some of my own emotion. I could even look back gratefully at my three grueling years. Nothing came easily even now. But there were no accidental successes. With my hated defects almost gone, I no longer regretted coping with them so late. Every nuance meant more, like a novel to someone old enough to have lived through what he is reading about.

In 1967 everything was linked to 1917. You couldn't go five minutes without slogans about the fifty glorious years of Soviet rule driving you mad. And of course, no artist would have achieved anything without the Revolution's inspiration.

The gala October Concert in Leningrad's October Hall was a "crucial" event even by the Party's standards for self-celebration. The expected arrival of Leonid Brezhnev and a swollen Politburo entourage made the evening more equal than a hundred other equal evenings that fall. Yuri Soloviev was almost accused of sabotage when he took sick just before the gala. The limousine fetching me to replace him rode the center of the streets with red flags streaming. Policemen saluting the grille at every corner amplified the thump of my heart, but my pas de deux went exceptionally well. Sergeyev took this as the full return of his gamble on me. At the banquet afterward he told Party leaders that holding me back was harming the Kirov and the country. Heads nodded at this obvious reference to my political limbo. My optimism revived slightly.

LATER IN THE SEASON Natalia Dudinskaya asked me to participate in a concert to show off the members of her classe de perfection. I was at a loss with most concert numbers—for just the reasons that some of my major roles worked. It was my opposites with perfect muscles and cool attitudes who produced ten splendid minutes at the drop of a hat. Except when "up," I could never get in the mood, never limber up my slow-warming muscles, never understand the point enough really to dance without being a fictional character.

The pas de deux from *Harlequinade* was the exception partly because it hadn't been done for twenty years. I was permitted to prepare my own version, and *this* became the standard for others! Besides, it was a miniature ballet in itself, with full opportunity to show off the Harlequin's personality. When I tried him the Kirov way, the result was disastrous in two minor previews. At last I dropped outside suggestions and worked on my own interpretation, inspired by photographs I had seen of the famous statuettes of Fokine in his *Carnaval*. The bronze looked so fluid that it threatened to melt. Fokine suggested a kind of motion I'd never imagined, a satyr's languidness, slack to the point of sexlessness.

I transformed every movement to fit this image of a sweet, harmless rake. Suddenly charged with passion, my Harlequin darted, flew, and cast spells in steps requiring clean, powerful technique. Then he slipped back to his neuterlike limpness. The extended coda actually earned backstage cheers. It was a series of ronds, pirouettes, and leaps fused into highly intricate patterns and performed with eye-blinking speed. I wanted to suggest a harlequin's legerdemain, especially this one's great captivating charm.

Carried away by the centrifugal spins one evening, I tore a groin muscle. Feeling as if my leg had been ripped off, I crawled to the nearest wing while trying to flash the Harlequin's naughty smile. Fear of a finished career tripled the pain. I passed out as the curtain came down.

"That's the end of Panov. He worked like a horse—and went out like one." I had come to in Sergeyev's arms, certain I'd never dance again. My groin was on fire; I couldn't move.

The ways of the artistic world were wondrous strange. No one in the Maly liked me until I left. And as I left the Kirov now, those who disliked my style offered the warmest sympathy. Tears fell as my stretcher entered the ambulance. It was time for a sumptuous funeral; all eyes were dry when I returned to class three weeks later.

Invitations to dance *Harlequinade* started pouring in while I was recuperating. Clive Barnes, the British-American dance critic, saw it soon after I was back. "It was Valery Panov's Harlequin that stole the show," he wrote of the "remarkable" Dudinskaya concert by a "group of the finest dancers in the world. . . . This, incidentally, was my first view of Panov, who was over a series of performances to impress me as one of the most remarkable male dancers of our day. Panov comes on stage, any stage, and offers an unmistakable image. His dance technique is fantastic, but it is his sense of dramatic conviction that truly impresses."

Rachinsky had another opinion. "Panov's thing is a disgrace to the Soviet stage," he muttered. But he had now less against me than against Dudinskaya, whose success disturbed him more than usual after Fedicheva dropped out of her concert without glory. And through Dudinskaya, Rachinsky wanted to get Sergeyev. As the country moved faster in the direction he approved of, his Artistic Director was a bone in his throat.

THE BALANCHINE VISIT in 1962 had come at the farthest point of our wobbly advance toward greater artistic freedom. Weeks later Khrushchev made his angry visit to an exhibition of paintings in Moscow and started backpedaling. The retreat became a rout when he was deposed. "Liberals" in the Party apparatus whose help I was hoping for now needed help for themselves.

Ballet creativity was battered and bruised. During the "new wave" capped by the Balanchine visit, dancers saw a few inventive choreographers who appeared as saviors from lifetimes of standard roles. But the Kirov had been last to experiment with anything and first to stop. The new men left for more congenial places: Igor Belsky for the Maly and Yuri Grigorovich for the Bolshoi. By the mid-1960s their departures from the old academic style were stuck in shallow grooves. The same pressures were exerted on them; they wanted to keep their new places in the establishment.

The exception was Leonid Jacobson, an aging balletmaster who had survived as one of Russia's few truly creative choreographers after Stalin's roundup. His *Spartacus* of the early Khrushchev years stunned everyone. Soviet rule prevented the world from knowing Jacobson's genius because it saw only the fraction left after his works had been made acceptable. He was always on the edge of disgrace. A "dangerous" urge to express his individual vision and to encourage individuality in general was in his bones. He fought battle after battle to preserve at least parts of his creations. He argued, pleaded, finagled. He compromised, too, twisting Mayakovsky's *The Bedbug*—and even Bulgakov's *The White Guard* and Blok's *The Twelve*—into pro-Soviet messages. This enabled him to stage these otherwise heretical works.

Jacobson was also enormously inventive in actual choreography. He *liked* contributions from his dancers that he could use—always with deft improvements—in his constant search for something new. Working with him was day-and-night excitement.

Land of Miracles, the ballet that provided this happiness—and the thrill of creating a new role, with no pattern to follow—was based on ancient tales of Russian folk heroes. Fair Maiden personified beauty, selflessness, and virtue. Yasny Sokol was the valorous leader in the people's fight against a tribe of evil monsters.

The new work's originality shone in sketches of the sets by elders of the town of Palekh, a famous home of icon painters for centuries. With the Bolshevik suppression of religion, Palekh's masters managed to preserve their craft by making resplendent gift boxes. The two artists who came to do the painting were deeply reverent of their work, but the administration dragged them to the usual Party meeting for talk, talk, talk and ideological analysis of the ballet's theme in the light of NATO's new aggressiveness. Finally, one of the timid men spoke up in a Volga accent. "Please, comrades, just tell us, and we'll do twenty more sketches if you want. We can't work with our tongues."

The completed sets had the vividness and imagination of the best Russian folk art. Brilliant colors and golden cupolas gleamed on a black background. It was the lining of a whole fairy-tale world, a genuine land of miracles, with all the flamboyant detail of Palekh boxes. In the complaints about "slanderously unrealistic" Russian horses and absurd demands for changes, the artists got a taste of what Jacobson had had to endure for thirty years. The saving factor was the theme: the triumph of the Russian masses and national spirit over all evil forces.

Yasny Sokol—otherwise known as Brave Warrior or Mighty Hawk—was an ancient Russian symbol of masculine strength. I liked Jacobson's vision of the part best for its abrupt changes from a primitive hero's dynamism to a surprisingly gentle lyricism. But Yuri Soloviev was planned for the first lead, and I rehearsed it with a certain reserve.

Makarova, for once, was my partner. She was constantly inventing little gifts for the choreography, each one underlining the Kirov's unfairness in still not treating her as a great star. Her repertoire was limited too much to the standard classical roles, where severe restrictions cramped her innate originality. When she at last got something new—the Fair Maiden, for example—she was inimitable. But her superiority over the methodical Irina Kolpakova was ignored. The older ballerina was not only a People's Artist of the USSR, but also active in the Party committee.

Then Kolpakova became pregnant, and Makarova was given to Soloviev, making a challenge to him by me even less possible. But as the company's leading male dancer—and rightly so—he was preoccupied with other things, including preparations for foreign trips. He was still completely free of ego problems and other backstage diseases. But the easygoing assurance his body had always given him also put him off hard competition. He much preferred a friendly drink to a Kirov conspiracy or to a struggle.

His absence encouraged me to make a real try. A give-and-take relationship with the choreographer had always charged my cells, and Jacobson was the most exciting I'd ever worked with. Classical steps as such meant nothing to him. To advance the story or to tell something about a character, a special touch had to be given to each turn, bend, and arabesque. "You leap perfectly, you land perfectly—what's the point?" he used to ask when seeking the spurt in the air to suggest an insight into Yasny Sokol's impulses.

My Maly fury reappeared just as Jacobson added even more to Yasny Sokol's variations. The new combinations came closer and closer to the expressiveness of character parts, a further obstacle to Soloviev, who was happiest with the movements he'd been practicing since childhood. The third candidate had already withdrawn, and Soloviev asked to join him. He was told to proceed with the dress rehearsal, which left him more exhausted then I'd ever seen him. "I'll never touch this fiendish part again," he swore and, after one performance, made this promise good.

With its strong character slant *Laurencia*'s Frondoso would have seemed made for me and wholly unsuitable for Soloviev, the lyric champion. Yet he was so much better than I when he tried Frondoso that eyes popped. His psychological barrier to mastering Yasny Sokol was the luck that advanced me from Kirov acceptance to the beginnings of stardom.

To be seen with foreigners was no more "recommended" than ever, even when they were "guests of the Soviet people." But the temptations for many of us were growing. Their faces were as free of wrinkles as their suits. Above all, they had a privileged scent, which worked like a potion on our girls. Westerners were color, contrast, and invigoration. Thanks to exchange programs started under Khrushchev, I could talk to the handful of young dancers who were training at the Kirov without drawing attention to myself. Yuri Maltsev always tagged at the heels of an English boy. The KGB had an unquenchable thirst for "just-in-case" information, especially political views and weaknesses.

Then a Parisian arrived. For a month he couldn't stop exclaiming about the huge Soviet studios, the aromatic Soviet borscht, the great and loving Soviet people. "You snap your fingers and zounds! Any girl you want comes to your room!" Like a practical Frenchman, he sold his underpants for sixteenth-century icons and amassed a trunkful of fantastic antiques. His voice trembled with the knowledge that he was *rich* when displaying them to his best Soviet friend.

Maltsev put his finger to his lips, suggested a good hiding place, and coordinated the police raid so the treasure would disappear two days before the Frenchman's return home. By this time our guest had learned more than he cared to know about Soviet life. He departed, its sworn enemy.

"Take home" KGB control reduced the need for elaborate shadowing. This consisted of two or three key people—including a lover, if at all possible—reporting on a foreigner's whereabouts. One girl from Brussels who was thought to have some connection with the Belgian court had day-and-night escorts. She shared a tiny apartment attached to the Academy on Rossi Street with a ballerina from Denmark and with Rosa, a Mexican girl with eyes that could have gone on the stage without makeup.

Rosa was a socialist but was impatient with Soviet rigidity in the arts. She seemed to know about every cultural trend in the world and insisted that modern dance was more relevant to our era than classical ballet. My offended reply was that no art could shine without traditions. Modern dance would have to take second place to ballet until it developed them. Isadora Duncan and Martha Graham made great contributions, but in personal style, not in the basic vocabulary, because they were offshoots from the fundamental tradition.

Rosa's sister was visiting from Paris, and Rosa proposed a foursome to see the city during the White Nights. The other man was Mischa Kozakov, an old friend in whose studio I used to sculpt and paint. A Russian artist to his nicotine-stained fingertips, Mischa drank constantly as medicine for his melancholy. We set out on a grand walking tour. As usual, the talk was of art—especially Western developments. The mood sank to Mischa's customary pessimism. He enthused about contemporary sculptors of whom I'd never heard. I said I'd soon be too old to try the new forms in classical ballet I yearned for. My joke about escaping to fulfill my dream of working under Balanchine or Béjart wasn't funny.

We came to the Fortress of Peter and Paul. A waiter in a barge restaurant recognized me from my nights of brooding there. The more we drank at the table he found us, the bigger our hopes grew for ourselves and for the world. Mischa sang folk songs while I stared into my vision of myself rehearsing Balanchine's *Prodigal Son*. He ordered yet another bottle, finished half of it, and jumped into the water with a smack like a cannon shot. "To the Winter Palace! A marathon! Hurrah!"

I dived into the current and miraculously coaxed him back for more vodka. Rosa's wide-eyed sister kept asking what all this meant. To me, it meant only that the White Nights were the time when the air itself was charged. Anything was possible. At least it was possible to dream of anything.

29

SOMETIMES THE WHITE NIGHTS FESTIVALS, WITH THEIR REAL AND artificial excitement, seemed elaborate frauds. The hodgepodge of ballets and concerts was put together with the single intention of pleasing Westerners. Even nature's never-setting sun was exploited. Yet I loved these early summer weeks when Leningrad filled up with tourists. Partly in compensation for not traveling, I danced more and more in the various programs. "Panov's got his trip abroad" was a standard joke each June.

During the 1967 Festival, Clive Barnes saw me in *Romeo and Juliet*. "The most remarkable performance," he wrote, ". . . came from neither Romeo nor Juliet but Mercutio. This was Valery Panov, a dancer virtually unknown in the West, yet a dancer of the most astonishing talent. His Mercutio was one of the greatest performances I have ever seen in the ballet theater." I heard a little of this on the BBC and danced like a flying horse. This was an affirmation like none other. For almost ten years—the time of my real schooling—Western critics had not seen me.

Barnes also watched Makarova and me in the *Land of Miracles*:

> The dancing—once again—was magnificent. Natalia Makarova is a dancer of rare gifts, of a sort of trembling passion combined with a precise formal statement. . . . The surprise of the performance was not, however, Makarova (since when has she not been good?) but rather the revelation of Valery Panov, who is unquestionably one of Russia's finest male dancers, and the least known in the West. He was dancing the role of the Brave Warrior—a symbol of dauntless virility rather than the opportunity for a characterization —and his brilliance lit up the stage. Technically (he is, incidentally, demi-caractère rather than pure classical) there is no one in the world to match him. As a pure classicist he is untidy—as a pure dancer he has genius.

Overnight the opinion of the members of my company, who should have known me better than anyone, soared. Only Sergeyev was immune to the magic power of Western judgment. His rejoicing for me was constant. "There you are, your debut abroad," he said. "Didn't I tell you you'd have one? And they like you best of all."

DURING HIS LENINGRAD VISIT Clive Barnes had attended a class of Alexander Pushkin. "Like all the Russian teachers I encounter," he wrote, "Pushkin has a fantastic rapport with his pupils. The class is a collective, discipline is self-imposed and the teacher is there, his proper work already accomplished during years of training, almost as a totem figurehead."

He went on to describe some members of the class, including me, who "arrived late in a flowered shirt, flashed cheerful grins at all and sundry, and danced brilliantly, like a scalded cat. . . . So in a different way did a very young boy, 18 or 19, fair-haired, cherubic, and the most perfect dancer I have ever seen. I asked his name. It was Yuri Baryshnikov."

Baryshnikov, who had just joined the Kirov, was in fact nineteen. His name wasn't Yuri but Mikhail: "Mischa" to almost everyone. Otherwise, Barnes was entirely right; Mischa was one of the few dancers of genius. Barnes mentioned my "good-natured teasing" of him in that class by "doing everything he did in the very free center work about twice as fast and twice as long." But Mischa remained unflustered because his technique was impeccable, and he knew how much it thrilled me. And he was so cheerful that everyone immediately became fond of him.

The following winter Baryshnikov made plans to attend the finals of a national competition among the top graduates of ballet academies. Like most potential stars without a partner, he was constantly on the lookout for one—and for pretty ballerinas in general. My own peeks at female classes now prompted banter about my stage "bachelorhood." The truth was I *did* look hard at every new ballerina. When I longed for my partner to appear, I saw her as the person with whom I could share everything.

Crossing the Kirov stage toward our seats one day, Mischa pointed to a girl as blond as a worker on a farm poster. She was obviously on her first trip to the big city but bustled about, all business and energy.

"What do you think?" he asked.

"Nothing to write home about," I answered with a familiar disappointment. Galina Ragozina was about to graduate from the Perm Academy, the one founded by Ekaterina Geidenreich, the Maly's female coach. Its contingent's superiority was obvious from the start of the program.

Seventeen-year-old Ragozina was already a minor event in ballet, and I had come with a secret hope that she might be the One. Her makeup dashed my fancy to pieces. She had smeared and troweled it onto her village face. Then she came onstage. Her tanklike doggedness gave way to the best female ballet proportions and foundation I'd ever seen. She could lift either leg over her ear and split both legs effortlessly in the air. Ballerinas with this "ballet step" usually suffer from lack of balance that hampers their leaps and turns, but all of Ragozina's movements were dazzling.

She danced again—even more furiously—after winning the competition. On our way to the stage exit, she passed us like a rubber band that had just snapped and was winding itself up again. All the other girls curtsied or giggled to a cluster of Kirov and Bolshoi balletmasters and teachers who might make their future, but Ragozina strode by as if the generations of stars were lighting fixtures. The stubborn little thing made me grin.

30

THE WHITE NIGHTS FESTIVAL OF 1968 WAS DEDICATED TO THE ONE hundred and fiftieth anniversary of the birth of Marius Petipa. "The father of classical ballet" had staged *Swan Lake, Sleeping Beauty, Nutcracker*, and sixty other major ballets in magnificent succession during his half-century reign at the Maryinsky. The tributes to him seemed worded to tell me what I had to be grateful for. The most famous dancers in history had created Petipa's roles. I was still a flop, and would always be, for those requiring soft, sweet gliding. Yet my contribution to the company that came closest to maintaining his standards was taken for granted.

In the long run, my late start, shifts, and interruptions turned out to be blessings. They lifted me off the path of the flawless dancer raised on ten seamless Academy years. The flukes of getting into the Kirov so late, then being saved from being sent away again gave me almost full polish without making me the ballet soldier that so many little boys became. I even owed a debt to the Kirov's monotony. In the Maly I'd learned how to dance through the dram-ballet's undanceable sections. Here the danced-to-death passages of the standard works forced me to think about what I wanted to say in them, so they wouldn't appear like exercises.

Clive Barnes returned for the 1968 Festival. We had champagne in the Kirov buffet with his wife, Patricia, my picture of an English lady. My half hour with the famous critic who had given me so much happiness was a crowning touch. I felt the personal contact would be crucial one day, and for once, this was not wishful thinking.

Barnes wrote about his Leningrad trip that year from the standpoint of the Petipa tradition and the Kirov's primacy of style. His praise of me surpassed the previous year's. But what mattered now was that he *understood.* "Here is a dancer who never appears in the West, although he is one of the few great male dancers in the world." His wife, also a critic, was even more generous in her reviews—and more direct in her conclusions. "If only he could come to the West, and soon."

The superlatives in Patricia's articles, and in Clive's, were the realization of all my dreams, everything I'd wanted for so long. Throughout the time when I was fighting almost alone for the finesse to merit full stardom, I never wholly believed it was achievable. I never trusted myself to become the equal of the full-fledged Academy products the Kirov had taken when and just before I went to the Maly. But judging by the assignment of roles and by professional opinion, I had done at least that. And in my own evaluation of my development, I knew I had triumphed. My goal of becoming as complete a dancer as I could had been reached. The destiny promised by the sun dawning after my graduation was attained.

Yet this awareness brought no relief. On the contrary, it opened me to deeper, more dismaying dissatisfaction than I'd ever known. For five years I'd been in a battle to make my body behave. Now I looked at what was happening outside me. The Soviet system was essentially the same. But the easing of my anxiety about my own problems allowed me to see it clearly. With ten star-kissed dancing years ahead of me, I realized that I was nothing *as a person*. All my talks with my physicist neighbor and with Alec's friends fell into place. My scrappy conversations with foreigners filled out the reading that Alec and others had seen to. I would never be able to do what I wanted even as a dancer, and this was no accident.

Apart from a few silent heroes whose best work was quashed, no one was creating anything real in Soviet ballet—because no one was allowed to. One Western company after another showed what free choreographers and directors could achieve. They proved that classical ballet had enormous relevance, range, and power to move when people conveyed *what they truly felt*. But from highest to lowest, we were numb. We served a political line that dismissed the very notion of personal expression. "Art is never the plaything of individuals. Art is always the Party's and people's inspiration in their struggle against bourgeois ideology and for the final victory of Communism."

Khrushchev had inspired a hope that this would change. That hope was gone. Now I recognized that the system was *designed* to kill real art. The heart of it remained Party control, which no "new wave" could wash away. Even genuinely creative men had to make so many compromises and curry so much favor that they became nearly as "Party-minded" as those they replaced. This was artistic suicide, and the opposite course—to fight—promised an even speedier death. When I woke from my trance of furious work, I looked at my fellow dancers. Their submissiveness to oppression was the major cause of my loneliness. From this moment ballet lost its hold as the meaning of my life. It would no longer be enough to dance what I wanted in the Kirov, even if this were magically allowed.

Somewhere I had known the whole truth long ago. But I had too many professional problems to cope with before admitting it. I hoped that if I overcame them, ballet triumphs would solve everything. I would win prizes, become a celebrity—and not notice that these were substitutes for living and creating. Now all I'd suppressed surfaced with double force.

One of the strongest influences was Solzhenitsyn's *One Day in the Life of Ivan Denisovich*. None of the atrocities was new. I had already known, heard, or guessed everything Solzhenitsyn described. I even knew much of what his later Gulag books would reveal, for I had met former political prisoners soon after they returned to Leningrad in the 1950s. An older man who loved ballet told me of starvation, unspeakable torture, and execution among the slaves who built the Volga-Don Canal and in the infamous Siberian camps. Bulldozers occasionally uncovered layers of bones, including those of Lenin Prize winners and Stalin's once-favorite singers. Another man, the brother of a famous Soviet hero, returned to Moscow from America in 1946 because he wanted to contribute to the building of Communism. Taken immediately to the dungeons, he saw only his torturers for ten years.

It was Solzhenitsyn's art that made this suffering real. It swept away the last doubts and brought on the ghastliness inside me. Soon after *One Day* appeared in 1962, I was invited to a meeting of Leningrad's "leading creative workers." I did not achieve this group merely as the Maly's male lead. Those invited included everyone who talked too enthusiastically about the new literature, who made too much of jazz, who were too interested in Western artistic developments. The KGB knew what heads to whack into line—the purpose of the meeting. Khrushchev had just begun his retreat. Leonid Ilichev, his cultural boss, had come to lay down the new line on orthodoxy.

Like a Nazi orator, Ilichev thundered that our "depravity" must stop immediately and that "all Western influences, every rotten one of them, must be rooted out." His way of reversing the liberalization was to terrify everyone. He even spoke of the need for "cleansing"—the same word as "purging."

Sergeyev, who already felt Party pressure on him, was one of those who dutifully rose for a promise of obedience. He mocked Balanchine and other "Western rubbish."

Only one veteran theatrical director dared object. "A razor has many good uses," he said. "But if resorted to for 'cleansing,' it can be dangerous even to the user."

This reference to Stalin's purge beheading its own henchmen infuriated Ilichev. "Write down his name for me," he demanded of his aides. "And I want a list of all abstractionists and 'liberals,' too."

Hearts stopped beating all around me. I could actually feel the fascist power of Soviet rule in the morbid silence. But the elderly director's refusal to be intimidated made a deep impression, too. Not everyone pretended.

The following year Joseph Brodsky was exiled from Leningrad to

Siberia. Brodsky was just a name then, but friends showed me some of his beautiful poems and a transcript of his trial. Ilichev's "Get him! Write down his name!" echoed throughout the sickening abuse of the law.

Then Khrushchev fell. He was the kind of man who might have helped on an impulse, and I had continued to write to him even after he had turned against art. Suddenly he was gone into a black hole. After a speechless twenty-four hours, the acolytes who had been extolling him as mankind's God learned their new chorus. "Naturally the Party had to get rid of the old fool, he made so many mistakes. . . ."

When my eyes finally opened, I saw that it wasn't just these incidents. The system's highest achievement lay in so befuddling people that they forgot what they had said the day before. No one could decide anything for himself. All of our society was a gigantic illustration of what was wrong with it.

For thirty years I had accepted drunkenness in Russians as a fact of life. The massive expression of despair I now recognized was spreading uncontrollably as we "marched ever on" to Communism's ultimate happiness. The average Russian guzzled twice as much hard liquor as the second hardest drinking country in the world, but UN statistics weren't needed to see the country sloshing in alcohol. Workers drank away half their wages to escape the pincers of meaningless work and crushing propaganda about its glory. Without travel, jazz, and a million forms of recreation available in other countries, vodka was the only refuge.

Whole villages sometimes went on monumental binges. I rubbed my eyes when I first saw this hopelessness, even though I knew why drinking among the intelligentsia had also increased fantastically. The best sculptors and painters sank deeper into demoralization. Many had large Artists' Union studios and lived well on canvases of Party Congresses and locomotives with red stars. But they had to hide their real work. They called themselves "impressionists," "expressionists," "futurists," or "nihilists"—anything not be be socialist realists. Everything new was good by definition. They smeared goo on icons, painted gaudy Christs, and attracted Western journalists eager to discover underground art. But at least they were searching—and that was their crime. One after another was punished for nothing more than having tried something different.

Any expression of individuality in the arts that interested me was precisely what incited the watchdogs' fury. I could never be standard. I would have to begin searching for my own new conceptions soon. What awaited me was worse than the artists' dead end. At least paintings could be done privately and shoved "to the wall." What about unorthodox ballets?

If I had admitted all this years before, it would have blunted my passion for dancing. I would never have conquered my problems, would have been left with nothing for fighting the larger fight. Now the truth was as clear to me as to Alec when his university journal had been raided. Besides, *they* hammered it home with their daily stamping on people's rights, thoughts, and hopes. I still loved dancing, especially new roles. I still kept my mouth shut and made compromises. But I knew. I even knew what I would have to do one day. All realizations fit one central design, which seemed ordained. Black realities outside ballet kept rushing at me.

31

THE ACCLAIM FOR DUDINSKAYA'S CLASSE DE PERFECTION CONCERT ended in an invitation to perform in Moscow's splendrous Hall of Columns. Late for warming up one August evening, I raced up its white staircase. An old Maly friend who had become Artistic Director of the Perm ballet was on the top landing. The ballerina with him looked like a teenager, yet had the cool assurance of someone important. Before I could remember where I'd seen her, my friend introduced her as the recent winner of the gold medal in Varna.

This was little Galina Ragozina. The moment I heard of her Varna victory, I knew I would meet her again. Her face was as bright as Fair Maiden's. It shone like her golden hair. She seemed the person I'd been waiting for. I went right on to the dressing room to keep myself from saying something silly.

Gold medals for Soviet competitors were always planned in advance, invariably for the upcoming stars of the "imperial" theaters. To win from outside Leningrad or Moscow required very rare talent. Doing it from the middle of the Urals, with no advance notice, no political connections, and no benefit to a cultural duke, amazed everyone.

The other miracle was my private one. In seven months the pudgy duckling who had won the Leningrad competition had turned into the partner of my daydreams. I had never seen anyone so immaculate. Her face was full of both will and modesty. My heart clenched.

Putting on my costume, I decided to dance for her alone. "God does everything right," I thought. If I had grown up as much as she in seven months, maybe . . .

The next morning I was up at a strange hour to track her down. When I found her hotel, she seemed unacquainted with how to use a telephone. Through her meek little yeses and nos, I finally learned that her Perm company, which was also touring in Moscow, was planning a farewell party that evening.

I arrived to see tears gather in her eyes. Together with the demure suit she was wearing, she had brought back a set of crystal goblets from Bulgaria. They were being filled with champagne, quickly drained, and tossed to the floor in the old Hussar custom. Each shatter sent splinters into her heart. I wanted to take her into my arms.

Instead, we went for a walk. I wondered about my sudden attachment to a deeply provincial child, probably more "Soviet" than Liya and all wrong for me. But she nodded her head as soon as I began talking about the Kirov's ultraconservatism. For years ballerinas had brushed aside my attempts to discuss this problem. Others avoided me for talking too openly about sensitive subjects. But Galya's brief answers were amazingly free of Soviet clichés. She seemed to understand.

It was both peculiar and utterly natural to expose my restlessness to a snippet who might misinterpret everything. I sensed that she always obeyed her instincts and that her strongest one was to be honest. Her veins showed under her transparent skin. Stubborn integrity ran through them. She never apologized for contradicting "accepted" opinion. Did she want to travel abroad? I asked.

"Oh, yes." The contrast between what she said and the country schoolgirl's voice it emerged in was delightful in itself.

Did she think the restrictions made sense?

"None of their stuff makes sense. I've got thirty years of *Swan Lake* ahead of me. I don't blame you for anything—I've wanted to leave for years."

"But you've just won a crucial prize. Just begun a wonderful career. Wouldn't that keep you back?"

"I don't like it here. Why are you looking at me? Nothing's nice here."

We arrived at my hotel after the deadline for entertaining guests in the rooms. "Where do you think you're going?" the watchwoman on my floor challenged while waddling after us.

"What business is it of yours?" Galya answered. She flashed a key— for *her* hotel—and walked on.

The corridor had a little bend into which the watchwoman couldn't quite see. Elastic Galya pressed herself against the wall like a coat of paint and inched to my door. But with the danger gone, being alone in my room with me seemed too much for her. I hoped it was this shyness, rather than the gap in our ages, that made her keep calling me "Valery Matveevich." She sat in the chair farthest from me, as self-contained as the hands clasped in her lap.

When she reached for a handkerchief, a newspaper clipping fell from her handbag. It was an old article about *Land of Miracles*, which she had seen on her Leningrad trip. Since then she had collected everything written about me. Yasny Sokol was what had started her dissatisfaction with ballet limited to sylphs floating in the moonlight. Her admission of this appalled her. She informed me that I had important ballet matters on my mind and must not be distracted by "unworthy" thoughts. Her back was straight as a convent girl's, but I could see resolution marching across her face. She made some daunting decision and ran toward me.

"I know you can't care for me, Valery Matveevich. I know you'll think this is terrible, but . . ."

Her kiss was like a cream puff I'd never tasted before. God did everything right.

WHEN MY HEART OPENED, Galya flew straight in. Her instinctive reaction to everything, even in situations she didn't understand, helped me be myself. The first thing I thought of was the relief of no longer pretending I wasn't Jewish.

A Leningrad reviewer had written of my "instant but incredibly natural" change from one emotion to another as Yasny Sokol. This was nothing compared to the transformation of Russian Jews by the Six-Day War. Backs bent over for generations straightened before my eyes. A massive transfusion of self-respect cured shame and defeatism so deep that Jews themselves had accepted this as part of "Jewish" nature. The force of feeling could have come only from the release of something hidden for lifetimes. It was a pity that bloodshed was needed for this transformation, but that is precisely what worked on the Jews—and even more on the Russians who had scorned them. The most anti-Semitic workers asked to shake the hand of Jews passing their beer stalls.

The amazement and appreciation for Israeli valor was so great that it "infected" even Communist activists—*especially* activists, since they were the type most impressed by armies. Scapegoats were needed to explain the defeat of the "progressive" Arab forces, and I was afraid that mass meetings called to condemn "bloodthirsty Zionist enemies of peace" might lead to pogroms. Then I saw that professional propagandists were pronouncing "Zionist militarists" and "Israeli aggressors" with a secret admiration. The miracle of stingy, feeble, cringing Jews risking their lives to defend their country—and then winning!—exhilarated them against their will.

Suddenly I could associate. Just because Jews were defending themselves instead of cowering, I recognized my relationship to the beatings they had suffered so long. The tremendous emotional uplift gave me a sunny new land in which to set some of my fantasies.

In the surge of Jewish morale a few Vilnius youngsters declared, simply but incredibly, that they wanted to be themselves in their true homeland. Vilnius was involved because people there still had much more contact with relatives abroad than was normal in the Soviet Union. The boys were sent to labor camps, where they remained long after the principle of emigration to Israel had been established. They were jailed to stop the movement. Instead, it grew. Demonstrations and hunger strikes showed the new determination not to submit. Eventually a trickle of Vilnius Jews was given exit visas. Faced with great potential unrest in the Baltic republics, the authorities hoped that releasing a few Jews would divert resentment from Russian domination. Only those with invitations from close relatives could go. As a half Jew I was entirely unaffected. Yet those first applicants were a lasting inspiration. They *had* to take action, even knowing what awaited them. It was another lesson about what the "meek cowards" could do, and more reason to be grateful for Israel's existence.

Finally, I realized that the real liberation was not from Soviet bondage, but from self-deception. My years of protesting that I had nothing in common with Jewishness had been shown up for what they were. For whatever my papers said and whatever I believed about myself, I had always been reacted to as a Jew.

Any Armenian, Lithuanian, Kirghizian who actually tried to live by the slogans about the happy Soviet family of nations was slapped into place. He could convince *himself*, but no one else, that he was sincere. He could explain why "petty nationalism" really was an evil disease of capitalism and why socialism promised eternal fraternal love. But his Russian overseers in the Party and the police would care most about the shape of his nose and the tint of his skin.

Jews had the least chance to escape the slime. Surely not work or willingness to pay the dues of assimilation could remove it. Maltsev told me that all my disliked characteristics were linked to my being a "cosmopolitan Jew." My interest in Western ballet was proof of this. If ever I wanted to read a non-Soviet magazine to make up my mind about anything, this was because "Panov has Jewish blood." Even my fondness for dancing the "little man" damned me. "Of course, he likes those underdog roles," I overheard. "They're typically Jewish."

I had demeaned myself in my senseless pretending to be a "Soviet" person. Most of all, I regretted changing my name. This clumsy dodge had only given people something extra to scorn. "He's one, but he took a Russian name. You know the kind." Party and personnel officials—that is, the KGB—were least fooled since their first question was always about a person's "origins." Now that a feat of arms by Jews threatened with actual extinction had given me the courage, I saw my life as a series of maskings.

AFTER THE DUDINSKAYA CONCERT I was invited to give several of my own in Moscow with any partner I wanted. Galya protested that she couldn't possibly appear with me. Only her eyes showed her delight. We were together every minute of the next two weeks. She was much heavier than she looked, but with strength, willingness to work, and astonishing endurance to match her amazingly elastic muscles.

Some of her shyness slowly wore off, but she rarely said more than two sentences together. Loud noises and sharp movements disturbed her as lacking taste. Public displays of excitement were the greatest offenders. Everything should be in its place. Hers was half-hidden at my side.

After our first hard rehearsal I wanted to treat her to a fancy restaurant. When I asked her what she preferred, she whispered a request for . . . ice cream. Finally, I persuaded her to eat. She ordered chicken. Her Perm Academy had served a wing on revolutionary holidays, but it was never enough. On ordinary bread-and-kasha days she was constantly hungry and had dreamed of a full portion of chicken throughout her student years. The waiter finally brought her order. She ate it with reverence, giving me a pleasure I couldn't remember. Everything Galya did gave me the delight I thought I could only have on the stage.

She was born in the far north, which explained her "Finnish" look, with the high forehead and extreme blondness. Her father eventually became a steelworks supervisor in a bleak, remote city. He was a kindly man who liked music and art. Galya was thirteen when he died. She believed the steady nagging of her mother, who had suffered a concussion during the war, had increased her father's drinking and speeded his death. Bringing up a family had always seemed too much for her, and it was a relief for both when Galya left to live in a dormitory. This had happened four years ago, after the local ballet teacher urged Galya to study full time. Her mother took her to the Perm Academy, which accepted her immediately.

Galya worked as if nothing else existed. Together with her talent, this made her the teachers' favorite. Hungry as she was, she remembered she had received less at home, with more scolding. On her mother's rare visits to Perm, she was a shrill stranger who bewailed the terrible sacrifices she had made for her daughter. Even now Galya would stop in the middle of relating a particularly humiliating incident, and I couldn't coax the end from her. She shrank from my every bouquet, as if expecting a blow to follow.

Galya was graduated as the Academy's star, and her teachers predicted she would conquer the ballet world. Bolshoi and Kirov coaches did travel to see her, but their recommendations could not get her even an audition. She had not been in the Moscow or Leningrad Academy's Plan.

She went directly to the top in Perm but felt that she could never do her best there. Her obstinacy in putting a strong personal touch into her dancing would always keep her in the shadow of the machine-stamped Leningrad ballerinas in *Swan Lake* and *Giselle*, Perm's steady diet. She was less vain than any soloist I'd ever met, but already frustrated. She wanted to reach her own opinion by seeing for herself, and she couldn't even move to Moscow without permission. Life was "wrong" without travel abroad—highly unlikely with her Perm company.

She couldn't understand why so much in the world's second richest country was so shabby and unpleasant, with perpetual poverty and grasping, snarling people, who lacked respect for themselves and for everyone else. Except in the countryside, there was no beauty to link with the Pushkin she read every evening. While the radio blared forth about Soviet society as the highest achievement of human civilization, her Urals had no meat for months, and people drank to escape the provincial squalor.

She had never read or talked about politics. Her every response was based on what she had seen. Even the illogic with which she defended her stubbornness in little things was dear because it came from *her*.

Almost everyone else who had won in Varna would have seen life from the perspective of the elite's privileges about to be received. Galya's trip had the opposite effect on her. Her partner had been abroad before and knew how things worked. He left half his Bulgarian purchases at the Ministry of Culture for the dozen officials who had sent him— Galya's introduction to the corruption at this level of Soviet culture.

Hypocrisy and lies affected her organically. The dirtying of the art she had trained for with such dedication—precisely to escape from what disturbed her in "real" life—startled and sickened her. "Now I understand," she told me. "It's all mixed up with pretense. Less depends on the dancing than on bribes and things."

We were staying in the gigantic Hotel Rossiya at the back of Red Square. We always had more to say when we returned from our walks and paced up and back below the Kremlin walls. Mornings I tried to wake up with the sun to gaze at her white skin and flaxen hair when she wouldn't blush. She was an alloy of innocence and tenacity.

One morning I heard a stampede of jittery feet running down the corridor and a chorus of porters' curses. "Have the bastards gone crazy? All checking out at goddamn once, as if their fat suitcases are a pleasure to lug." I slipped out of bed. The elevators looked as if someone had been screaming "fire" into the three thousand rooms. But since cars for the airport choked the roadways outside, maybe the foreigners were evacuating the entire country rather than just the hotel. Their fear was tinged with disgust. I pushed to a newspaper kiosk. The news of our invasion of Czechoslovakia, in the form of *Pravda*'s account of the Czech comrades' request for fraternal assistance, battered me.

This hideous lie troubled even staunchly pro-Soviet artists. Ulanova was quickly sent to Prague to help cement the new "friendship." On her return I saw her trying to hide her shame and dismay when Bolshoi personnel questioned her. But the small number of democratically minded Russians truly suffered—even more, in a way, than the Czechs and Slovaks themselves. We had been holding our breath throughout the thrilling, inspiring, rejuvenating Prague Spring. We could hardly believe such honesty could exist under socialism. We were right.

I went to Galya in a kind of shock. We set out for our rehearsal, but Red Square was completely cordoned off and crawling with KGB agents. Orders for this precaution apparently went out together with those for the invasion itself, in case some courageous Soviet citizens might risk a protest.

Galya shuddered at the ugly atmosphere but did not know what the invasion really implied. I sensed she was too young and too fragile to be told. I had visions of Soviet tanks in Prague and of the men just across the Kremlin wall who had ordered them to murder Alexander Dubček's goodness. The pus of evil drawn to Czechoslovakia's striving for justice was the final proof of what our system was.

32

IF I WERE MAKING A BALLET OF MY LIFE, I'D HAVE DROPPED THE CURTAIN at this point. I was so opposed to everything Soviet that my main problem was how to keep my mouth shut: not enough internal conflict for another act. My long years of whimpering for understanding had been nonsense. There was no mistake, no rotten luck, nothing personally directed against me. Bigger stars in other arts were persecuted for even flimsier reasons. The best Red Army Ensemble dancer, a man with a phenomenal leap, saw a girl twice in Mexico City, in the same 1959 as my disgrace. He never traveled again and never would.

Yes, we could rise higher than average citizens—as the serf-dancers had in the nineteenth century—but we still belonged to our masters. As their pets we accepted closer control in return for our privileges, including the privilege of performing. We had fewer real rights than ever because the country's new owners were less educated, liberal, and gracious than the tsarist landowners who started private theaters for their own pleasure. Since it was now clear to me that I'd always been a serf, the point was to get out, not to plead for personal justice.

The uselessness of my new understanding drove me further toward despair or temporarily repressed what had to be repressed. Dancing was a way to separate myself from the good people who had started hating themselves as well as the system after Dubček's elimination. The joke was that everything I'd dreamed of in ballet was starting to come true, especially more new roles than I could ever have hoped for. The next was in *The Mountain Girl* by Oleg Vinogradov.

A graduate in Nureyev's class in the Academy, Vinogradov had been assigned to the Novosibirsk theater deep in Siberia. That was considered the end of him until reports drifted back that he was re-staging the classics with interesting touches. The Ministry of Culture overrode all objections and returned him to Leningrad.

The Mountain Girl delighted the Kirov's supervisors. A new socialist-realist work that might actually interest an audience was a gold strike. Huge grants to create new Soviet ballets usually produced scenarios about mining victories, choreographed with as much flair as a Five-Year Plan. *The Mountain Girl*, by contrast, had a genuine story. The underlying theme was the establishment of Soviet rule in mountainous Moslem Dagestan, a remote Caucasus region, where men are proud and women serve them. A village beauty flouts the strict customs and rules by opting for education and professional independence through the Soviet system's new, liberated way of life. Her suitor is the tribe's strongest, bravest shepherd-warrior. Osman takes his duty as the repository of his people's spirit so seriously that he is eventually driven to kill his beloved, despite his fierce love for her.

Everyone acknowledged Osman as one of the great roles of Soviet ballet. He was a thrilling exception to the near-constitutional law that the heroes of major Soviet works be "positive." His endurance and devotion to tradition were the pride of his people. They called him a *dzhigit*, a fearless brave no doubt descended from Genghis Khan's warriors. Thus, he represented not Progress Through Soviet Consciousness, but the doomed way of life—almost the enemy. He was quite different from the smiling cosmonaut.

Competition for a role could no longer be the full meaning of my life, but this one pulled me deep into ballet again. Most dancers wait all their lives for a part this rich. It came close to character dancing throughout, a kind of Georgian folk dance, with wild leaps and other "savage" steps, but all translated into the language of classical ballet. The role also drew on everything we had learned in the Academy and after about fencing, "Eastern" plasticity, and bravura technique. It could have been composed only in Russia, with its emphasis on the heroic and the dynamic in male dancing.

Vinogradov was too new to Leningrad and too nervous to miss a single rehearsal. He usually wanted to add yet another midair twist to choreography that was already fantastically difficult. He seemed to be trying to kill us with impossible passages that jumped the line between natural exuberance and artificial sensation. Maybe because of his scant experience dancing leading roles, he didn't understand that an audience always senses when a performer strains to meet a challenge. They hold their breaths. Art becomes sport. But Vinogradov was open to suggestions. Unlike the balletmasters who killed their ideas by pronouncing them law, he improved many of his concepts by encouraging dancers to shape them. Baryshnikov and I turned on everything we had for him. Some of the rehearsal sessions were inspired.

Baryshnikov's virtuosity dumbfounded spectators who saw him for the first time. At the age of twenty he was just short of perfect. His weak arms and chest made his lifts—and therefore his partnering in general—wobbly at times. In heroic roles he had to struggle to project an image of himself almost opposite to that of his baby face. But this was only proof that ballet gave even geniuses problems. He was the most naturally gifted dancer I had ever seen.

Even he was just different enough from the "proper" Kirov forms to have prompted derision when he first joined. "What is he, a hockey puck or something?" the established soloists complained. "I can hardly follow his darting around. What kind of dancing is that?" Now everyone had to recognize that it was a magnificent kind and that his endowment might prove to be finer than anyone's in the history of ballet.

Meanwhile, the fight for the part of the Mountain Girl became as intense as a feud in the Caucasus itself. For almost ten months of rehearsal, the choice had been between Gabriella Komleva and Natasha Makarova, both of whom were excellent in their characteristic ways. Komleva meticulously rendered Vinogradov's designs, and Makarova was often behind in the drudging battle of the rehearsal studio. But when her mood was right, she was more expressive than choreography alone could make anyone.

Each ballerina got better daily, and the competition was conducted on the highest professional level. The contrast between the finely tuned women of opposite approaches was itself artistic. Then the ballet caught the attention of leading Party and Ministry of Culture officials. Now Fedicheva leaped into the competition. Before this she and Rachinsky had belittled the ballet. She instinctively avoided a new work until convinced she would look good in it or that there were other advantages to participating. Then she would enter the contest, displacing others who'd been shaping a role for months. Once she had been able to carry this off. Now the spoiled, heavy star was as expressive as a broom compared to the other two. But vulnerable Makarova could predict the outcome and withdrew.

The Minister of Culture and members of the Central Committee's Cultural Department came from Moscow to see the premiere. The made-for-me part worked so well by now that my borrowing from the opera singer's technique of holding certain notes an extra second had become unconscious. An inner ear tuned into the audience and told me when to take this slight liberty. I could concentrate utterly. Everything I knew about life formed a unity between me and the music.

Backslaps from Rasul Gamsatov, the author of the narrative epic on which the ballet was based, also fitted the rhythm. The stupendous event of a Kirov ballet generated from his work made him an even greater cultural hero back home. He arrived in Leningrad with almost the entire Dagestan government in tow, wiry mountain men with ministerial titles. They had come to bless the city for the immense honor and to have the fling of their lives.

Gamsatov himself was the most engaging of these men. As round as an old owl, he turned pink from noon to midnight with the finest Dagestan cognac and was always trying to pour some for others—or at least fill them with amusing talk—so they too could enjoy life. I was the beneficiary of the delegation's special largess. Osman's every swashbuckling, midair configuration brought a separate cheer; each wave of the sword produced a war cry. The delegation saw their images of themselves in the role, and a band commanded by the Dagestan Council of Ministers lay in ambush for me everywhere.

"There is Panov. He must to relieve thirst with us."

"Fierce Dagestan hero. Panov is *dzhigit*."

The artlessness of a simple people bubbled in Gamsatov, but underneath his being best friends with everyone, I sensed an equally hot hatred of bureaucracy. He pulled me aside one day to ask whether some capitalist monopoly had "captured" the Kirov. Rachinsky's clumsy attempts to show paternal concern for me before the Moscow dignitaries troubled him, and he composed a furious protest the minute he heard that I—who was already half Dagestanian—was discriminated against.

Then I saw him whispering with the Dagestan Minister of Culture. Before their triumphant return home they announced that I was an Honored Artist of the Dagestan Republic. The question of a title for me had been dragging on since my early Maly years. I had even signed the papers several times. Now the whole matter had been settled in twenty-four hours—for one ballet on a Dagestan theme. The cultural officials of my own Russian Republic scratched their heads.

I HAD TO SEE GALYA AGAIN. The easiest way was to be invited to dance in Perm. I arranged this through my old acquaintance, the chief choreographer there.

The Director of the Perm ballet met me at the airport. The minute he left me in my hotel I called her. As she ran in, I saw that everything I remembered about her was true. But she shrank from my hug and sat on the edge of a chair, all prim and spotless.

"Naturally I mean nothing to you," she whispered. "You don't want to see me anymore."

I wanted to laugh and cry at the same time. It had taken much maneuvering and a trip of twelve hundred miles for this moment, which her sweet silliness made even better than I had hoped for.

During the next ten days I pushed through some of her reserve. She had prepared Kitri for our performances of *Don Quixote*. Her technique astonished me again, and she herself was gentle, candid, and artless. "What if something happens to pull us apart?" she kept asking. "Something to make you lose all interest in me, which could happen just overnight. It's terrible."

Her gray native habitat made me appreciate her inner luster even more. Perm was swarming with military staffs that ran huge defense establishments. Provincial patriotism that snarled at everything "different from ours" weighed down the air. Galya had kept free of all corrupting influences partly by staying as far away from them as possible. I had never met anyone who took daily class so seriously. Afterward she rehearsed all day, every day. On the evenings she wasn't dancing, she stayed home and read Russian classics. Only food could tempt her from her permanent campaign for self-improvement. After a few days I knew that she had understated her hunger in the Perm Academy. There had been absolutely nothing fresh from October to June, and meat often disappeared for months. She rarely saw an orange. As Perm's pride after her Varna victory, she was awarded a special ration card reserved for top stars, Party officials, and other elite personnel. This entitled her to an edible brand of sausage and to twenty eggs on May Day and the Anniversary of the Revolution. But potatoes were often unavailable, and on the day of a performance she would stand in line for some form of protein until her feet froze.

By opening her up to both the unattainable world abroad and ballet politics at home, the Varna trip had ended her innocence. She was picked for a foreign tour with a small brigade of dancers and removed shortly before departure when someone else bought or traded her way on. Six or seven similar treats were on their way to her. She said that if she traveled again, it would be even worse than if she never did, for it would show she had sacrificed her self-respect to the mess of bribes and submission to sponsors.

We escaped from Perm's raw autumn drizzle to the countryside as often as we could. I never knew the name of the village I had been evacuated to during the war and couldn't find it now. Our brief search was strangely mystical. Could I have believed I would return to the outskirts of Perm a quarter of a century later—and with the woman I loved? I still felt as if my life were caught up in a huge spiral that kept returning me to "forgotten" places always at some higher level.

Galya also took me to her apartment, but only when her mother was on duty as a medical attendant in some stadium. She kept apologizing for her, and I wanted to see the woman for myself. Finally, Galya admitted that she never invited anyone home while her mother was there, even though it was her own apartment, which came with her position in the Perm ballet. Her mother had moved in as soon as she got it, strengthening Galya's determination to be opposite to her in everything. When she returned from Varna with the Bulgarian suit I liked so much, her mother hid the "foreign thing." Galya protested. Her mother chased her with a hatchet aimed at her legs. "If you can't respect me, you'll go to work in a factory like everybody else."

Galya's great worry was that I might find something in common between her mother and herself and lose my interest in her forever. Rummaging in her things, her mother had found the articles about me and somehow uncovered the terrible truth. "He's twice your age and a Jew," she hissed. "What's this twaddle about his ballet ideas, his 'teaching' you? I'm going to write to his wife."

I returned to Leningrad just before the Anniversary of the Revolution. Galya was scheduled to dance during the holidays but announced she was coming to see me instead. "I'm not listening, so please stop telling me why it's impossible," she said with a pout. "I know you don't need me, but I'll tell the theater I must go. And if they don't let me, I'll do it anyway."

MY PERFORMANCE IN *The Mountain Girl* won me a bundle of prizes from various theatrical societies. After much embarrassment because I was a Dagestan "Knight" but still untitled at home, the Russian Republic too made me an Honored Artist. The climax was a state prize for the best male role of 1968.

The awards—to winners in painting, filmmaking, ceramics, everything—were presented in the Council of Ministers. Circles of sentries around the Moscow building examined every pass ten times as the bearers tried to pick their way through the forest of red flags and toward the banquet table. We were rounded up at the last door anyway and sent to the auditorium. Production statistics and speeches about Lenin had to come before the food and drink. "Thank you, dear Soviet rule, for our opportunities and our success. Thank you for guiding my brush on the canvas, for allowing me to serve. . . ."

All the other men were dressed in the prescribed gray suits and black ties. I was in the best of gifts from the Western ballet friends I was beginning to make: a tan suede jacket, yellow checked trousers, and an orange shirt. Now I saw that my tie alone would have caused trouble. It was a knitted one—unknown in our Soviet capital. My father's admonition to be "like everybody else" sounded in my ear.

Rachinsky summoned me on my first morning back in Leningrad. "Why do you have to mess up everything? The whole Council of Ministers has been calling me. Get hold of yourself and buy some proper *clothes*." My body had always rejected suits like an unwanted kidney, but the next time I visited Vilnius, Alec's highest contacts got me into a clothing warehouse. I picked out a suit that should have ended one problem at least. If it's Belgian, I thought, it can't be as bad as it feels.

Then I set out on my most memorable reward for Osman: a trip to Dagestan as an official guest. Honored Artists Komleva and Vinogradov were invited, too. We arrived by plane in the Caspian port of Makhachkala, where sturgeon was relieved of its caviar. Lambs were cut up for shashlik with equal enthusiasm—and people for pleasure if the local lords took a dislike to them. In case anyone failed to sense that the wrong word could start a blood feud, cold steel in every other belt made this pointedly clear. *The Mountain Girl* was supposed to be about Soviet rule changing the violent old order, but the mountain mood was obviously intact from the days of Hadjim Murat, the great Dagestan warrior who fought savagely against Russian colonization.

Nothing less than a national holiday had been declared in honor of us brother-heroes who had upheld Dagestan's honor in the Russian badlands. Every restaurant in the capital rang with "Glory to ballet!" and to us, its "greatest masters." The final rodeo of hospitality was in the house of *The Mountain Girl*'s composer, Murat Kazhlaev. We sat on cushions surrounded by rugs, bottles, and the nobility of the arts and sciences. Every tribal chief seemed to have several large wives.

After countless tumblers of cognac, Rasul Gamsatov stood up with a grave expression on his face and a bayonet-sized dagger in his hand. He waved it. We dropped our forks. Our replies to the toasts had obviously contained some accidental insult. *Our* time for being sliced up had arrived. Oleg Vinogradov went from his usual wanness to a ghostly white. The frail balletmaster hated the sight of weapons. Once when a Kirov stagehand cut his hand, a stretcher had to be brought—for Oleg. Rasul Gamsatov was the color of young wine. He raised the dagger higher.

"Hadjim Murat, I demand blood oath from all," he cried. His Russian had reverted to something resembling his native tongue. "After great victory of *Mountain Girl* made sacred new date in Dagestan calendar, I swear to give other scenario. Hadjim Murat, my friend Kazhlaev must swear to make music for new ballet. Great Vinogradov must swear on blood drawn from same dagger to write heroic dances, Hadjim Murat. And brother Panov will give much blood to become one of us."

He kissed the blade and brought it down. Blood spurted from his arm. "Woman!" he bellowed. His wife brought him a sheaf of paper. Dipping a thick fingernail in his blood, he traced "Gamsatov" on his oath, then solemnly handed the huge blade to composer Kazhlaev. Well before it reached Vinogradov, he started swaying. He begged for a pin instead, then pricked himself laboriously to produce two drops for his initials. Rasul stared heavenward and muttered prayers through his mustaches. But Komleva restored our honor by bravely cutting her finger and plunging it in the antiseptic of cognac.

"That's not woman," the guests shouted in what was apparently their greatest compliment. "That's real *dzhigit!*"

After a few hours' sleep we set out on a triumphant tour of the republic. Ten minutes out of Makhachkala, we were in the mountains of Lermontov's wild, tragic extravagance. The jeep drivers were eager to prove their courage on so-called roads along demonic drops. Tinkling sheep bells faintly penetrated the fog on craggy peaks. We seemed as doomed as the animals.

The villages we visited were scatterings of houses stuck to the mountainsides like eagles' nests. We were greeted by the Party Secretary, the chairman of the local soviet, and the chairman of the collective sheep ranch—miniature Stalins in boots and tunics. One of the first rules of hospitality was for guests to see blood gush from the newborn lambs slaughtered for the coming feast. Not to eat would have been a mortal insult. It did not matter that we had just come from three similar orgies in which thirty similar animals had been consumed.

Cases of vodka had been waiting—under guard—since the night before, and the toasts began even before we reached the table. My requests for Dagestan wine brought only laughs. Wine was for girls or for export to lily-livered Russia. A kind of torture by gluttony went on for a week. Toasting welcomes, gorging, toasting good-byes. Stepping across the next border and into the arms of a new set of officials impatient to show us another pile of bloody lambs. It started early in the morning and continued until we crawled back into bed. Vinogradov grew delirious and imagined rescue by helicopter. I tried to hold up his end by drinking that little bit more. Komleva asked to visit mountain streams, where she would fill up her perfume flask and try to get some into her glass at the table. Otherwise, the only water available was in pitchers in the outhouses. It was intended for a different purpose, but we gulped it down in secret before going out to face a new day.

Back in Leningrad, Komleva and Vinogradov went directly into a rest home. I was declared ambulatory but blacked out when a second effusive invitation from Dagestan arrived.

33

I COULD NOT GO BACK TO LIYA AFTER PERM AND RENTED A TINY ROOM. Galya's promise to visit sounded like teenage fantasy, but one morning I saw her standing like a frozen sentry outside the Kirov. My joy lasted only until Liya encamped outside my studio and pushed Andrei toward me when I emerged. "Papa, why are you doing this to us?" he whimpered, as she had trained him. "Papa, let's go home."

It was a mortifying week. One child had come to see me, all on her own, from Perm. "Galya, how long have you been in this cold?" I shouted when I saw her scarlet nose. "Just a few hours," she answered with her adorable pout. But the other child was my own innocent son. His face mirrored painful confusion when he saw me. I could not explain.

Galya saw everything. "Shouldn't you go back to your family?" her meek voice kept asking. Knowing how often I *had* gone back, I didn't tell her what I really felt. Anyway, I couldn't trust myself to carry through any plans.

Not even spring brought relief from the dead-end winter. Each time before, I had gone back to Liya when she had fetched me with some proof of how hopeless I was without her help. This time I surrendered because I'd awakened to what I owed Andrei. It was all the more miserable because nothing was Liya's fault. I didn't know what to do except to pour out my weakness to Maltsev. "If only she gave me an excuse to break with her. Andrei's only nine. Anyway, I'm the guilty party. Somehow I can't be the one to do it."

Maltsev studied me. "You don't need an excuse," he said very slowly. "Husbands are always the last to find out what everybody else knows."

I broke my pencil in half writing a note to declare our marriage finished. Aware that the sight of Liya might snap my control completely, I asked her not to see me until Andrei returned from his vacation.

Maltsev's revelation provided the easy way out I'd hoped for from a dishonest marriage of inertia. Yet I choked wth hot shame and fury. Liya's "terrible deed"—taking as a lover a Maly corps de ballet dancer— had dishonored me unbearably. My double standard was only fuel for the hellish fire. Even the talk of her lover as "a total nothing except for his motorcycle" was a personal insult.

Liya did not stay away as I'd asked but arrived to measure the blaze and to establish strict conditions—"no more little country ballerinas"— under which we could live in the future. As she saw it, her use of the ultimate weapon of provoking my sexual jealousy had properly humbled me. Now the marriage could resume.

Her total lack of understanding drove me berserk. I ran full speed into the kitchen and banged my head on the refrigerator. Dents in the metal and inquiries from the neighbors did nothing for my anguish. I dashed outside and into a small wood, where I howled until blood seemed ready to pour from my throat.

Maltsev's "Everybody knows" reverberated in my ears. The gossipers were feasting on *our* garbage. But wounded pride was only the beginning. For eleven years, we had given each other no intellectual understanding, no spiritual growth. . . . We had so little respect for each other after living most of our "adult" lives as man and wife that we couldn't even part with honor. I was sick with disappointment—above all, in myself. The marriage had always been based on my weakness.

Insignificance was the final humiliation. Instead of attacking my real oppressors, I took out my accumulated frustration on Liya. Although I knew she had acted within her rights, this no longer mattered. What did matter was that they'd never let me out. I'd never know my own artistic limits. Liya and I were a foretaste of the greater waste waiting for me.

Maltsev dropped everything to spend whole days with me. He was abashed that his revelation had brought on my frenzy and did everything he could to temper it. His personal loyalty was my comfort.

At last the misery passed. My first normal feeling was a longing for Galya. After hours of waiting, wrong numbers, and slammed receivers, my call got through to Perm, and I learned she was on a summer tour. The rest of the day went to tracing her by telephone deeper into the north. Finally, I found her—in Archangel, her birthplace. It was the dead of night. Her "hello" was full of furry sleep.

"Come to Leningrad," I pleaded. "Everything's empty without you."

When she arrived, she looked at me with big eyes and said I needn't explain because it didn't matter how long we lasted. I kept wondering whether she might just be the latest of my inventions, but she put me deeper under her spell every day. This was no act, but the real Galya, who still worried about not "deserving" me.

"Now you can see for yourself," she whispered when we returned from an all-day walk. "You need someone better. I can't cook a single thing."

I COULDN'T WAIT FOR THE DIVORCE to come through to leave the apartment on Cosmonaut Street. Only one suitcase with spare underwear and ballet shoes left with me. Someone's comment that separation from a wife must be performed "with honor" relieved me of the headache of packing, and the Kirov saved me from the quagmire of hunting for a room.

Divorces hit the company as often as sprained ankles. To smooth things over enough to keep dancers on the stage, erstwhile husbands and wives were quickly found temporary quarters. I got the luxury of an apartment on Rossi Street, on the same courtyard that led to the Academy dormitory.

After eleven years of Liya's depicting my collapse without her personal management, I loved my second bachelorhood. Leading Maryinsky soloists and choreographers—even Fokine, I was told—once lived in the same apartment. Now the miniature rooms were empty except for two iron cots, a four-inch television set, and a table that kept the color of an old frying pan through every painting. But my cord was cut. Peace of mind enriched the air.

THE FRONT OFFICE KEPT ASSURING ME that I was on the list for the London tour next year. I swallowed and prayed. The tidings that I couldn't be spared just then came with solemn promises for Japan the following spring. I tricked myself into believing again.

Then came the thunderbolt of Makarova's defection in London. Before I had time to be glad for her, I mourned what seemed the last lost chance for myself. In the aftermath of this second sensational defection no one would dream of taking the risk of letting *me* out. The crackdown was angrier than I expected. One certainty was that there would be more defectors if the victims got the chance.

The most dismaying aspect of Soviet propaganda was that it did not work only on the selfish and the stupid. Its greatest success was in perverting the good. My elderly fans were generous, discriminating, and utterly truthful. They had their own forceful thoughts about almost every subject—except Soviet rule. As soon as we veered in that direction, they changed to pawns. Everyone knew by now that Nureyev hadn't been eaten alive in the Western jungle, yet ballet devotees went around describing the jaws that would shred Makarova. I tried to understand the Soviet anesthetic that obliterates what the eyes have seen and the brain has recorded. Most people capable of independent thought had had their heads cut off long ago. Fear or despair paralyzed almost everyone among the tiny percentage that survived and understood. This left the great majority, or the products of Soviet education, where the huge apparatus for befuddling brains did its best work. Momentary inklings about the system's absurdities and lies came and went like lightning. Yet all in all, they believed.

When I recovered, I applauded Makarova—and louder than ever for her dancing, which came from the same source as her courage to rescue herself. Most of her colleagues chanted that she was a fool and a mediocre talent.

"A birdbrained egotist. We never needed her anyway."

"Just wants to cash in—in dollars—for her Soviet training. And make it worse for *us*."

"She only got where she did in the Kirov by pushing herself forward."

It was the prisoners justifying their imprisonment, poor cousins hating one who'd suddenly got rich, many things at once. Even a kind of compassion was involved, since most members of the company genuinely couldn't understand how an artist could want to sacrifice the Kirov and the motherland to make her own way in the outside world. But above all, it was our propaganda, and now I thought I understood how it worked.

Only geniuses reached their conclusions in isolation. Whatever our political inclinations, the rest of us needed information to make up our minds. But Soviet rule had eliminated facts and ideas for so long that we didn't know how to use them. Worse than this, we had been taught to hide our real feelings and trained to act against our instincts. The black-is-white hammering was so relentless early in life that most Russians had simply stopped thinking. When President Kennedy was assassinated, the majority of the company did not know how to react until the official telegram of condolence in *Pravda* neutralized the chemical, and genuine grief poured out.

Cessation of thought might explain the mysterious phenomenon of people returning from the West with no "obvious" conclusions about what they'd seen or listening to shortwave broadcasts without really hearing them. In London, Makarova said very clearly that she'd simply had enough of the Kirov repertoire and needed to express herself in other ways. The people who knew her best complained of BBC "inventions" and "anti-Soviet slander." A coach who had considered Makarova the darling of Soviet ballet predicted she would starve in the West but saw no contradiction in also denouncing the "slut's" future riches. Jingoism wrapped in socialistic rhetoric had fed our nationalistic fear and jealousy since childhood. The real message, which everyone received in his gut, was to strike back at the Western lords who were supposedly striking at us. We were poor only because they somehow kept us down. Makarova was therefore a rotten traitor.

WHEN I WAS FINALLY ALLOWED TO TRAVEL in 1970, it was not really abroad but to Poland and Rumania. Since their borders were equivalent to Soviet ones, there was no risk in letting me out that far. Having tossed me this bone, the authorities could answer all questions self-righteously. "What do you mean, Panov never goes abroad? He's just returned from Poland and Rumania. The lucky bastard travels all the time."

For extra insurance, Maltsev came along. Irina Kolpakova was the major ballerina of our little group. She was still one of the Kirov's major Party activists, and it was suitable that we'd come for some Soviet-Polish brotherhood "festival." But the raw memory of Czechoslovakia had multiplied the resentment of Soviet domination tenfold since my 1958 trip. I walked around Warsaw with a silent appeal to every Pole. "I understand how you feel, I'm *with* you. I'd hit back too if I could, but anyway, I apologize for my country."

Rumania was even more depressing. I joined the large contingent that was returning from London without Makarova. For ten years Kolpakova had worked the Party plots against Sergeyev. The opportunity to expel him after Nureyev's "treachery" had been missed, but she resolved not to fail in this second great chance.

She asked Maltsev to her hotel room. I went too because he hadn't let go of my hand since we crossed the Soviet border. She sat on the edge of the bathtub and turned on its tap to drown out any microphone. She probably understood that the Rumanian secret police were not bursting to learn her plans to dispose of a balletmaster, but long years of Party work had made conspiracy second nature. The gist of their whisperings came through. "This is the moment. Everybody must refuse to work with him."

I knew that our finest balletmaster was finished. I had to turn my face to the door.

As Kolpakova schemed, I thought of Sergeyev's life and accomplishments. Of course, he had faults. As he moved into middle age, continued adoration of the glorious roles of his youth hardly helped him lead new developments. He could be stubborn, distant, and fussy. But he was still the Kirov's jewel. Even in terms of the coldest calculation it would be idiocy to ease him out. The West paid its hard currency for his classical ballets and rightly shunned the socialist-realist disasters.

Sergeyev had been central to the birth of Soviet ballet in the 1930s, with its new accent on male dancing. A whole generation strived to be as good as he. If some ended by sacrificing expressiveness, he was no more responsible than anyone whose excellence makes him an example. Great gains in art everywhere often became fortifications for equally great conservatism. In our country, the breastworks were thickened many times by the dogma that it was Soviet rule that had bestowed everything good. Thus, the slavish adherence to models of the earliest (still-favored) period, of which Sergeyev was the ideal. He couldn't be blamed for dancing brilliantly in the style of his time. Not he but Rachinsky, Vartanyan, and their Central Committee bosses were depriving ballet of its life-force by mummifying his creative achievements.

Maybe Sergeyev didn't recognize this. He was still oblivious to the designs against him and would tolerate no plotting, even in his own defense. He seemed unable to contemplate what others wanted to make of the art he produced or of his belief in God. During the decades of truly militant atheism, churches were dynamited and believers tortured.

But he maintained his faith and his loyalty to his mother, the leader of a minor religious sect.

Deep respect for Sergeyev's kind of believer had been building up in me. They had to sacrifice so much for their commitment, and most—like Sergeyev—became stronger and purer for this. Maybe when the majority were religious, it was easy and profitable to believe. Now their faith had to come from within, as an expression of the individuality I loved—and also as a kind of protest.

Sergeyev never demonstrated his belief. An Artistic Director who publicly crossed himself in the "temple of Soviet art" would be out the same day. A few years from now, when he would be homeless in the sense that the Kirov had been his home for forty years, his son would die in a car crash. The grieving father took great pains to have the funeral conducted according to all Orthodox rites, but to avoid attention to this. The man he turned to for help with the "confidential" burial was a KGB informer, a symbol of what infected his life.

But Sergeyev never degraded his religion either. Well ahead of Solzhenitsyn's call to "at least not lie," if we couldn't always tell the truth, Sergeyev had always done just this. Everyone knew he was a believer, just as all knew why he wouldn't join the Party. He could not violate his relationship to God and to himself. Even when he stood to deliver a "Soviet" message at a public meeting, his true allegiances were unmistakable.

The inner strength that kept him a whole man while others were ground-down toadies was also his undoing. The Party-KGB wanted their flunky in his vital position. His dedication to art for art's sake was a nuisance, but what really griped them was the moral and spiritual independence on which this was based. I realized the real cause of his approaching punishment when Kolpakova turned on the bath tap to drown out her imaginary microphone. I did not want to stay in Rumania, did not want to go back to Russia, wondered whether I would ever have the strength to fight.

A few days later I witnessed Sergeyev's first defensive moves. For the first time in his life he drank beyond control—and with people not worth his little finger. Enlisting everyone he could, especially young soloists who knew little about the longstanding Kirov rivalries, he entertained them with banquet supplies unused in London after Makarova's defection had canceled the usual peace-and-friendship receptions. He had never resorted to the slightest pandering, even to the highest Party bosses, but the doom he suddenly sensed for Dudinskaya and himself temporarily unhinged him.

The young boys and girls did hold their tongues, but only long enough to savor another mouthful of caviar and down another glass of vodka. Relatively few of them—and of the troupe as a whole—had KGB commitments. But they were already clamoring for new positions and opportunities the Artistic Director's demise might open up. A kind of exhilaration developed in which the dancers urged one another to "get the old guy." The old guy's fumblings to indulge them were pitiful.

A major new ballet he was staging would keep him going as balletmaster for five more months. But Dudinskaya was relieved of her classe de perfection almost immediately. She was also virtually barred from the Kirov—after forty years of immeasurable contributions there. Makarova had been her star pupil.

Soviet ballet had known even more shameful episodes. I was happy to have missed them. The charge was that Dudinskaya had perverted her ballerinas with glory-seeking notions in place of their duty to the people. The truth was that she had taught them to perform magnificently. And having achieved this, the best wanted to *dance*, not mark time.

Great teachers are as important as great dancers. Dudinskaya was one of the world's best and lived only for her teaching. Her class was the pride of the company. All the leading ballerinas took it. Two of them risked staying with her after her public disgrace when the tour returned.

Sergeyev begged and pleaded. Eventually Dudinskaya was allowed to keep the Academy class she had also conducted for many years. Her mastery was lost on pupils there. Her gift was for bringing professionals with full-fledged stage experience to their highest level of development in a theater, not for a school. It was in the demonstration and polishing of specific roles for actual productions, the perfection that distinguished the Kirov.

Other measures in response to Makarova's defection were as irrationally destructive. A dozen forms of control were tightened, and even greater stress was placed on ideological indoctrination. Foreign ballet lovers could no longer approach the stage door without a pass from the Ministry of Culture. Party membership became one of the important factors in the selection of teachers. We were being converted into a political fortress.

Soon half a dozen Kirov stars with the strongest individuality would be in the West. Wits would begin calling us the "Kirov Theater of Opera and Corps de Ballet." "What a strange company," went a melancholy saying. "All the exciting soloists live abroad, but the corps is at home." The exodus was not only abroad. A lopsided percentage of the most interesting talents were also leaving for other Soviet jobs, often at great cost in money and prestige.

Meanwhile, the generation of teachers who had preserved the St. Petersburg tradition had died, retired, or been dispatched. The conformity that was left had been carefully prepared. The juice of life was gone. Dancers had neither rest from constant repetition of the romantic classics nor the contrast that would enable them to re-discover their emotional truths. The treatment of choreographers was a death sentence. The Party and KGB were getting a company with no personality and standards except their own, exactly what they wanted.

Although it still seemed farfetched to most, this would eventually lead to mediocrity, then even to shoddiness. Ballet may include many schools and tendencies, but all must struggle to be at their outer limit of human endeavor. Imitation and routine are deadly even to the most meticulous expression of art.

In this respect, the "people's art" of Soviet ballet—whose heroes were extraordinary figures and whose performers were uniquely pampered —had always been a contradiction in terms. All of the Ministry of Culture's attempts to speed up its production with gimmicks borrowed from factories—the bestowing of "Honored Artist of Amateur Art" and other titles, the pretense that workers could dance *Swan Lake* in their spare time—were only further proof of how far the bureaucrats were from understanding where art had always come from and what it had always tried to do.

True elegance is an intensely individual creation, containing an element of revolt against the ordinary and the average. Without Sergeyev's blue blood, the Kirov's style was on the way to becoming empty pretentiousness. When Italy, the "birthplace of ballet" turned from true expression to empty technique in the nineteenth century, Italian virtuosos continued to astound the world briefly, but the art died so fast that in our day "Italian ballet" sounded like a feeble joke. Increasingly barren reproductions of the classics joined the sterile new productions as a threat that the same could happen to the once-exalted Kirov.

34

MY APARTMENT WAS THE ONLY ONE WITH A PRIVATE ENTRANCE FROM the courtyard, an ancient cast-iron staircase that spiraled its way to my second floor. The alternate method was up a fire escape to the roof, then through my kitchen window—and, for many, directly into a cubicle next to the sink. It was not a kitchen cabinet, but the toilet. From there, newcomers would join the party. Everyone knew he was welcome.

This could have been my happiest year in Leningrad. After support for Andrei, my handsome principal's salary was my own, meaning that it disappeared into food and drink in the first few days of the month. This was the way I'd always wanted to spend. Not having to buy an ashtray or a bedspread was a kind of liberation.

I chose my own friends, and foreigners took first place. With my own place in which to entertain, the trickle that had been seeking me out since Clive Barnes's articles rapidly swelled. Many came just to sample "real" Russian life by making the forbidden step into a native apartment. Western ballet and film people, critics, and scholars mingled with lovers of art and the Russian soul. Their presence also made it an adventure for Russians, although *they* couldn't fly home when tired.

In the days when I still nourished my hope for a passport, I had observed some elementary precautions. Before smiling to Professor X from this university and Mr. Y from that theater, I'd dash to a telephone and ask permission. Later Maltsev said I could dispense with the calls if I remembered to take him along. The attraction for him was the possibility of meeting some foreign lovely while keeping his eye on me.

Despite the general tightening of screws, the KGB was becoming slightly more sophisticated in granting minor mercies. Instead of punishing all disapproved activities as anti-Soviet, a few presenting no direct threat to their power were tolerated, especially if the perpetrator was otherwise useful. Eyes were closed to weaknesses for alcohol, women, and sometimes religion. The contacts with visitors that had become so important to me were considered a relatively harmless deviation if they helped keep me in good dancing form. Still, most Kirov dancers saw my open house for foreigners as a new reason for avoiding me. Even fun-loving Baryshnikov shrank from the pretty English ballet lovers who besieged him after his London debut. But I could no more shut off my hunger for communication with the world than stop dancing.

There was wild, wonderful Suzanne Massie, an American who then lived in Paris but who considered Leningrad her spiritual home. The "special link" to the country she was always talking about was based on a mixture of sensitivity and sentimentality. But what mattered to her was a certainty that she had "come home" to us with her Russian soul. She had studied the Kirov for several years. She had even written about me, for ballet criticism was one of a dozen outlets for her energy, which could have run a perpetual-motion machine. Suzanne was already on good terms with almost everyone in Leningrad ballet and knew the city's most interesting artists and writers. Her closest friends were semiunderground poets about whom she was writing a book. Later the KGB would accuse her of grabbing Leningrad's talents for the West—the same talents who couldn't publish a line in Russia.

Two other foreigners who meant a great deal to me were Jennie Walton, a dancer turned ballet photographer, who had already made several tourist pilgrimages to the Kirov, and her close friend Rosemary Winckley. The twin sister of Clive Barnes's wife, Patricia, Rosemary had been sending me ballet magazines from London because a mutual friend from Leningrad had told her how much I would treasure them. Both were tall, "typical" English girls in well-made suits and blushes of modesty. The company all loved them. Jennie was noticed first for her statuesque beauty, while a luminous kindness radiated from Rosemary. The only quality I didn't detect in her was her ability to fight fiercely for others, as well as sacrifice for them—a quality hard to imagine in someone so quiet and gentle.

Rosemary and Jennie knew nothing of real Soviet backstage life, saw no stain on its ballet glory, and seemed too innocent anyway to understand. I wanted to pour out my heart to them, but that might break theirs. Their very goodness made them unequipped to understand the risks and debts people assumed in order to spend time with them. On our long walks, their love for the Kirov reminded me of what my own once had been. No one should spoil this kind of innocent reverence. Yet I yearned to tell them my secret; they seemed like my sisters. They would be leaving soon, and I already missed their gentleness and honesty.

Finally, I couldn't contain myself any longer and told them I had only one real dream left: of leaving the country.

They looked at me in disbelief. Both protested that it was a disastrous impulse. "But who will dance your parts?" they whispered. "And how can you give them up? You'll never find a company comparable to the Kirov."

I said I had to get out even if I never danced again.

IN THE FALL OF 1969 I had arranged a guest appearance with Galya in Vilnius, then two in Leningrad. The Kirov sent for her again the following spring as a temporary replacement for an ailing ballerina. This was the best I could do for her after months of campaigning.

Ulanova led the Bolshoi people who now wanted Galya. She had helped prepare her for Varna and coached her on her every trip to Moscow. She said—and Plisetskaya agreed—that she had the best basic technique in the country. It became a special project of Ulanova's to get Galya into her highly restricted Bolshoi class. But unplanned praise was as ineffective as the unplanned gold medal. No bureaucrat stood to gain from the transfer. Invitations were canceled at the last minute.

Galya's alternative was to accept one of the proposals from men in the Ministry of Culture. "Marry me," went the most courteous, "and I'll get you into the Bolshoi for certain." It was now clear that this was the only way she would get a residence permit for Moscow or Leningrad. I would have married her myself in a flash, if only I could have believed I was cut out for married life.

When she danced *Swan Lake* for national television in the spring of 1970, Sergeyev and Dudinskaya stood to applaud the screen. Her image there answered all my doubts. I proposed on the telephone the minute the program ended.

We borrowed a white dress for the ceremony. She was the embodiment of her own purity. She hardly spoke or breathed. Whatever she was thinking remained deep within her separate self.

The next morning she began buying chicken. It all went bad eventually, but the refrigerator had to be full at all times.

"Galya, if you put another bird in there, it'll bust."

"But what if we get *hungry?*"

The notion that I had known her before seemed odd until I

recognized that she was a living ballet heroine. When others were present, my own wife could hardly raise her eyes to mine. If I looked at her, she blushed. *Giselle* reveals what happens if such innocence is shattered. I loved her even more for showing me I could love.

The only shadow was her mother. Bit by bit, I learned how strong her opposition to "that old Jew" had been. Galya winced whenever she heard her mother's phrases. Some of her kindest, most enlightening teachers in the Perm Academy had been Jewish, exiles from Moscow and Leningrad during the purges. By nature, she was one of those rare, crystal Russians who believe that the person is what matters, not his nationality or religion. She truly believed in the universal virtues taught in fairy tales, not in class-war lectures. But her mother had continually urged her to accept invitations from Jews because "they always give you a good meal."

Now, when Galya cringed in a corner, I could guess what she had in her hand. Letters from Perm had begun to arrive.

"What's the trouble?" I asked.

"She wants to come see us."

"Should we worry about that?"

"But it really means she wants to move in with us. She thinks you're rich."

Several weeks later I heard a scuffle at the kitchen door. When the victor forced herself in, her hefty arms showed why Galya hadn't stopped her. Her bleached hair was crimped into a tight permanent; her orange lips were closed like a purse. She opened them to berate Galya—"What are you trying to pull? Who is your *mother?*"—while her blistering look at me announced that she had indeed come to round out our happy household.

"I told you," Galya whispered, pleading with me not to look. "Didn't I tell you?"

"I'm very glad to meet you," I spluttered. "Won't you join us for some tea?"

The angry woman wanted to know whether I too was "against people's mothers." Explanations about parents living with grown children clearly wouldn't do for her, so I elaborated on our minuscule rooms and my failure to achieve bliss with Liya's mother. These defenses held, and I soon heard my new mother-in-law was moving to a town several hours away by train. She insisted on getting an exact equivalent of her

—actually, Galya's—Perm apartment, and since no one in his right mind would exchange two hundred square feet in Leningrad for the same space in Perm, the town was as close as she could get.

THE BALLET THAT KEPT SERGEYEV in the Kirov until the end of 1970 was *Hamlet*, the dream of his life. It was also a summary of his creative achievements, which fell well below his performing gifts. His formative years were those when every "non-Soviet" feeling was being pummeled out of the Soviet people. The very phrase "an artist's individual vision" could mark a man for destruction. Yet more than any other recent ballet, *Hamlet* needed inner vision and conviction to probe the human condition as the play did. Unless the inspiration came from the deepest personal source, it could only be a watered-down imitation of Shakespeare.

Sergeyev's choreography included some brilliant ideas, such as Hamlet and Laertes fighting their duel with their legs and Hamlet swearing revenge by leaping across the stage in a scissorslike movement that cut the air of the whole theater. Hamlet's stretched limbs suggesting swords pointing at himself or others was a display of Sergeyev's mastery of using the male body to produce pure technique and a faint hint of what the work was really about. But on the whole, everything was undermined by not getting to the true meaning of the conflict.

Sergeyev gave furious movement in place of depth. As a performer and coach he knew better than anyone the danger of forcing a dancer to sweat and strain instead of expressing himself freely in his chosen language. But this is precisely what he did as a choreographer. His inventions reached the highest aesthetic and technical levels, therefore were fascinating to perform—but as exercises. The huge collection of steps in Hamlet's particularly overladen part served only to interfere with communicating a sense of character. Having polished his every design to the highest perfection over years of mental preparation, Sergeyev now forced them all on us with the same scrupulousness. I begged him to lighten the burden. I was certain that slight adaptations would enhance some of his own effects. He would watch, close his eyes, and pronounce himself "not convinced."

The "To be or not to be" scene was the crux. It should have brought Hamlet's dilemma starkly to life, dispelling all doubt about the ballet's meaning. It should have shown what Shakespeare's genius did:

a self-critical, self-doubting protagonist being driven to despair—less by circumstances than by the nagging questioning of his rage against the circumstances. The conflict between his conscience and his animal instinct for revenge had tremendous theatrical potential. When the Prince mistrusts and fears his own motives on the verge of taking action, audiences should agonize with him. Hamlet's vacillation should be a time of deep self-examination for everyone old enough to remember what he had wanted to be compared to what he was.

Sergeyev sought refuge in his whirlwind of superbly difficult movements. Instead of compelling thoughts about everyone's humiliating hesitations in crucial decisions, the scene was an enormously complicated marathon of feat following technical feat in the blink of an eye. The choreographic intricacy did give a magnificent opportunity for displaying virtuosity, but even this presented another problem: Hamlet's worry about collapsing during the fifteen-minute "soliloquy."

I tried to understand why Sergeyev shied so far away from the central conflict. For one thing, Hamlet was a great departure from the romantic leads he was accustomed to. Instead of the handsome figure agonizing over how to capture his lady's heart, *this* Prince brooded about life itself. He was far more complex than a "Kirov" hero, and all his problems were chaotic inner ones.

Just to depart from the lyrical lover image, I studied photographs of English Hamlets. Elizabethan actors supposedly used a Titian portrait of mature, bearded Impolito Riminaldi for their inspiration. But when I based my makeup on this riveting painting, Sergeyev led the storm of protest. He felt his hero must win public affection by being the "pure" youth of *his* inspiration. This automatically excluded a beard, which, in the Kirov code, identified the wearer as a villain. The Hamlet the audience eventually saw came on with the famous Sergeyev cape: the very symbol of romanticism, borrowed from his own Count Albrecht in *Giselle*.

This reminded me again of what he had survived in his heyday, when terror taught choreographers that only socialist-realist conflicts were permissible. No wonder he backed away from Hamlet's quandary. *It* provoked just the kind of ambiguous questions that had to be suppressed since they might interfere with "revolutionary" explanations.

But gradually I realized that Sergeyev was not the problem, but his love for *Hamlet*, which was pathetically misplaced. A Fokine or a

Balanchine could not have staged it properly in a Soviet imperial theater. *Hamlet* remained eternal because it was not merely historical, but a vehicle for expressing something universal. To "solve" a new production, its director had to provoke a contemporary response to contemporary issues, an emotional understanding for *our* day in *our* country. The court intrigues and murderous lust for power would have had to cast a reflection on similar goings-on among Communist royalty.

Above all, any real new *Hamlet* had to illuminate its epoch's problem of submission to authority, which is what Hamlet's wavering is all about. What confronted him was not peculiar to medieval Denmark. Soviet lies, arrogance, and corruption were the modern equivalents. Hamlet's torment could be felt in Russia only through this connection. State power was the evil that made our lives unbearable. Yet we had to tolerate it because, like Hamlet, we feared the alternatives. He hesitated, faltered, and compromised just as every one of us did. Watching this ought to have been an excruciating revelation for a Soviet audience. But the very tyranny the ballet should have exposed suffocated its meaning.

The play within a play that was being acted out backstage had more emotional content than all five of Sergeyev's acts. Dudinskaya was the first to be stricken. Ever since Sergeyev conceived of his *Hamlet*, she had danced before his eyes as Gertrude. After Makarova's defection, she could not even assist as the chief female coach. Gertrude herself had no worse punishment.

Fedicheva, the replacement, was also falling from grace. With a new husband, her life was as full of impossible conflict as the once self-satisfied Gertrude's. She too dropped out of the part for the time being. Polonius was Yuri Maltsev. Until now, he had done the KGB's work with a certain finesse. Like a successful thief, he was even secretly admired for his skill. But he followed his orders to sabotage *Hamlet* too openly and slavishly. Losing everyone's respect for this was a disaster for him, for he loved the theater as much as ever. He and I could never be the same again.

Ophelia was Makarova and only Makarova. She had worked on the part for six months before defecting in London, just before starting to rehearse her mad scene. Her dancing was more brilliant than ever. Now she was gone, and Sergeyev knew what this foreshadowed for him. "My Ophelia has already gone mad," he kept saying. "And she is driving the rest of us mad with her."

Yuri Soloviev had already bowed out of rehearsals, considering Hamlet's characterization too complex for him. This widened the opportunity for Mischa Baryshnikov. Baryshnikov needed more depth of precisely the Hamlet variety to help raise his acting to the level of his dancing. But sadly for his development, he became trapped in the web woven by the anti-Sergeyev spiders.

As the other Hamlet, I associated with my role as never before. The last reason for remaining in Russia was dying with Sergeyev. The feeling choked me that I *must* get out, must avenge his assassination, must become the person I was intended to be. My Kremlin Claudiuses loomed up before me, taunting me for being too weak-willed to stand up for my honor. I despised myself, yet could not act, could not be sure of anything except my self-doubt and self-contempt. If I followed my instinct, I would destroy myself as a dancer, probably as a person, too. If I held back, I faced a life of Hamlet's humiliation with no hope of respect for myself. My puny resolution sometimes pushed me toward madness, but I couldn't stop its raging. Shakespeare knew it came from the deepest level—most of all, in someone who must make up his mind once and for all what kind of man he is going to be.

I looked at my weary fellow dancers and sensed that we all were doomed. Everyone involved in the production would soon fall from the Kirov. *Hamlet's* legitimate father was already being foully murdered. A bloodthirsty viciousness had been injected into the anti-Sergeyev campaign. Ballet's noblest Prince was dragged to Party sessions and vilified at meetings of a dozen Kirov committees. The purpose was to make his life unbearable and to wreck the production. For it was not enough to fire him as a scapegoat. In keeping with Soviet practice, a "reason" had to be found. Since his person was immaculate, this could only be achieved by denouncing his art—and so demolishing the love of his life.

The Kirov's anti-artistic cliques happily joined forces. Maltsev's supervisors obviously liked the Party approach that Kolpakova had suggested in Rumania. As soon as we returned to Leningrad, Maltsev led the undermining of confidence in Sergeyev. "You're a fool to waste your time on his disaster. You should be working with people worthy of your talent."

At the Party-sponsored meetings that disgraced the final months of rehearsal, many of the younger soloists were especially active in condemning Sergeyev as "empty" and *Hamlet* as "a sorry farce." With little experience of these things, Baryshnikov dropped out after only two performances, saying that he couldn't understand what the ballet was about. In the summer of 1974, when I was silently cheering Mischa for his defection, this incident came back to me. Maybe he was already thinking of escape and therefore could not take any strong stand. In any case, how good it was that he was *out,* where the wide world would have him and his career could take its own glorious course.

My own respect for the master gave me no immunity to the anti-Sergeyev virus. At one point during the struggle with the massively overburdened choreography, I almost agreed that the ballet wasn't worth fighting for. Sergeyev continued to press his demands on me, and some scenes simply didn't work. I lost my enthusiasm for several crucial weeks —a terrible blow to Sergeyev. He had been talking to me about dancing Hamlet since my earliest days in the Kirov. Until he took me in, he had eyes only for his own kind of pure dancer. I was a new kind of animal for him, but before I could tackle the part as he saw it, I had to acquire the style it required. This was one reason he had worked so hard for so many years to groom me.

Instead of rehearsing as I usually did, I showed my lack of faith in the production by dillydallying. Instead of damning the talk that the work must be scrapped, I listened with one ear. Then Dudinskaya took me aside for a little talk. Her bloodshot eyes woke me up to what I was doing to Sergeyev.

I found Sergeyev alone and apologized. He said I should take no notice if *he* seemed distraught; so much depended on him now, and this production, which meant more than ever to him, was giving him "many worries." "I know you're in a difficult situation, too," he said. "You've always had so much pressure on you." This was the closest we ever came to a real talk. We understood each other perfectly.

From then on I gave him everything I could. *Hamlet* was going to be his last ballet, and his version of it, just like himself, was worth more than his enemies could understand. This was borne out by the clutch of prizes it eventually won—including a state prize for the best ballet of the year—despite everything. After this, place was made for it as a major production in the Kirov's permanent repertoire.

I danced the premiere in December 1970. This was the clearest case of emotional inspiration making a deeper impression than sheer excellence. One evening I overheard an elderly coach saying he'd lived to see something extraordinary in the Kirov: a dancer with only average endowment giving more to a ballet than a genius, perhaps the best dancer Leningrad had ever seen. "Panov comes closer to the meaning, opens it up as a work of art," he said. "He must do it by hypnotism, since Baryshnikov is physically better in every way."

Another teacher said it more simply. "Baryshnikov may be greater than even Nijinsky. He is a magnificent Hamlet. But Panov *is* Hamlet."

The huge ovation at the premiere had been mostly a show of solidarity with Sergeyev: ballet enthusiasts' attempt to save the city's pride. The production itself was embarrassingly raw, thanks to the forbidding choreography and to Sergeyev's impossible working conditions. After his departure I pared down the overly complex patterns, using my ideas, but trying to control them with his eyes. It was a year before I felt really comfortable with the role and thought the ballet as a whole deserved its early acclaim.

During this time Sergeyev was hardly in the Kirov. But he did come on the evening of December 31, 1971, almost twelve months to the day after the premiere. I knew of his arrival from the roar of applause while I was warming up backstage. The Leningrad public had remained faithful to him. As the immaculately groomed Artistic Director, he had always watched every performance from a front seat in the Director's box. He was conscious that the audience used to wait for him to take his seat and set the tone of a Kirov evening. The flighty Dudinskaya would invariably scuttle in during the middle of the first act, but Sergeyev was always as prompt as he was elegant—a living monument to his art.

After his dismissal as Artistic Director the two seats remained empty for a time. Even Rachinsky's Party guests hesitated to sit where the whole ballet world knew Sergeyev belonged. When he came back the first time, an electrician swung his spotlight around, and the theater rose to cheer the man who had brought fame and glory to Soviet ballet. It was as close as possible to a public protest. The electrician was fired the next day.

Now Sergeyev rarely attended performances. Only *Hamlet* still pulled him there, but he came as an ordinary member of the public and, to avoid more fuss, waited for the last moment before taking his seat. But devotees spotted his unmistakable figure and let him know how his destruction dismayed them. Galya rushed backstage. "How magnificent he is. Sergeyev is . . . a real Pushkin hero. Everyone's crying." It was beyond her understanding how a man who represented everything she had always worshiped could be treated as he had been. I understood perfectly. The lump in my throat commanded me to dance in his honor.

He came to my dressing room after the second act. I noticed that he had to sit down. "It's magnificent," he said, looking up and down me as never before. "I can hardly believe I created such a thing. Your New Year's present fills me with optimism." After the final curtain he said this wasn't true; we had choreographed it together. "I didn't recognize some of it myself, but you could never have done it differently. That's what I was always dreaming of—for us, for ballet. You *convinced* me."

Neither of us suspected that this would be my last appearance as Hamlet.

35

THE URGE FOR EXPRESSION GREW AS THE URGE SIMPLY TO DANCE ONCE had. There was nothing to do but bottle it up, together with the growing sense of imprisonment.

My "ingratitude" mystified many. Although I was still the black sheep, professional attitudes toward me had flipped. In their twenty-year careers most dancers performed six or seven major traditional roles and considered themselves lucky to get two new ones to create. I now had fame, relative riches, maximum prerogatives onstage. "What else could you possibly want?" people asked. "Why aren't you *satisfied?*"

Dancers of other countries who sensed themselves suffocating in a particular artistic atmosphere merely moved to a theater with a divergent approach. But all our theaters played the same broken records. For Soviet performers who felt differently, the only alternatives were to stop dancing or to defect. But defection was a huge gamble and a total ripping away from your old life, a frightening sacrifice for anyone. This is why even those who once wanted to achieve something special with their work knuckled under. A few combative spirits wrangled for

Esmeralda—*part of the final examination at the Kirov school*

Also for the Kirov final exam: The Pearl *with Marina Cherednichenko*

On the Eve *with Galina Pakryshkina, at the Maly*

Daphnis and Chloe *with Ludmilla Kamilova at the Maly*

Laurencia *with Kaleria Fedicheva*

Scriabin Etude

The Seven Beauties

As Yasny Sokol in Leonid Jacobson's Land of Miracles

With Natalia Makarova in the Blue Bird pas de deux from a film of Sleeping Beauty

*As Mercutio in Leonid
Lavrovsky's* Romeo and Juliet

Jacobson's The Blind Girl *with Alla Shelest*

The Lady and the Hooligan

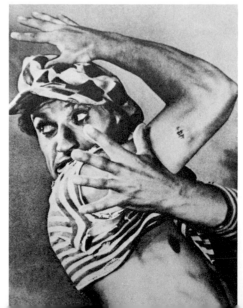

Making up for Petrushka *(opposite)*

As Osman in The Mountain Girl

Rehearsing The Creation of the World *(Mikhail Baryshnikov at center)*

The Creation of the World *with Baryshnikov*

Practicing leaps

Harlequinade

(Opposite and above) Rehearsing Hamlet

Rehearsing Hamlet *with Alla Sizova (Boris Blankov is watching at left) and (below) the same moment in performance*

Galina as Aurora in Sleeping Beauty

Galina in The Creation of the World *(Baryshnikov at right)*

Galina and Valery in The Bronze Horseman

Together in Nutcracker

Harlequinade

Le Corsaire

Le Corsaire

Albinoni's Adagio

Harlequinade

individual mercies. But the majority of the potentially creative people gave up their insights and visions. The best ideas were killed before being born.

Well-meaning soloists returned from trips to tell me how childish my dissatisfaction was. "Ye gods, ballet gets nothing in the West. No studios, no coaches, no Academy. A tenth of our budget, a hundredth of our advantages." To me, it didn't matter whether foreign theaters were better or worse, only that they offered growth. The magnificent Kirov had nurtured and groomed me as none other could, but rightly or wrongly, I believed I had farther to go and more to give.

I was sick of being able to predict every rehearsal and production, of knowing in advance what might be possible and what I "categorically" must not try. I dreamed of tasting something besides the Soviet cud and my own carcass. When nothing new is permitted, a dancer can only repeat himself, which is a form of cannibalism.

Once I'd been flattered when my *Don Quixote* was chosen to impress visiting dignitaries. Whatever my hurt, going out onto the stage brought exhilaration. Now I felt nothing for Basilio but a fatal weariness. I had done all I could with the role. It was taking me nowhere except to an early artistic graveyard.

Or I'd be in my dressing room when the orchestra began warming up with themes from *The Bronze Horseman*. When first preparing the role, I had played the record in my room for months and learned more on the thousandth hearing. Now the music hounded me. The audience stirred when I came on. For a second I tried to hear the inspiration I needed. But the stage was quicksand. The Kirov professionalism had hardened into iron bars.

Years before, Maya Plisetskaya complained to a friend about Petipa's eternal *Swan Lake*. The public adored it, she said, and she once had too. But she had danced it so often that the opening themes made her sick. "The most wonderful ballet music ever written. Maybe the best ballet ever created. And I want to pull my hair out and stuff it down the directorate's throat—that's what they've done to me." At that time I thought she was carrying on in her "Plisetskaya" way. Now my whole body understood. She would never get the new things she needed. She was gagging on force-feeding of the standards, yet starving at the same time. The future in store for me was even worse, in proportion to the Kirov's greater rigidity than the Bolshoi's. It would never change because its masters took it for art's highest achievement. Even in roles I'd once loved with all my being, dancing was no longer a joy. I wanted to choreograph and already knew that nothing I felt strongly about was fit for this theater. I hated Soviet rule for this. I hated it for everything else.

Alec called my new dream—for the Japanese tour planned for the spring of 1971—a reversion to childhood. "They'll *never* let you out; you *still* don't understand them," he said—correctly, for no matter how stupid it was, part of me continued to hope for an accident or a miracle. I had also begun to imagine escape routes. I would find a weak point in an Asian mountain frontier or attach myself to the hull of a ship leaving Leningrad for international waters.

Maltsev kept assuring me I *was* on the list for Japan. He'd been told to keep me quiet but also truly believed "they" had to let me travel. He had convinced himself that his anti-*Hamlet* campaign was really to save me from going down with Sergeyev. He genuinely wanted me to be satisfied, so that I wouldn't become an outright opponent of Soviet rule.

He insisted that my rehabilitation had to come soon. Since a Kirov star and a suspect were mutually exclusive in the official mind, my participation in all the important new ballets *had* to change the attitude toward me. There was simply no provision for someone to crawl out of the political doghouse for one successful premiere after another in Leningrad's top artistic palace. All I had to do was help people overcome their mistrust.

"I know them," he coaxed. "Words alone can never do anything. What they need is documentation, something they can't throw out." He was referring to the common practice known as going abroad on someone else's bones. What you said about the fellow dancer you denounced didn't even have to be accurate. False "documentation" was sometimes better received than real information. It put the accuser in the KGB's moral as well as physical power. Maltsev knew they were better disposed to applicants who wallowed in communal dirt.

He plied me to name Soloviev and especially Baryshnikov. The KGB had decided to hinder Mischa's progress too. He'd been abroad only once, watched by dozens of "helpers." Instead of delighting in his enormous London success, the policemen were resentfully suspicious.

"Just think of something, *anything* about Baryshnikov. It's so damn easy. I'll do the writing."

Selling old classmates had become more blatant since Makarova's defection and Sergeyev's departure, so he was right in his way. He was also right about my case being reviewed. This was no tranquilizing rumor; the reasons were obvious.

A three-minute variation by one of my understudies touring in New York was more newsworthy to local critics than all my Kirov seasons together. Mention of me had as much relevance to their readers as a statue in a Leningrad park. Therefore, only a handful of Westerners had heard of me—but they were all balletomanes. Some had begun inquiring about me in Intourist offices before visiting Leningrad. Naturally, export departments wanted to cash in on my growing reputation.

For some Party officials my recent nomination for People's Artist of the Russian Soviet Federal Republic—the next step up the ladder of awards—presented a more painful dilemma. For years I'd been untitled because "How can we give such a high state honor to a suspect person?" Now it was: "How can we *not* give more titles to someone who keeps creating leading roles in our leading theater?" The question was deadly serious. Titles played a crucial part in the hierarchy of ranks, rewards, and privileges that propped up the Soviet system. Not to give the proper one to a Kirov mainstay was an implied insult to Soviet culture.

Things had gone too far; they had to be put in order. To settle once and for all who I was and what I'd done, Leningrad Party headquarters ordered a full investigation from the head of the KGB's department that supervised the Kirov. There had once been a popular series of jokes about "Vasily Ivanovich," a thick but sly commissar who came to stand for secret policemen in general. My major was a living example of the breed, and Vasily Ivanovich was actually his name.

Maltsev begged me to pay a visit to "someone who really wants to help in your case." The duty matron in one of Leningrad's two luxury hotels motioned me on, as if this use of a room were the most normal thing in the world. Inside, Vasily Ivanovich was waiting to oil me with a veteran interrogator's false courtesy, which was intended to remind me of his power. He suggested I write the full story of my life. "We need complete material for a new evaluation."

"My whole life? You must be joking."

"All right, I'll make a concession. Start with everything you did in America—in detail. We'll get at it like that."

It was the favored approach, based on the victim's supplying his own incrimination. The major was upset by my reluctance to cooperate. My file lay on his desk. Evidently the highest authority had ordered him to clear me, if at all possible. The wasted hard currency and the titles impasse had suddenly become urgent.

After this meeting a swarm of his men questioned my friends about "Panov's real thoughts." He kept the most exacting job for himself: trying to worm the truth directly from the suspect. What skill and experience it took! "But what do you really think? About the world struggle, for example. All right, you're in ballet now. But what if you had to pick up a rifle and pass the real test? . . . You're not as dumb as they say, Comrade Panov. But why not do something really wise? Write what you have to. For *your* sake, I'm *asking* you."

He must have dropped all his other work for a month while buzzing around me like a fly. Then he announced that his liver was in bad shape again; he'd have to leave me for several weeks. "But when I get out, we'll really tie one on, you and I. And have a real heart-to-heart."

I managed to avoid this pleasure. Vasily Ivanovich looked less jaundiced when he returned, but his line was harder. Now he wanted me to incriminate others along with myself. He pressed me to write "what you think" about several of my artist friends. Then it was back to Baryshnikov.

"You want him to get ahead, don't you? Then help eliminate any questions about his attitudes. Write just a couple of words about that. It's very important to you."

The major pushed a glass of vodka in my direction. He looked at me and waited.

"Honestly, Comrade Major, I don't know how to write."

Finally, he left, muttering about his "stupid goose chase" with me. "Anyway, it's crazy to clear somebody they've got something against." Labels stuck fast even when high Party people wanted to pull them off to see what was underneath.

The next night I was walking home after missing the last metro train. Shouts echoed off a large department store. A huge poster of Brezhnev embracing Husak suddenly ignited in an orange flame. Policemen closed in instantly on a young man walking away from the blaze. They beat him viciously with boots and clubs, tossed him into a car, and drove off. Checkpoints were immediately set up on all surrounding streets in case of "group sedition," and a whitewashing team arrived within minutes. By morning no one would see the slightest sign of the protest. When I described this to Alec, he told me about a book called *1984.*

THE NEXT MAJOR PRODUCTION AFTER *Hamlet* might have been staged to show the Kirov's decline. *The Creation of the World* originated with two French Communists' chic debunking of the Bible. "Let there be light"—and God ignites the sun with a cigarette lighter. "Let there be life" —and He tosses a can of sardines into the sea. Our far cruder version smacked of the atheistic propaganda that bombarded us from our first day of kindergarten. Vulgar sneers at the Scriptures was another example of Marxism-Leninism serving as a mighty advertisement for the faiths it supposedly exposed.

The choreographic portraits of God, Adam and Eve, the Devil, and others were twisted and frenetic. The music was a slick blend of Bach, Gluck, Penderecki, and Beethoven's Choral Symphony. Yet the ballet was even more popular than old favorites such as *Don Quixote.* No Leningrader without contacts had much hope of seeing a Kirov ballet on even the least wanted evenings. In this case, spare tickets were begged at bus stops across the Neva, while speculators were busy making fortunes in the lobby.

The attraction was *five* principals showing off their specialties in the leading roles. Choice bits from everywhere had been spliced together into a parade of virtuosities. Yuri Soloviev leaped so high as God that people were awed despite the mockery. Soloviev's perfect style and sweetness of personality were truly heavenly. Mischa Baryshnikov awed Leningrad with his fantastic gyrations, thrilling everyone. People's Artist Irina Kolpakova was a skillful Eve, while Galina Ragozina was only relatively less amazing than Baryshnikov. The Kirov had taken Galya as a leading soloist soon after we were married and she had been issued a Leningrad residence permit. Her first roles were in the classics. Now audiences saw her as a ballerina who could do everything.

She danced the premiere and a few subsequent performances before leaving—unexpectedly—on the Japanese trip. I stayed behind and continued to dance the Devil, an outlet for my full bag of "tricks." Cheers resounded, but the role was artistically frivolous. Our production's cheap blasphemy repelled me. Aside from a little irony of myself in the underworld, I could find nothing to make my Devil meaningful.

But the ballet sharpened my interest in the Bible. I listened to people who had studied it and borrowed a prerevolutionary copy to start reading myself. The rare object brought light to the darkness of our existence. What surprised me most was how rich in genuine feeling it was.

Galya and I spent hours in front of the Hermitage's religious paintings. I picked up Bulgakov's *The Master and Margarita* again, at the scene where Christ tells Pontius Pilate that lust for power has doomed him to eternal misery. He was thirty-three when Pilate had him crucified. Suddenly I realized that the number "3" had been involved in everything crucial in my life, even the day I first saw Galya. And I knew that superstitious instincts like this could mean more than anything "real."

My thirty-third birthday had come just before the premiere in March 1971.

36

DRINK, TALK, AND DAYS IN THE COUNTRY WERE THE TRADITIONAL escapes. Especially in spring, the countryside outside Leningrad offered a mystical peacefulness. A sense of total harmony with nature wafted there, as if to wash away all disappointments.

Galya left for Japan in May 1971. Soon after that the tireless Suzanne Massie arranged a picnic in the park of a glorious estate. In the evening we went to visit Dimitri Okhtorsky, whose reputation as a rare combination of stagy nonconformist and talented underground artist was steadily growing. The elevator was out of order; we mounted a steep stairway with a sharp smell of urine. A gloomy man with a prominent mustache followed closely behind, giving me a spooky feeling. Since meeting us in the courtyard, he had pronounced three words— "You want Okhtorsky?"—and had given one nod toward the stairs. His bizarre haircut was my first unknowing view of Okhtorsky's art.

Suddenly a door opened at the dark end of a long corridor. It framed an outdoorsman with his sleeves rolled up to display powerful arms. Although leaning against the doorjamb, he swaggered somehow. The uninhibited individuality I'd always admired made a deep impression on me even before I could distinguish his features. As we approached, he looked more and more like an Inca peasant, but his face also showed European refinement, somehow enlarged by a pair of obviously imported eyeglasses. These alone would have set him apart.

He locked the door behind us. It was lined with homemade insulation. As another way to prevent conversation from reaching the corridor, the Rolling Stones were blaring from an excellent Western phonograph. A small delegation from Leningrad's sprinkling of jazz freaks and hippie imitators was enjoying the earsplitting "anti-Soviet" concert for its own sake. More music could be provided by a small organ recently "lifted from a house of God," as Okhtorsky promptly informed me. He and his common-law wife had become Catholics, and religious artifacts lay everywhere. The principle of their collecting was that it was better they get things than the state, which was robbing the country blind, churches first of all.

Okhtorsky claimed that his dramatic antique furniture came from rubbish dumps. "Our people unload their treasures the moment they see the ugliest Soviet imitation of the cheapest Scandinavian modern," he said with a sneer. His young daughter slept on the first four-poster bed with a canopy I had seen outside a museum. Now she was wafting about in a caftan of his design. Unwilling to truck even with Soviet dolls, he had beautifully carved and assembled his own for her, which included carefully sculpted genital organs. When I came to know the girl, it seemed to me that his "unwillingness to lie even in this" placed a burden on her.

Okhtorsky's wife was wrapped in white like a nun and surrounded by photographs of the couple's naked friends disporting themselves. As if competing in kinkiness, a cat howled feverishly and thrust her hindquarters toward the resident dog's nose. Okhtorsky proudly observed that *his* pussies were *always* in heat.

His graphics on the walls included some illustrations for Dostoyevsky with cold but striking forms. The walls themselves were painted as I imagined an avant-garde nightclub would be. But patches of plaster had been chipped away to the brickwork, especially of the chimney, since this was supposedly a favorite place for KGB microphones. Okhtorsky's precautions seemed dramatized, like the rest of him.

But the talk we soon plunged into showed he had reason to be careful. By dawn the impression he made on me was overwhelming.

More than an enormously striking personality, he was a force, because everything he said came from himself, not from what others taught. His formal education hardly existed; the spelling blunders in our notes to each other could have been part of a code. His religious interest assured him precious little schooling, even if he'd wanted more; principals kept throwing him out for making the sign of the cross. Later the Repin Academy of Art also expelled him, and he stayed alive as a warehouse loader, night watchman, and street sweeper. But he managed to have several exhibitions of his exciting graphics and paintings in the relatively liberal mid-1960s. These were quickly closed, with punishment for the brave gallery and museum officials who had sponsored the "garbage."

Okhtorsky took out his hatred of Soviet rule on the house's other residents. When up in time, he would scatter the morning line to his communal bathroom with a roar and display of his biceps or hands, which bore bruises from his demonstrative karate blows and kiln burns. The tenants all were terrified of him and of the silent Sorokin, who hovered behind, willingly submitting to his master's spell. Okhtorsky had named him Mustachio and added him to the bit players in his life theater. His friends played the audience, and his possessions served as props. His religious interests were also dramatized but grew out of genuine conviction. He gave me a beautifully illustrated Russian Bible, smuggled in from Stockholm. When Galya returned from Japan, I read aloud to her, and we started visiting churches. Okhtorsky knew them all.

For weeks after the party Okhtorsky and I were together day and night. Most of all, we talked about what kept us peons of a system we despised. He too was suffocating. I used to admire a poet's line about being able to tolerate even anguish in magnificent Leningrad. It was precisely because we could *not* tolerate ours that Okhtorsky and I understood each other's deepest longing.

Despite his precautions against listening devices, he felt relatively safe only outdoors. Our walks started after my performances and sometimes ended at dawn. The mute Sorokin followed behind us, examining anyone who approached on the deserted streets. Galya returned from Japan to many new Kirov roles. After rehearsing them furiously all day, she slept the sleep of the innocent while we three crossed the city night after night. I dragged myself home in the morning and was up again for groggy rehearsals a few hours later. For the first time I could not

take them seriously. I waited all day for the "escape" of cursing our fate
at night.

Walking along the Neva, we prattled about jumping in, swimming
away, and coming up in Sweden, Iceland, anywhere. We fantasized
about stealing a diving suit and about the day when chemicals would
rubberize the skin. Suitably equipped, we could slide into the river and
emerge *free*. Gradually plans formed for a genuine escape. The land
borders were fanatically guarded, as I knew from my trip to entertain
frontier troops near Finland. The air route was eliminated when we
realized that there was no way to learn in advance how a forged passport or a person in a crate might be examined at an airport. Water was
our only hope.

Weeks of talk committed us to a do-or-die attempt, and pure desire
produced a dozen schemes. We'd bribe local fishermen to take us out to
the Gulf of Finland, overtake a Western ship headed for open water,
and persuade a sailor to throw down a rope. Rumors circulated that two
or three men had got free this way. But further investigation established
that all outward-bound ships were so closely watched into international
waters that a piece of driftwood couldn't approach one undetected.

We designed a homemade aqualung. Outfitted with it and
properly weighted, we'd attach ourselves to a departing vessel's rudder.
The vision of a severed hose and of currents dragging us into the
propeller shelved these blueprints.

We switched from the Baltic Sea to the much warmer Black, where
Soviet passenger ships plied between the major ports. We'd board one
and jump overboard at its farthest point from land. A tiny Western
transmitter bleeping on a preestablished wavelength would signal a
yacht provided by a certain Frenchman who much admired Okhtorsky
and his drawings. This plan was our most promising until we learned
of the day-and-night KGB patrol of all decks of all Soviet cruise ships.
The dreaded "Man overboard!" would sound before we hit the water.

Okhtorsky returned to a scheme from the previous summer. He had
almost persuaded some Black Sea fishermen, whom he sometimes called
his friends or his relatives, to smuggle him past the security inspections
and drop him at sea, near the waiting yacht. The price equaled almost
two years of my wages. While more nights went to scrutinizing this
alternative, the principal decision grew firmer: *we were going to try*. In
the end, we picked a port much closer to Turkey. On-the-spot investigation in the town of Batumi would determine our final plans.

Our tiny apartment was a showroom for the latest amplifiers, tape decks, tweeters, and woofers that Galya had bought for me in Tokyo. To cover the costs of travel and training, I sold the entire collection of gear I'd been dreaming about for years. Sorokin ran down for a celebratory bottle. When I dropped a hint over the telephone to Vilnius, Alec rushed to Leningrad to see what he fervently hoped would be my last performance in Russia—and to help.

It was as natural to seek Alec's advice as to keep everything from my parents. He had flirted with danger as long and insistently as I, but instead of shooting off half-cocked, he minimized risks with pragmatic battle plans. The attempt needed his powers to seize the essentials of a problem and stay with it until all aspects had been analyzed. And if we were going to be separated for years, I needed to tell him what he meant to me. As my day approached, I realized how long and patiently he had been preparing me for it. Twenty-five years of talks and books followed the pattern of the candy he'd brought for me from his wartime evacuation.

He arrived and put his expertise directly to work. It had been impossible to get an idea of Batumi's outlines in Soviet publications; such information about coastal areas was a state secret. But Alec knew where to look for loopholes. Sure enough, a Czech military atlas on sale in a specialist store for East European books provided excellent charts. Much later my father ran from the room when he saw the huge volume. "A military publication in private hands—what is this? And with strategic maps! Are you crazy or something?"

But after a week of Alec's help I began to sense that our roles were reversing. He had long felt that I must get out first—by defecting if possible—because I'd be lost if left alone in Russia. Now I saw that despite his problem-solving skills, I had become the older brother. Still the supervisor of his amateur movie club, he remained true to his principle of doing only enough work for the dictatorship to earn his food. The discrepancy between his abilities and his achievements was growing as time to correct it was running out. Only I could help now, and with me on my way, he revealed how much his hope rested on his brother's being abroad. Just that thought would inspire him, and I might be able to campaign for his freedom, too. I swore to myself not to fail him. This was my only way to deal with the pain of his sacrificed life.

The single awkward element in our planning was some alternative plan that Okhtorsky seemed to be developing in whispers to his wife and telephone calls from Paris. It was odd that he was keeping something important from me at this critical time, but I felt it wrong to question him and tried to learn more about Batumi instead. All that mattered was completing the physical process of leaving.

Late one night Okhtorsky appeared unexpectedly at the Rossi Street apartment. His eyes avoiding mine, he immediately launched into a harangue about the egg—apparently me—being unable to teach the chicken. This performance ended with a command that we leave for Batumi the following morning. His reasons—that he was being followed, that his wife and child were already waiting for him in Paris!—were so illogical that I took them as some attempt at humor. But his raving became more vicious. Suddenly I felt ill. Okhtorsky was trying to provoke a fight, but *why?*

I said I could not go until the end of the week. I was leaving Galya behind, after all; it was my duty to provide for her in at least some basic ways. He knew that the final papers for an apartment promised us— where she could live in my absence—would be ready in two or three days. This would make her life somewhat easier without conceivably affecting the success of our plan. But my explanation only infuriated him.

"So you're a little baby, after all. What's the double cross of trying to drag your Galya into *our* affair?" His shouting reminded me that he'd just announced that *his* wife, who was *his* reason for insisting we change our plans, was already abroad. It was strange that he'd told me nothing about this startling achievement, stranger still that she had suddenly got a visa. I tried to brush away these sickening questions and return to the spirit of our months together. But he had been drinking. I could hardly believe he'd come to discuss life-and-death matters in that condition. Worse, I sensed that he'd had just enough to *play* drunk but knew exactly what he was doing.

"When I decide something, that's how it's going to be. You're nowhere until you understand that."

There was only one answer. His alternative plan appealed to him more. He was trying to shed the obstacle I'd become by inciting me to break with him. Of course, he had every right to scrap our dangerous method for a better one. Maybe my impulsiveness and urge to talk were genuinely worrying. In some ways, I not only appeared, but still *was,* childish.

Okhtorsky could have said all this with no loss of honor. It was the obscenities perverting our friendship that I couldn't digest. "You're with me or you're against me," he shouted, in Lenin's favorite words. "And if I get arrested or into some 'accident,' my Mafia boys will zip from Paris to St. Petersburg and cut you up. I thought you'd like to know."

Eventually I was to realize that hatred of the Soviet system was in itself no foundation for a friendship. I had been so happy to find someone who loathed the same things I did that I took everything else for granted. But bitterness *against* something was no guarantee of wisdom, goodness, or honesty—Okhtorsky's or mine. My backwardness had kept me from understanding that a society of lies and oppression produces more twisted characters than pure ones, even in the minority who resented their enslavement.

These thoughts came much later. Now Okhtorsky's behavior produced only a silent cry. *But we had trusted our lives to each other because we believed in the truth.* Beneath all the embellishments, Okhtorsky's artistic vision and religious conviction were genuine. How could such a man betray our mission?

ALEC, GALYA, AND I waited only a few days until we took possession of our new apartment. We threw everything into it and left the same morning for Vilnius. From there, my brother and I rode his motorbike every morning to Green Lake, a deep loop lying in an unspoiled gorge a dozen miles from the city. But we chose it not for its beauty, but for its virtual emptiness on weekdays. We rented a boat from the tumbledown station and rowed out of sight. My training began in early August. I had decided to escape alone.

The first requirement was flippers for swimming long distances underwater. The tenth pair we tested were flexible enough without constantly slipping off. Next we enlarged snorkling tubes to provide the oxygen for the hardest possible swimming. I weighted myself so that only the tip of the snorkle showed. A breaststroke with flutter kick that never broke the surface was the best combination for headway over many hours.

Our destination was still Batumi; meanwhile, I needed to prepare without a wet suit. I'd asked Jennie Walton to send me one when she returned from her latest White Nights visit to Leningrad. No rational person would carry this little item into our country, but a brave friend of hers did bring an underwater compass from London. Even with this, maintaining a true direction underwater was very difficult. I would pick out a tree, swim a mile or two, and come up to check. It took two weeks to work out the compass correction and stroke control for a fairly straight line.

Nervous tension had killed my appetite during the final weeks of planning with Okhtorsky. I lost weight even faster after our break. Now I swam until I couldn't take another stroke and was near shock when Alec pulled me out of the water. Appalled by our failure of judgment about Okhtorsky, Alec and I merged in total trust. As chief of operations he was greatly concerned about building back my weight as protection against the water's cold. But I vomited up the bread and lard he tried to stuff me with. My sister-in-law, still chief chef of the Lithuanian Central Committee's restaurant, brought home its finest delicacies. I managed to swallow a few mouthfuls of the Party's caviar.

The cold of the water was like nothing I'd ever known. After two hours I was hauled into the rowboat like a purple corpse. Vodka kept my blood from actually congealing in the wind, but the swimming sessions almost broke me every time. I was afraid to tell Alec their true pain. The Black Sea would be much warmer than this mountain lake, but Alec's reading had shown that the greatest danger on coastal marathons was from cramp produced in icy underwater patches fed by mountain streams, of which the snow-capped Caucasus had many. After more research he began experimenting with protective greases. Proportions of lamb, pig, and goose fat were varied daily and boiled into a new "brand." The only problem was the stink of the boiling, which was so bad we thought someone would surely call the police.

At last everything was ready. Alec spooned his thick concoctions into movie film cans. It was mid-August, the best time. The final plans would be made in Batumi.

WHEN THE STEWARDESS WAS OUT OF SIGHT, we uncovered our binoculars for a view of the coast and an estimate of whether an underwater swimmer could be spotted from the air. The first glance took in a constant patrol by motor boats and helicopters, running far out to sea. Our confidence in our preparations collapsed. The realization of what pitiful amateurs we were produced a kind of shame; Galya avoided my eyes.

Posing as vacationers, we rented a room, left our things, and climbed a hill overlooking the city. Our hearts sank. It was obvious why the authorities discouraged tourism in Batumi: the border was *right there* on our left—far nearer than it appeared on Soviet maps. But crossing a mined strip would have been easier. Over the water, Turkey was no more than twelve miles away from the municipal beach. Even a big circle around the port and its anchored ships would have needed a swim of only thirty miles. But armed cutters patrolled a band from the coast to the horizon like precision-timed troops; as one passed by where a swimmer might get through, the next one appeared. Faster-moving helicopters whirled constantly above. And an awesome forest of radar installations, watchtowers, and searchlights stood at every place of access to the water, especially on the six miles of the prohibited zone's shoreline.

Feeling foolish even looking for somewhere to slip into the water pushed us back to thoughts of the land. Cool as a movie spy, Galya strolled toward the frontier to probe reactions. She approached within an incredible three miles of the border before being stopped and sent back. Our hopes soared—until we established that the guards, who had followed her for half an hour before descending, really took her for the flower-gathering country girl she pretended to be. I would not get the same leniency, especially after sunset, when anyone penetrating the zone was likely to be shot.

We returned to the sea. My fins and breathing apparatus alarmed the legion of guards watching the bathers. Patrol boats intercepted me after about two and a half miles of my first practice swim, and when my grease made it hard to fish me out, they told me to train for marathons elsewhere. The first time they checked my papers. The second time they warned I would be sent "to somewhere a lot farther away than Leningrad" unless I stopped.

A detention-camp atmosphere descended at sunset. The beach was cleared at 5:30 p.m., and squads searched every inch of it, while cutters moved into the swimming area. Switching on their searchlights at dusk, they maneuvered like destroyers hunting an enemy submarine. Shore-based searchlights illuminated every conceivable access to the water, and sentries patrolled at regular intervals. Departing ships were also floodlit to the horizon, eliminating all chance of climbing aboard one for a later swim across to Turkey. Bright, deserted Batumi was a macabre parody of a seaside resort.

We spent days reconnoitering the city outskirts open to the public. Evenings went to strolling in bathrobes over bathing suits—to pretend, if questioned, that we were planning an innocent midnight swim. Actually, I wanted to slip into the water at the first security lapse we spied. But we only saw more batteries of searchlights being added. We also sensed we were being followed. Eroded nerves left us constantly shaky.

The last hope was for some act of God to interrupt normal procedures. This hope dwindled even faster than our money. When Alec ran out of suggestions, he talked of a storm, painfully deluding himself in the blaze of an orange sun on a glassy sea. I felt that my broken promise to myself would break *me* if I left without an attempt. Our departure day approached unmentioned, like a bad family secret.

One afternoon dark clouds suddenly covered everything, and waves thrashing the beach drove all bathers home. By evening the downpour was so strong that it blocked out the banks of searchlights and, Alec guessed, "snowed in" the radar screens. Even the beach patrols were suspended. The sea's rumble was like a drumroll building toward the climax of our project—and a cue for suppressed thoughts. The storm seemed both a miraculous stroke of luck and part of my pattern of succeeding at the last minute. But I also knew that the surf would probably soon be washing my corpse back to shore.

No, I couldn't die. What I really feared was capture, the conceivable defeat. "Illegal flight" was often classified as treason and brought ten to fifteen years' imprisonment or execution. One month in a labor colony would end my dancing forever, and with the Party and KGB machine turned on lonely Galya, she would eventually crumble. She was too pure even to tie her toe shoes for fame or riches. But she needed to dance as others needed food; how could she hold out against the threat of being deprived forever?

The gale lashed at the window, but our room stayed unbearably hot. I tried to ignore my fear and concentrate on little preparations I'd worked out but could only wonder whether Galya, smearing me with grease, was touching me for the last time. I had always loved her more than she knew. And we had five minutes more together before our insane separation.

Naturally, we told ourselves that when we were reunited *over there*, our love would expand with our artistic and spiritual lives. I had coached her how to report my disappearance: a story about the current carrying me away. If I made it ashore, she was to play a patriot outraged by my "cringing" betrayal of Russia. She would allow the KGB to use this as they wished, then obtain an immediate divorce and marry a Party-oriented husband we'd already selected. Still publicly denouncing me, she would track down the source of forged passports we'd heard of, buy one, and fly to me. Or she would be included in a foreign tour after a year or two of loud contrition and brilliant Kirov success. There she would bolt from the group and into my arms. . . . The vital move was *my* breaking free. The second step of liberating her would be easier from the West, where publicity had power and everything was possible.

The truth was that if I escaped or were caught on the way, Galya would never leave the country again. We were not quite so naïve. Underneath our self-deceptive plans, I told myself it was only fair to leave her temporarily. The Party lords whose whims fashioned careers were beaming at her. With her gifts *and* crucial patronage she would become the Kirov's prima, the ballet world at her quicksilver feet. If she were willing to sacrifice this for me, it would confirm that our love was truly exalted, which meant that she *would* find a way out. But surely she deserved freedom from me while making the decision of her life.

But beneath *this* lay a deeper reason. For all of Galya's immunity to political propaganda, vast gaps of experience separated us. What mattered most to her—as it once had to me—was perfecting her battements tendus and Rachinsky's promise to give her Giselle. If my adoration came instead of, rather than together with, the huge happiness this role would give her, she would quickly see it as a secondary meaning in her life.

I tried to stop these thoughts. But the moment of action was also a moment of truth. Galya didn't like Soviet rule but didn't know it as I did. At her age she had no way of knowing it so. It would have been selfish to let her in on my grim political education while her star was rising. This is why I had always held back from burdening her with *my* loathing. Only when she felt the dead hands on her own movements would she wholly understand what I had to flee from. The lessons would be quicker if she were alone, but was I wishing them on her? Or with me gone, she might become *one of them* in time. Her feeling for me would gradually take second place to the thrill of Odette-Odile before a gala audience.

A premonition of this blow dazed me. Galya's desertion would be worse than drowning. . . . But was this a self-deception to help me abandon *her*? Suddenly I realized I might be sacrificing even her to my obsession to live outside the corrupt Soviet system. My own corruption sickened me.

The wind shrieked. The sea was a cement mixer crunching the shoreline. Nature was out of control. Alec grabbed the film cans like stolen gold, and we fought our way toward the beach. Walking, let alone swimming, was risky; the patrols had left without worry. Lightning revealed that the motorboats were also gone. And the avalanche of water inactivated the searchlights.

Furious rain and spray soaked my bathrobe. I took it off and waited for my old need to conquer physical challenge to click into place and march me into the sea. I couldn't see the nearest watchtower from its edge or the huge rocks thrashing around on the beach. Suddenly the absurdity struck home. The whole plan had been crazy; here was the lunatic proof. I shrank from the water. No one could have survived two steps into it. Cursing this weakness, I peered into the foamy blackness for somewhere to enter. All such attempts succeeded only in wild circumstances, precisely *because* of the risk. There would never be a better chance. If I let this one go, I didn't deserve to get out.

Galya and Alec huddled together as I inched forward. Waves crashing on underwater rocks sent mammoth cascades over my head and stopped me again. In the past few years I had been trying to *think* instead of always blindly following my instincts. I saw that the seething water and galloping boulders were not a challenge, but a summons to suicide. Driftwood timbers snapped like twigs. I didn't want Galya to watch me die like this. But Alec counted on my strength and my lucky star. And I felt I must trust myself to the elements. They would spare me. I could rehearse all day and perform every night, could swim as far as anyone I knew. My stamina had always rescued me and couldn't abandon me at this final moment.

It was now or never. My thought about not blindly following my instincts was a coward's excuse. Hamlet knew it was not worth living as a slave. I had to overcome my humiliating terror. I shouted this to myself through the howling storm.

Rocks shot back at me through the downpour. I shouted again, but my limbs would not move. Gradually, yet in a moment, the past months reclaimed their mortgages. The all-night talks, the training sessions, and the suspense sucked away my strength and left me too weak for what I had to do. I stood at the edge, watching the pounding of the waves. I *was* a little man.

37

I WAS A CORPSE, LENINGRAD THE COFFIN. THE LAST *Pravda* ARTICLE about me in the previous season spoke of a "perpetual search for new colors and insights. Panov's huge appetite for work and relentless self-analysis bring out constant new meanings in his interpretations. This is why his dancing brings great art to so many—art fused with great happiness." The sick irony fitted. I had to force myself onto the stage. Except for Hamlet's scenes of despair, my muscles wouldn't flex. They were stronger than ever after the training in the water but couldn't respond to music.

Afternoons I wandered through the city like a being from another planet. I couldn't understand why the hordes were thrusting into stores and smiling at the Indian summer. Did they really want to live?

Yet the failure of my strength contained an offering of peace. I was part of the universe in a way I hadn't felt before. It no longer seemed disastrous that I would never dance in London. Instead, I thought of ancient Greece, Rome, Egypt—above all, of Palestine. The Bible was my book; the desert, my homeland. Painting the colors I imagined there linked me to whatever it was that made civilization sprout.

The defendants in the Leningrad skyjack case had been condemned to death—although they had not laid a finger on anyone—and were saved only by a world outcry. I knew some of the participants and felt certain the episode was a KGB provocation. The group went to the airport knowing they could not succeed. Despair drove them there, and despair grew after their sentence. Yet Israel's existence comforted me. It was a miraculously resurrected descendant of the ancient Palestine from which mankind's best values came. I began to think of myself as an exiled Israelite and to take pride in the few Jews now allowed to emigrate.

Without permission even to apply, I had no hope of going myself. But I kept myself informed to feed my affection for the emigrants. Some of Leningrad's best minds endlessly analyzed every half hint about changes in emigration policy. Sandrik M. passed on their discoveries to me. His "candlelight" evenings went on, although in far greater gloom than before. Too numb for them, I saw him only to learn who was leaving and who had been ruined for having applied. I wondered how to get through the winter.

To LEAVE OUR LAND OF THE DEAD, Galya and I accepted an invitation to head a gala Vilnius concert. When I was onstage, the local dignitaries remembered that my ballet start had been in the nearby Pioneer Palace. The next day the General Secretary of the Lithuanian Communist Party asked me to become balletmaster of a group moving to a new theater nearing completion in the city. It was my former Vilnius company.

I spent most of the winter there, flying back to Leningrad mainly for Kirov performances. The new Vilnius theater, the country's most modern and lavishly equipped, offered a way back to life through the one remaining artistic challenge. Volodya Sverdlin's jazz records had begun my feeling that everything in my work was leading to choreography. After my Kirov roles had been learned, I would wake up in the morning with an outline of whole scenes. There was no opportunity to work on these raw ideas, but I did adapt all my roles within permissible limits. I took the acceptance of these rearrangements and slight transformations as confirmation of my potential, but Vilnius would be the test.

The three one-act ballets I began with were completed in a single breath. The least original was a brief number to Vivaldi's Concerto Grosso, a kind of bodily étude in my conception of the Balanchine manner, with a touch of the early Renaissance, when painters introduced perspective. Pleasing to the eye, it said nothing of any importance. The second effort, a thirty-five-minute fable in four scenes, was also derivative—in this case, of Alvin Ailey, José Limón, and other Western groups I'd seen. The music was a song called "The Gates of Happiness," performed by Blood, Sweat and Tears, the American rock group. Spanish Tragedy, the third work, was mine. Spain had captivated me almost as long as Spanish dances had. It seemed strange that such terrible catastrophes, including a civil war as destructive as our own, had happened in a land of sun and Latin people. The story was of a little man who tries to make his way to a circle of happy people on an otherwise-darkened stage. Monsters in Stalinist tunics taunt and beat him.

Alec's most important help came in getting things right for Spanish Tragedy. When I mentioned an image, he went to the library for research on the cultural mood of the time and place. At the same time he learned how I wanted to use *my* language. When I talked of how I'd try to choreograph my deepest ideas if I ever got a chance, he ran to his typewriter. "It's not just twirls around the stage; you've got some real *thoughts*," he puffed. "Keep talking, and I'll get them down. We'll need them for reference one day."

The "inspection preview" was for Ministry of Culture overseers and emissaries from the Central Committee's Ideological Section. Spontaneous applause sounded at the end, especially for the "Gates of Happiness" number, which had no hope of being passed even if each inspector liked it individually.

For all the usual reasons, my notes to *Spanish Tragedy* spoke of "fascism's brutality to the people," a transparent disguise for the ballet's clear analogy to Russia. But the preview prompted fierce arguments instead of outraged rejection. No one even mentioned artistic short-comings. All speakers went immediately to "fundamentals."

This was my preview of what to expect as a choreographer, even when my work excited the Baltic bureaucrats, who were distinctly less rigid than those in Russia itself. They immediately began teaching me how to "save" my work—that is, where to depart from what I felt. The first suggestion was to keep Blood, Sweat and Tears off the posters, to-gether with all mention of anything American. "Present the thing as your own from top to bottom, I tell you. Why drag in Uncle Sam or rock music anyway?" The next feature marked for removal was the four-piece combo I'd intended to have play on a platform suspended above the stage. Everyone warned that the intrusion of a tenor saxophone was unthinkable in a Soviet theater bearing the title "Academic."

It was merely a question of changing enough details so that some-thing pro-Soviet would be read into the program. If I agreed, the works would appear in some recognizable form. Posters had already been de-signed for this event in Baltic cultural life, and the Lithuanian Ministry of Culture urged me to leave the Kirov because the theater needed a full-time balletmaster.

But there was nothing to decide. Before Batumi, I might have joined the adjusters and accommodators. After it, I couldn't accept a life of deals to save bits and pieces. Only a few very strong men who began begging for small mercies escaped bureaucratic hands around their throats. Compromise suffocated everyone's art.

Whenever I thought of acceding, I remembered Leonid Jacobson, who should have been another Balanchine. His love of ballet somehow sustained him through thirty years of persuading, pleading, and re-working to the instructions of Party secretaries—even allowed him to achieve some brilliant scenes. He had accepted the nightmarish grind as necessary. I could never do the same.

Besides, I'd come to Vilnius more to take my own pulse as a choreographer than to get my ideas produced. No one else realized how much copying the Vivaldi and rock ballets had involved, therefore how little they achieved. But something real, if very minor, now existed. I could continue believing in myself.

DURING A BOUT OF DEPRESSION the year before, I had awakened from a nightmare with an almost completed synopsis for a ballet. Sections of fully choreographed scenes came later in dreams. I couldn't sleep undisturbed until everything was out of me.

The protagonist was Emelyan Pugachev, leader of a popular revolt under Catherine II. Pugachev captured the Volga region, burned the city of Kazan, and terrorized every noble and landlord in the country. Our textbooks presented him as a revolutionary forerunner, impatient to ease the people's plight. He came to me as a bloody tyrant. A Pushkin article Alec found confirmed that he was closer to a drunken bandit with huge popularity than to a political reformer.

Alec helped me write a scenario for a full-scale ballet. It began with my vision of ax blows and fearful screams blending with the wind of the steppe and with peasant wailing. I tried to project an image of this enduring burden of Russian tortures and mass murders through Pugachev's public execution. In flashbacks, the story of the beheaded and quartered rebel is told by the stump of Pugachev's torso and by three doubles, dancing on different platforms. This is all interspersed with scenes from servile St. Petersburg, with its counterfeit gentility. Silk ribbons for its minuets turn to ropes for Pugachev to drag himself toward the audience. Vanka, the symbol of the Russian people, plays three sad notes on his battered balalaika.

The central focus was the rebel himself. In Vilnius I worked to achieve the desired effects without exhausting the dancers. In *Pugachev* I tried to avoid Sergeyev's much more serious mistake of borrowing from others instead of bringing a personal interpretation to a historical theme. All Russians knew Pugachev's story even better than Hamlet's. Retelling it without some insight into my generation's dilemmas would have been the old dead translation from one medium to another. My Pugachev emerged as no idealist summoning the Russian people to freedom, but as a robber-demagogue, twisted by tsarist oppression. His revolt was a discharge of pent-up violence and superstition, not an early struggle for justice. One of the most sacred Party lines was that the heroic Russian people led the world to enlightened socialism. I had a ragtag, morally stunted mob on their knees before the Cossack rebel.

The Kirov had awarded me a personal "creative" evening for the following spring. I said I would not just string together parts of my best roles—the usual offering for this honor—but include some *Pugachev* scenes. The administration encouraged me to do a major ballet about our national hero.

The Party Secretary and Rachinsky's representatives came to my preliminary presentation with more than the usual expectation for this promising theme. They watched my interpretation in shock. One muttered about "this wrecking of Soviet culture" in a voice that itself seemed wrecked. Another cited me as precisely the kind of renegade against whom the new campaign for fortifying art's ideological content was directed. "In the current world conditions of sharpened class conflict, every work must strengthen our people's socialist resolve. Your shocking profanation is undermining our cause."

Later a friendly assistant director took me aside. "Maybe you have the makings of something, but no one is going to lose his job for your private perceptions. Take my advice, and don't try throwing such ideological bombshells anymore. There's not going to be a revolution in the Kirov."

For me, choreography was the supreme contribution to ballet, a natural growth from dancing. If it were stopped, a person's development as a performer would be cut off too. *Pugachev* was the most highly developed of a dozen scenarios I had worked on in private. The assistant director's words made it official: ballet was finished for me.

SOME FOREIGNERS who came to our apartment brought disillusionment with them. My friends and I had expected Westerners to know more than we did, but their knowledge of our lives was often as defective as ours of theirs. Thanks to Russian isolation, we knew nothing of each other's problems, and we idealized. But the strange part was how few of them wanted to learn. Here they were in our country, as we would never be in theirs, and very few ventured to explore. They let their Intourist guides lead them around the way our "spare artists" led us. Yet they were free, weren't they?

Many had apparently come to Russia in search of the "exotic," which meant vodka, caviar, and onion domes. Soviet rule had been fooling foreigners since 1917. And here they were in their special hotels and restaurants, telling us what good and interesting lives we led.

John Cranko of the Stuttgart Ballet stood out like a revelation from all such gullibility. I did not know how rare it was for Western artists to follow their own creative instincts when large sums had to be raised, as in ballet. Cranko "merely" seemed to me Europe's most interesting choreographer. Even his flops were inspiring because they showed a free man *searching*.

Cranko himself represented all that beckoned from the West. His dedication to art did not put him "above" politics. Every form of injustice upset this true man of conscience, who instinctively fought for all underdogs. He was a South African who could not live under apartheid. The silver necklace with a Mogen David star he wore under his open collar was a gift from dancers in Tel Aviv, for whom he had staged a ballet about the Holocaust. Jews were persecuted; therefore, he considered himself Jewish. He did not hide his opinion of the military government when he was in Greece or of our regime when he was a Soviet guest. This "insolence" amazed the Party and KGB. But everyone who met him, especially those who worked for him, called him the gentlest, kindest man they knew.

He arrived with his company in February 1972. It was no "miracle" that he had made it one of the world's best in ten years, but a natural outcome of his character and talent. Watching them rehearse was a joy. In an imperial theater serving the Central Committee and its ideology, intrigues and betrayals *had* to be the norm. But Cranko's people really had the "love for the collective" that rang with such hypocrisy throughout the Soviet Union. They genuinely wanted to help each other, sincerely believed in themselves as a group, which was a remarkably international one, with dancers from a dozen diverse countries. Their art, which came through love for Cranko, held them together. His principals blessed the day they left "bigger" theaters to work for him. It was my dream of the ideal company, and all the more because Cranko's vivid story-ballets were just what I believed ballet should be doing.

Amazed by Baryshnikov, Cranko predicted a future for him as bright as Nureyev's if ever Mischa "settled" in the West. He said this in my apartment, after a performance of *The Creation of the World*. For he and I were friends from the moment he saw how his own ballets affected me. An East German friend of mine served as translator for our meetings, which the authorities tolerated as professional discussions. I took him to evenings of food, wine, and song in my artist friends' icon-covered apartments. His dancers all worried about what alcohol might do to him—and to themselves—if it disabled him. Yet strange as it seemed, his constant drinking came from an urge for life, not for oblivion; it never interfered with his clarity or wit.

His talk about his work convinced me that anything was possible, given his honesty and vision. My few criticisms—especially of his *Onegin*, which missed the spirit of Russia and therefore was a disaster in Pushkin's native city—moved him to ask for more because "we speak the same language." Eventually I sketched and danced some of my own choreographic hopes for him. One night he said the time for talk was over, then asked me to become his assistant in Stuttgart. I would have my own troupe of thirty dancers. "You can choreograph what you want, with you and Galya as principals. We'll try it for a year, to find your feet. After that you can work where you want to in Europe. We've got to get your ideas on the stage."

I had told him how desperate I was to leave. I thought he was mocking me, the first lapse of his generosity. He asked for a pen so he could draw up a contract there and then. I took his head in my hands. Just spending time with him had been happiness. He was the man I hoped to be. To work for him was precisely what I wanted, only what I wanted.

To get me to Stuttgart, he promised to badger our Ministry of Culture. For insurance he would arrange an invitation from Israel on his next trip there. While he tried these impossibilities, I knew I would not risk dying in an escape across some border.

For our last day together I arranged a trip to a glorious country estate. We sang in the winter countryside, took a steam bath, drank again. When he walked off for a moment, one of his coaches held up his silver necklace. "John's very shy but wants to give you this," she said. "He'd never part with it otherwise. But since you're a Jew who can't go there, he wants you to have it." This first Israeli object I'd ever touched was proof that the country really existed. The little inlaid stones of the Mogen David were like palms in the desert. I ran toward my friend.

When cranko returned to the west, Galya and I traveled in the opposite direction. We had been asked to perform *Don Quixote* in Ufa, the capital of the Bashkir Republic. The local balletmaster and leading dancer—two of my happiest dormitory torturers among the Academy's Asian band—had arranged the invitation. We went for the fresh air.

But Ufa's air smelled of sprawling, spuming factories. If not for the freakish A+ on my graduation exam, I would have spent twenty years in similar grittiness somewhere. Still, a surprisingly good theater of opera and ballet existed even in such a place. The soloists were strong, and the thousand-seat building with the familiar Russian classical columns was impressive. At least Soviet rule hadn't crushed the inherent Russian love of fantasy and beauty that sprang out through the performing arts.

Galya and I walked all afternoon, searching for fruit juice. The most interesting sights were dinosaur-sized snow piles and, in the distance, trains beckoning us to flee the forlorn encampment. No one could remember having seen any juice, but a few merchants happened to have some bumptious fur hats in the style of a bandit lieutenant of Pugachev. They jammed them over our ears so that our visit to their stores would not be a total loss. Eventually we bought two for just this reason; there was nothing else.

To guide us on the important occasions, we were passed from the chief of the railway station to the Director of the theater to the First Secretary of the Communist Party. Each of the notables put out his hand and introduced himself.

"How do you do, I'm Nureyev."

"Welcome to Ufa, my name is Nureyev."

"You must be the Panovs, I'm Nureyev."

Just because every official bore the same clan name, we thought all the more of the one individual who had broken free. Rudolf Nureyev had started with the same Ufa theater. Even with his endowment, it was a miracle that he had made his way to the Leningrad Academy, and a second one that he hadn't been expelled and sent back. Maybe he had some pleasant memories of his birthplace, but we could tell him to thank God for escaping. All Ufa was a shout of "Get out of here. Go to Cranko."

WITH THE NEW REASON TO LIVE, the unthinkable loss wasn't ballet, but Galya. Her Japanese trip had delighted me at first, especially since the Personnel Department let it be known that she was going in compensation for the "change of plans" about me. Without the wish to pacify me for the broken promise—and to do *something* after Vasily Ivanovich's failure to resolve my case—she would have stayed at home with me. Her Kirov successes had not penetrated to the selectors. She was still the outsider who would never learn how to play the game.

The Tokyo critics adored her—a special triumph because of the Japanese enthusiasm for classical ballet. Squinting in the dazzling praise, the Kirov management looked for themselves and discovered the diamond under their feet. Back in Leningrad, the new asset in international prestige and hard currency became an official darling. But Party favor meant Party property. She suddenly had obligations, such as curtsying to ambassadors and smiling for delegations. Rachinsky would rather not waste his drinking time on me. The best receptions were closed except to "one-of-us" artists. My personal problems and "exaggerated" artistic notions would spoil the mood. "Not that you're always unlikable, Panov," one of the regulars explained. "But you're so . . . well, un-Russian."

But the largest reason for not inviting Galya's husband was that the Director always had other plans for his prettiest singers and dancers. He liked to escort them himself or offer the pleasure to someone from Party headquarters. This helped advance his career, of course. In fact, it was what his career consisted of: compiling guest lists and juggling the Kirov's programs to suit the whims of his Party protectors. Some Party bosses enjoyed a kind of droit de seigneur. Even if it didn't come to bed, the flattering company of famous ballerinas was awarded on a priority system, just like consumer goods. Providing one with Galya's looks was a big feather in Rachinsky's beaver hat.

A recent loss intensified his interest in her. Fedicheva's dancing had long been declining. Maltsev told me that she was even more imperious on foreign trips than in Leningrad. Rachinsky stayed loyal as long as he could, but Makarova's defection had weakened even his position.

Rachinsky had taken an immediate fancy to Galya's pretty new face, and as Fedicheva fell, he became more and more attentive to her. When we took curtain calls together, he kissed her cheek and handed her an envelope. Both coming and going, he clumped past me as if I were a total stranger to him *and* to my wife.

Galya opened the envelope. "How nice!" she chirped. "We're invited to the Japanese Embassy." I looked at the card. The "Two" in "Admit Two Persons" had been scratched out, and "One" scrawled in above it. Even someone who didn't know Rachinsky could have deduced that these weren't the Japanese ambassador's tricks. Galya's eyes widened when I pointed this out. "It's wrong, isn't it?" she asked. "Rachinsky always inviting me with that funny look in his eyes; it's not polite." When I assured her it wasn't, she asked me to keep a close watch on her. "These things can get me all mixed up; I don't know how they should work. I do know I'm not going to any embassy." She ripped up the invitation. But she'd have gone if I were in Vilnius. And I was there half the winter.

Galya was as pure as ever. But she was too young, too preoccupied with work, and too naïve to understand what lay behind Rachinsky's pimping or why it was impossible to keep aloof forever from the corruption of Soviet art. I believed that Galya loved ballet more than she loved me—why shouldn't she? And I could see the bosses calculating that *their* new star would be better off without the likes of me for a husband. I had taken everything up to now. This attempt to steal the one person precious to me was too much.

Then Maltsev joined the campaign. In little tête-à-têtes with her while I was in Vilnius, he said she was making a serious mistake by being so standoffish. "All right, you love Valery now. But you don't have to compromise any principles. Being alone in a room with some-body much more important than him—somebody who loves *you*—has nothing nasty about it. Talk to the man about Valery's being so mis-understood. It's your chance to pay him back for all he's done for you. But the main thing is *you*. A little sweetness to them, and you'll have trips abroad, top stardom, everything." To drive the message home, he said her prudery was foolish since I had a flock of mistresses. This knife in the back was beyond anything I expected from him. Before this he had stopped short of personal hurt. I could have accepted even more if it concerned only me and ballet. But Galya was sacred.

My rage didn't last. The limits of our friendship had long been clear. I should have known he would attack me when he had to. His greater loyalty was to the KGB, and no one but I bore the responsibility for maintaining the relationship. It was finished forever.

Breaking a man was a common Soviet spectacle. Maltsev's case went one step further. For I knew about the greatest contradiction within him: his father had been an early idealistic Communist. When Stalin's NKVD shot him in 1937, Maltsev was just old enough to have idolized him. Yet he talked of socialism's triumph justifying "minor mistakes" and even *joined* his father's murderers, whom he somewhere fiercely hated. The harder his masters hit, the more he respected them for their punches. Russia's curse was to have so many mesmerized subjects such as this.

He was obviously miserable that I would no longer see him, and I suffered, too. As he fell lower and lower into KGB work, I had to hold myself back from writing him a long letter. I wanted to tell him that although I had to conceal certain things, I never lied to him. I wanted him to hear *from me* how I felt about life in Russia. I had been closer to him than anyone and knew what he was capable of. The waste of his originality, curiosity, and warmth—above all, his passion for life and for art—was a tragedy. Without his mental imprisonment, he would have given much to ballet and to his friends. What a man he could have been!

The overtures to galya intensified as her dancing flowered. The blackness of our world had swallowed Cranko, as if his visit had been a mirage. But something would turn up. Nothingness couldn't last long in nature. As if to fill the vacuum, a motor started whirring in my head. A Vilnius doctor had said I was on the verge of nervous exhaustion. I couldn't tell him the causes. The dread of losing Galya was worse than all my failures. There was nowhere to turn. Back in Leningrad, the motor picked up speed and activated shrieks at the base of my neck. The whirring began the moment I got up. Then I couldn't sleep at night.

I tried all available diversions. One evening I went to a showing of *Wild Strawberries* in the Union of Cinema Workers. As much as I could follow the story, Bergman's protagonist with his atrophied feelings seemed to predict full withdrawal into myself. The movie ended. I saw Sandrik M. running toward me from across the hall. When I made out what he was shouting, the motor stopped.

"Valery, wait. They're *going!*"

He was frightened to blurt out more. Those words were enough. The "they" were half-Jewish men and women who had applied for visas.

We had a chance to go to Israel!

Nothing else mattered.

I plunged toward the light with all my heart and soul.

RIDING THE WIDE ESTABLISHMENT TRACK to fame, Galya had far less reason than I to leave Russia—and no reason to go to Israel. She knew we faced at least a few tense months. But her answer was immediate. "Of course I'll go if you want to." I was furiously happy. The opportunity to take action brought everything back to life.

The first step was to gather information and documents. Almost all the cases of half Jews were in Moscow, where a kind of Jewish emigration center had been established. With introductions from mutual friends, I went to see one of the leaders, a tough fighter named Vladimir Slepak. He suggested I apply on the basis of an affidavit testifying I would be admitted to live in Israel. Since family reunification was the sole official ground for granting emigration, this was not as "legal" as an invitation from a relative in Israel. But Slepak and others assured me that Jews had been let out with an affidavit in recent years. He told me how to get one from the Dutch Embassy, which represented Israel's interests. Armed with it, I returned to Leningrad.

According to the Ministry of the Interior's "Rule 7," applicants for exit visas had to obtain their parents' consent in writing. The age of the applicants didn't matter, nor whether they had seen their parents in twenty years. The requirement itself was nonsense in Soviet law, since the "Basic Principles" established that adults were fully responsible for their own behavior.

This wasn't for me to argue. And so that I wouldn't have to argue with my parents, I asked Alec to break the news. Raging and cursing, my father shouted what he had been trying to prove to himself for fifty years: that our family wasn't Jewish, but Russian. He shrieked as if trying to force the truth of his past into a bottle. At last Alec convinced him that it would be worse for everyone if he withheld his permission.

Galya's mother took less persuasion. She was worried about her old age. Since her wartime concussion, she had been trying to win a small disability allowance. Although nervous about having to later sign the necessary paper, she brightened at the thought of a handsome retirement with Galya and me in Switzerland, which is where she chose to imagine us.

The checking, consulting, and arranging took ten days. Galya had to spend the last of them in a hospital seeing to a minor complaint. When everything was ready, I was like a horse at the starting gate.

38

THE EARLY LIGHT OF MARCH 21, 1972, ILLUMINATED OUR BEDROOM like sun shining through stained glass. I got up and inhaled the morning's sweet sorrow of leaving.

When Russian sailors heard their ships were steaming into battle, they rushed belowdecks to change. It was important to die in clean underwear. This happy association came to me when I realized I was putting on my Belgian suit. Anything could happen to us.

But I didn't believe it. Serious trouble seemed farfetched in the rare blueness of the early spring day and in my happiness. The luxury of acting on my deepest impulse had washed away the hesitations, half measures, and compromises. At last I was taking an unequivocal, unretractable step that allowed me to respect myself. I felt liberated already.

I was going to inform the powers this morning by asking the Kirov for a statement of our character, attitudes, and job performance. Since we wanted to leave the country, not apply for a new job or for membership in some organization, this lightly camouflaged security evaluation was an absurd irrelevancy in our case. According to normal reason, the greater a would-be emigrant's "deviations" from the norm, the better for Soviet society to dump him onto the ideological enemy. But the iron rule was that this document, known as a *kharakteristika*, had to accompany all visa applications. The authorities simply ordered the candidate's place of work not to provide it when they wanted an extra obstacle. But the request for it was decisive, for it declared your intentions—and on paper.

At the theater I went directly to Rachinsky's Command Post, as he like to call it. His secretary was guarding the office from her usual place. For her delicate mastery of the bureaucratic arts, the old girl was known as the bulldog. She understood the relationship of power to paper shuffling better than the many directors she had served. The bulldog always stiffened at the faintest whiff of political complication in any paper that neared her desk. After setting down our request as if it were a declaration of war, she stared straight ahead and said nothing.

I went upstairs to change for the morning class. Midway through it, the assistant to the theater's Party Secretary entered. He was so frantic that he kept bumping into the chairman of the Komsomol* organization, who accompanied him. Both kept adding "immediately" and "without the slightest delay" to their hoarse whispers that I was wanted in the Party office.

An emigration application sent wheels spinning with amazing speed. Four dark-browed men were indeed waiting. They aimed black stares at me, as if to announce what agency had dispatched them here so quickly. Their prologue was establishing that I was in fact Panov and had actually submitted "this terrible request." They tried to inform me I couldn't be serious about it but were hampered by an aversion to pronouncing the name "Israel."

"That militaristic, fascist country. And you're not even a full Jew!"

Later their leader took charge. "Let's drop this horseplay. You tell us what's bothering you. Are you dissatisfied with something?" I tried to suppress my smile. "Dissatisfied" was not exactly how I'd have put it, but there would be no sense in trying to explain anything to the present company. "What's troubling you, that's what we can't understand. You're picking up the top Kirov salary, and a packet in Vilnius to boot. So what is it—your apartment? You want a better one; we'll *give* you a better one. Just say the word."

I restrained myself. "Let's just say that I want to join my people," I said. "It's time for me to live in my own homeland."

After the long pause this earned, the leader of the quartet was first to find his place again. "You're hurt because you haven't been going on foreign tours. That's ridiculous. Millions of people don't go abroad, and they don't commit suicide. But don't worry, we'll fix up even that."

* Young Communist League.

As the agents' faces grew angrier, they pulled their chairs closer. Obviously, their orders had been to make "that bastard dancer" retreat from his villainous deed. "Do you realize what might happen now? Why ruin your career, finish your life?"

Of course, it wasn't *my* career that worried them, but their own. As always, someone would have to pay for the trouble. The punishment would fit the unforgivable publicity of two Kirov principals, supposedly the happiest people on earth, asking to depart. And this was the team directly responsible for protecting the theater from ideological subversion.

At last they gave up. The Party Secretary scurried after me as I walked down the corridor. He looked as if Count Albrecht had lowered his leotards in front of a full house. "For heaven's sake, *why?* You have . . . we have . . . we want to help you get your choreographic ideas on the stage." He realized this wouldn't work even before I said *Pugachev*. Shifting ground, he said that I was "no kid" any longer. "You don't understand how these things work. There are always ways of getting around obstacles. You just have to—"

For the first time that morning I interrupted. "Why don't you save yourself lots of trouble and just let me *go?*"

Class had ended, but the pianos seemed to rear on their hind legs as I walked past the studios. I smiled at the good old Russia I was leaving, where everything was secret, but word-of-mouth news traveled faster than teletype. Wide arcs were negotiated around me in the corridors. Coaches peered from behind cracks in doors, as if I had amputated my own legs. Members of the orchestra looked at me as if I were the first aborigine in Europe.

Cleaning women were the first who actually dared say farewell. Their red eyes flowed with tears for the wretch who was about to be cut off from Mother Russia. Their children stared at me as if I were going to my beheading. "My God, those poor people!" one granny actually wailed.

A hypnotist had obviously convinced most of my fellow dancers that I didn't exist. Someone I'd known since the Academy would pass me as if I were air. If I'd put out my hand and said my name was Valery, he would not have believed me. I was no longer the person he once knew.

As eyes full of compassion or horror followed me constantly over the next days, whispers of "Israel!" and "Jew!" went along. They sounded in the same half-frightened, half-disgusted tone as used for "Third

Reich!" and "Nazi!" The company had been so laced with propaganda that most perceived Zionism and Hitlerism as roughly the same evil and the same threat. This fear partly explained the avoidance of me. Something had stirred in the Kirov's swamp of compromises, intrigues, and half-truths. Now the thing had emerged and was trying to . . . leave!

At the top, furious consultations went on about what measures to take. Every other matter in the life of the great theater was dropped, while Rachinsky rocketed back and forth to Moscow like a steam-powered shuttlecock. "What a selfish bastard you are," his assistant sputtered. "This damn emergency, the unbelievable trouble—all for *you* and your terrible unfairness. A real comrade would never think of giving us so much work."

The Personnel Director had a more personal complaint. Frantic because of a favorable recommendation of me on the latest KGB questionnaire, she screamed about my heartlessness. "I called you a *Soviet* person. I put it in *writing*. Now look what you've done to me."

Rachinsky's every return from Moscow increased the feeling that retribution was coming, but no one took any action while senior politicians were deciding what it should be. The few members of the company who continued to see me were fully conscious of their valor. Driving me home one day, a colleague suddenly became apprehensive for his new Moskvich. "Be a pal, and hop out at the next light, okay? They might be fixing up a crash for you. Why should an innocent buggy take it on the chin?"

Another young friend gave a straightforward answer to my teasing. "Yeah, I *am* scared. Which proves *I'm* not crazy."

Oleg Vinogradov of *The Mountain Girl* was one of the exceptions who offered sympathy, although he disagreed with my decision. Losing dancers was a personal blow to him. And he knew more defections would follow. "Ye gods, how stupid it is. How opposite to everything in art. Where is our crudeness leading us?"

The plan Rachinsky finally returned with from Moscow was to isolate me entirely from the Kirov in preparation for expelling me. I was to have no contact, no coaching, above all, no performances. But I had already given one. Months before, I had been scheduled to dance *The Creation of the World* on March 27. No stand-in for the Devil was available, and rather than cancel the ballet, I danced this final time.

High Party and KGB officials stuffed the boxes that evening. They had come to be outraged in person by the dancer who was trying to defile Soviet art. What was the animal that had committed this terrible crime? Why had the responsible comrades allowed it to happen—in the Kirov of all places? But another part of the audience sensed they would never see me again and felt that *this* was the disgrace. The interaction of bureaucrats controlling their fury and admirers controlling their sorrow generated its own electricity.

The current reached me as I waited beneath the stage, from where the Devil first emerges. When I realized that this was going to be my final appearance in Russia, nostalgia and love surged through my system. I wanted to hold the props, the wings, the set against my face.

Hell blazed above me in the form of pyrotechnic flames. A small elevator lifted me through the Devil's trapdoor. Applause of a kind I'd never received before filled the Kirov.

For the first time since Batumi, I heard my old music, telling me I could dance again. My muscles themselves had stayed sound during this deathly season. Now that my reflexes were back, everything worked as well as it used to. But this wasn't enough. I wanted to be truly extraordinary and show the Party bosses what they were losing. Something else also summoned. The part of me that would always belong to the Kirov demanded tribute to ballet while I was still there.

Crowds of dancers, stagehands, and the entire administrative staff watched me from backstage. Instead of the customary "Fantastic!" and "Marvelous!" when a soloist exited to the wings, I received silence. A hundred eyes burned my back as I walked alone to my dressing room.

As word of my swan song spread, people rushed to buy flowers at stalls just outside the theater. It was an old Kirov tradition to present each performer with his bouquets at the curtain calls following every act. Although Rachinsky could do nothing about the farewell cheers, he took decisive action to prevent a non-Soviet rat from receiving visible evidence of public esteem. This further disgrace would have been too much while district, city, and regional overlords watched, beady-eyed, from Tolstikov's boxes. I wasn't even given an individual curtain call after the second act, but this was a kind of compliment.

Yuri Soloviev was dancing God with his usual brilliance, and Mischa Baryshnikov was a genius as Adam. Our styles were too different to speak of a "winner" in our friendly competition, but miracles were taking place. I amazed myself. I leaped higher than ever, did more turns in the air than during my experimental rehearsals. My Devil risked his own special steps—double assemblé while spinning horizontally in the air—with a charmed immunity to physical hazards. This is how I wanted to be remembered; it was the way *I* wanted to remember what Russian ballet had given me. Chaliapin's bells tolled for the first time in years.

My flowers were again withheld after the final curtain. The enormous pile lay out of public sight, like offerings for a secret funeral. But the applause almost became a demonstration.

Several weeks later the middle-aged official responsible for scheduling Kirov performances was summoned to a stern Party meeting. "Comrade Ukhov, why didn't you *prevent* it?" Ukhov tried to protest that in the absence of instructions, he could only wait, together with everyone else.

"No. In a terrible case like this, your duty was to have foreseen all possibilities. You should have had a spare Devil to substitute . . . for him."

Ukhov's defense was useless. Rachinsky had indeed brought back his orders too late from Moscow. And since *someone* had to answer for the mistake thousands had seen on the Kirov stage, Comrade Ukhov was severely reprimanded and told that his Party card might be recalled. He had a heart attack.

NOT EVEN THE ELDERLY PROPS MAN dared visit me after my last performance. Galya was home from the hospital, but not strong enough to have danced her She-devil role. She and I were alone in my dressing room when the door was opened and the floral mountain dumped inside. Fear was lurking, threatening, growing in the aftermath of the exhilaration on stage. But Galya gazed at the luxurious bouquets as if nothing else existed in the world. "Just think," she whispered. "The whole audience knew. It's even a little exciting, don't you think?"

What I thought was that we'd had a taste of what awaited us. The theater's willingness to flout its solemn traditions for petty slaps at us showed what the great machine of state could do to "enemies." But this didn't occur to her. Having decided what was right and acted upon it, she was free of all anxiety. "Look at our flowers, how beautiful they are."

For the hundredth time in our few years together, her innocence soothed me. Whatever form the battle would take, it would be easier with her as my partner. Throughout the coming years, her "Let them say what they want about us, we know what counts" would save me again and again.

39

EVEN WHILE HE WAS COMMUTING TO MOSCOW FOR INSTRUCTIONS ON how to handle me, Rachinsky knew what to do about Galya. He sent Party ballerinas to work on her while she was still in the hospital. In his first free moment he himself was at her bedside, his voice tender. "I don't believe it! There's some kind of silly paper on my desk. Why should that oddball ruin *you*? What on earth does a Russian girl have to do with Israel? Let him go; nobody cares about him anyway. But you're our darling." I was a lost cause, but she was savable and *must be saved*. "You know how the people who matter feel about you. It would be tragic to lose the fantastic career and the marvelous life that are awaiting you."

A Party ballerina called to chat about what fun it had been having three husbands. The next visitor simply had to tell Galya what a terrible husband I was. I had exploited all my Kirov mistresses very selfishly, she said, and now was trying to work a new nasty trick on Galya.

Galya and I wrote to Rachinsky, with a copy to Party headquarters. We asked to be spared such advice in the future, which, since the marriage was sanctified by Soviet law, could qualify under the criminal code. However, this only fed their efforts. The instinctive reaction to try to split us up seemed more than just tactics. It was the first lunge of revenge.

The first official shots were notices that began appearing on the company bulletin board. "A reprimand to V. M. Panov is hereby announced for being five minutes late for a rehearsal of *Hamlet*." (The average delay in getting to rehearsals was a good half hour, and no one had complained before.) "A reprimand is hereby announced to V. M. Panov for having performed *The Creation of the World* without a wig." (I had dispensed with the thing a year before.)

Then an order not to notice me must have been issued, for people started pretending I was a sheet of glass. When Galya returned to class, everybody looked straight through her, too, and her teacher didn't even glance in her direction. But after a few days of this she suddenly became a princess for whom every door was opened. The exaggerated courtliness to her was intended to underscore that she was the maiden of pure native stock, sadly corrupted by an evil foreigner. No one spoke to her without emphasizing her "Russianness" in every other sentence, while whispers of "Jew, Jewish" followed me everywhere.

I also heard rumors of a "court of conscience" being planned on orders Rachinsky had brought home from his last Moscow trip. Passing me in a corridor, one dancer whispered that I'd "better be careful: a Party meeting has decided on your condemnation—by the collective." I supposed this meant an article in our wall newspaper. There was nothing to do but keep calm and hope the attacks stayed harmless.

Two days after Galya's first class following her hospitalization we arrived at the theater early to avoid more rebukes for tardiness. Galya went to her dressing room, and I to the men's, which was several degrees more frigid than previously. Yuri Soloviev was particularly out of character. He had remained an exceptionally decent man who simply couldn't do anything devious. His stunningly tragic suicide a few years hence would remain a mystery, but it must have grown out of Kirov disappointments; in this sense, it could be called an internal defection and added to the list of those who escaped abroad. Now it obviously distressed him to have to avoid my eyes.

I changed and went upstairs to Kaplan's class in Studio Number One. Still early, I was one of the first to begin limbering up. Just as I started, a young Jewish boy whispered, "Watch out!" and hurried away. Then Alexander Pavlovsky, the man who had been graduated from the Academy the year before me and never fulfilled his promise, announced he found it "shaming and disgusting" to be near me. It was certain that something was brewing. If not keyed up for it, Pavlovsky would never have had the courage.

After five minutes of warming up, I was ready for work. After ten, I wondered whether the class had been canceled. The Party Secretary nervously stopped me on my way to find out. "If you'd please wait just a minute more. You're . . . er, needed here."

Needed? I had an image of Colosseum lions clawing at human

meat. Just then Galya crossed the studio on her way to the one next door, where the women trained. After the missed days in the hospital, practice called her even more insistently than usual. She went toward it with the same determination on her face as when I first saw her at the competition.

A few minutes later the thunder of a driven pack shook the corridor. They weren't lions, but they didn't sound like dancers either. The doors burst open. A vanguard of Party activists rushed in, followed by the entire company, with administrators, accompanists, and coaching staff. Almost three hundred people spilled around the studio's perimeter, pushing me against the piano in the far corner. Then I heard voices trying to pry Galya loose from her warming up. Her impatient face finally appeared among the crowd at the door, opposite me.

The silence was as if a conductor's baton had been raised. A dancer who divided his time between lyric roles and Party work strode to the center of the studio and assumed the pose of an opera hero attacking a tragic aria. His deeply melodramatic voice echoed off the mirrors. "Despicable . . . treachery . . . has . . . been . . . committed . . . in . . . our . . . Temple . . . of . . . Art . . . and . . . of . . . Love . . . for . . . Humanity. . . . I . . . call . . . upon . . . the . . . collective . . . to . . . drive . . . the . . . traitor . . . out."

Then Maltsev had the floor. "Shulman, a Jew, has submitted an application to go to Israel. Having fattened himself like a swine on the art of the Soviet people, he now wants to sell it elsewhere. But that's not all. If he goes, foreign newspapers will carry the stink of his slander and lies. We must stop our enemy from carrying out his hateful intentions."

Few had heard of our recent split. Everyone knew that he had been my best friend. And despite the preparation for this "court of conscience," despite the universal knowledge of Maltsev's outside work, people gasped. Private life was something separate and sacrosanct, even— or especially—under Soviet conditions. This language from a man who had shared so much of my life was startling.

After ten more minutes nothing startled anyone. One of my neighbors in the old Rossi Street apartment confessed his shame for having borrowed bread from me there. His roommate, a young corps dancer I sometimes fed and with whom I had worked for months on his stage presence, said he wanted to "vomit up all the putrid leftovers Panov gave me." Pavlovsky shook while announcing that "Panov and Ragozina have sold themselves to a foreign intelligence service. We must fix a punishment for them usually not provided for in humane Soviet law. We must exile them to Siberia for the rest of their lives."

The calls for vengeance followed in smooth succession. It was absolutely clear that the Party had planned the order and the content of this nightmare, but for whom? I looked at Galya and froze. Her face was a pool of shame and distress. Everyone else was staring at her and waiting.

A character dancer named Konstantin Rassadin was now explaining that "Panov wants to betray the greatest art in the world for the West's dirty degradation. We are revolted by this cheater who never understood that the only true art is Soviet. If he wants to sell what the Soviet people gave him, he is a thief and must be punished. If he wants to trade the best ballet in the world to rummage in moneymaking garbage, he is an animal, and we must treat him as such."

Fighting instinct told me to hit back at the same level. But the Party activists growled orders for me to hold my tongue. Obviously the program did not include an answer by me.

Next, People's Artist Irina Kolpakova described her reaction when she first heard of the "loathsome betrayal. . . . But what really hurt was a young girl's surrender, a Russian girl agreeing to go to Israel with him. This disgusting scum befouling our theater—I wanted to throw up. Now I want to spit in their direction. Out! I say. Out forever, you Zionist fascists. And may your traitorous feet never again defile our sacred studio."

After Party stalwarts had led the attack, Komsomol activists eager to get ahead and abroad marched right behind them. I observed this with a surprising detachment, trying to decipher what it might mean for our future. A major article about me by Suzanne Massie in the *International Herald Tribune* was less than a year old, and the tappers knew we sometimes talked on the telephone. I'd been hoping that her access to the press on top of my other foreign contacts would persuade the authorities to let us go quietly. I had badly underestimated their desire for revenge.

Maybe these Stalinist-style accusations were the prelude to his kind of punishment. Or maybe the one good discharge of resentment—and the scare for my fellow dancers—was the climax of the campaign: a sign that we *were* about to go. But the flush-faced accusers had warmed too happily to their roles. The stage-managed speeches were going beyond the call of duty, building up a thirst for personal vengeance. The increase in pressure boiled away my analytical coolness. All I had left was an urge for self-protection.

Not hacks were yelling now, but dancers with whom I'd worked closely and I had learned to respect. "We took him into our ranks and gave him a title," shouted a ballerina who had kept coming to see me after my divorce. "Now let's throw the bastard out." My old friend and frequent partner Gabriella Komleva demanded that I "tell us once and for all what you did in America. Tell us what filth you're preparing to write about our art." While these spontaneous threats came from the sidelines, corps de ballet boys with eyes full of unrehearsed menace muttered, "Israel," "Shulman," "enemy."

The hatred spread like fire. Everyone welcomed it for settling every kind of score: women who had liked me; men who sought my roles; Kirov patriots who had always despised my style. For the first time I felt the power of a mob kicking a fallen man. The front ranks seemed about to lose control and actually start doing this. My eyes sought out Galya's. She was rigid and white.

Enough hysteria had been whipped up so that the People would "demand" a "fitting" sentence. This *was* Stalin's legacy, but the collective hatred also had older roots. The attackers' common ground was anti-Semitism. The dislike of me as an outsider had all come down to this. While the Party fanned it, the spirit of the pogroms filled the studio.

Kaplan had to say what he did to demonstrate *he* wasn't really a Jew. Another reason was to stay on a tour of Spain starting in two weeks. But despite the extra pressure on him to prove himself, despite his terrible training under Stalin, Kaplan's reaction was dismaying. When the order went out, he had stopped looking at me. For ten years he had lived for me. In one instant I had become Judas.

Several years before, he had written the scenario for a ballet based on Gogol's *Taras Bulba*. All Soviet textbooks treated the hero's murder of his son, who had committed a political betrayal, as a splendid act. Kaplan found his answer in this. "Taras Bulba tells us what we must do. We gave birth to Panov. Now we must kill him."

· · ·

WHEN I WAS FINALLY ALLOWED to speak, so much needed answering that I couldn't think of any logical order. I said that since my American trip my working conditions seemed designed to keep me depressed. After thirteen years as an outcast I wanted to leave, and my company called it treason. But this was a specific crime under Soviet law. If applying to emigrate was indeed treason, I should be tried.

I had started as a Young Communist who believed as much as most. With suspicion, slander, scapegoating, the state did everything it could to destroy my belief. Not one official I had turned to since 1959 had given me the truth. Now it was time to end the hypocritical courtesies. I mistrusted the Soviet regime as much as it mistrusted me. The solution was a quiet parting.

I had somewhere to go now, my historical homeland. I would not be an outsider there. The speeches just delivered were the best evidence that I did not belong where I was. . . .

Jeers went up at "historical homeland" together with catcalls of "*Shulman!*" I said that my right to leave was written into the Soviet Union's own laws and international agreements it had signed. I broke off when this brought more laughs and boos.

My comments had been a mistake. I hadn't developed them into a forceful whole, had not, somehow, even got to the main points. I knew how to move, not how to talk. But at least I'd stopped the assault. A tense quiet descended. As on the stage, each minute seemed like ten. Party people were evidently not fully satisfied with their presentation either. "Who wants to add something?" they coaxed.

Suddenly the ballerina who had led the attack on "the traitor's accomplice" broke the sick silence. Others had called out to Galya to "leave the Jew" and "divorce that criminal," but Ninel Kurgapkina, a respected principal and teacher, had been the most explicit. "We can't expect anything from *him*, he's a Jew. But a Russian girl agreeing to leave with someone she can't respect or love is a terrible thing. Great days can be yours in the Kirov—if you free yourself of his foul influence."

That had been near the beginning. Now Kurgapkina was calling for Galya's answer. "You, Ragozina, why are you standing there? Speak up and say something—like a Russian girl."

This was the finale I had been praying wouldn't come. I knew what the company was demanding. It was the Soviet way, perhaps based on Russian tradition, to beg forgiveness and re-instatement into the "collective." Enormous psychological pressure for public confession and repentance pressed on any Russian who stood alone. The Party had to be seen as flawless by showing how woefully the doubter had erred.

Galya's nose was crimson. Veins swelled beneath her transparent skin. Kurgapkina's third call was like Svengali's command. My hypnotized bride detached herself from the far corner. Tears from her swollen eyes spotted the floor. Losing her this way was the worst thing that could happen to me. I could already hear her pronouncing the compulsory apology: "Save me, comrades, I didn't know. You have opened my eyes to the monster he is." Shame and misery twisted Galya's teenaged face. "It's all right, I understand," I said to myself. The ballerinas who cursed me had been her idols since she could remember. They were crushing her like a doll under a tank.

She had reached the center of the floor, hesitated there. I wanted to run. But she did not kneel down. I saw her advancing to me like a stricken Giselle, from some realm of purity. She did not try to speak. She stopped at my side and soundlessly laid her head on my chest. I kept myself from crying. I had never been so happy in my life.

She was what ballet was meant to be about. The grace and loyalty of her gesture in ballet language said a hundred times more than my attempted speech. The "judges" were stunned.

So I was not alone. She truly loved me. While her supple figure clung to me and her face sought my heart, I swore I would never live a day without remembering her gift.

40

THE NEXT MASS FLAILING TOOK PLACE AT A MEETING OF THE KIROV'S trade-union branch. The threats—of what "the scum deserves," of what would have been "simple and quick" under Stalin—were more direct here, but at least I managed to keep Galya from coming. The trade-union chairman kept calling for my exile to Siberia. "Let him rot there. Let him never see the light of day. It's a disgrace that he's walking the streets of our Leningrad." The assistant director talked of a "filthy station calling itself Radio Liberty, filling the airwaves with terrible lies about our theater. And fascist Israel." He could not understand how he had once praised my dancing.

The "terrible lies" were the fact of my application and a brief summary of the official reaction. These had been relayed to Western correspondents in Moscow by Fedya Medina, a charming young cellist from Bogotá. He had come to study in the Leningrad Conservatory but fell in love with ballet and spent more time with dancers—especially with me—than with musicians. The moment the trouble started, he dropped his studies to devote every moment to Galya and me.

Fedya was appalled by the thought of not seeing us dance again. After I had been ten days without class, he thought he saw signs of my losing my form. "I know you don't believe me," he said. "But if something happens to you, I'm going to do what Jan Palach did. Right on the Kirov steps. I'll pour kerosene on myself and light a match."

I *did* believe him and told some jokes to lighten his resolve and stop his troubling. His reckless dropping of the Conservatory for us showed he was even younger than his years. But we needed him badly. With his English, Spanish, German, and French, he took calls day and night from the whole corps of Moscow correspondents. This infuriated Leningrad officials, especially when Western shortwave broadcasts beamed back into Russia the information he had passed on. His efforts are what saved us from those quick, quiet measures we "deserved." Publicity in the West was our only protection. So few people there had heard of us, but Fedya's frantic work kept us from despair. He slept in our living room, and I was selfish enough not to insist that he at least make a daily appearance at the Conservatory.

When correspondents did not call us, he contacted them. In free moments he begged the American and British consulates to take an interest in our case. Most important of all, he interpreted for our foreign "protectors": John Cranko, Patricia Barnes, and Rosemary Winckley. The twins became a kind of transatlantic link for me—the center of a network of helpers.

THE KGB HAD GONE TO WORK on our parents the day after we submitted our application. Their first question to my father in Vilnius was whether a member of our family lived in Israel. One woman did, although we hadn't heard from her for forty years. But my father had kept "Auntie Riva's" existence as secret as if she were a lunatic. In the thousand questionnaires he had filled out since his youth, he always answered "none" to the lethal question about relatives abroad.

Now he insisted that Auntie Riva had left before the Revolution, although he knew it was during Soviet rule. The exposure of this skeleton in the closet frightened him. He swore to the visiting agents that he'd see me dead rather than "collaborate" in my "double dealing." Fingers wagged in his face during meetings of his Party organization increased his humiliation. How—the good members asked—could a trusted Party worker have reared such a son? He was so ashamed that he avoided busy streets, so outraged by my decision that he threatened physical retaliation.

Besides, my mother broke precedent by not falling in behind his political lead, but arguing that I ought to be allowed to go. She was in the habit of examining Alec's coat pockets when he dropped by, and my letters to him over the past few years had apparently given her some understanding of me. After two weeks' resistance from her he gave in and signed my parental "release." "Let the scum go that wants to leave for Israel," his new line went. "This will only clean up the motherland."

Galya's mother was a better subject for the KGB. The apparent lunacy of requiring parents' permission for fully responsible adults to emigrate was concocted for bludgeoning a no from any of the overwhelming majority of Russians who wanted to keep their names off incriminating documents. Although we already had her verbal consent, the KGB team that called on her on March 22 quickly changed her mind.

Galya and I were unaware of this visit when we took the train to Volkhov, the town she had settled in. The release form was in Galya's handbag. Her mother opened the door and ranted about the bloodsucking Jew who wanted to steal her child for sale abroad. As her pronunciation of "outlaws, fascists, traitors" turned more menacing, I remembered her chasing Galya with a hatchet.

Eventually she got to "our Stalin." "If he were alive your kind would be shot on the spot," she said. "And I'd be glad, for me and for my daughter." This particular smell of trouble was familiar, but my wish to leave was no match for Galya's stubbornness. She had remembered a large pile of her treasured poetry collections and ballet histories her mother had brought from Perm. She disappeared into the bedroom to make a selection.

Her mother raced after her as if a thief were stealing her life savings. "They're *my* books," she screamed.

"No, mine."

"Leave those things there, you bitch."

Galya's feeble "Help, Valera!" sounded a split second after a fist thudded onto her cheekbone.

In the bedroom I saw Galya's mother, teeth clenched in exertion, while she pulled so ferociously at Galya's hair that clumps ripped out, leaving splotches of blood. Her hands were like the jaws of a bulldog that would hang on even if the animal was dying. All I could do was to push as hard as possible on the pressure points under her wrists.

"The maniac's killing me!" she shrieked.

Galya had at last taken my point about leaving. When her mother eventually relaxed her grip, we scrambled for the door. I held it shut while Galya flew down the stairs. When I caught up with her outside, her mother flung open a window and squealed like a stabbed pig. "Help! Police! Anybody! Murder!"

SINCE NO ONE AT THE KIROV was speaking to me, hints about a criminal charge reached Galya first. They came just before an "ideological interview" scheduled for us with the Party Secretary of our city district. If we didn't give in there, the rumors went, a full offensive would be launched, starting with my imprisonment.

The Party Secretary began by assuring us that our application would make things worse for Jews who wanted to live peacefully in Russia. "You're doing something disgracefully selfish. Why don't you think of your fellow Jews?" I said that Galya was Russian and *she* wanted to leave, and as for Jews, his kind of advice was exactly what many of them felt they had to get away from. The conversation ended with a reminder that "we'll do anything we want with you anyway."

My summons to appear in Volkhov came a few days later. It charged me with "malicious hooliganism" in assaulting Galya's mother and warned that I'd be taken there by force if I didn't go on my own. The two men who came to tell me this stressed that they were from the Volkhov procuracy, which was interested only in upholding local law and order there. The next day they made the mistake of buying round-trip tickets just before me in a Leningrad railway station.

"Malicious hooliganism" was almost always a police matter, far too small for the procuracy. The punishment for a first offense was invariably a warning or a fine. The two men kept referring to my sentence as if it had already been passed: three years in a labor colony.

Our train trip took just under three hours. Volkhov was a faceless collection of buildings that had somehow pushed up from the northern plains. Its most respectable inhabitants seemed to be forced laborers who had built a dam and poisonous chemical plants on the Volkhov River, then stayed on. Chiefly to keep Leningrad presentable for foreign tourists, its deported drifters, alcoholics, layabouts, and thugs were not permitted to return within sixty miles. Volkhov was sixty-one miles away. Its small army of "undesirable elements" was watched by hordes of policemen and KGB teams.

At least I'd learned enough to fight. I stuck to my story all day, objecting to every invention in the list of charges, which included depositions from complete strangers that they had seen me through the window assaulting Galya's mother. I was told to return a second day—and a third, fourth, and fifth. The daily trips and endless repetition of absurd questions were meant to wear me down and frighten me with the grimness of an interrogation. But the larger reason was the same one that lay behind all of the Kirov's moves. At all costs, Galya and I had to be pulled apart.

Our protest against this campaign had enraged Rachinsky. He could hardly believe that two of his dancing serfs had written him our kind of letter, let alone sent a copy to Party headquarters, which was growing impatient with his failure to put my case in order. He kept at Galya constantly. While repeating his speeches about her Russianness and her wonderful prospects, he had his most trusted ballerinas talk to her about divorce and nothing but divorce.

The criminal charge against me grew out of this strategy. At the Kirov, Galya was told exactly what the Volkhov investigators kept repeating to me. Expert witnesses would "prove beyond any doubt" that I had inflicted bodily injury on her mother. The court would send me away for three years, and she would be fired from the Kirov. But if she left me and withdrew her application, the case would be dropped, and she would be flown to join the troupe in Spain.

"You can save him if you love him. You must *divorce*."

With the stakes so drastically changed, I had to give Galya the chance to leave the game. I told her I'd probably never dance again. Would she wait the three years, or should we do as they wanted and end the pressure?

"You know the answer," she said. "Let's not talk about this anymore."

The next day I told the Volkhov investigators that whatever they did, Galya wasn't going to leave me, and I would not withdraw my application. Meanwhile, I'd been trying to find witnesses for our side. One friend of Galya's confirmed that her mother had tried to chop her leg muscles but wouldn't testify because "it serves anyone right who does what you're doing." The Kirov's Komsomol organization had passed a resolution declaring her mother's hatchet waving justified.

At last I obtained a confrontation with my mother-in-law. By neglecting to word his questions as before, an inexperienced lieutenant confused his star witness. "But what about your wrists?" he pleaded. "Didn't you say you were in pain for a week?"

Galya's mother bristled. "Nothing ever hurts me—certainly not *that* so-called dancer." This opened the way to my cross-examination, which got her to admit that she had never lodged a complaint. Rachinsky's men had promised that they knew how to save her daughter. For cooperating, she got a free trip to a sanatorium and her long-sought disability allowance for her brain concussion.

Three weeks after the charge had been brought, I was informed that it had been dropped "for lack of evidence." I tried to work out the real reason. My mother-in-law's weak performance surely wasn't the full answer; they could have got around the inconvenience with written depositions. No doubt our resolve had been equally important. After Maltsev's evaluation of us as ballet freaks, they clearly hadn't expected our willingness to accept three years of imprisonment. Lacking a plan that provided for real resistance from us, they probably felt uncertain of their tactics, especially since President Nixon was about to arrive on a state visit.

But foreign newspapers were the crucial factor. While Fedya ran his one-man press agency, Moscow journalists kept calling to ask what was happening and whether I was "still alive." They were the ones who were keeping me so.

AFTER GALYA HAD STUNNED THE "COURT OF CONSCIENCE" into silence, Party activist Irina Kolpakova was the first to recover. "Get out of here," she shouted. "I don't even want to spit in your direction."

We assumed we'd been fired and did not go to class the next day. A reprimand was on the wall the following morning, and I was asked for my immediate resignation. When I didn't give it, I was told I'd been expelled for "immoral behavior, intolerable in our collective and incompatible with the title of 'Soviet Citizen.'"

I asked for this charge in writing and drafted protests about such an absurdity. A decree with a different kind of nonsense was posted soon afterward. I'd been discharged for "economic reasons"—in this case, a staff reduction. The decision had been made by the Central Trade-Union Bureau in Moscow and could not be appealed. Even if this weren't another illegal reason for firing, a principal dancer performing major roles in half the repertoire wouldn't exactly be the first cost to be cut. But this explanation might sound less ludicrous to Westerners not acquainted with Soviet law.

Galya presented a more complicated problem. She was immediately transferred to the corps de ballet and driven out of its class by the other girls' complaints that her presence "spoiled the studio's air." While the company stars and supervisors were in Spain, petty officials practiced petty harassment on us. One hall was supposed to be permanently open for individual training. Other dancers kept us out when they were there, and caretakers did the same when it was empty. Galya managed to slip in only on occasional evenings.

It was a cruel month for her. Not a single ballerina even whispered, "Sorry." The kindest gesture she could hope for from a member of her new company was that he merely turn his back, rather than attacking her.

Suddenly the attitude toward her completely flip-flopped again. She was given small parts and asked to rehearse her old solo roles. Everyone was elaborately solicitous, and kind friends appeared to offer her chocolates wrapped in advice. "For goodness sake, don't rush a decision that can destroy your whole life."

Then came the pressure to save me from the Volkhov sentence by divorce. This was not merely insulting but also dangerous; access to her alone at the theater was their best chance of separating us.

Galya's surface calm hid a storm underneath. Her deep emotions could destroy her; that was why she hid them. Hostility that she didn't want to accept intellectually was especially dangerous. Her support for me was entirely instinctive, a woman's urge to protect her man. After a day of police and other official encounters, all I could do in the evening was down a glass of vodka. But she was still so involved in ballet that she couldn't understand why I didn't drop everything for a few hours' exercises. I wanted her to hold onto this and to her hope that she'd soon be dancing *over there*. But the risk of her staying at the Kirov alone outweighed all others. Hard as the decision was, we agreed she must resign. She did this as she did everything else and turned away when I tried to thank her for it.

Outdoor celebrating began with May Day. While workers tippled in doorways and families went to the countryside, I paced the cage of our apartment. KGB patriots playing drunk were good at clobbering dissidents with the poles of their red flags and picking fights so that their friends could do a job on them. Fedya heard telephone tappings. New neighbors had suddenly moved into nearby apartments. Angry eyes followed us—and sometimes shouts of "Traitor!"—whenever we went out.

We had to accept this for a few more weeks. If we could lie low, we'd probably have our happy ending. Yes, they were totally unscrupulous and brimming with hatred. But now they knew *my* determination to fight. The dropping of the hooliganism charge seemed to indicate I'd passed the crucial test. They were probably looking for the easiest way out of the problem we were making for them.

The "few more weeks" was because President Nixon was coming to Leningrad later in May. Jews who had been waiting much longer than I were counting the days, for the visit of a Western statesman could pull miraculously liberal acts out of our system. Because the Politburo respected only strength, we banked on America's might almost exclusively. The other NATO countries were too small and too spineless to be taken seriously.

Since we would be profiting from the deception called détente, a certain guilt rode along with our reliance on America. Détente was really innocent America drawing closer to the wolf, while Russian workers heartily approved. "Great, we'll drink Pepsi-Cola along with our vodka. And maybe some cans of Spam will show up, like during the war." More thoughtful foremen and engineers liked the idea because our industry wasn't ready for the coming war with China. It was good of the Americans to help with our consumer and computer messes, allowing even more Soviet resources to go into arms.

Only those who really studied Russia were appalled. Anyone familiar with events since 1917 knew that the driving Soviet interest in détente was how to dupe America. If there was no time to learn this from history, an honest hour with the men in power would make the same point. The goal of the Brezhnevs was to diddle, destroy, and defeat. To them, tricking capitalists was just as moral as beating them in a fair fight. Without this mentality, a man would never rise in the Party. It was what he had been trained for, what his success depended on.

Even after our wheat dealers had tricked America as crudely and cynically as they could, the cultivated Dr. Kissinger didn't understand that the people he was dealing with had an urge to dominate in their bones and in their blood. It wasn't his fault; Soviet ruthlessness was outside the experience of Americans. And although some Russian liberals argued that *only* contact with the West, no matter how one-sided at first, could tame the bullies, the Soviet war machine seemed to be growing faster than its civilized attitudes.

Like everyone else in my position, I loved and longed for America more than any Americans I'd ever met. But while praying that its illusions wouldn't undermine it, I also prayed that they'd last long enough to get me out. Selfish interest triumphed. The only thing I feared more than the State Department learning its lessons the hard way was its learning them before Nixon arrived.

Everyone in opposition sweated as the day approached. I was often on the telephone with some "names" of the dissident and Jewish emigration movements in Moscow, and it was natural to sign a statement protesting the "security measures" already beginning. To prevent any possibility of a demonstration Nixon might witness, Jews from Riga, Vilnius, and other cities were being removed from trains, buses, and planes going to the capital. They were picked out by their identity papers and their "looks."

The little demonstration my friends and I were planning for the President never took place because the leaders in Moscow were arrested well ahead of time. But signing the petition was enough to attract a new kind of attention to myself.

Leningrad's less sinister preparations were also in full swing. The road from the airport, for years a cause of almost-daily fatal accidents, was at last widened to four lanes. New asphalt was spread over every farther inch of Nixon's route. Traffic was also paralyzed by flower planting everywhere and the washing and painting of every building he would see—those that didn't actually disappear, that is. The dynamited architectural landmarks included some two-hundred-year-old warehouses serving the railway station near our apartment. These picturesque old structures were considered inappropriate for Presidential eyes.

Unsightly people along the route were disposed of just as efficiently. The merely "undesirable" were politely told to clear out for the period. Some were dispatched on distant official trips. More disreputable types were rounded up for jail.

The President was scheduled to ride up Moscow Prospekt, directly below us. It was prohibited to open the windows that morning. A year before I had adopted a witty stray cat near Oreshek, Peter the Great's fortress. As Nixon's cavalcade approached, the wily little thing managed to get onto our balcony for a look. KGB officers had been watching us long enough to know its name. "Galina Ragozina," they shouted up from the street, "remove Oreshek from the balcony immediately."

Days before this, things had grown tense. Moscow arrests were increasing, following an order to "neutralize" everyone who might "interfere with the success of the historic visit." All "suspicious elements" who might try to get in touch with the President's entourage, especially American journalists open to victims' stories, fell into this category. From Moscow, Vladimir Slepak urged us to take precautions; but, confident that *I'd* have no more trouble, I decided not to leave Leningrad.

My optimism was more than a fond wish. I'd been telephoning the Kirov daily about my *kharakteristika*. Three days before Nixon's arrival in Leningrad the Personnel Department blandly answered that it had already been processed. I was off and running to the visa office before I put down the telephone. No one there knew exactly where my file was, but everyone assured me that things would go smoothly now. So Nixon's visit *had* done the trick. I'd be in Israel soon, dancing in my own ballets!

The telephone awoke us at seven o'clock on Friday morning, but the caller hung up as soon as he heard my voice. A few minutes later our door almost splintered open. Our experience with the men who'd come to invite us to Volkhov suggested who was doing the pounding and that the door would be broken down if we pretended to be out. But when I opened it, this visitor seemed different. He didn't *look* like your average policeman.

"They want you to come with me," he said almost meekly. "Have a quick talk, help you find work."

Why this urgency at dawn? His use of "help" worried me almost as much. But he went white when I said I didn't feel well.

"No, no. I beg you. You *must* come."

Remembering Slepak's warning, I asked what "must" meant. He produced a summons to appear immediately before the chief criminal detective of my district. But Volkhov had taught me to examine official documents. This one was neither stamped nor signed. When I said I wouldn't go, my caller was so unnerved that he could hardly dial my telephone. "He won't come," he whined, and cringed while listening before handing me the receiver.

The chief detective identified himself and asked me to visit him. "For five minutes. Just to clear up a few things about why you're not working. If you don't want to cooperate, we'll have to . . ."

This was one of the moments when resistance was useless. The captain's tone of voice said it all: that there was nowhere to run in our country, nowhere to hide. Futile gestures were a waste of strength—and might worsen Galya's nerves. Her whole face seemed to be a pair of panicky eyes. "Here we go again," I said, trying to remind her of our victory in Volkhov.

I put on the gray Belgian suit that made her proud of me. My policeman's breath on the short trolley ride to the station indicated that he had downed a lot of daybreak vodka. I could have done with some myself. The first hour of a new threat always led me into a bundle of mistakes.

The police station's red flags were already fluttering for Nixon. The building reeked of antiseptic, and the bars down its windows were a projection of the chief detective's smile. "See? Nothing so terrible," he said beneath the Lenin portrait in his office. "I just want to chat about—well, what's all this about some application to go somewhere?" He so dragged out his silly questions—"You're still at the same address?"—that the waste of time became painful. He kept picking up one of his telephones to ask whether something was ready. I assumed he was waiting to give his boss the pleasure of arresting me.

Finally, someone called him on the same telephone. "All okay, you're *sure*?" he asked in a military voice. Then he told me I was free to go. "I just wanted to make personal contact with you, thanks for coming."

I wondered whether I'd get out of the building. Then whether I'd get past my policeman-visitor, who, together with a group of colleagues, was staring at me outside. The morning was the color of my suit, and I had a strange taste in my mouth. I walked quickly to get home and reassure Galya as soon as possible.

Moscow Prospekt was empty except for a car that pulled up, discharged two men, and spurted off again. Looking over my shoulder was already a habit. When I was a hundred yards farther along, I saw a third man getting out of the same car behind me.

I didn't notice him again until he grabbed my shoulder. "Hey, you, what do you mean by this? You *spit* on me."

A few months later I happened to see him receiving a medal on television, as a model citizen devoted to upholding the law. He was introduced as the commander of a city district's volunteer police, whose officers are as "voluntary" as submarine captains. He smiled like a poster then. Now his wrestler's face was red with fury.

He shoved his sweater under my nose. A neat spot of spittle lay near the cuff. In case I missed this challenge to fight, he began shoving me. There was still nowhere to hide, but instinct told me to get out of reach. This activist assigned to provoke the chief detective's new frameup was the kind who broke "anti-Soviet" arms for purely personal satisfaction. By flushing out the full team, my sprint lessened the chances for individual action. I covered thirty yards before being surrounded. The car leaped forward. I was bundled in.

In the farce that followed, the activist was also booked for hooliganism. A witness "just happened to be passing by" and volunteered to testify to everything. He just happened to be Jewish, too, eliminating any complaints on that score.

The officer who had banged on my door two hours before was still outside the police station. Seeing me under arrest did more than the vodka for his courage, and he sneered to his colleagues about my "resistance" when he had come for me. The chief detective seemed happier, too. "Yes," he agreed with the activist, but loud enough for my benefit. "We can't rest until we cleanse our streets of his kind." Instead of simply cutting off his victims' heads, Ivan the Terrible would arrange a gala affair with music and dancing bears. Now we were struggling through this terribly acted melodrama when I could just as easily have been arrested in my own apartment.

"Why did you have to do it?" the chief detective asked in a moment of frankness. "I just don't understand why an Honored Artist could want to ruin himself in a hopeless cause. I don't understand how the Kirov's Party organization could let you even dream about Israel."

The little basement jail for people awaiting their hearings served police stations in the district. Separate cells for men and women were linked by shouts across the corridor—"Masha, show us how you pee"— and duty policemen growling, "Shut your filthy trap." The men's cells had jagged walls to prevent graffiti, an electric bulb constantly shining through frosted glass, and a wooden platform slightly raised above the floor. I stood on it to stay free of the bugs. Then I joined them in a position I would use more and more often in the coming years. Curling up with my head in my hands seemed to conserve my mental energy and help me think. I had to fight down my self-pity and nausea.

Luckily, the surroundings were too new to me and the questions too intensive for extended brooding. The first trouble I expected was from toughs who had a perpetual grudge against what they considered overfed cultural types. But my glum face—or maybe the muscles under my suit—provoked sympathy instead.

The rest of the day was filled with explanations of what everyone was in for. Most were drunks and disturbers of the peace who had been locked up a hundred times before. Yet, by his own account, each was completely innocent. Choruses of "You're crazy, you liar" interrupted every tale. The loudest shouters then went on to protest their own purity just as fervently.

The most repetitive stories came from the Nofiplorows, men arrested for having *No fixed place of residence or work*. They were proud of this title. Considering the pressure to get everyone to a lathe, it was an achievement to remain a bum in the Soviet Union. The other men were also ragged and unshaven, except for a young Siberian engineer who had crowned his Leningrad spree by breaking a department-store window. The only man truly appalled by his arrest was a dark Azerbaijani who had found his blond girlfriend in bed with a rival when he arrived for a weekend with her. He faced a year in a labor camp for flashing his knife but was more worried about his head being shaved. In his land, which was full of ex-convicts exiled there after their terms, this was a terrible disgrace. He detested Soviet rule and wrung his hands for me too when I told him my story.

We slept on the same wooden platform. The others courageously snored through the bites of the bedbugs, which came out in swarms at night. On Saturday, the day of Nixon's arrival, we were joined by a new batch of men puffed up by weekend drink and blows. They too assured me I'd get used to the conditions. These were worse than during the week because everything was closed down until Monday, when we would be brought before a judge. After my case only one other—that of a man and woman screaming accusations at each other—had been heard by the investigator. The weekend-reduced police staff coped by taking us all to the toilet together. A man who begged to go quickly because he'd messed his pants was told to wait until everyone else had finished.

Except for scraps from the police table, our food during the three days was a couple of bowls of something that looked like uncooked kasha. My cellmates were furiously hungry, yet fully resigned; this was the regular weekend diet. They only complained about "this fucking 'knickson' business, what a pain in the ass." I thought they were cursing "the *Nixon* preparations," which they'd heard so often that they made it into one word. But some of them knew nothing of the President. They understood the term as *knicksen*, which meant curtsying to superiors. It was practically the same thing, and I laughed even louder.

"When's this shit-eating knicksen going to be over so we can get out of here?"

Late that afternoon a prisoner came back from sweeping out the upper floors to whisper that my "three wives" were waiting outside and had asked him to tell me that I'd been on Moscow Radio all day. He also gave me five rubles from them. I learned the facts much later: *foreign* radio stations had been steadily reporting my arrest; and he'd been given *ten* rubles by the three women. Galya had done the talking. The other two were Liya and an art historian named Lara, who was beginning to play a crucial role in my life. Ordinarily, the three could barely tolerate each other, but they had contacted each other in the emergency and marched arm in arm to the station to "save" me.

Of course Galya's bundle of provisions featured a chicken, which the policemen must surely have appreciated. Everything disappeared, but the chief detective called me into his office on Sunday, asked me not to tell the others, and handed me a bun and a jar of yogurt. Maybe he'd heard a broadcast; instead of swaggering, he seemed slightly ashamed.

Early Monday morning we were taken upstairs in a group and seated in a cubicle behind two thick panes of glass. Grinning KGB officers pointed me out among the school of others in this aquarium. My "three wives" tried to push into the space that served as a courtroom. While Liya and Lara sobbed, Galya bristled at the policemen.

In a way, I was even happier to see Andrei. We had started to develop a real relationship after Liya and I separated. It slowly grew into mutual respect and fondness, and the twelve-year-old boy wanted to know why his father was being called a hooligan. During difficulties with Liya I used to ask him not to listen to anyone, but to look with his own eyes and make up his own mind. All I could do now was repeat our private motto. "Watch everything carefully. Try to work out the rights and wrongs for yourself."

The only thing the judge worked on was her own indignation. She was Galya's mother, with bright red instead of bright yellow hair. The painting of Brezhnev behind her could have been a family portrait.

"Panov, Valery Matveevich? Did you spit on Citizen ——? . . . All right, there's nothing mysterious here." Her voice picked up more righteousness. "It means nothing that you're an Honored Artist. Hooligans spoil those ranks too. *You're* an example." This was the only opinion she allowed herself, and her eyes stayed on her papers even then. Evidently I wasn't worth a look. There was hardly time for one anyway. Petty offenders passed before her like sausages on a conveyor.

"Ten days."

The sentence could not be appealed. Through tears, Andrei asked me to be brave, and Galya told me that this was a "silly nothing." Suddenly it *was* something. All prospects that went with my Nixon hope had been shattered. More than this. Since the KGB was not just putting me away while the President was in Leningrad, I dreaded what might follow the ten days. My dream of freedom had already disintegrated.

41

THE BLACK MARIA BARELY MOVED UNDER ITS LOAD. MEN AND WOMEN were packed like herring into the back cage, which, even after a weekend of drying out, reeked of the vodka breath that went with that very fish. All possible male and female odors mingled together, and as we rode, drunks, prostitutes, and pickpockets laughed and cursed.

When I found a crack in the side of the truck, I saw a monumental gate automatically closing behind us. Ten iron doors later we were in a huge courtyard of a gigantic prison. A plaque on the wall proclaimed that Lenin had been incarcerated here.

The size of the place indicated it was part of the Big House, which included the city's KGB headquarters. To avoid the impression that this vast compound—Leningrad's Lubyanka—would have created in the center of town, the buildings were disguised by façades of various architectural styles.

Black Marias from other districts discharged their loads. Eventually a mass of wretched-looking prisoners was led inside for photographing and skull shaving, a form of humiliation passed off as protection against lice. After two minutes with an electric cutter we were indistinguishable from the jailbirds and soldiers that make up 20 percent of the country's male population. The searches—mainly for knives and food, according to veterans—were performed with mechanical scorn. "Hey, you, spread your stinking ass apart. *Next*, shove on." Hoarse whispers for cigarettes were background music for these rasping orders. The prohibition against smoking—another way of bringing the men down, old-timers insisted—was the hardest punishment for many.

Rules were bellowed at us throughout the processing. We must not cover ourselves with anything while sleeping, must not keep any uneaten food, must not . . . Any violation would automatically bring a year in prison, and I foresaw a provocation to give me that extension. Meanwhile, a lieutenant went around announcing that this was "not a prison but a dispensary that cures through collective labor."

We were sorted into details to receive that miracle medicine. The largest went to garbage dumps and other municipal dirty work. The least trusted inmates were kept "inside" to prevent contact with friends or family. I was pushed into this lot as it marched to the fifth floor. Our work was pasting together sloppy cardboard boxes for candy and removing the last bits of fabric from textile rolls. It was exhausting because nobody had eaten all day. Cries for "fodder" grew weaker and weaker as the afternoon dragged by. When the immense line formed for the evening feed, men swayed and fainted from hunger. Others shook violently. While warders led them away, some said they were epileptics; others called them drug addicts in need of a fix. The line was from an icon of the Descent into Hell. Reading Solzhenitsyn wasn't enough to picture the debasement of human beings in Soviet prisons. As he said, you had to live it yourself.

At last I got my rations. "Fodder" was no prison slang; a piece of bread was all that came with the liquid called potato soup. I was one of the lucky ones with something floating in his bowl. It wasn't the color of any potato I'd ever seen.

Still starving, we were taken to our cells. Thousands of them hung like grotesque bird cages along the corridors. The design prevented an occupant of one cell from seeing any other. Another feature was Catherine II's immensely thick walls, which the warders proudly called "as sound for modern needs" as anything in Leningrad. As I was led in, an antique cast-iron judas-hole caught my eye. It had a beautifully wrought hinge.

The cell was too dark to make out more than rust and dirt. It was like entering a toilet last cleaned in some previous century. I understood why wire had been strung all along the corridor: to prevent suicide jumps.

Four of the five bunks were occupied. I crawled up to the empty one, my body craving sleep as much as my mind. The rub was the impossible cold. It was late May, but six feet of stone in the walls retained rawness like a refrigerator, while hunger kept down body heat. The absence of blankets was part of the policy to make the petty hooligans' sentences nasty enough to deter the most hardened offenders. I could hardly touch my work jacket when it had been issued in the morning. But it no longer mattered whether its slime came from a garage or a sewer. I pulled the cotton quilting gratefully around my neck and felt the first fingers of sweet unconsciousness.

But something threatening dropped to the floor. I peered into the dust. If not for the fright my father once gave me, I might not have recognized the objects being unscrewed from stumps. The man beneath me had one leg. Another prisoner was whispering to his artificial arm. And the bottom bunk held a completely legless man. Only one of my cellmates was physically sound. He was studying my reaction with a weird smile.

This theater was too strong for me. My mind couldn't cope with what I'd seen since morning. I felt myself losing control, as when fairytale monsters had stalked the evacuation home.

Artificial body parts clanked against the walls. This cell was to tell me what Soviet rule could do to me. My future as a dancer was as clear as these amputated limbs, and I couldn't understand why I had worked so hard to train my limbs or had ever believed in ballet's beauty. This ghoulish world revealed the truth I'd always considered most important as a mockery. Life and ballet had nothing in common, after all.

THE COLD WATER I SPLASHED ON MYSELF whenever I got to a sink did not interrupt the nightmare. The monsters kept me terrified. The breakdown of a spoiled professor's son in the adjoining cell heightened my worst fears. He had been on the arrest list because he loved foreign clothes, the English language, and jazz—and because his window overlooked the Leningrad City Soviet, where the American delegation would make an important courtesy visit. By the third night he was sobbing uncontrollably and begging for his Brubeck records. Attendants took him away in a straitjacket, but I kept hearing his screams.

Many prisoners had bad stomachs, which the diet made worse. In the half hour between six o'clock reveille and the start of work, disgusting sounds and smells overtook the prison as humiliating fighting for the slops bucket took place in every cell. Breakfast was delivered while people were still using it. A lump of black bread came with the caulk called kasha. Unless eaten quickly, it turned hard enough to crack a head. I soon learned to lick the bowl. The next feed was the evening one.

Warders checked that not even a few bits of bread were stored anywhere for nibbling to soften the hunger. They were also vigilant in preventing anything that might help a prisoner sleep. One night I slipped a piece of plywood under my head as a pillow for my iron bunk. A guard instantly shouted, "That's solitary if you try it again." In the morning I got my personal harrying. "Your buddies, them cripples," the jailers kept grinning. "They can't eat or shit without their lost pins. Why don't you give them a hand, ha-ha?"

The nightmare turned into a trance. When I was summoned for "a meeting with someone" in the middle of my sentence, I was certain that extra punishment was about to begin. Then a policeman led Liya into the room where I was waiting. This was amazing; visits to petty hooligans were strictly prohibited. But Liya had just gone on pension from the Maly and begun working as an ice-skating coach for the sporting club of the Ministry of Internal Affairs, which was, in fact, run by the KGB.

Our relationship had been uneven in recent years. A friend who had seen the files told me that Liya had warned the KGB that I'd defect if ever taken abroad. Yet she liked to visit me more and more often, sometimes volunteering to bring Andrei. Since I needed an emigration release from her, too—as Andrei's mother—she could have taken harsh revenge when we applied to leave. She could have got even further ahead by blackening me. But when the campaign began, she behaved better toward me than she ever had while we were married.

Like a true Russian woman, she knew what people in trouble needed most—and had brought it in a little bag. For the first time, I fully understood what food could mean. I was profoundly grateful for her sausages and cheese. She cried with happiness while I gorged—and with distress at the sight of me, which was far worse than what she'd expected. This was after five days in the Big House. Political prisoners were serving ten to fifteen years.

I WAS SO MUCH BETTER after Liya broke my isolation that I volunteered to sweep the corridor every evening. The others thought I was cracking up. I hoped exercise might retard my physical deterioration.

The work norms for each brigade and individual did not prevent prison talk, which I could now take in. Everyone here also protested his innocence, and one timid man *was* in for nothing. A policeman had insulted him. His son answered by pushing at the uniform. The man asked to serve his son's sentence, and this request was magnanimously granted.

An aging alcoholic across the table from him squealed all day about rats that came for him all night. His opposite was a strapping young Nofiplorow whose jazz addiction had got him into trouble in every city he wandered to. He laughed at anyone who wasn't having a good time, insisting that the Big House was a hotel compared to provincial jails.

Another vagabond claimed he'd been taken because someone mugged *him* on a street but also hinted at his contribution to a daring burglary. He questioned me eagerly about how foreign broadcasts painted Russia, then pulled me aside. "Tell you what," he whispered. "I'm so sick of Soviet rule that I'm going to back you to smash it. One whistle will muster an army of twenty thousand to overthrow the whole farce. Why not, when it was rabble who made the first revolution?"

My best friend was the Azerbaijani from the police cell. In our final day of cleaning putrid toilets, we worked out a plan for compensation. I unscrewed the beautiful old judas-hole in my oak cell door. It waited in place for our morning of liberation, when I slipped it into my pocket, passed it to my pal while I was searched on the way out, and took it back when he was worked over. His blonde was at the prison gate to forgive him when we emerged—two bald idiots with a souvenir to win him straight back into her heart.

GALYA SAID I WAS WHITE AND SHIVERING. I only remember running up our apartment stairway toward a bath. She came in and couldn't make up her mind whether to pity me more for my skinniness—I'd lost twelve pounds—or for my smell. Then she went out to sell my Belgian suit, which I'd worn on March 21 and on the day of my arrest. She didn't want that bad luck even in the closet.

The next morning we were informed that another ten days awaited me unless we paid ten rubles for my Big House board. I couldn't face more prison officials and waited on a bench while Galya went to make the payment. I was thinking of what went on behind the elegant architectural façades when a man appeared to check what my shaved head was doing so near the compound. "Come with me. Let's see what you're up to here."

My paranoia ignited as in my first days inside. I was certain the fine was a trick to put me away again. During the following weeks I remained a hunted animal, afraid to go outdoors where another incident might be waiting, searching for refuge whenever someone approached our door.

The worst was that the visa office had forced our papers back on Galya. The day Nixon left the country they called her in, said the application lacked a proper invitation from a relative in Israel, and promised a reprimand for the official who had accepted it. This terrible news put me in shock. Our last card had been proved worthless. There was no way out, no hope, nothing to plan for.

In my panic, I grasped for further help from the West. Suzanne Massie won a promise from a leader of the French National Assembly to intervene. Later I heard that the chairman of the Confederation of French Trade Unions raised my case with Moscow worthies, including Brezhnev. In Stuttgart, John Cranko said he would move heaven and earth. But purely by instinct, I counted most on the least influential of my friends. From London, Rosemary Winckley shared my horror. I pleaded into the telephone for help.

Rosemary wept, tried to reassure me with news of the well-publicized petitions being gathered all over the world, begged me not to do anything foolish. Her frenzy so matched mine that just talking to her was some comfort. I did not grasp the scope of what she immediately undertook. But I blessed her for understanding our terrifying dead end.

Fedya Medina still linked me with most of my other foreign friends and with the Moscow correspondents. In June the director of the Conservatory, a celebrated pianist, called him in for abuse. The Soviet people did not want such students, he declared. Fedya must leave immediately. This new blow was almost more than I could bear. Fedya was my dear friend and faithful helper. We kissed good-bye at the airport, and I took a bus back, lonely and totally defeated.

By now, almost all my former Russian acquaintances were hiding from me. Friends unconnected with the Kirov, my true ones, scurried across the street at the first glimpse of me. The exceptions were so few that they froze me up.

Vladimir Lorionov was among the country's best poetry readers, always an important performing art in Russia. Ten years before, after he had read Lermontov and I danced to a Scriabin étude on the same bill in a famous theater, he had taken me home and started introducing me to new realms of art. I had been a regular guest at his private readings and at candlelight suppers produced by his equally artistic wife. We had joined the annual pilgrimage to Pushkin's country house.

Lorionov's reverence for art had constantly elevated my life and work. After Fedya's departure I needed its solace. My old friend and teacher always had known me before I even said hello on the telephone. Now he pronounced a chilling "Who?" when I called.

"But it's me, Valery."

"I don't know anyone by that name. Please don't call again."

His son had once been closer to me than my own Andrei was. Lorionov forbade him to talk to me.

Lorionov was one of the good men who had long understood everything. But he wanted to continue his own work—and to *live*. Most members of the intelligentsia were more frightened than people who had nothing to lose and nothing to strive for. But in my fear for myself I could not accept his.

I choked when my two or three loyal friends urged patience. More time would finish me. Finally, I lost control and began shouting at people I loved. A snarl welled up in me when Galya approached. My physical decline was too personal to share even with her.

Disgraced writers could continue working, even "publish" in samizdat. Dissident artists could find critics and customers in Moscow's foreign community; mathematicians could read scholarly journals. But a performer had to perform. At the very least a dancer had to exercise. Without the daily bread of the daily class, death came quickly. This pertained especially to me. My muscles weren't pliant like Galya's or Vasiliev's. They had to be warmed up slowly every day: kneaded, stretched, and demanded from. I had an athlete's heavier oil, not a dancer's fluid stuff. Without the daily battle my body would turn thick.

Friends tried to cheer me up by saying I could slip into other branches of dance. But I had seen too many sagging muscles accommodated to new forms—most of which were coarsenings of those they could no longer perform. Some aging dancers persuaded critics that their tricks to stay in the spotlight were "improvements"—and took back from ballet's development almost as much as they'd once given it.

I hated this picture of myself disguising my degeneration. Something else fed my panic. Rodin took the body as the measure of a man, Chaliapin invited anyone who appealed to him straight to the baths—and I knew why. The body was self-expression, self-affirmation. For the first time since I was seven years old, mine was deteriorating. Ballet was too demanding to prevent this with living-room exercises—and I couldn't exercise anyway if there were no performances. I couldn't even think under the constant threat of another arrest.

A layer of fat was creeping over my jail skinniness. The sickly slackness of my muscles was advancing toward incurable rot. Stretching myself to the outer limit, I set a deadline. If we weren't out by July, I was finished: they would have won.

42

AUGUST PASSED IN THE WOODS OUTSIDE ALEC'S APARTMENT. A MONTH of sun and long swims and of talking with Alec was treatment for the nerves. Then Israel's Olympic athletes were murdered in Munich. I

left immediately to join Moscow's emigration leaders and to share the
funereal mood. Terrorists machine-gunning *our* people like firing squads,
and we couldn't even fight for them. All we could do was hear Soviet
commentators exonerating the killers and blaming "the rapacious Zionists," as if Israeli platoons had shot their own children.

We *had* to answer with a demonstration. We debated where to
hold it, put on black armbands, and positioned ourselves outside the
Dutch Embassy, Israel's representative in Russia. We spaced ourselves
far apart to try to avoid arrest for "blocking a public pathway"—a
pathetic fiction, since the sight of us scattered all passersby. Only
swarms of policemen crowded around, while Dutch diplomats ran back
and forth to their windows before deciding not to accept our message
of condolence.

After more debate we transferred to the Lebanese Embassy, to protest Lebanon's use as a terrorist training camp and refuge. We arrived
just in time to see a separate group of demonstrators being corralled
into police buses. Only Andrei Sakharov wasn't manhandled, but respectfully led away, together with his family. His presence prevented
serious police violence.

Several days later the Jewish New Year began in the gloom of the
Munich slaughter. The throng around the Moscow synagogue was apprehensive since the building had been almost completely cordoned off.
Using a back-alley route, activists managed to take me to within sight of
it. The crowd huddled together in hushed mourning while policemen
and KGB officers shouted through megaphones that "this unauthorized
jamup must immediately disperse." The hundreds of regular and secret
police evidently needed re-inforcements, for armed soldiers were crammed
into troop carriers parked in side streets. This first celebration I'd ever
attended of our holy, happy Rosh Hashanah told me everything about
my people's fate.

Few people did disperse. The police re-routed heavy trucks from
a major artery through the synagogue's quiet street. The roaring traffic's
clouds of dust and exhaust fumes drowned out the services, as intended.
The bullhorn bellowing continued: "Break it up, you. This is a public
place." Black-suited KGB detectives competed with thugs called "volunteer militiamen" in snarling at people who wanted to pray.

The shouts, the traffic, the soldiers at the ready became an image of
fascists ravaging Jewish ghettos. But we had survived worse intimidation.

EVEN THOUGH SOME SEEMED at the end of their rope, Moscow's Jewish leaders bolstered me as much as my baptism of fire as a demonstrator. Swarms of informers tried to make them quarrel among themselves and spoil their reputations. But if these beleaguered men could fight, so could I.

New friendships in Leningrad's more modest Jewish movement pulled me further back from loneliness. A prominent historian named Leonid Tarassuk had applied to leave on the same March 21 as Galya and I. Lenya Tarassuk looked like a strapping Ukrainian hussar, but his Ukrainian name was a coincidence; all Jews in a district where one of his ancestors lived had got it by fiat.

He was in his early twenties and living in Leningrad when Stalin planned his mass exile of Jews to Siberia in 1952. A friend told him that trains were already being assembled. Deciding not to submit without a fight, Tarassuk and his brother gathered some arms and other equipment and dug a cache in Crimea. Some years later rainstorms washed it into view. The act had little significance in the changed political circumstances of 1958, but the KGB had to punish anyone who had dared even to think of armed resistance. They traced Tarassuk to Leningrad. Only Khrushchev's recent boast that Russia had no political prisoners saved him from a crippling sentence for anti-Soviet conspiracy.

Convicted of anti-Soviet slander instead, he taught himself two languages in his three years in the labor camp. His parents launched a Herculean campaign to gain his freedom, but his father died before Tarassuk's release, and his mother became a complete invalid. She lived in a communal apartment on the other side of Leningrad from Tarassuk's family. Every day he traveled twelve miles to wash and feed her, then back to his two children and wife.

Before his persecution, people marveled at how he had survived his domestic load to write his excellent books and win his many degrees. Now his catalogue of cares, from hustling for food and medicines without money to coping with his suffering, made mine seem easy. But he never lost his intellectual curiosity or his wit. When new attacks occurred, or one of our friends was arrested, the world was wretched. Lenya Tarassuk's zestful plan for a counterattack allowed no thought of defeat.

. . .

WHEN THE FALL THEATRICAL SEASON reached full swing, threats of exile from Leningrad became explicit. Anyone who hadn't worked for three months could be sent to chop wood in Siberia. The law also stipulated that unemployed specialists must be offered a job in their field, but the officers who summoned me for warnings laughed when I mentioned this. "You'll never dance again in the Soviet Union," one clarified. "Why beat around the bush? You'll never dance anywhere."

A later invitation to join Galya's former company was a trick to neutralize our only weapon. Especially after the break with China, publicity that might interfere with manipulation of Western governments was the only thing the authorities feared. But Perm was still closed to foreigners. We would have disappeared from there without a trace.

Meanwhile, I hunted throughout Leningrad. Igor Belsky's laugh echoed in a Maly corridor. "You don't want to apply to the Artistic Director," he said, "but to . . . another office." The balletmaster of the Musical Comedy Theater whispered that he would love to have me but was simply afraid. Others did not even say *that*.

Then someone took the risk, on condition that my identity stay secret. A few experimental cabarets had recently opened in Baltic restaurants. They called themselves nightclubs, enough by itself to cause pandemonium at ticket windows. The director of one of the Vilnius revues used to dance with me at the Maly. He hired me to prepare his program.

To thumb their nose at Russia, the tiny Lithuanian troupe gave me full support. I quickly choreographed one number on a Gypsy theme and another to a Rolling Stones song. Without my name attached to them, they won first prize when the acts were judged at the end of the year. But my job disappeared before our opening night. When the KGB, which packed the audience anyway, discovered our secret, four agents approached my generous friend in the restaurant toilet. They showed him their cards, informed him of his offense, and beat him bloody.

I could not do this again to anyone. And without work, we worried about what to eat. By fall we were so poor that food was a daily problem.

In the euphoria of first submitting our applications, we had spent money as if we had been on vacation. Without classes to attend, Galya turned to packing the refrigerator with produce from the peasant market.

We invited friends to celebrate, "refusenik" Jews who had been living hand to mouth since being fired for making their own applications. Their hunger at a full table showed us they needed something more serious than celebration, and we asked them over regularly.

The blood money extracted from departing Jews included four hundred rubles for their exit visas and five hundred rubles for the obligatory renouncing of Soviet citizenship. I made loans to people trying to cope with this state robbery and strove to settle my own debts. Then things started going badly for us, and we spent wildly for foreign telephone calls. In weeks we were completely broke.

Each item sold from the living room provided a week's food to supplement Alec's salamis. The bedroom couldn't help because it was too small for more than mattresses on the floor. Photographs of us at work still lined the otherwise bare walls. I stared at them for hours.

Sweaters and tights from visiting foreigners were our salvation. Galya ran down to sell them for groceries as soon as the donors were out of sight. She was good about parting with her treasured books and about preparing snacks for our famished refusenik callers. We had to feed them *something*, and I faced prosecution for yet another offense unless I contributed to Andrei's support.

It sounded noble to be fighting for our principles, but the dreary truth was that we were spending as much time thinking about what to eat. Suddenly Baroness Batsheva Rothschild, Tel Aviv's patron of modern dance, saved us from this. She had first called us months before, soon after John Cranko told her about the start of our troubles. Now she sent manna from heaven in the form of American dollars.

But nothing could save us from the surveillance. KGB faces leering into mine were the constant of my new existence. The presence of henchmen was the first thing I felt on walking into a room. Most of the agents were Big House warders in serge. The extras who did some of their tailing for them might have been recruited from the prisoners. By providing work for a small army of them—two cars full on many days, in addition to scouts posted at strategic doorways and bus stops—I should have won a Hero of Socialist Labor award. How many alcoholics I kept from vodka and petty theft!

When I ran out of the house, it was: "He's going out—out! Get into the car, the car!" If I turned back for something, I bumped into a running hulk. Sometimes I tried to lose myself by making a break for the neighboring courtyard. When I dashed into its telephone booth for a preliminary look in three directions, I saw panic.

Since one function of shadowing was to frighten foreigners from seeing me, some of the ugliest toughs were posted outside my door or jammed their boots *into* our door as Americans or Englishmen arrived. KGB teams often pushed their way in—without a warrant, of course— just after someone had arrived to see me. Their job was to prevent firsthand communication with the outside world. They threatened to expel Western correspondents for interviewing me and tried to confiscate their film.

The horde of agents who burst in when a Texan associate of Dr. Armand Hammer was visiting remained five hours to intimidate us by writing up "protocols." Before this, the surest thing the dumbfounded American knew about the Soviet Union was that Dr. Hammer was its big friend and that his Occidental Petroleum Corporation had just completed an eight-*billion*-dollar deal with the Ministry of Foreign Trade. "But I'm a friend of Dr. Armand *Hammer*," he kept repeating. "I'm planning to trade with your country, too—how can this happen?"

The dismal guard mushroomed during visits of Western statesmen. A look out my window confirmed that someone important had arrived in Moscow. A small row of cars with unmistakable occupants would be waiting outside. A cluster of joyous anniversaries, including several marking the development of collective agriculture, was being celebrated just now. These happened to coincide with yet another disastrous crop failure, double reason for intensifying surveillance of "rebels." Sheer economic need was forcing the authorities to let in more and more American businessmen.

To keep us from spoiling the Anniversary of the Revolution, we were picked up as counterfeiters. At a peasant market Galya handed a vendor a large bill—part of the ruble proceeds of the Rothschild transfer— for some cucumbers. Men from our escort delivered us to a day in the local police station. In the end our interrogator ripped up the fifty-ruble note "evidence" and released us.

Our friends were constantly intimidated. The few who hung on from before our application were threatened with losing their jobs and their permission to live in Leningrad. One who had already been fired managed to keep his car and drove me to emigration consultations and on other business. When his tires were slashed—eight times in a row— the blades were purposely left in.

Other "friends" were stooges whose noses appeared in our door whenever a foreigner arrived or we were planning our defense or a new attack. Tarassuk and I shook off the worst pests by naming them on a bugged telephone. "That rat again? Don't mention anything in *his* presence." He would disappear within a few days.

Thanks to Patricia and Clive Barnes, my case was becoming known in New York, and when Mayor John Lindsay arrived in Moscow, he told friends of mine that he wanted to see me on his Leningrad swing. One of the KGB men asked his usual morning question about my plans for the day. I said I'd show the mayor my new KGB summons, take him along to the police building, and give him firsthand news of Jews' treatment that he could use very effectively—and for his own standing, too—in New York. Sure enough, the headquarters was practically shuttered tight when I arrived. On my first step inside, someone whipped my summons out of my hand and politely asked me to call again the following week.

The following week—when the Mayor had gone—I was read an angry accusation of anti-Soviet slander and reminded of what happened to others convicted of this crime. This was the primary purpose of the day-and-night hounding. The game was to wear me down, take me out of action. Agents called constantly to snarl questions to which they knew the answers better than we did. Where did we get our money? What foreigners had we met? Who were our chief anti-Soviet contacts? "Your spreading of slanderous information about the homeland falls under Article Seventy," they said, holding up folders of evidence. "Don't have any doubts about it. You'll get ten years."

Since the same men had given this sentence to others, we *had* no doubts—or about their other threats. The "friends" warned of plans to break my legs, crush my Achilles' tendons, or "just plain smash your head in"—as had just been done to an acquaintance who applied after us. Poison was mentioned even more frequently. The stooges told of overhearing their bosses talk about cancer-producing needles. "They said the prick can happen anywhere. On your stairway, for example. You won't feel anything until months later. Honestly, you're crazy to keep provoking them."

The Leningrad KGB was traditionally fonder of outright criminal methods than the Moscow branch. Every corner I came to might conceal a gang of thugs. I took cover indoors, hiding in our tiny pantry at the sound of every knock. The jail atmosphere strained me to the limit; they waited for the snap. Galya gasped for fresh air, and somehow believed the black cars went away at dusk. "So what if they do follow us? Don't pay any attention to them." But when fear gripped badly, I couldn't go out at all after dark.

Sometimes we went far out of town to get away from them. We'd find a shop to buy some milk—and one of them would be waiting inside. I was afraid the brutal faces everywhere I turned might break me even without a beating. But the surrender they were driving for would be worse.

THE ARRIVAL OF the New York City Ballet in the fall of 1972 reminded me of thoughts I used to have as a dancer. A lifetime had passed since the stunning revelation of Balanchine's first visit. The company was still beautifully schooled and polished. Balanchine's great contribution to ballet, especially through his marriage of movement to music, struck me even harder. However, I felt a certain dehumanization of company talents in the brilliant but easily forgettable scenes. The expression of the choreographer's genius reduced dancers to marvelously precise moving parts of his schematic machine. I could actually feel their subordination to his will—which is why I saw Balanchine and only Balanchine, even in his most gifted ballerinas. Alvin Ailey's group had been far less professional, but the celebration of individuality in his works made them more exciting to me. Evidently not only Soviet ballet had trouble combining a high degree of schooling with personal expression. But maybe I wanted to lose my infatuation for Balanchine.

My hopes for help had resurfaced when he arrived. I told some of his dancers how I had worshiped him and how much I wanted to meet him. They answered that he had suggested to his company that they avoid me, fearing great danger to me—and warning of serious company consequences to them—if they did see me. Edward Villella's dismay at this was re-inforced by the fate of a young ballet lover who had been waiting for the Americans outside the Leningrad City Soviet. In sight of everyone, the police shoved the boy into a car and began beating him as it pulled away. Villella felt that this display told him more about Soviet rule—and my yearning to escape it—than all the official receptions he would ever attend.

Villella and the few others who did visit Galya and me despite the warning spoke with great respect for Balanchine's genius, but regretted his attitude toward us. They felt that *we* should decide what meetings would help or hurt.

These first celebrities to come and see us were the most beautiful of people, as inspiring for us as their messages from Patricia and Clive Barnes. They made Balanchine's unwillingness to listen to my despair even harder to accept. The authorities he dealt with were fully aware of his international prestige, which might have given us just a trace of protection.

Balanchine didn't realize what he had done. How different Sergeyev was! Ballet eyes still followed him whenever he appeared in public. In full view of everyone, including all the policemen in the audience, he shook my hand during a New York City Ballet intermission and asked how he could help me out of my "hell."

LATE THAT FALL a United States Senate committee visited Russia to investigate the vexing questions of trade, emigration, and détente. On the urging of the Barneses, an aide of Edward Kennedy's contacted me and asked for an outline of my situation. The short document I wrote for them was confiscated during the delegation's airport search.

The crop failures had made the authorities hypersensitive to any publicity that might affect purchases from America. A car came immediately to take me to the Party headquarters of my district, where young Stalinists grilled me about my "foreign contacts and payments." They were visibly impatient with this new warning someone had ordered and with the Brezhnev government's general weakness. What they wanted was action to finish me off.

The next day's summons was from the Big House. The building was guarded like an ammunition dump, and wooden-soldier lieutenants flanked the desk I was led to. The man behind it was the KGB's assistant chief for Cultural Affairs. In his job of purifying literature and the performing arts, Colonel Pavlov had already crushed many lives. Public opinion meant nothing to him; victory was everything. "Your moment for going abroad hasn't come yet," he scoffed. "Give us a little time. . . ." I was intended to finish his sentence: "To control the world."

Pavlov warned that I was about to be exiled for parasitism. He banged down a thick dossier, thundering that my case would "now begin." Suddenly he withdrew my letter to Senator Kennedy from the file and launched into a furious accusation of my "slander of Soviet reality." I said the confiscation might have been a mistake; the Soviet government presumably wanted good relations with the Kennedy family.

"Don't tell us what to do. I'll tell *you* that no President is going to speak up for your petty little 'cause.' And we spit on all other appeals, they mean nothing. . . . Just remember this, we're going to get you for your anti-Soviet activity. Just a couple of more days. . . ."

He raged for two hours. Acute anxiety took over when I was released, but the "couple of more days" passed with no arrest, and one week was again much like another.

EACH MORNING A RATTLING bedroom window began our day at 5 a.m. In the frantic hours before leaving to train for Batumi, we had grabbed the first apartment available, a 1960s prefab with a crumbling stairway. Thank God we'd taken possession of *it*, at least. If we had followed Okhtorsky's urging and not bothered, we'd have been thrown out of the Rossi Street dormitory when expelled from the Kirov. The KGB would have arranged that we had no other residence in Leningrad, and we'd have had to leave. In this sense, our new apartment was a sanctuary. But after a few days of living there, we knew exactly why the previous occupants had left.

The district's major landmarks were factories for tanks, rockets, and submarine equipment. Making for the freight depots attached to the Warsaw railroad station, two blocks away, steady lines of heavy diesel trucks roared up Moscow Prospekt, four floors below us. I would go to bed a few hours before the truck route hit its morning peak. Without proper exercise, sleeping at night was even harder for me. When I finally dozed off, my ballets often passed before my eyes like old films. Then came the combustion music for their twisted endings.

We got up when the first visitor arrived. Sometimes a small group came, or several together. Most were refuseniks, but occasional dissidents also looked in. The news they brought was almost always bad: a new arrest, another visa denied, one more family facing breakup because the father had been allowed to leave, within forty-eight hours, without his wife and children. Other crises concerned money, threats of physical violence, and uncontrollable despair. Someone with hungry children had been fired without his back pay; someone else had been indicted on a false charge. Only quick countermeasures might work.

We fought back chiefly through statements to various Soviet offices detailing the illegality of the new harassments. When these were ignored, we sent them to the Western press. In minutes the living room was a legal office and operations room. We discussed cases, devised plans, passed on news and advice telephoned from the emigration leaders in Moscow. For what it was worth, the radio was on full blast. Our apartment was so bugged that an electronic squeak went up from pieces of equipment placed too close together. For more delicate matters, we crammed into the kitchen and turned on the faucets. But anything truly secret had to be discussed by writing on scraps of paper or by going outdoors.

Jewish applicants came to our apartment—one of the city's few places of refuge, comfort, and consultation—as dancers once had to my Rossi Street den. But if no victim dropped in on a particular morning, I studied my Talmuds—criminal codes, legal commentaries, and foreign studies of the rights of man—and drafted petitions:

> Respected Comrade Podgorny. . . . In connection with your position as Chairman of the Supreme Soviet, therefore the protector of Soviet legality, I should like to remind you that my wife and I have applied to emigrate to the State of Israel, an action sanctioned by the Soviet Constitution and by the United Nations' Declaration on Human Rights (adopted December 16, 1966, by the XXI session of the General Assembly), to which the Soviet Union is a signatory (in accordance with Article 569 of the Civil Code of the Russian Republic). . . .

The law required members of the government to answer such messages within two weeks. I might as well have thrown mine down a well. But in their hundreds, they were doing what no school could: I was learning how to write. The acts themselves were like memorized verses.

Our marriage ceremony had been sanctified by a reading from the Family Code about the Soviet government's solemn protection of the sacred institution, the same government that was trying harder than ever to separate us. When Fedya left, our telephone was disconnected. Then every piece of our mail was stopped. From the post office to our building's management office, every agency obediently trampled over its own statutes. The major rights to work, to demonstrate—and to emigrate—all were violated.

"The law's like a pair of horses," goes the old Russian saying. "Jerk the reins, it always follows the strongest force." Brezhnev announced to the world that only Jews who had national security secrets weren't free to emigrate—as if my work had been in jet fuels. To silence Tarrasuk, an officer quoted chapter and verse of an international agreement he had supposedly broken. No such agreement existed.

Yet only the dissenters saw anything unusual in legal institutions practicing lawlessness. People blinked when I objected to something in terms of a legal code or of the Constitution. The law was for idiots, for propaganda, or for tricks—most of all, for the still foolable Italian and French comrades. The national boss of all visa offices had recently told a Moscow emigration leader he was "nuts to keep quoting laws to me. . . . We're as strong as this wall right here. You can bang your head to a pulp against it, recite your legal rights until doomsday. You won't get out unless we want you out."

I kept at my petitions and appeals because sitting around without *some* activity deepened my depression, and I wanted my shadows to report me as alert and pushing. An old or new fault in our application was adduced whenever I went to inquire about our case. When I received a proper invitation from a woman in Israel, some other document was found invalid. The only purpose of the visa office was to send me packing—to the City Soviet, for example. The City Soviet would get a brainstorm: why didn't I try the visa office? The Soviet bureaucracy could give lessons in the old shuttle game.

The visa office was called OVIR, an acronym for the Department of Visas and Registrations. The officials themselves plastered a smile on top of their power over their vassals' lives. KGB agents in police uniforms were in charge of the waiting room. Applicants sat in this room, imagining what was going on in the interviewing cubicles. When one of the doors opened and things had gone well inside—with an engineer assigned to a job in Milan, for example—a beaming official pumped the lucky man's hand long and hard. "So you're off, Vasilich? Don't forget us, Vasilich. Have a wonderful trip."

Weeping and pleading from the nonofficial supplicants were much more frequent. Children were refused permission to join their parents.

Grandparents, wearing rows of Soviet medals to impress the interviewers, could not go to see their grandchildren. Sobs, prayers, and fits took place every morning. Seasoned emigration hands took along smelling salts for applicants who had come with too much hope.

The other great consumer of time was calling on friends who were making up their minds about whether or not to apply. Since one visit from Tarassuk or me was enough to mark a man, we spent hours throwing off our shadows. Tarassuk's support grew more vital as the winter days shortened. If we hadn't met earlier in the day, I made sure to see him during the late afternoon, an important time to spend with a friend. He told me much about his difficulties in the Hermitage, where he had been curator of ancient arms and armor before his emigration application.

Everyone outside saw the magnificent museum as a model of love and care for national treasures, and it was true that the underpaid staff, which included some of Leningrad's most cultured people, worked with rare dedication. But backstage the Party manipulated the Hermitage even more cynically than it did the Kirov. Although KGB agents watched the curators' every move, none objected to stunning Party giveaways to visiting royalty. "You like that?" Khrushchev would ask about a fabulous diamond peeking out between his thick fingers. "Here, it's yours." Unique, priceless treasures were handed over in return for Detroit cars and swimming-pool equipment. Tarassuk saved an antique dagger—and earned himself a bad name—only by announcing that it would have to leave over his dead body. Since no one knew precisely what the Hermitage held, the Party treated "the people's" wealth as its private horde. The lack of accounting and control was possible because gems had been acquired through liquidation of private collectors. Tarassuk's accounts of rich Russians arrested for this purpose, and of the Soviet army's vast looting in postwar Europe, would have curled the hair of hardened criminals. Vanished collections for which owners were still searching lay crated in the basement.

THE EVENING WAS THE MOST LIKELY TIME for foreigners to appear. Some would boost us with promises to help; others would disappoint us with their naïveté. A certain percentage came just to look at us, for we had become a kind of tourist attraction.

We pulled away for our evening radio listening. Our lives depended on intimate knowledge of current events. If the French and Soviet governments were considering a new accommodation, we had to adapt our tactics. If foreigners were coming to a Moscow conference or the Kremlin had made a lying statement, we had to act while the subject was still in Western newspapers. Without up-to-the-minute information, it made more sense to stand in line for potatoes than to try to continue our kind of fight. We simply couldn't understand the crusade of some Americans to cut off Radio Liberty's appropriation. Although not our favorite station, it always carried hard news that the others didn't about Soviet abuses. Détente temporarily protected the cautious Voice of America, but all other stations were at least selectively jammed, and Liberty was jammed to death. Finding a place and angle where the receiver would catch wisps of speech was an art as delicate as positioning arms in ballet.

Unless an emergency appeal needed composing, telephoning was the late-night entertainment. The time difference for international calls—our midnight was 10 p.m. in London and late afternoon in New York—made the early hours the best for this. After our telephone was cut off, we had to rely on a handful of sympathizers who volunteered theirs.

A few phones of dissidents continued to work until one Soviet hand caught up with what the other was doing. Others remained connected in large communal apartments because the authorities sometimes hesitated to deprive the dozen other tenants. This led to the curious spectacle of Tarassuk speaking to the Israeli Embassy in Washington from a dark corridor where the resident informer gnashed his teeth. Of course, this phone too would soon be disconnected, probably in the middle of a conversation. More and more people learned not to let us in at night.

For outgoing calls, we could still go to the telephone exchange, where the operators would make us wait till 3 or 4 a.m. for a connection, when they granted it at all. We took our nervous tension to bed. A few hours later Moscow Prospekt's truck traffic shifted into its rush-hour gear.

As THE SIEGE DRAGGED ON, Alec kept calming me with his dry wit, while my father raved and ranted about teaching me the lesson I deserved. Waving a *Pravda* in my face, he would curse me in its words. "They know about you. All the newspapers have exposed you for what you are." When I suggested that the London *Times* did not fall in with his "all," he leaped on me for my "blasphemy."

Somewhere he must have known everything was a lie. Soviet methods were too clear by now for him to miss the terrible trick played on his life. But his fear and submissiveness were still so great that he could allow these thoughts to escape only in his sleep, if even there.

Only my mother departed from character. She had worried more and more about me since our application. Alec and I kept everything we could from her, but we couldn't stop the KGB threats to destroy the family as punishment for her having signed my release. She'd begun listening—fearfully—to shortwave broadcasts about me. The scare tactics my father's institute used on him gave her pains in her chest. The KGB grilled both my parents about whom I was selling my possessions to. Their policy of getting at me by frightening her worked so well that she talked only of my "terrible end" whenever we met.

Something had snapped in her late middle age. The missing attachment for me when I was a child now emerged. A year of constant anxiety had weakened her so much that she took to bed after every KGB visit. Finally, she needed a hospital stay, which much improved her. When Galya called me on a Moscow trip to read out a telegram, it sounded like a variant of the ruse used on my 1959 American tour.

ELIZAVETA PETROVNA SHULMAN DIED 9:45 23RD MARCH
(SIGNED) PAPA

Surely a husband and a father couldn't have composed this official communiqué? I called Alec. My mother had indeed died. She stepped out of bed the morning she was going home from the hospital and fell over, seized by a blood clot.

When I arrived in Vilnius the next day, my mother had been buried. My father had done it in a hysterical rush, as he was now running from the house to smash every bottle of her pills he could find in the garbage can. I stepped forward, expecting him to throw things at me instead. But I did not recognize him. He was no longer as strong as re-inforced concrete or as angry as hot steel, but as helpless as a child. Too bewildered to put on his artificial arm, he used the empty sleeve as a handkerchief. It was sopping wet.

Suddenly I realized that all his normal emotion had been given to my mother and only my mother. "She was my partner in life," he choked. "I always loved her."

His howling tore us apart. We wondered what could possibly keep him sane now. Trying to apologize for my part in this tragedy, I said Mama had received what should have happened to me. "I never imagined that she would be the one to go under."

"No, this was fate," he blubbered. "It's not your fault. I tell you, this came from above." He had never before used "from above" to indicate anything other than the Party. I felt he must mean God. We reached for each other and wept. This is what it took for our first sharing of real feeling.

Three weeks later he was telling Alec that I alone was responsible for my mother's death. His Party organization had decided this. He was back to fulfilling instructions, the only pattern that could keep him going.

43

WHEN WE RESUMED OUR DREARY ROUTINE, WE MADE A STAB AT A BALLET class sometime during the day. We had tried to give ourselves one in a studio, but every little Palace of Culture slammed its doors. If we did use one that only a cleaning lady had been guarding, it would be protected by officials the next day. Leonid Jacobson might have risked letting us sneak in at night, but his new company's Young Communist organization announced they would not tolerate our using their facilities.

The only alternative was to make our own. A friendly engineer put up a three-foot barre for us from his factory's timber. The living room was empty enough, but we could barely turn around in the ten-by-sixteen-foot box. We could use the barre only one at a time; center work was impossible. Water sprinkled on the floor warped the boards without stopping us from thudding into the walls. My hands hit the ceiling on small turns, and my head bumped on a medium jump, which I couldn't take anyway, since our well-organized neighbors threatened to start eviction proceedings.

Despite everything, Galya was as solemn as ever about "class" and chided me to keep up with her. But the standard exercises had always been mumbo jumbo to me without a coming performance to make sense of them. Now they meant even less. An hour of pretending only made me more miserable. My hand recoiled from my flabby stomach.

To discharge my desperation into something physical, I took a karate class until I saw how easily a neck could be broken there. A large contingent of KGB types trained in all combat sports. Home workouts were the final resort. I forced myself to lift heavier weights than I ever had. Without rehearsals to smooth them out, my muscles thickened.

Galya didn't believe we could die as dancers. Our mirror had no such illusions. Day by day the KGB tactic of killing all hope that I would dance again was further vindicated. I had the beetle-like torso I so despised, supported by toothpick legs, dead for dancing. Certain abilities simply had disappeared. Five months without proper work was probably the limit beyond which someone my age could never return to his previous form. We had not danced a full year.

We spent most of the time in our apartment prison. I disliked leaving it because signs of searches were obvious when we returned. Not one of my letters to Brezhnev, Podgorny, and the Central Committee produced a reply. Their henchmen were certain of wearing us down into surrender: after the initial publicity about us, the West's attention would surely shift to something else. KGB officers kept repeating that "you are going to oblivion; nothing will help you."

The hardest thing to face was that this strategy was working. I was going down again. Each time it pulled away, the barre was harder to re-attach to our flaky plaster. Days passed before I could pick up a screwdriver. I didn't want to hear the maddening tapping from the tenants below or the signals from my own brain. To replace my load of classes, rehearsals, and two three-act ballets a week, I began drinking with Tarassuk whenever we had a few rubles.

The living room had only two old armchairs left. Sunk in mine, I felt partially protected. My radio was on one arm, and my cat was in my lap. I took to eating, drinking, and sleeping in this home within a home. Sometimes I ran to the *banya* and beat myself with birch besoms until my skin was bloody. Panic blocked out the absurdity of trying to get into shape this way. When I calmed down, I looked to see whether my leg muscles had stopped collapsing.

Fantasy was the most alluring escape. I refused to see even Tarassuk. After several days of my staring at a smudge on the wall, Galya became alarmed. Whole ballets passed before my eyes there. I danced my favorite variations to my own orchestra and tried not to wake up into the cold sweat of real life on a dark planet whose masters could do what they wanted with us.

Galya and I used to tell each other that we couldn't live without dancing, which was truly our lives. Now we clutched at straws—I would be her coach; she would dance for both of us—but we no longer discussed our wonderful plans as partners. Instead, I heard her weeping.

When the snow melted, the refuge that gave most peace was the cemetery of an abandoned monastery near the apartment. The grave of the brilliant painter Mikhail Vrubel was totally neglected, a symbol of the fate of nonapproved artists. Galya and I cleaned it up and planted flowers. Death became a little less unfriendly.

The Batsheva, a modern dance company in Tel Aviv, dedicated its Passover program to us and asked that we be available for an interview to be transmitted directly to the audience. The telephone line was slashed as soon as they named the number at which they were going to call us. A week later, when a Batsheva official accidentally reached me at another apartment, her sobbing for us broke my will. The last of my strength passed over the line to her. I heard myself saying we were near collapse and begging for help. "Suicide" surprised me as it came out, but the thought had been there for months.

To protect each other's feelings, Galya and I had not considered it openly. What we did discuss was taking our chances on a border crossing. We decided that if we were not out in another year, we'd risk an attempt whose result God would determine. For months after my telephone breakdown, I did not return to this plan in Galya's presence. Only part of us was preparing for it—the part that knew when we reached for each other's hands.

LOOKING BACK, I SEE US as desert flowers that spring back to life with a drop of water. A call from Rosemary in London could do this, or an afternoon at the Hermitage. Galya's reading of a favorite Pushkin poem sometimes worked. Most of the rescues fell to Lenya Tarassuk. His example of uncomplaining acceptance of his own problems was re-inforced by his coaxing us not to give the KGB the collapse they were counting on. He also suggested new, soul-saving action: writing letters to the hope of the entire emigration movement.

U.S. Senator Henry Jackson's perception of the real working of the Soviet system pierced the smoke screen of lies and tricks, allowing him to see the use of Jews as a commodity to obtain trade concessions from Congress. In our experience, straightforward exposure of such extortion was the only way to deal successfully with the dictatorship.

My letter was a simple chronicle of our treatment since we had applied. It included a short description of my physical state—I had a strange shortage of oxygen even when breathing deeply—but almost no other commentary. Galya tucked it into her panties, and we left the house, very nervous because we might have spilled something to the microphones while composing it. But we arrived safely in Moscow and searched for a diplomat willing to transmit it through a secure route. A call from Washington a few days later confirmed its arrival.

Soon a dozen theatrical and dance luminaries—Harold Prince, Joanne Woodward, Theodore Bikel, Paddy Chayevsky, and others—led a solidarity meeting on New York's Broadway. It was in response to my chronicle but, even more, to a campaign of letterwriting, petitions, and demonstrations by Americans. Deeply moving articles by Clive Barnes called on people who were planning to invite the Kirov to New York while our "savage" treatment continued to resign in shame.

Our support was even greater in London, or seemed so because we were nearer. The thousands of performers who had already petitioned the Kremlin to allow us to leave included Lord Laurence Olivier, Paul Scofield, Dame Peggy Ashcroft, Sir Frederick Ashton, Dame Marie Rambert—what a BBC commentator called a "Who's Who" of British theater and dance.

Lord Olivier, in a letter to the *Times* of London, asked Minister of Culture Ekaterina Furtseva to "take from us the shocking sense of disillusion which has shattered our belief" in Soviet artistic appearances as a force for good. Broadcasts made clear that Lord Olivier ordinarily stayed aloof from all political causes. His support became my symbol for what thousands of strangers were doing for me. Yet the honor sometimes made me feel like a thief. I feared I'd never be able to dance for these people, to show them what I'd once striven for.

After my letter to Jackson, a hundred or so performers, led by Janet Suzman, Fenella Fielding, Malcolm McDowell, and Lindsay Anderson, staged a new demonstration outside the Soviet Embassy in London. A young dancer named Michael Vernon appeared in the costume of

Petrushka, an appropriate symbol of persecution. Giants of the British and American artistic community kept joining the campaign: Harold Pinter, Peter Hall, Irene Worth, Dustin Hoffman, Arthur Miller, Joel Grey, Alvin Ailey, Paul Taylor, Merce Cunningham, Tennessee Williams . . . an endless list.

When the Kirov appeared in Manchester, Leningrad's "twin city," members of the Jewish community there bought three rows in the orchestra stalls and held up letters spelling out "Panov" during the playing of the Soviet anthem. Then they silently filed out, leaving the empty seats to symbolize our isolation.

In many of these extraordinary acts of solidarity, I saw the hand of my guardian angel. Rosemary Winckley would call me to say, "There's going to be another demonstration." I realized that she—with the help of Jennie Walton in London and Patricia Barnes in New York—had *organized* the new demonstration by distributing my every new appeal overnight around the world and by mobilizing support from an amazing number of celebrities. While Jennie's photographs of us were flying around the globe, Rosemary described the work and sacrifice of hundreds of people, including four indefatigable London ladies, who had never heard of us a year ago but were now involved almost full time in the campaign for our release. But I did not know the people she named. I did know that Rosemary never slept because she had taken my despair on herself. One of her ways to cheer us was to persuade English ballet lovers to visit us during their Leningrad trips. From her many telephone calls and seeming day-and-night work for us, we had assumed that she was the daughter of a millionaire. When I suggested this to London friends, they said that in fact she worked for a sympathetic television network. Her apartment was as modest as ours. She had managed the calls only because of a small inheritance she'd recently been bequeathed—and was spending on us.

NOTHING IMPROVED, but the spectacular foreign support was why nothing worsened either. We could actually feel the KGB's worry over adverse publicity holding off their urge to finish me. They shook their fists, threatened to break my neck, pointed to where they would throw me under the wheels of a metro car. They broke out in a sweat—and held back. Why feed the enemy press with this when we would soon die natural deaths anyway? "Panov's already dead," I overheard. "Give us a couple more months, and Ragozina will join him."

Between the bouts of depression, my morale had actually improved. Reports that the KGB considered me Leningrad's public enemy number one strengthened my sense of responsibility to those who considered me a symbol. Refuseniks urged me not to weaken their resolve and the spirits of their families. If someone lucky enough to make Western headlines caved in, how could *they* keep going?

The KGB's mood shifted as often as mine. Battle experience was teaching me how to fight. After each blow, I crawled on all fours to a telephone booth, knowing that if I could get through to certain correspondents in Moscow, news of the latest pranks would soon be circling the globe. In the periods of respite this provided, I tried to analyze why they were willing to tolerate the running sore of the truly terrible publicity they were inflicting on themselves. The most obvious motive was to frighten others not to follow our example. If they couldn't stop all defections, what they could do was teach all dancers that no one would be allowed to make his own way to the West.

They had to demonstrate that treachery from the *privileged* would never be tolerated. "You were at the top," Party officials whined to Galya. "We gave you everything." This was their way of shaming her for relinquishing her reward of twenty eggs every May Day; and to make the same point to me, they ordered me to hand in my titles. When I remarked that this detail was slightly crazy while they were busy killing me, they passed a decree stripping me of them.

Madame Furtseva let slip yet another reason for our treatment: I knew too much. "We can't let Panov out to start a school to compete with ours," she had said, scolding a Kirov administrator. Considering the resources required to found a ballet school, this was her usual hyperbole about foreigners stealing Russian culture. But she *had* heard of my dream to combine elements of Russian ballet education with the West's freedom of choreography.

The strongest reason of all was probably the momentum our case had built up. It had grown to such international proportions that the KGB really did consider me "the leader of the local counterrevolution." No one in the West had ever heard of other applicants who were worse off than we were, but who hadn't been on the stage and who had no Rosemary. We could only hope that the articles and broadcasts about us would make clear what the struggle was like for all those who had no foreign help at all: a truly terrible dead end. On the other hand, it was precisely our publicity value that had locked us into our position. Since the KGB had either to break us or to lose face, victory was more important to them than it was to our Western friends. Every headline swelled their hatred of us.

MY AWE OF MOSCOW'S JEWISH LEADERS started to dim when I realized how deeply divided they were. One major split was between the Jewish cause itself—that is, the striving to emigrate—and what was known as the democratic movement, composed of Jews and non-Jews. This handful of brave souls was fighting for reform, mostly by protesting the persecution of people who had spoken up against state crimes. The captains of emigration, by contrast, cared nothing for Soviet developments except as they affected Jews getting out. Several former "democrats" who had edged toward emigration after losing hope for their doomed country were among the fiercest believers that it was not the business of a Jew to concern himself with any—futile—struggle for Russia's betterment.

As a further complication, some of the most prominent "democrats" were Jews. And the government silenced some of these by making them involuntary émigrés to Israel. Not all democrats approved of people leaving Russia. Not even all religious Jews did.

Whatever our religious and political beliefs, Moscow's synagogue was our common meeting place. It was a center and a base, a place where we could absorb some of the tradition we were struggling to join. For those like me who had avoided it all their lives, it proved that the Jews were a community of fate, not of origin. But many congregation elders wanted to throw us out as "stupid, rebel troublemakers." Soviet rule actually allowed them to cower together in fear and to pray with a handful of prayer books that hadn't been burned. They aspired to nothing more.

"Stop coming to our synagogue," they kept sputtering. "You crazy young people, you've never understood it. You don't care if you destroy it." Except for worshiping a Jewish God, they were just like all other Soviet slaves who were grateful to the Party for not killing them. "Our life is fine here; who could want to leave?"

The emigration spokesmen all saw this ingrown terror as the most compelling reason to leave, but they differed sharply over policies. Some insisted it was our duty to go to Israel and would tolerate no word of criticism against it. Others said Russian Jews had had enough hardships and were entitled to settle anywhere in order to *live* at last. Struggles for authority and for *personal advantage* divided these real issues among a welter of antagonistic splinter groups. Everyone wanted to be a *leader* and broke away as soon as he could find a single follower. At urgent meetings to discuss a new arrest there were as many platforms as people in the room. It was as if each person were preparing himself for a leading role in the Knesset the minute he arrived in Jerusalem.

Most of these rivals were historians or scientists who had first regarded me with Alec's old conviction that no serious man would waste his time jigging about a stage. But they knew Russia was a strange land. The latest proof of it was the name I'd somehow achieved abroad and my quick access to Western headlines, which their "organizations" needed. Each felt he had to take me in, indoctrinate me, and warn me off the others. Often for personal prestige, each had to prove that his stand, and only his, was "right." All rejected the thought that a ballet bumpkin might want just to emigrate without joining their inflamed debate about degrees of Zionism. Their intolerance of my staying independent sometimes smacked of what I was trying to escape from.

With no time or taste for this infighting, I gained hemming and hawing time by playing the simpleton's role expected of me. Meanwhile, I tried to work out my personal view. The more I thought about Russia's future, the less I felt in common with the democratic movement. I bowed down before the fighters for human rights, especially before Andrei Sakharov, that gentle hero. But his genuinely democratic inclinations were so untypical—even among the dictatorship's opponents— that he only increased my pessimism. What *could* be developed in a hundred ways was Israel. A state existed where Jews could feel their own land under their feet and not feel a need to apologize for what they were. After two thousand years of begging for mercies in other people's countries, I felt we should go home.

For my liking, the Moscow leaders' constant use of "homeland," "fatherland," and "motherland" came too close to the birch-tree-and-Russian-meadow propaganda that had submerged us all our lives. Some zealots' "Chosen People" talk was uncomfortably similar to the "Great Soviet People" pronouncements, and there was no need to denigrate *everything* Russian. But in the sense of believing that Jews should first contribute to their own country, I myself had become a nationalist. Anyone who wanted to work for mankind's improvement could find the perfect place for it in Israel.

Soviet lies, deceit, beatings, and rottenness had done more than anything to teach me that Jews would never escape persecution unless they had their own homeland. But the Moscow leaders helped me understand this basic Zionist tenet more clearly, and I was deeply grateful to them. Compared to their help in pointing emigrants toward Palestine, their faults were minor.

In the fall of 1973 I was informed that I had been made a citizen of Israel. I memorized the number of my Israeli passport.

EMIGRATION POLITICS WERE ONE THING, learning about Judaism something else. *A Chronicle of the Jewish People*, published in an American paperback edition, answered our sharpest questions about our origins and history. It was in enormous demand among Soviet Jews. Even gentiles sought out a remarkable old man named Pavel Vinkovetsky for enlightenment about Biblical subjects. He provided many moving stories for Galya and me about early Jewish history.

Vinkovetsky was high on the list of refusenik hardship cases. Year after year his application was rejected because he had been a shipbuilding engineer specializing in interior design. That was ten years ago, before his retirement. He was now seventy-five and lived only to get his wife and children to Israel. His library of Judaica was the largest in Leningrad. His knowledge of culture and customs—all gathered from original Hebrew sources—was even more prodigious. On top of this, he could explain the most serious matters in a wistful, humorous way, with love for all faiths and peoples.

He rarely talked about religion itself except as it influenced history. I vaguely believed that a kind of God or higher force must exist somewhere. The heavenly inspiration I had occasionally felt while dancing must have come from this source, and the Communists' desperate attempts to deny Him only confirmed that something better than absurdly weak man, something we ought to feel a responsibility to, surely existed. Vinkovetsky left this side of me unchanged, while giving me an enchanted introduction to what I most sorely missed.

His hobby was Jewish folklore, from recent ghettos to ancient desert settlements. Yiddish melodies from his vast anthology prompted ideas for ballets. The Bar Kokba rebellion and revolt of the Maccabees emphasized suffering and heroism. But more than these, I wanted to choreograph themes expressing the spirituality that had allowed the Jews to survive and contribute so much to human civilization. Vinkovetsky had made me see our people's yearning for freedom, like Christ's teachings, as part of the best of mankind.

44

EARLY IN JUNE 1973 WORD HAD REACHED US THAT GALYA AND I WOULD BE freed if we cooperated in a two-month truce. A left-wing Israeli theatrical director vacationing in Moscow relayed the bargain to us. The highest cultural officials had promised him to let us out if we lay low during the summer. With Brezhnev about to leave on a détente-with-trade visit to America, everyone knew the authorities wanted to reduce attention to Soviet oppression. A face-saving way to end the notoriety of our case made sense for them.

When the two months came to an end, the Israeli returned. Through friends, he assured Tarassuk and me that we'd be on our way when the bureaucrats came home from their summer vacations. The president of New York City's borough of the Bronx, Robert Abrams, also had encouraging news. Visiting Moscow in August, he raised some hardship cases in meetings with high officials of OVIR and the ministries of Internal Affairs and Foreign Affairs. In the presence of witnesses, deputy ministers and generals gave him a "clear and unequivocal" commitment that Galya and I would leave "shortly." In various ways, it was stressed that the *quid pro quo* was more time to cool our case. I tacitly accepted the bargain.

JOHN CRANKO'S MESSAGES and telephone calls never stopped, even during this summer "armistice." During his Leningrad visit two years before, I'd asked him to arrange an invitation from Israel just in case those with one Jewish parent would be permitted to apply. This was the least of his work for us since then. He personally badgered officials all over Europe, then sent us invitations from Germany, Austria, and elsewhere—which never arrived. He despaired that nothing was working and would choke into silence when he heard the tones of our voices.

It was not merely the hope of working with him that kept us thinking about him constantly, but also gratitude for his fighting instincts. He had been the first celebrity to reach out to us and the first to strike at Soviet prestige where it counted. In refusing to accept a Bolshoi team in a Stuttgart ballet festival, he made people think about what lay behind cultural missions sent out from Moscow to win foreigners' hearts. "My friends Galina and Valery Panov are being tortured," he wrote in an explanatory article. "Their daily suffering is inconceivable to anyone who loves art. Until they can visit me in my home, Soviet dancers will not perform here."

He dedicated a new ballet called *Traces* to us. The theme was a girl reviewing her life in a totalitarian state; the traces in the dark included a lover in a labor camp. No one could have expected what Cranko gave. An artist who *felt*, he was also a friend who *took action*, even at sacrifice to himself, as he sacrificed his whole Soviet "market" for us. *Traces* meant more to us than anyone could understand. He was helping us enormously just by being himself and reminding us of what we were fighting for.

Then the BBC announced his death. We were in Vilnius. Alec had not known him, but I grieved so that he did too. We stumbled to the post office to cable Stuttgart. "A great choreographer, a magnificent man is gone. We weep with you." Just before his death Cranko had been full of optimism and choreographing as never before. A pill he took because he hated flying made him vomit, and he suffocated. He was forty-five.

My inspiration was gone. My artistic bulwark had fallen. Losing the person who was everything I wanted to become obscured for me what a tragedy his senseless death was for all ballet.

THE KGB SHADOW LIGHTENED SLIGHTLY during the summer truce. It merely consisted of preventing us from obtaining scores for our old ballets, just in case, and of warning that "frolicking" in public parks—where we sometimes tried a lift when no one was near—was illegal. When our money ran out, we visited Alec for food and for taking stock. Far fewer people avoided us in Vilnius, and members of my old company actually came to visit. Alec's intellectual circle was as loyal to us as he was.

The KGB cars that followed us into the woods seemed less menacing. When a friend of Alec's locked his keys in his car, the agents graciously opened the door with their skeleton key. It had become dark, and they were hungry for their supper. Thanks to the reduced surveillance, another friend slipped unnoticed into the bushes for a call of nature one lovely summer morning. Several minutes later a man with a walkie-talkie crept past. "Panovs are looking at flowers in the center of the clearing, center of the clearing," he reported in a battle-urgent tone. Still squatting, my friend chimed in, "And I'm helping the flowers on the side, on the side."

Sometimes I felt a debt to the KGB. Thanks to them, I'd met some of Russia's finest people—the persecuted and the resisting. I had had time away from my little world of the rehearsal studio to sort out what mattered in life, to form my own views about good and bad. They had given me an abundance of risk that pushing oneself to the edge of safety on a motorcycle could never provide. People might plan for a decade but not really know what they would be like in crises. I had seen myself paralyzed with fear—and also standing up to pressure that crushed fighters who were better prepared, both politically and morally.

The best of me had been a ballet boy who wanted to express himself and take curtain calls. *They* had made me a husband who felt responsibility to his wife. Their persecution had taught me that I was Jewish; I would always be grateful for this. They had forced me to look at mankind and its history, to sympathize with sufferers, to *think* about how and where I wanted to fit in if I ever got out of Russia.

Something deep in me now warned that I might never dance again. Something else was grateful for the compensations.

WHEN WE WERE PENNILESS, Madame Rothschild's generosity kept saving us. The thirst for hard currency restrained the government from eliminating her five-hundred-dollar transfers. Instead, it stole a mere third in "exchange charges."

When the residue was counted out in hard-currency certificates, I was better off than I'd been during fifteen years on the stage. The previous winter my unemployed feet had been warm for the first time—in sheepskin boots available only with the certificates. They were sold when we were back to crusts, but meanwhile we enjoyed some high-flying weeks. We bought cuts of meat we'd never seen before, a better shortwave receiver—which would also be traded away when hard times returned—and jazz records that would provide two weeks' food apiece when they had to be sold.

I returned from Moscow loaded with cans, jars, bottles, and net bags stuffed with fruits and vegetables. When these were distributed to refuseniks actually weak from hunger, Galya set our table for those who would be coming for loans. Stories of their families' plights melted away the money, some of which had already gone for Swedish aquavit, scotch, and other exotic fuels.

This could be our last chance to run riot before the madness that might finish us off tomorrow. All that mattered was using the moment to celebrate the good fortune of the money—and of life—with a few close friends. We drank so much and sang so wildly that Oreshek crawled her way up the wall and hissed. With some of the sickness sweated out, we were rock steady for at least two weeks.

OF THE PEOPLE WHO CONTINUED to see us now, those with no connection to the dissident or emigration movements had a special courage. They were not crusading to change anything in Russia and didn't dream of leaving it. They simply refused to abandon friends, no matter how many times they were interrogated and intimidated.

It came as no surprise that the one dancer who felt for us was from Moscow. This was my old Bolshoi friend Vladimir Vasiliev, now dancing more spectacularly than ever. When I bumped into him, he had won every prize going and was a Deputy to the Supreme Soviet. He suggested a walk.

"In your position, aren't you scared to be seen with me?" I asked.

"You're damn right I'm scared, who isn't?"

But he went on to say what he thought of our treatment. On trips abroad, while others were calling me "an unknown, third-rate hack, an invention of the Western press," his remarks to Western journalists required real bravery. It was a delight to love someone as a person as well as an artist. When most Russian ballet bored me stiff, his work was thrilling.

In Leningrad my artistic interests were sustained largely by Lara, the third woman who had stormed the police station when I was held as a "hooligan." She was something from another century: a passionate patriot who lived and breathed Russian culture—and hated injustice.

Lara was an art historian and a lover of poetry, painting, architecture, every good that Russia had produced. Solzhenitsyn's Matryona was the symbol of the Russian peasant woman, and Lara was the spirit of the old intelligentsia, one of the handful whose passionate devotion kept it alive. She knew everything about styles, schools, artistic personalities. She also insisted that my dancing was purely Russian and that I had nothing in common with Israel or Jews. But personal loyalty was what mattered to her most.

It was Lara who kept me from the persecuted person's self-destructive hatred of all things Russian. When I was going mad in the prison of my apartment, she took me out to Raskolnikov's lodgings and to the building where Dostoyevsky lived when writing *Crime and Punishment*. She described daily life in Pushkin's house on the Moika River and what happened on a particular footbridge over a canal on the night Lermontov died. The courtyards and cobblestones came alive. And when I was too low for literary touring, she urged *me* to write about my childhood. Her therapy worked almost immediately. To pump some life into me and to preserve something of my career for Russia, she pressed me to remember everything. This book was born in her notebook.

IN OCTOBER 1973, GALYA AND I took a trip to the village of Mikhailovskoye, where the exiled Pushkin had written some of his most famous works. It was deep in the most picturesque Russian countryside we'd ever seen. Away from the KGB, we soaked up the peace of the woods and meadows immortalized in the verses. I sat on "Eugene Onegin's" bench, on the beautiful estate of Pushkin's mother. As always, my radio was at my side. Its news of the beginning of the Yom Kippur War sent us back to Leningrad in shock. I went to cable our solidarity to Golda Meir and Moshe Dayan. The post-office clerks stuttered that they could not accept such "terrible things."

As the threat to Israel grew, I could not leave the radio. Egypt's surprise-attack victories were worsened by the West's submission to Arab blackmail, which only America and Holland found the conscience to resist. The other countries accommodated Arab demands with a servile smile: Jewish blood was cheaper than oil, after all. Perhaps those Europeans who did not themselves live under bandits saw it differently. But Russian democrats despaired that appeasement of Hitler had taught the world nothing.

Confident that few would willingly go to a battle zone, OVIR's new form of mocking was suddenly to issue visas to refuseniks. But most, including my closest friends, did go. Meanwhile, Moscow Radio spewed out more anti-Israeli hatred than ever, and Jews were followed more threateningly than before, especially those who had tried to send telegrams like mine.

The propaganda's most rewarding results were in the countryside: half the peasants regarded the war as their personal one, especially since Israel seemed to be losing. In Leningrad, Jewish residents of communal apartments found cockroaches floating in their soup pots. Two hundred ancient Jewish tombstones were vandalized in the Preobrazhensky Cemetery. A friend of mine saw a note pinned to the wall when he opened his door one morning: "Jews living in RUSSIA, go where you BELONG."

Once again I saw how little had changed in Russia. In any emergency the Soviet government instinctively reached for the ugliest weapon of all, and the potential for a pogrom was so great that police officers at the cemetery seemed worried that the little Jew-baiting might race out of control.

45

LEONID TARASSUK'S DEPARTURE WITH SOME OF LENINGRAD'S HARDSHIP cases left me without my best friend and closest collaborator just when the KGB encirclement of "Zionist fascists" tightened another notch. On top of this, I'd been tricked again. Experts had told the KGB that two years in limbo would finish us beyond recovery. I now realized that their "lay-low" bargain had been concocted to drag out time toward this goal. When I recovered from the depression of this latest deceit, it was time for new action.

A hunger strike seemed the best plan, especially because we had no other weapons. I did not want to be traded for a concession extracted from the West. I had to go to my own limit first, although I counted on persuading Galya to give up after a symbolic few days. It was a natural decision, requiring no bravery. I was convinced that this kind of death would be no melodramatic gesture, but a demonstration to the world of what Soviet rule did to people who tried to be themselves. Only the irony disconcerted us. We were at the stage where not eating, the negation of life, was the most positive "action" we could take.

We read yoga literature about fasting and waited until just before the Anniversary of the Revolution, when the publicity would have maximum effect. When we ate the last of our stunted apples on the evening of November 2, 1973, Galya was somber.

I read a despairing statement to a Moscow correspondent about my intention to fast "to the end." "Day by day our strength is draining away. We understand perfectly that we will never be allowed to leave the country. Our physical death will now follow our professional one." But the next morning my mood was excellent. I was taking some action at last; this had an immediate effect. Several cars were parked outside our apartment house by evening. We had the added pleasure of calls by informers sniffing out our plans, the best sign that their bosses were worried.

Jewish communities all over the world began demonstrating outside Soviet missions. A vigil of theater people was held at the Soviet Embassy in London, led by Nicol Williamson, Dame Peggy Ashcroft, Claire Bloom, Joan Plowright, Irene Worth, Lindsay Anderson, Malcolm McDowell, and many others who explained our motives for television audiences. Lord Olivier, Paul Scofield, Judi Dench, and Janet Suzman asked to see the Soviet ambassador and were informed that he was un-available to meet them for a discussion of our case.

Despite all such mockery, the demonstrations *worked*. Two dozen leading Americans in all branches of the arts wired Dr. Kissinger about the "increasing outrage felt throughout the cultural community at the desperate plight of the Panovs, those innocent victims." We were sum-moned to OVIR on the hunger strike's fifth day. Its chief called us "slimy blackmailers" for "doing this" to spoil the revolutionary holidays. "What's your carrying on all about, nobody's arrested you?" These jeers seemed the reason for the interview, but in the middle of it the chief said some-thing casually as if mentioning the time of day. OVIR had accepted our application.

After twenty months we had apparently won. I used the victory—and the argument that I needed looking after—to persuade Galya to stop fasting. Her psychological need for food had made the five days agony for her, and she was exhausted after being dragged to various offices. She went to the far corner of the kitchen to spare me, but her whole being so embraced her first plate of cottage cheese that the sounds carried throughout the empty apartment.

I didn't eat. They were probably trying to trick me into breaking my fast; then they would ridicule the whole affair. They had taken our documents once before and thrown them back when the crisis subsided.

They summoned me again a few days later. To process my application, my nationality had to be officially changed to Jewish. The five-minute exercise was dragged out over morning and afternoon interviews, with a hundred corrections, erasures, and afterthoughts. Other sessions were called to tell me that the hunger strike was stupid, useless, and "unsalutary." "Why don't you drop this ridiculous self-torture so we can get down to the business of arranging your departure?"

Stressing that the greatest danger was of the psyche weakening along with the body, the yoga literature specified tranquillity as the most important condition for fasting. The KGB knew more than I about hunger strikes and continued with the summonses. I shook and weaved on my way to ovir. Raw hunger had given way to dizziness and nausea. "Haven't you done enough now?" Galya whimpered. "Don't *they* punish you enough?" Hiding the yoga warnings about nervous strain, I showed her passages stating that fasting up to forty days wasn't harmful.

To preserve her for the slow walks and massages I needed to keep *me* going, it was essential to keep her from consciously recognizing my pain. Galya had to be able to tell herself that we were in a kind of ballet, which would end—very soon now—with the Prince and Princess living happily ever after.

When I returned from ovir, I would lie down on a cot in the living room, while she brought me water and fussed over me. Our door was open. Visitors gathered as if at my wake. They represented the best and the worst Leningrad types I knew. The best were friends who worried more about me—the symbol—than about themselves. They brought information about emigration affairs, but their real purpose, even when they urged me to stop, was to help me continue. They sensed a great victory for the KGB if I surrendered. Vinkovetsky came with his family to thank me for "being my friend. You are half Jewish, and we are all of the same mankind. You are giving us the courage to live."

One of the regular visitors was Polina Epelman, whose husband had defected during a trip to Helsinki three years before. OVIR told her that she would "never join the traitor." She was fired from her job as a large hospital's chief pharmacist and lived in hopeless poverty with her persecuted daughter.

Sasha de Ribas—the last in the line of the great family for whom Odessa's main street was named—came daily to help. The Civil War had destroyed all of Sasha's relatives except his old mother, whom tragedy had so demented that she'd beaten Sasha's wife blind. He himself owned only two pairs of overalls and had almost forgotten how to eat. He also stuttered so badly that the authorities thought him retarded. But he knew European literature in four languages—and yoga, which he had introduced us to, originally for body maintenance. Desperately as he hoped to get out, he risked everything to help us in our hardest moments. It never seemed to occur to him that he was more downtrodden than I.

The worst types were informers masquerading as admirers and supplying the KGB with the information it longed for about my health and whether I was swallowing caviar on the sly. They included a Jewish doctor who examined my symptoms—a scary-looking rash and a black liquid I kept vomiting up—and warned me to stop instantly. He said I had ulcers and a possibly irreparable loss of white corpuscles. The younger informers all but brought scales to weigh me. Their eyes popped trying to read the amateur medical chart I kept to help me stay in control of myself.

One day someone rushed to give me news he thought would cheer me up. "Your pal has fallen," he exulted. "You know, the great preacher of Soviet morals, Rachinsky. He's caught it for contraband." Stripped of his post, the Director was in a hospital suffering from a general breakdown. Eventually the criminal investigation being conducted would send him to a labor camp for three years, and his accomplice, a certain Sergei Sorokin, for fifteen.

Girl-loving Sorokin was one of the Party pals who had pulled Rachinsky's career steadily upward while his own went even higher—to the directorship of Leningrad's Intourist. Embezzlement was taken for granted in this kind of position. Sorokin stretched his too far. The case began with the pocketing of change in the hard-currency bars. The barmen—all KGB agents or informers—were paying kickbacks to Sorokin. Since this was in foreign coins, they were rich men. And since Sorokin also controlled the bars of international cruise ships operating out of Leningrad, he was *very* rich. But he couldn't be seen splashing dollars on his foreign trips. Rachinsky came in as a buyer of the hardware for re-sale. Now both were finished, but I found it impossible to rejoice. This was an aria from another opera, another era.

THE KGB GRILLINGS INCREASED after the fifteenth day of my fast, and the local draft board was told to keep calling me in. My appearance frightened both friends and informers. I couldn't understand why the friends didn't understand my need to persevere. The informers dashed to the cars outside to report my condition, but maybe they couldn't bear to stay in the room with me. A body with nothing to eat turns on itself, producing a stench of sour juices. Galya pretended not to notice.

The shortwave broadcasts made up for everything. I was always conscious of the "unknown" victims who were suffering with none of my support. The first Jews who had applied in 1968 were still imprisoned, while I had a world campaign behind me. Galya and I hoped that the publicity for us would help those worse off by focusing attention on the general problem. But none of those desperate people enjoyed my rewards. Switching on my radio each evening, I would hear a summary of what had happened to me that very day!

I remembered my childhood feeling about the radio as being incapable of telling any important truth. Now it was my shortwave set that allowed me to feel I wasn't abandoned—something too terrible to imagine.

THE KGB'S ONLY ALTERNATIVE was to arrest and force-feed me. Instead, they kept grinding away at my nerves. I comforted myself with the thought that war with China would break out soon. Then I had nightmares of being forced to fight for Marxism-Leninism, the world's most ominous lie. The scene shifted, and I was aiming a rifle at Uncle Sam, who had the features of dear old Vinkovetsky.

A freezing cold snap came. Late on the twenty-first night I felt an irresistible need for oxygen. On the stairway I realized I was going out into the snow in my pajamas. I went back inside and tried to think. The greatest danger was losing mental control. The fact that a neighbor had seen me outside might have been enough for the worst of all Soviet punishments: committal to an asylum, with mind-destroying drugs. Fearing this more than anything, I decided that my touch of delirium signaled the time for surrender.

I drank a swallow of juice the next morning and informed Moscow reporters. On the third day, I took some yogurt; nothing heavier went down. But my depression at yet another failure was brief. The international reaction to the hunger strike was about to produce results.

More demonstrations had been held and petitions signed in New York and London. Despite the story's repetitiveness, the major newspapers kept running articles about us. Shortly after I broke the fast, I was asked to visit OVIR. I said I would go only to pick up our visas. The official replied as if we had recently applied for a dog license. "Yeah, your matter has been settled."

Galya leaped up to hunt for a suitcase. "It's all over," she announced. "Just a little misunderstanding, now let's pack." But I felt the same old atmosphere the minute we stepped onto the street. I hopped on a trolley with Galya, ran to the back window, and saw two black cars spurting after us. "It's not all over, Galya. It's the beginning of something new."

OVIR's secretary played her usual game of not recognizing me. When I gave our names, she told us to wait. Five minutes later she asked me to follow her down a corridor. "Why alone?" I asked.

"It's done alone. Your wife will be called in a minute."

I stepped back from the door she opened. The room was rigged up with newsreel cameras, cine lights, and tape recorders. Half a dozen reporters from the major Soviet newspapers were seated under portraits of Lenin and Brezhnev. Colonel Viktor Bokov, OVIR's headman, pointed to my chair.

My first hesitation was whether to sit in it. A refusenik acquaintance of mine had recently joined several friends in a silent, meticulously peaceful demonstration outside an Intourist hotel. The others were arrested, and he was taken here to OVIR, with a hint that his visa was waiting for him. He was put in an office empty except for a single chair. His buttocks began stinging just before an official appeared and told him his papers were being studied, he could go now. Outside, the pain became fierce. When he was taken to the hospital, huge, violent blisters kept him from moving. His skin dropped off in chunks and tissues split. The doctors diagnosed "a nervous disorder." A chemist friend found his trousers full of etheric poison. The victim remained in the hospital ten full weeks. When I visited him, his deepest burns still hadn't healed, but his broken spirit was worse. He begged me to mention nothing, in case an accusation by him would land him in a mental asylum.

I studied the chair set out for me. The same method was unlikely in a room full of reporters, but I sat down on the very edge, with my legs taking most of my weight. In this elegant position I heard a string of magical words pronounced in a single breath. "Citizen Panov, after a full review of your entire case with all its documents, we have decided to give you permission to leave for the State of Israel; please sign this declaration that you have received such permission and agree to leave."

The paper Bokov pushed at me blurred. Could it really be true that we had won out over the monstrous machine? I didn't quite believe it. Bokov shoved the statement farther under my nose and pressed a pen into my hand. Midway through my signature, I stopped.

"What about my wife? Where does she sign?"

"Your wife will sign her own statement. We are a governmental organization, you can believe us."

Flashbulbs popped as I completed my signature. Smiling now, the OVIR chief asked me to "have a chat with these few representatives of the press. After, ahem, all the interviews you've given foreign correspondents, our own comrades are surely entitled to a brief one."

A TASS correspondent dripped scorn into a question about why I hadn't listed my nationality as Jewish when my identity papers were issued. I said that I deeply regretted that now, but at the age of sixteen, I naturally followed my parents' insistence. "If you want me to elaborate about anti-Semitism in the country, I will. But maybe it's enough to say that parents' natural instinct is to protect their children from harm."

"And later you changed your name," an *Izvestia* reporter tried to counterattack. I said I regretted this stupidity just as deeply, but the same factors applied. Years of sniggering about "Jewish" in school registers and of "Yid" on blackboards didn't exactly spark yearning to be a Jew. Beyond this, my first theater had told me in so many words that "Shulman" would be an obstacle on the Soviet stage.

Total silence enveloped the room. Not a single pencil moved.

"How can you want to take a Russian girl from her own country?" asked the *Trud* man. "And to that fascist-militaristic nightmare, that miserable Zionist nest!"

"That's not a 'Russian girl' but my wife. We want to go where we can work and we can live. We want to be where we won't hear the kind of horror you have just pronounced."

"Work in Israel?" a contributor to *Soviet Culture* huffed. "Surely you know there's no art there."

"Of course, you journalists know the country much better than I do since your newspapers describe it so accurately. The only thing you left out is that my wife and I are kept alive by aid from . . . an Israeli dance company." This produced another hush. No one moved.

The hardest question was whether I had "retained any gratitude to the motherland, after all." I assumed that this press conference had been planned for edited propaganda showings after we'd left. The questions that were letting me proclaim what had been building up for two years were obviously conceived as bombshells to expose me as a villain. I wanted to give them nothing to use or to manipulate into thanks for their "humanity." I was deeply grateful to everyone in Russia who had developed me as a dancer and a person. But none of these people had anything to do with Soviet rule, and I would do no service to the Sergeyevs, Frangopolos, and Laras by naming them. So I merely said that for anyone acquainted with my recent life, the question was foolish.

"Okay, you cross our border," the *Izvestia* man shouted. "Will you start spreading your political poison? Tell cock-and-bull stories about the . . . er, circumstances of your emigration?"

"I can only repeat what I've said to a hundred policemen: I don't want to change anything in the Soviet Union; I just want to leave it. I won't hide anything if people ask me. But first of all, I want to rest and recuperate from your treatment."

The time for resting seemed to have started. I thanked the reporters and went to Galya. She was bursting with suspense. I told her that everything seemed okay but warned her to give no complicated answers. When she came out after three minutes in the room, she was splotched with red and teetering on the edge of hysteria. "They . . . won't . . . let me go," she choked out between sobs. "It's my . . . mother again."

I rushed back inside. Bokov was gloating. "The press conference has ended," he commanded, trying to push me out. I said nothing had ended and that I was going nowhere without my wife. The subterfuge had obviously been based on the theory that I was exhausted and would rush to the airport with my visa—and without Galya.

One of the hunger-strike informers was waiting outside. "Go pack your things," he urged. "I tell you honestly: Galya will get out too after a few face-saving weeks for them. But if you stay, they'll poison you—I *know*."

Three KGB toughs waved fists outside the telephone booth glass while I described the press conference to Moscow correspondents. We went home and sat in despair with Polina Epelman. Goons followed her when she left late that night, and a lone man was waiting on the staircase of her building. Her escorts often spat obscenities at her. "You whore, we'll fix your cunt-face right here and now. The bunch of us are going to fuck you around that corner just over there."

No doubt the KGB reasoned that this was the quickest way to break the morale of a woman who had been without a man for years. The agent waiting in the dark went one step further by exposing himself and chasing Polina home.

46

I WAS NOT PREPARED FOR MORE STRUGGLE. I STARTED DRINKING BEFORE my stomach could take solid food and flared up at "insults" from Donutya and Alec. The escape was more alcohol.

After he had visited me from Copenhagen the previous spring, the American dancer Bruce Marks had written an open appeal.

We are the same person, Panov and I. We are both of Russian-Jewish descent, both in our mid-thirties, both married to extraordinary ballerinas. We both wished to dance and choreograph in new repertoires—to expand as all artists must. With an invitation from the people of Denmark, my life has become all I hoped it might. With an invitation from the people of Israel, Panov's life has become a nightmare.

Self-pity tightened my throat. I used our barre as a coat rack and told myself a good layoff was just what I needed to put me in shape for returning "refreshed" to my exercises. This doublethink blasphemy for a dancer who needed daily work and had lived on it through fever, torn ligaments, and hernia reduced me further in my own eyes. The body's weakening always started in the mind.

The KGB summoned me for long, gruelling interviews after the press conference. They threatened exile, draft into the army, and other administrative measures. "Your life isn't worth talking about if you keep lying to Western sheets." News "leaked" that the Leningrad Communist Party had ordered a trial, and a pack of "friends" dropped by to report overhearing plans to break my legs. "For God's sake, be careful. Maybe it's set for tonight."

When Henry Kissinger arrived a few months later, I evaded my shadowers by leaping from one courtyard to another and changing clothes in waiting cars. If I couldn't meet the Secretary of State, I might at least make a headline that would bring me to his attention while he was there. In the panicked search for me everyone I'd recently seen was grilled. Then Galya used an intercity telephone booth to call the Moscow apartment—of a refusenik—where I was staying. Two hours later a squad charged up the stairs. The telephone was disconnected, and I was imprisoned inside for three days, until Kissinger's plane took off.

GALYA BEHAVED BEAUTIFULLY, but she had counted on winning. This was the real cause of my moral collapse. I drank to block out what I was doing to her. Once or twice she cried. A few times she lost her patience. "But you promised five months. We've waited two years." Mostly she simply faded away before my eyes. I was filled with pity for this beautiful woman whose only crime was to have believed in me. Instead of glowing in the center of applause, she was losing her hair and developing circles under her eyes. She always used to play with the children present in any company. The eternal child in her would show them her toe shoes because the stage still dazzled her. This preciousness was what the forces of evil were grinding out of her, and I bore a terrible responsibility for it. She used to look at me with radiant confidence that I would save her, as a hero-husband should. Now she stood alone in a corner.

"What's the matter?" I would ask when I saw tears.

"I've just danced all of *Don Quixote* in a dream," she said. "It was so beautiful, do you understand?"

But I also understood what would happen to her if I left her to them. The attempts to separate us had gone on so long that a sporting interest had sprung up among the most gentlemanly of the KGB. The most vindictive would crush her if I left. So I would *not* go alone to Israel. I would stay and witness what I had done to her. It was far worse than what had happened to me, who had known somehow what to expect. I had led her into a hideous reversal of a fairy tale.

WITHOUT INTENSE ECONOMIC PRESSURE, my hunger strike would have been a joke. Protests were already swelling against the Kirov's first American tour in ten years, planned for the spring of 1974. No one could remember anything comparable to the outspokenness of Clive Barnes's moving articles in the *New York Times*. "The Russians use art for politics and money," he wrote. "They will recognize a firm stand when they see one. . . . This is a matter of conscience—and a man's life." I had never dreamed of such support.

The American impresarios tried to convince Moscow that Kirov triumph would become Soviet disaster unless we were freed. Madame Furtseva faced a genuine dilemma. . . . But we could see nothing good from our black pit.

Galya wrote Prime Minister Kosygin about the new attempt to separate us by making me leave alone. "If this is the government's treatment of citizens," she asked, "what was the point of the October Revolution?" The answer was a letter from her mother to *Soviet Culture*, a newspaper celebrated for its "discreet" anti-Semitism. The staff-written lines bristled with lies about Shulman's million-dollar Western contracts. Its complaint against the "young Jews who keep besieging me with demands regarding the State of Israel" was a dangerous playing on the fantasy of Jewish "oppression" of Mother Russia:

My daughter was born into an ordinary Russian family. She was raised in the Soviet state of workers and peasants, who gave her a higher education. Galya owes everything to her motherland and her people. . . . Panov-Shulman is eleven years older, an unscrupulous, depraved man whose *evil influence* estranged my daughter from me and who is trying to use her to attain his money-grubbing ends abroad. Galya does not fully realize what awaits her in *alien lands* without friends, relatives, and the Soviet way of life that made her what she is. I never gave my permission and never will, for I know how bitter bread can be in somebody else's country.

Russian readers immediately caught the signals. The patriotic woman was trying to protect her pure-blooded daughter from hook-nosed predators in alien lands. But the key message was for Galya herself: that she had no hope.

Then came "Israeli" letters pleading that my only rational course was to leave now to save my body and my talent. For eighteen months our letter box had been completely empty. Suddenly these communications arrived, with Israeli stamps and postmarks from the KGB store of such things—and without signs of having been opened. Nothing so neat had ever reached us from "abroad."

The worst was addressed to Galya from a woman supposedly from Tel Aviv. In English—a direct translation of the Soviet phrases we knew so well—it begged Galya not to come to Israel. "Things are not very happy here, and why should they be? I tell you, a Russian girl has no business in a Jewish state. . . . I happen to have information that you will definitely be allowed to come, if only you do your duty and let your husband go first where he belongs. My heart wishes only the best for you. . . ."

Friends who laughed at the crudeness didn't understand. The new campaign penetrated to Galya's weakest point and shattered her. She wept apologies for her mother and moaned that if she hadn't married me, I'd be free now. "If one of us is there, it will be great happiness for both of us," she pleaded. "*Please* go. I'm lucky; I know I'll be able to follow."

Saving me had become her *idée fixe*. I had a duty to ballet, she wailed, and my friends who had never known the hidden Galya encouraged her to feel that she was killing a great talent. They pointed to her deep gloom as evidence that she was weakening and was ready to return to the Kirov. But her hounding me was for the opposite reason. It came from her suffering *for me* that she couldn't express in anyone else's presence.

"I've loved your art longer than I've loved you. I can't bear to see it destroyed any longer. I beg you to go. Can't you see that it will be easier for me?"

I couldn't think of leaving such a person, even if my persecutors weren't waiting to write about the coward who had abandoned his wife. But the paper I'd been tricked into signing at the "press conference" obligated me to leave the country within one month. I kept being called in for warnings that my visa would be withdrawn *tomorrow*, and I'd never get another.

Galya was near the brink. All her hope had switched to the crazy notion that she would revive only when I left. My head ached constantly. Is this what our struggle had come to?

"Break their morale, destroy them spiritually," they'd been ordered. I looked back to the relative happiness of when I was in jail and we had had the luxury of fighting a "clean" fight.

To mark my thirty-sixth birthday, Sir John Gielgud, Alan Bates, Keith Baxter, and Wayne Sleep headed a contingent of London theater people and well-wishers who met at Speakers' Corner and marched to the Soviet Embassy. They sang "Happy Birthday" and drank toasts to us. Outside New York's Plaza Hotel a similar group also drank our health and sang birthday greetings, which we heard over a foreign broadcast station a few hours later. Lotte Lenya, Betty Comden, Hal Prince, and Carol Channing were among the hundreds present. Pearl Lang read a statement from Martha Graham:

> Dancers are a shining thing. They give delight and rekindle memories, and to a certain extent are gods and goddesses.
>
> I have always thought that the Soviet Union had understood this, but evidently this is not so.
>
> I appeal to the Soviet Union, as an older dancer, to let the Panovs choose their own lives.
>
> No shame will descend on Russia for this decision, only honor.
>
> *11 March 1974*

ALEXANDER SOLZHENITSYN'S PROPOSALS for curing what he had so brilliantly exposed made many haters of the Soviet regime wary. He seemed to seek salvation in a mythical Russian past, the very source—although he denied it—of certain Soviet atrocities against modern civilization. The true democrats of Moscow, Leningrad, and Vilnius saw him as the latest of a long line of Russian "prophets" who went around telling *everyone* how he should behave in regard to *everything*. The contrast with modest Andrei Sakharov, our political hero, showed up Solzhenitsyn's imperious tendencies even more clearly.

But this did not reduce the vileness of Solzhenitsyn's expulsion, which had occurred in February 1974. The repulsive deportation of a giant and a genius showed what our gangster-rulers were still doing to Russian culture. I was terrified, as well as sickened, since the next step in the drive to evict me and destroy Galya might be putting me, too, on a plane.

GALYA'S FEELING FOR CHILDREN had led to more than the usual talk about having one. I had been reluctant, but this was the time. As soon as we were sure, I told OVIR that if they threw me out now, the world would know how they separated a father from his unborn child, not only a husband from his wife.

The tiny protection of the coming baby relieved me slightly and changed Galya completely. Nothing worried her except preparing for the birth of our child. She lectured herself about avoiding all excitement and had soon convinced herself of the benefits of not dancing again. Russians have always poured out more physical love on their babies than people of happier lands. But Galya's orphanlike childhood must also have contributed to the strength of her reaction. As if motherhood had always been her real calling, she grew soft and pink and no longer implored me to go alone.

Senator Edward Kennedy and President Georges Pompidou came and went with no change except more ugly faces in doorways while they visited Russia. In the spring we went to Vilnius for air. Three months of pregnancy were filling Galya out to a sweeter femininity than ever, but something wasn't quite right. Donutya took her to her relative, an excellent gynecologist.

My escorts were happy not to be puffing after me, now that I felt too low for running in the woods. On warm May evenings Alec and I tried to think. Despair was no inspiration for action, but I sensed the time for physical retribution was approaching and felt a great compulsion to document Soviet methods before it was too late. It was like my old urge to dance. I locked myself in a room for two days and poured out my memories to a tape recorder. My nervousness about not being able to express myself grew into terror that the KGB would destroy the machine or steal the tapes. They patrolled under the window as I recorded, subject to a wild anxiety building up from minute to minute that they would break in. When I finished, the relief was immediate. I was amazed at the importance I'd come to attach to words.

We were still in Vilnius when notice came of another Rothschild "stipend." We hesitated about going to Moscow to fetch it because a new Washington committee was investigating Soviet conditions and the KGB were gnashing their teeth, especially because of Politburo dis-agreement—the exit tax levied depending on your level of education went on and off; visa procedures were tightened or loosened—about handling the emigration problem. The authorities' first instinct in such periods was to silence headline makers. But we needed the emigration leaders' advice and encouragement almost as much as the money.

Alec insisted on going with me since Galya wasn't well enough to travel. We crawled out of his window and took a twisting back-street route to the station. But two men on the platform ended our self-congratulations at not being followed. Both looked like demobilized sergeants who had spent the day in a beer hall. They signaled to another pair that closed in from the opposite side.

The train was an international run back and forth to Berlin, which gave us a little extra security. We found our luxury compartment—there'd been no cheaper seats—and a conductress with a spotless uniform helped us to settle in. Fifteen minutes out, she genially offered to bring us supper. Donutya had just fed us, but the proposal of "nice thick steaks" warmed the atmosphere. Soviet train service was obviously picking up!

We politely declined and returned to our thoughts. Alec and I could read each other's even when neither spoke. The prospect of a night in the homey compartment relaxed us, especially since the signs were growing that we were about to reach the final act.

The relief of my recording was much re-inforced by a change in the attitude toward us that we both clearly felt. The campaign against the Kirov's appearing in Manchester the year before seemed to be striking home now. This time it was the Bolshoi's London tour the coming month, against which the protests were so strong that the trip was in doubt. British Equity had formally asked that Bolshoi dancers be denied per-mission to perform until we were freed. If they did reach the stage, the electricians' union promised to switch off all the lights. Newspapers reported a growing revulsion at our treatment all over Europe and a reluctance to do cultural business of any kind with Soviet groups.

The specter of an international boycott had already become real in New York. The Kirov's first American tour in ten years had been all set for this very May. The excuse for canceling it was something about a shortage of air transportation, but Americans knew that rising disgust with Soviet emigration policy—of which Galya and I had been made the test case—was the reason why "it will be intolerable to have the Kirov here," as a leading American writer wrote. "Just how stupid can the Russian bureaucracy be?" Clive Barnes asked in a stinging article about the threat to the cultural exchange program itself.

Unless Brezhnev was willing to scrap his entire détente venture, something would have to give. For the first time, Alec and I felt optimistic—especially since the two years calculated to finish Galya and me were over. . . .

The conductress knocked again to ask if we were thirsty. Compared to the usual women in her job, she was remarkably groomed and attentive. The third time around she put two steaming glasses on our table. "I won't hear of another no," she insisted. "It's very good tea."

In fact it was so tasteless that Alec interrupted our abstracted sipping to mention this. Five minutes later I was in a strange sweat. Water was also running down Alec's red-splotched face, as the most intense nausea I'd ever felt spread through my system. We barely had time to wonder what we'd eaten before we were lunging for the basin.

When vomiting wasn't enough, we ran to the toilets at opposite ends of the carriage. The violence forced out my insides. Massive diarrhea led to a breakdown of everything. While I bent over the toilet, the bottom hole went fuzzy; then the bowl itself faded into a haze. I had to lie on the floor until the next discharge.

I felt my way back to the other toilet, shouting for Alec. Some barely working part of my brain remembered the KGB threats to cut my tendons, smash my head in, or *give me a drink to finish me off*. If Alec died because of me, my whole fight had been a hideous mistake. Thank God his sight went only as we groped back to the compartment. Half his tea was still in the glass. But his heart had long been weak. Mine was pumping strangely, so I could imagine why he was gasping. I took his face in my hands. All I could see were eyes bulging from a ghastly whiteness.

We shouted for help. The other compartments were empty. Holding hands, we crawled back to the toilet. We tried to reason whether we should attempt to stop the train and escape. The minute we realized what was happening, I told Alec I was getting out. In a final swipe of revenge, the KGB often beat people *after* they had their visas. This was my punishment—but had we got an overdose by mistake?

Our groans finally produced people. Alec recognized a frantic voice: a man who'd gone to school with him and who was pouring water down our throats. The conductress appeared, chanting that we must have eaten something "at home, at home, at home." Her voice tried to control her panic; evidently we were in worse condition than she'd been told to expect. I remembered a man looking at me with icy hatred from her compartment as we boarded the train. And two of the platform goons were in the cabin next to the back toilet.

No one knew that water cannot flush out chemical poisoning. We drank so many pitchers that it ran out of our nostrils, then were led to the toilet because our basin was clogged. We could barely breathe. Our insides had gone, and our skin was numb.

The station lights in Minsk slightly lit up our blindness. An ambulance was waiting. We vomited again and felt needles going into our arms, which immediately made our heart fluttering more spasmodic. I wanted to protest when I heard mutterings about an isolation ward. They could hold us for months there or finish off what the injections had apparently started. But I was too weak; nothing mattered. At least the clinical smell seemed assurance that we were entering a hospital, not somewhere else. . . .

THE FIRST THING I MADE OUT was the ceiling. Finally, a line appeared where it met the wall. Then I recognized bottles of drip solution: one for Alec's arm, two for both of mine. The doctors parroted the official diagnosis of "severe food poisoning from an unknown source." We said nothing about the tea. The KGB might send us to a mental hospital for "dangerous hallucinations."

The doctors were most worried about my heart. A group of specialists hovered over me for hours. The professor who led them prompted everyone's great respect. He advised me to forget about dancing. "You have prodromal symptoms of a heart attack. You must never again try anything strenuous."

My heart did seem to be failing but would suddenly start pumping in little explosions. The next day Alec sat on my bed during my worst moments. Since his weaker heart had partially recovered, he was sure I'd swallowed far more "hemlock." "They probably just rinsed your spoon in my glass," he said bitterly.

The hospital could not have imagined the consequences when it allowed us to check on the "food poisoning" in Vilnius. Return calls from Moscow and Leningrad, then London and New York were bombshells for the local KGB. More heart specialists arrived, then Leningrad friends. Alec was strong enough to walk them down the corridor.

When Galya arrived with Donutya, she was so sweet and plump that I giggled. As an expectant mother she felt obligated to take charge of the family's health and scolded me for "eating that greasy train stuff." But Alec was too worried about me not to let a few words about the poison slip. Galya's pregnant sparkle changed to horror. She stepped back as if to protect the baby. "But you're all . . . *blue*," she gasped. She seemed calmer when she left with Donutya the same evening, but if my head had been clearer, I might have remembered she was in no shape to travel. And how could I have forgotten how tenaciously she composed herself whenever she feared her deepest emotions might break her apart?

On the fifth day, gloomy new "patients" were evidence of the Minsk KGB shifting into second gear. I felt I couldn't stay my prescribed week more in this hospital. Recuperation would be faster in Vilnius—if we had enough money to feed ourselves. Carloads of agents followed on our way to the station. A more sophisticated brigade relieved them in Moscow, but none of this mattered because I still saw our Russian tea as the beginning of the end.

Moscow friends helped me to the bank, then to the airport. When the plane landed in Vilnius, I learned that Galya was in the hospital. The doctors said shock had caused a bad hemorrhage. They could not save the baby.

I extracted the full truth from Donutya. Our telephone call from the Minsk hospital had weakened Galya. She was shaky on the trip, but Donutya and Alec kept this from me because of my heart. Back in Vilnius, she deteriorated rapidly. My condition forced her to face what she never quite had faced before. For the first time she looked straight into the pit of Soviet rule. Her fear broke through; the miscarriage became inevitable.

The doctors said only that Galya's physical strength prevented serious internal damage. When I reached her bed, she tried to mutter that it was "nothing." She was stricken and feeble. The connection between her reason and her emotion had shattered. She raised her eyes toward mine. "You see?" she said. "There's no hope. Nothing works out for us."

I couldn't speak. I knew I would break down if I tried to say anything. Since I was her only support, this would have ripped at her wounds. I wanted to give her a new baby. I wanted to give me one, too. All I could do was buy her something beautiful.

My heart couldn't take a run to Vilnius' hard-currency store, but I managed a respectable walk. I looked for something white, but the pulse explosions and dizziness delayed me. The man who approached me as I braced myself on a counter was obviously KGB, yet I wasn't afraid. I even knew what it was when he asked me to go to the telephone. A colonel at the other end told me to come immediately to the Ministry of Internal Affairs to "receive permission for you and your wife to leave the country."

Somehow I got back to Galya. I stroked her hair and gave her the only possible medicine—slowly, to break through her indifference: "We'll have other babies. They're letting us go. *Together*."

An hour later she was Galya again, telling *me* to stop worrying, reckoning which Russian souvenirs to buy. She even raised her cheek for a kiss, which had never happened when Alec and Donutya were present.

47

WHEN THE MINISTRY OF INTERNAL AFFAIRS ORDERED GALYA OUT OF the hospital, the frightened superintendent came to do her duty. But the doctor who had tried to save the baby now saved Galya by insisting on blood transfusions. This gave her another day to recover.

With this settled, I flew to Leningrad. Collecting the permissions for emigration—from the police, the draft board, the apartment house commission, the installment-plan administration to testify nothing was owed on a refrigerator—usually took months. We had three days to leave the country. And as a parting gift of absurdity, I had been ordered to drag myself through the full run of legal niceties.

Galya and I would have left in our underpants as soon as she was strong enough to walk. Instead, I had to fill out forms I could barely read. I certified that I had no debts and would pay for redecorating our apartment. It was a surrealistic journey in a single day to all the offices that circumscribe a Soviet life. There was no time even to grab a sandwich.

The next morning I flew to Moscow to collect our passports and buy our tickets. Western correspondents drove me to the necessary doors, and I managed to walk through them, but I was close to collapse on the train. The professor was apparently right about the permanent damage of the poisoning.

When I fell into my own bed at midnight, the fact that we had our visas began to seep into my system. Galya would be here in the morning. Now I needed only sleep. But my heart beat louder and louder with nightmares of form filling in dozens more offices. My pulse seemed to be pumping away my life. I took off my clothes and managed to open a window to get the air I was gasping for. A pinkish dawn was already in the east. The White Nights had always alluded to the something wonderful waiting for me—and now promised Jerusalem, my dream. But I was suffocating. My body was still a bundle of muscles trained for living. I looked at it and tried to understand why they no longer worked.

Only God could resolve the baffling contradictions. He had planned everything so well until now and wouldn't let me die here. "Please give me more help. Just until I get there."

It was worse than in the hospital because there was nothing left; I could not draw breath. Panic pushed me out of bed again. I remembered a bottle of brandy under my armchair. At the first sip I crumpled to the floor. The alcohol had dissolved the last calorie of strength. Sensing that the slightest jerk might burst my heart, I crawled inch by inch to my door. It took fifteen minutes to open it and another fifteen to reach up to my neighbor's bell. She screamed and ran inside.

When a doctor arrived, she checked the pulse of the "disgraceful drunkard" while surveying the empty apartment in contempt. "You're all alike, you bohemians. Selling everything for a drink. Boozing yourselves to death, and now you're in the preliminary stage of a heart attack. I could give you an injection but you'd only—"

She broke off to ask if I was "that dancer." My answer filled her with embarrassment. "I'll give you these injections around the heart," she said soothingly. "You'll feel better in half an hour."

I was better almost immediately, starting with some feeling returning to my hands. Israeli earth would nourish me, even if I were a permanent invalid. I would never forget God for giving me the bonus of strength to get me there—which was my last thought before I dropped off to sleep.

THE NEXT MORNING I FELT MUCH STRONGER. Two more certificates were needed, and our exit visas had to be registered with the police. The KGB cars did not stop a Western crew from filming these errands on my last day in Russia.

But Galya didn't arrive. The worst possible thoughts came as the afternoon dragged on. She had left the hospital in the morning for an hour's flight from Vilnius. They might have arrested her, even tampered with the plane. At last her ghost limped into the apartment. Fog had delayed her takeoff, then kept her circling Leningrad for hours. I did not let go of her until we were assured we could postpone our departure for two days.

As instructed, I went to Moscow again to re-register our exit visas. While I was there, Galya was informed that she would not be allowed to leave, after all; her mother had telegraphed a new refusal. She could barely wail this over the telephone to me. It was a final KGB attempt to crush her while I was away, and she was at her weakest.

With Western correspondents at my side and KGB captains just behind, I said that if Galya's tickets were not validated, this would be in a hundred headlines tomorrow. Two miserable hours later our papers were signed and stamped.

AT THE LAST MINUTE A BBC CORRESPONDENT kindly asked whether we would like a final look at Leningrad. Galya was too exhausted, but some outside energy kept me going. Opposite the Winter Palace, Vasiliev Island's "arrow" divides the Neva in two. I got out of the car, went down to the water, wet my face with the coldness. Then we sped along St. Petersburg's most evocative literary streets, past Pushkin's house on the

Moika River, the Dostoyevskian courtyards that were alive with old Russian deathliness. The last stop was where my nighttime meditations during the hard Kirov times had always ended. The Fortress of Peter and Paul commanded a view of Leningrad's golden center. I looked at the glorious architecture for the last time and felt the spirit it had so often inspired. I said farewell to many of my best dreams and thoughts.

The correspondent and his wife did not understand why the Soviet government wreaked so much pain on so many who loved Russian culture. I could not explain that the country had always done just this. I only knew that, although some friends insisted I'd return when life was better one day, I would never see Russia again. I had to absorb its best in this moment. I had to supply enough memories of the great majesty and the great sadness.

OUR DELAY IN ARRIVING AT THE AIRPORT had frightened a small band of waiting friends. Now they pressed around us while cameras clicked. Except for suitcases filled with Galya's books, we had only the clothes on our backs. Customs officers who subjected other emigrants to the most humiliating searches didn't bother to look at our things. After twenty-seven months the KGB knew every inch of our apartment.

Friends who had ignored this final risk for us were raising glasses, crying for our happiness and in the knowledge that we would never meet again. I tried to respond, but a strange new depression separated what my eyes took in from what I felt. I couldn't make sense of the jumpy talk and tight handclasps. I owed too much to too many, and where we were going, I did not even know my benefactors' names. We were leaving with beggars' debts we could never repay.

The numbness blocked out the jet noise. We were flying over Soviet territory, where we still could be brought down at any moment. Then we were in Warsaw, but Galya and I could not talk to each other. We were too empty to ache. The air bombarded our skin with meanings we couldn't understand.

In the Budapest transit lounge there were incomprehensible toasts and a siege by correspondents. Twenty-seven months as a captive had supposedly taught me how to be interviewed, how to provide good angles for newspaper copy. Now I could say nothing. Questions about our past —and our future—were gibberish. Galya was still a ghost.

In Vienna swarthy, shouting men rushed us out of the plane. Large pistols bulged from under their jackets, and the cars with tires smoking in pursuit of us also bristled with guns. Our captors' claim of being Israeli security men strengthened our worst suspicions: they were terrorist kidnappers from some Arab brigade. Lest I say something stupid in shock, I decided to remain silent. Their Hebrew finally disposed of that paranoiac fear, but after we had raced around a block many times and dashed into the Israeli Embassy, we were instructed to pass through the electronic devices and enter the inner door one at a time. The "press conference" trick prevented me from obeying; I would not be separated from Galya. And I couldn't understand the fear everywhere—everything we thought we were fleeing from.

The ambassador courteously apologized and explained that these distressing measures were necessary to prevent publicity that could close the most important route to Tel Aviv if Soviet anger were provoked. I could not take this in. Nor the undercurrent of nervousness that we might be planning to stay in Europe or go to America. We needed no prompting or convincing to know that Israel was our home.

The next day we were given a delicious lunch in the Vienna woods. Security men would not let us take a little walk alone. But a full sleep had dulled my pulse explosions. And my sense of perspective was returning. I had no right to expect the West that had saved us to be perfect. No matter how much higher, freer, and more civilized life was here, it was still *life*, not the dreamworld I had visualized. Nothing could ever reduce us to what we had been *there*. Sipping coffee in a café, we saw television pictures of our arrival at the airport: two run-down, wild-eyed captives. So much for my complaints. In a few hours here we felt almost like new.

Our El Al plane left that afternoon. This time Galya and I held hands. I had been waiting to speak to her alone. I wanted to tell her how wrong I'd been from the beginning. Not only had the KGB and my friends underestimated her strength, but I also—because I had put too much emphasis on her lack of experience compared to mine. But of course her feelings were what mattered. Every attempt to separate us had driven her closer to me. One such person is a hope for mankind.

I said this as well as I could, thanked her for her courage—but in my dreams, for I apparently fell asleep during takeoff. When I awoke, I sensed the entire passenger cabin had been staying quiet for us. I kept my eyes shut. Images of Alec came, and of the other martyrs I'd left behind. God grant them what we now had! The old heart was probably kaput even if my body could be made to remember the stage. But choreography was as important as dancing. The material from our bitter years would have to wait. I wanted to do "happy" ballets first.

An air current lifted the plane. I remembered a family story that my Vitebsk grandfather had wanted to come to Palestine before he died. So another spiral was nearing completion. The pity was the skipped generation. My father deserved to get to Israel more than anyone else and probably would have if not for history's trick, twisting his hope for the Revolution as the dawn of mankind's final renaissance. But maybe he'd free himself one day. I'd write him a postcard when we landed. "Dear Papa, I'm not sure what my new country will be like, but maybe you'll investigate it with me. You might find something interesting here. . . ." But first, I would write my son, Andrei, who was so much more grown up than I at his age.

The nose of the plane dipped. A stewardess was bringing champagne on a tray. Our fellow passengers gathered around, laughing, clapping, crying, shouting "Mazel tov!" They were singing the "Hava Nagila" I'd heard on a thousand Radio Israel broadcasts. Sunshine lit up the night. The whole plane was a joyous "l'chaim," to life. Tears streamed down Galya's face. "Everyone's so happy for us," she cried.

Tel Aviv was a spray of lights along the sea. The plane kept taxiing while Galya put her emotion back into place with worry about when we'd attend class in the morning. The big jet's front door was opened for us. A million stars twinkled overhead, and flashbulbs answered from below. The air was balmy. There were flowers, a blue-black sky, more flowers—and a dizzying desert scent.

A crowd pushed up to the ramp. "You've come *home!*" someone shouted. Kisses covered our faces. I made out Jennie Walton galloping toward us. Bouquets tumbled from Rosemary's arms as she tried to keep pace. Sweet, shy Rosemary had liberated us and now was welcoming us to our land—not because she was or wasn't Jewish, but because she belonged to the higher community of angels. So fairy-tale endings did happen in life. I was so happy I had to dance.

Index

A Note on the Type

THE TEXT OF THIS BOOK was set on the Linotype in Fairfield, the first typeface from the hand of the distinguished American artist and engraver Rudolph Ruzicka. In its structure Fairfield displays the sober and sane qualities of a master craftsman whose talent has long been dedicated to clarity. It is this trait that accounts for the trim grace and virility, the spirited design and sensitive balance of this original face.

Rudolph Ruzicka was born in Bohemia in 1883 and came to America in 1894. He has designed and illustrated many books and has created a considerable list of individual prints—wood engravings, line engravings on copper, and aquatints.

This book was composed by Maryland Linotype Composition Company, Inc., Baltimore, Maryland, and printed and bound by American Book—Stratford Press, Inc., Saddle Brook, New Jersey.

Typography and binding design by Virginia Tan